The White Nuns

THE MIDDLE AGES SERIES

Ruth Mazo Karras, Series Editor
Edward Peters, Founding Editor

A complete list of books in the series
is available from the publisher.

THE WHITE NUNS

Cistercian Abbeys for Women
in Medieval France

Constance Hoffman Berman

PENN

UNIVERSITY OF PENNSYLVANIA PRESS

PHILADELPHIA

Published by
University of Pennsylvania Press
Philadelphia, Pennsylvania 19104-4112
www.upenn.edu/pennpress

Printed in the United States of America on acid-free paper
1 3 5 7 9 10 8 6 4 2

Library of Congress Cataloging-in-Publication Data
ISBN 978-0-8122-5010-7

To my sister Mary
Only she knows how much she has done

CONTENTS

PART III. COMPARISONS AND CONCLUSIONS

Modern descriptions of the religious reform movement of the central Middle
Ages have often depended on accounts written by monks from the Cistercian
Order, who were in many ways the great winners in that reform movement.
Those accounts made central the Cistercian monks in the history of monasticism. Reliance on those monks' accounts, indeed, has led modern historians
to remark on the rapid expansion of the Cistercians in the first half of the
twelfth century. In contrast, historians have given almost no attention to the
equally remarkable expansion of abbeys of Cistercian women, primarily in
the first half of the thirteenth century. This is so, despite the facts that by
circa 1300 the number of houses of Cistercian nuns would come to nearly
equal that of the order's monks and that abbots in the General Chapter had
begun to legislate about those Cistercian nuns by early in the thirteenth
century.[1]

When I began this study, historians of monasticism still argued that
abbeys of Cistercian nuns did not exist—either denying their appearance
altogether or suggesting that abbeys claiming to be of Cistercian nuns were
"only imitating" the order's practices, or asserting that only a tiny number of
houses of Cistercian nuns were ever incorporated by the order and then only
during the first decades of the early thirteenth century. This study, based on
a large number of archival sources, contradicts those conclusions. It goes so
far as to suggest that by the thirteenth century, Cistercian nuns were becoming more prominent because they were replacing Cistercian monks in popularity. The early history of such abbeys for Cistercian women has had to be
established from the ground up: foundation dates and founders, abbey and
grange locations, and their very existence as Cistercians.[2]

To demonstrate the presence of such abbeys of Cistercian nuns within
the order and to show their early appearance have required a considerable
rethinking of the early history of the order itself, one that posits a gradual

process through which one of the most important innovations of the twelfth century appeared: the religious order. The earlier consensus (drawn from triumphalist Cistercian accounts) was that late eleventh- and early twelfth-century reformers, including those who came to be Cistercians, had moved away from earlier monastic groups. Many earlier monasteries had become extremely wealthy, were organized in hierarchical or monarchical form, and had members who were almost entirely elites. In the twelfth century reformers sought to recapture notions of asceticism, poverty, and equality that had been present at monasticism's origins. The reformers eventually organized themselves into more democratic congregations of monastic communities in which all abbeys (at least all abbeys of monks) were equal. Cistercian monks were often seen as the leaders of such a movement, founding a universal and mandatory general chapter of all abbots who met annually at Cîteaux: it was they who established the Cistercian Order. Such a religious order was a distinctly new institution, what might be called an organizational "umbrella group" that oversaw many houses of monks and nuns.

Through my attempts to incorporate women's communities into the early history of the Cistercians, I came to conclude that although the creation of a religious order had been attributed to the very early twelfth century, its development was more gradual. Over the course of the twelfth century the developing institution, the religious order, was characterized by an exchange of ideas from one group to the next. There is no clear reference to a Cistercian General Chapter (as opposed to local chapter meetings) from earlier than the 1150s. What had once been piecemeal papal grants of exemption from tithes "on their own labor and management" to individual abbeys of monks like Clairvaux were only extended across the order in the 1180s along with exemption from local episcopal visitation.[3] In place of visitation by bishops, internal visitation by father abbots was instituted by the Cistercians by the early to mid-thirteenth century when the General Chapter finally resolved disputes about where individual abbeys or groups of abbeys fit into the filiations, the five family trees used to organize such visitation, but also used to establish precedence in ceremonial entrances into General Chapter meetings.[4] That process was described in my earlier book, *The Cistercian Evolution*.[5] Only once it has been established that the religious order and the Cistercian Order were evolving twelfth-century institutions does the "narrative space" become accessible for an account of the Cistercian Order that includes its women's communities.

But as this study shows, Cistercian nuns and their communities and the economic bases of their lives were much like those of Cistercian monks. There were differences. Only nuns recruited lay sisters. Nuns appear to have recruited fewer lay brothers, depending instead on hired or tenant cultivators. Perhaps more significant is that visitors for the order's early communities of nuns could vary both formally and informally. Many houses of nuns were formally visited by bishops, but informally visited by mother abbesses. It was only circa 1240 that the Cistercian General Chapter began to regularize the visitation of these nuns' communities, asserting that it was to be undertaken solely by father abbots and that mother abbesses were not to contradict those father visitors.

Still, confirmations of the founding of such communities of nuns by popes and bishops that describe communities "following the Rule of Saint Benedict and the customs of the brothers of Cîteaux" were in words identical to those used in confirmations for the order's monks, like this for Clairvaux: "Ut ordo monasticus, qui secundum Deum et beati Benedicti regulam et cistercensium fratrum institutionem."[6] There were rich and poor houses of Cistercian nuns as well as of Cistercian monks. Some foundations were made de novo. In other cases, communities of religious women becoming Cistercians, like the order's men's houses, had originated in anonymous, semi-eremitical religious groups.[7] The new Cistercian communities of women thus shared in the same larger reform movement as Cistercian monks; they were not a separate women's movement. Like houses of monks, most abbeys of nuns soon acquired endowments of associated granges and properties, sometimes in numbers equal to those for the order's abbeys of monks. Like abbots and other officials, abbesses and other female officers could leave the monastic enclosure to negotiate their abbeys' business.[8] Like abbots receiving lay brothers, abbesses might recruit lay brothers who then took their monastic vows directly from those abbesses.[9]

This study is not primarily about the religious motives or the spirituality of those women who became Cistercian nuns but about their economic successes.[10] Several of its important findings may be mentioned. First, this study shows that women made positive choices to enter new communities of Cistercian nuns, as asserted by the bishop Jacques de Vitry in his *Historia Occidentalis*: "These were women, often young ones, who had given up their wealth and fineries to pursue a celestial future."[11] Second, moreover, it shows that population increase freed twelfth-century women to live religious lives. More women were free to follow their religious inclinations and enter religious communities because economic expansion and population growth meant that a much smaller portion of the female population of western

Europe was required for reproduction than in the early Middle Ages.[12] In the period from A.D. 1050 to 1250 better harvests and diet, lower infant mortality and that of mothers in childbirth improved the gender ratio in favor of women. Those with religious inclinations could enter religious life as young girls, as widows with grown children, or just before death, *ad succurrendum*.[13]

Third, an unanticipated finding of this study is that the documents for new abbeys of Cistercian nuns often reveal the existence of secular women of considerable power and authority, the *dominae*, or lady/lords, who were founders and supporters of such communities of nuns. It was to provide themselves with surrogates in prayer that those powerful secular women most often sponsored religious women. Many such secular women rulers would have lost wealth and power if they had entered religious life before their deaths and many entered their own foundations only near or after death for burial.[14] Those secular women might have wholly escaped our notice were it not for their appearance as founders and patrons in the documents used in this study.

Fourth, this study confirms what other recent studies have shown, that nuns used written records to organize their own rule and were rarely wholly illiterate, even if sometimes they did not compose in Latin, and it finds no evidence that abbeys and priories of Cistercian women were used to house unwanted, disabled, or superfluous daughters. This was once thought to be the case by Eileen Power: "The novice who entered a nunnery, to live there as a nun for the rest of her natural life, might do so for various reasons. For those who entered young and of their own will . . . might take the veil because it offered an honourable career for superfluous girls."[15] Recently Emilie Amt has returned to the evidence cited by Power of English convents' "poverty of learning," identifying it as coming from a Middle English translation in the 1460s of an earlier Latin cartulary, made by a "poor brother" who described why he made this translation: "For as much as women of religion, in reading books of Latin, are excused of great understanding" (cited by Power), but as Amt points out, the poor brother continued, describing those nuns as "for the most part in English books well learned."[16] Power's arguments about the evidence of the bishop's registers have also been shown to be distorted and overstated.[17]

This study contradicts assumptions that nuns did not use written documents to manage property and shows that, despite the fact that there were few large stretches of unoccupied land to be granted to new religious communities, Cistercian nuns actively acquired the substantial endowment necessary to become self-sufficient religious communities. It shows that despite assumptions that women's inability to celebrate mass would have been detrimental to nuns' ability to attract patronage, medieval populations believed strongly in the efficacy of those nuns' prayers, hastening to make gifts to those nuns for their own and others' souls (see in particular, Chapter 7 on Saint-Antoine). It also shows that the misogynous language used by Cistercian monks to describe the nuns in their midst, particularly after 1400, often derived from attempts by those Cistercian abbots to take over the property that had been given to support the nuns. The abbots justified their actions by attacking those nuns using ill-founded, misogynous clichés about religious women's failures.

*   *   *

This study of Cistercian nuns is divided into two main parts, and a third that consists of conclusions, followed by various appendices. Part I uses a wider lens to turn a more European-wide gaze on Cistercian nuns. In this first part, Chapters 1 and 2 describe recent historiography on Cistercian nuns and how the Cistercian General Chapter's abbots came to recognize and regularize those nuns. Chapter 3 considers how nuns' communities adapted Cistercian economic practices to a variety of environments across Europe.

Part II provides a more focused account of Cistercian nuns in a single ecclesiastical province in northern France in the thirteenth century, the ecclesiastical province of Sens. In the Middle Ages that archbishopric comprised seven dioceses stretching from Chartres and Orléans to Auxerre, Troyes, and Meaux, including in the center those of Paris (not a separate archbishopric until 1622) and of Sens itself.[18] About twenty-five communities of Cistercian nuns were founded there between the 1190s and 1250, a number similar to that of the earlier foundations for Cistercian monks in the same region—most of them founded two or three generations earlier. The communities of Cistercian nuns founded in the archbishopric of Sens ranged in size from as few as 20 to as many as 140 nuns (see Map 1 and Appendix 4).

Part II treats individual abbeys or groups of abbeys in chapters arranged primarily according to the identities of their women founders and only secondarily according to foundation dates and geography. Such an organization of the material, at first sight not compelling, turns out to underline the importance of those thirteenth-century noble women founders whose histories have for too long been ignored and whose presence in this story might otherwise have been missed.

Chapter 4 considers houses of nuns founded in the western parts of the archbishopric, several of them founded by widows whose husbands died before fulfilling crusader vows. These widows made such foundations as dowagers, using assets specified by husbands and income from their dower lands. In some cases the Crusade in question was one launched against Albigensian heretics. Chapter 5 considers great heiresses, women like Isabelle, Countess of Chartres, and her daughter, Matilda of Amboise, who had inherited familial land and titles after the deaths of cousins or nephews. For these two countesses of Chartres, considerable documentation reveals their generosity in founding houses of Cistercian nuns and their considerable transfer of lands from secular elites in the countryside into the hands of Cistercian nuns. Less well documented are foundations made to the east of Paris by another equally important heiress, Matilda of Courtenay, Countess of Auxerre, Nevers, and Tonnerre, often called "the Great." Surviving documents for her foundations are sparse, although there are some for the foundation made at Pont-aux-Dames for the soul of Matilda's daughter, Agnes, who had married into the family of the lords of Saint-Pol.

Chapter 6 turns to Blanche of Castile, queen of France, and her foundations for Cistercian nuns at Maubuisson, begun in 1236 and dedicated in 1242, and at Lys, begun in 1244 and dedicated in 1248. Her two abbeys for nuns are compared to that for Cistercian monks at Royaumont, which was begun in 1228 for the soul of her late husband Louis VIII and with the participation of their young son, King Louis IX. The large expenditures to acquire consolidated properties that were made by Louis IX for Royaumont are compared to his mother's more piecemeal acquisitions at Maubuisson. For Blanche's foundation for nuns at Maubuisson many small claims even to the abbey site itself had still to be acquired after the nuns arrived. Thus, John of Maubuisson received sixteen livres for an arpent of meadow located just behind the abbey wall; he may also have received two livres for a house located next to the abbey's well; Dreux of Maubuisson and Aiceline, his wife, received twenty livres for their claims to a nearby quarry. The knight Lord Thibaut and his wife Martaria were paid for a bridge located next to the abbey; two women from Aulnay were paid two and a half livres for land next to the abbey's garden and a right-of-way; Richard Borin was paid nearly thirteen livres for his holdings there. Roger Redbeard and his wife received three and a half livres for land located next to the abbey wall, which they held from the church of Saint-Lazare; Gerald of Saint-Ouen received eight livres for a single arpent of land, but one located inside the nuns' enclosure, which he held from the prior of Saint-Peter of Pontoise.[19] Part of the point of such listing of the slowness of acquisitions is to suggest that Blanche had to approach the founding and endowment of her abbeys very much like other widows discussed in Chapter 4, using dower/dowry income to purchase rights.[20] Chapter 6 also examines the record book *Achatz d'héritages*, made for Blanche's construction at Maubuisson as evidence for construction as well as of the acquisition of endowment.

Chapter 7 is devoted to a single abbey, that of Saint-Antoine-des-Champs founded just outside the walls of thirteenth-century Paris. Begun circa 1198 by a group of male and female penitents inspired by Fulk de Neuilly, preacher of reform, Saint-Antoine came to be among the most important abbeys of Cistercian nuns. Its abbesses ruled the Faubourg-Saint-Antoine right up to the French Revolution, and even in the thirteenth century they had begun to amass both important granges in the countryside and a considerable endowment of rental houses in the city of Paris itself.

Chapter 8 considers the more suburban abbeys of nuns founded in the eastern parts of the ecclesiastical province, some of them in the county of Champagne. Among founders and supporters were contenders for the countship of Champagne during an early thirteenth-century comital minority, bourgeois and citizens of towns and cities associated with the international Champagne fairs, and the archbishop of Sens. While some of these abbeys appear at first glance to be associated with leprosariums, a second glance suggests that this was often only an issue of proximity. It was in this region of Champagne that some of the abbeys of nuns were suppressed beginning circa 1400.

Finally, Part III and Chapter 9 open with a query about the province of Sens. Were the paltry numbers of foundations for Cistercian women made in the twelfth century attributable to the presence of rival reform groups that included women: Fontevraud, Prémontrée, and the abbess Heloise's Paraclete? Did those other twelfth-century reform groups that included women occupy the same societal "niche" in the province of Sens that Cistercian nuns did elsewhere? How similar were economic structures between those other groups and those of Cistercian nuns? What a brief overview of the available studies suggests is a shared competency among the female leaders of all such communities.

Thus, my conclusions in this study show abbeys of Cistercian nuns that were not poor and not unable to manage property. The findings about how very successful they were may be extended not only to other regions but beyond the Cistercian Order to medieval nuns more generally. Medieval authors' biased and self-serving rhetoric should not be taken at face value for medieval nuns. Such conclusions about evaluating medieval statements about nuns according to the contexts in which they were produced bear more widely on our considerations of medieval women, secular and religious alike. They should challenge a hyperromanticized view of the Middle Ages as consisting only of strong and knightly men fighting dragons.

Please note that all translations of non-English works are my own unless otherwise specified and that Appendix 1 provides definitions of technical terms and some of the more obscure legal practices with regard to landownership. Abbreviations are listed at the start of the notes.

The White Nuns

PART I

Were There Cistercian Nuns in Medieval Europe?

CHAPTER I

Reform Monasticism and Cistercian Nuns
in Western Europe

It is now widely accepted that communities of nuns associated with the Cistercians began to appear less than a generation after the foundation of Cîteaux in 1098 and that many more houses of those Cistercian nuns had appeared by circa 1250.[1] Yet the presence of nuns within the Cistercian Order, as part of the *ordo cisterciensis*, has been denied until recently. Indeed, for many monastic historians, to acknowledge the presence of women among those early reformed monks would upset a time-honored narrative of a golden age in which heroic men went off (without women) to found new religious communities in the deserts of western Europe. In that narrative, pioneering and frontiers were particularly associated with the new, reformed Cistercian monks, while Cistercian women were denied any place at all. That such a narrative long held sway was because it had been written by the most successful monastic reformers of the time, Cistercian monks themselves.[2] Cistercian "control of the discourse," as modern historians would have it, meant that the nuns' role as part of the order has long been obscured. Indeed, one of the underlying themes of this study is how much we must reject the narrative of those monks.

The monastic reform movement in which the Cistercians would be so successful was part of a church-wide reform movement, the Gregorian Reform, which may be said to have begun when Emperor Henry III called for a reform synod at Sutri in 1046, which deposed three popes and established a fourth. Such secular intervention in church reform was soon disavowed by reforming clerics. Clerical and monastic reformers instead sought to bring back into ecclesiastical control both election and investiture to church office, condemning the buying and selling of church office (simony) and outlawing clerical marriage (nicholaitism).[3] Some reformers attacked clerical marriage because they were convinced that married priests had alienated church property to their children; others attacked it because of its threat to the purity of the sacraments.[4] Reformers' assertions of the superiority of the celibate clergy over all other Christians undermined the power once exercised by kings and emperors over the church, but also introduced an antifeminine rhetoric, which undermined the power and authority of abbesses, queens, and countesses for at least part of the eleventh and twelfth centuries.[5] By the thirteenth century, however, such women of power and authority were back; it had become necessary to have such women available to defend the castle and rule the realm while men were away on military adventures.

One aspect of the Gregorian Reform was a reassertion among churchmen of their own rights to power and property, with the consequent attempts to restore existing monastic and episcopal estates, accompanied often by bishops preaching about the return of tithes to the church. Such advocacy for the return of tithes from lay hands, as Giles Constable has pointed out, encouraged secular owners to return such tithes, but often they were returned to monastic communities rather than to the bishops to whom they belonged. In doing that lay owners could rid themselves of forbidden ecclesiastical revenues but at the same time received monastic prayers. This process not only benefited established monasteries but also appears to have benefited the new eremitical reforming groups, including Cistercian monks and nuns.[6] Moreover, those reformers also benefited from exemptions from tithes granted by popes and bishops, who saw that they were poor and working their own fields and exempted them from tithes "on their own labor and management." At first made to individual abbeys of monks like Clairvaux, those grants were extended across the order in the 1180s. By 1215 the Fourth Lateran Council had heard complaints about their avaricious land acquisitions and limited the order's tithe exemption from all lands managed by the order to holdings already in Cistercian hands or to *novales* (by which they appear to have meant either land never used before or new tithes.)[7] This "grandfathering" of the Cistercian tithe exemption might imply that the ability of early thirteenth-century houses of Cistercian nuns to acquire tithe-free holdings would be more difficult than it had been for Cistercian monks. In fact, acquisition of tithe-free lands had changed little, for both earlier abbeys of monks and later abbeys of nuns often had to repurchase existing tithes from earlier owners and would dispute over what constituted *novales*; only through the practice of repurchasing rights from existing tithe owners could Cistercian monks and nuns exercise their exemption from ecclesiastical tithes.[8]

In attempts to reassume control of tithes and other income sources once held or claimed to have been held, bishops and abbots of established monasteries in this reform period searched archives to document their claims or fabricated documents if they were missing; this was, indeed, a great period of ecclesiastical forgery.[9] Such ecclesiastics at this time also removed assets long hidden in their treasuries to use as cash substitutes: books, jewels, silk vestments, and altar furnishings were all turned into productive assets.[10] Abbots of Benedictine monasteries associated with pilgrimage routes to Compostela constructed more expensive and impressive buildings that could accommodate pilgrims and attract their gifts, but they were also demanding new accountability from their managers.[11] In contrast, many of the new monastic reformers avoided providing hospitality or medical care to pilgrims, seeking instead a new simplicity in architecture, practice, and decoration.

Established abbots also divested themselves of more distant cells and properties in order to consolidate income-producing assets closer to home. As a consequence some of those distant properties found their ways into the hands of the new hermit monks, who could ensure continuation of divine service.[12] Often those sites came into the hands of wandering preachers who gathered followers who eventually needed rules and a more permanent site, and references to such sites often marked the first appearance of a preacher or hermit's followers being normalized into a more permanent monastic community.[13]

The most successful of such hermit monks and nuns were, of course, those for whom no record survives. Very ephemeral references may be found in other cases, as in that of a certain Bona and her tiny chapel in Gascony, first absorbed by a church called Artigues (literally, the clearances), she disappeared from further records after the church of Artigues and its properties were absorbed by the Cistercian monks of Berdoues and became that abbey's grange.[14]

Nuns and Twelfth-Century Cîteaux and Clairvaux

Accounts of the origins of a community of monks that came to settle at Cîteaux resemble accounts of other such eremitical/monastic communities seeking lives of asceticism as they renounced the decadence of traditional monasticism.[15] In emulation of the desert fathers and the apostles, these groups sought to support themselves with manual labor, presenting themselves as having abandoned cities and towns for the marshy and forested wilderness of the new deserts of Western Europe.[16] Thus the foundation story of Cîteaux told in the order's *Exordium Parvum* describes a group of monks and their abbot Robert abandoning the only slightly earlier reform foundation at Molesme to seek a stricter life for their New Monastery at Cîteaux.[17] Despite the fact that Molesme's surviving documents reveal the presence of women and children there, accounts for Cîteaux omit any mention of religious women.[18] Was the move triggered by the presence of women at Molesme?

Such a move away from women was short-lived. When Bernard, future abbot of Clairvaux, led a group of followers to the door of Cîteaux circa 1112, most of them had female friends and relations who also wanted to live religious lives. Bernard's sister, Humbelina, and other female relatives of Clairvaux's monks established themselves at a new priory at Jully, eventually identified as a daughter house of Molesme, as was Cîteaux.[19] Documents dating from between 1128 and 1142 reveal Bernard's close ties to Jully's nuns. He is seen accepting property for those women and even receiving the vows of women entering that community.[20] Moreover, as Father Jean Leclercq remarked in 1990, Jully's practices closely resembled those of the early Cistercians, as described in an undated early document:

> Those women should be allowed to serve God there undisturbed under the direction of the abbot of Molesme, and their food and daily routine established by Lord Abbot Guy of Molesme and his community, so that payments in kind and labor and from their oxen in the fields and the alms of the faithful provide for the women's food and clothing, but that the nuns themselves will have neither male nor female serfs, nor income from churches, tithes, or villages. And if any man or woman should give them such things, those possessions will be kept for the nuns by the church of Molesme, so that the church of Jully should continue without having to manage any type of property. Thus, if anyone should give them land the nuns should not seek to cultivate it using their own plows, but it should be conceded to Molesme. For the enforcement of this regime, designed for both their bodies and their souls, four monks

should be sent by the abbot of Molesme so that any use of private property or wandering by the nuns may be terminated according to the Lord.[21]

There are other traces of Bernard of Clairvaux's concern for religious women. Bernard had cousins, "the devout Emeline" (d. 1178) and "the blessed Asceline" (d. 1195), both members of a double community at Boulancourt, or Lieu-lez-Boulancourt, the abbey of ladies (*locus dominarum prope Bulencuriam*).[22] According to Anne Bondéelle-Souchier, there was also the abbess Adeline (d. 1170) of the abbey of Poulagny in the diocese of Langres, who was a relative of Bernard's.[23]

Bernard's letters of condolence to the abbess Heloise and the Paraclete upon the death of Abelard also suggest an association, as do the liturgical similarities between the Paraclete and the Cistercians.[24] Additionally, Bernard was also likely involved as one of the leading Cistercian abbots in the foundation of a house of nuns at Tart by Stephen Harding, abbot of Cîteaux. Tart's first abbess, Elizabeth of Vergy, was the daughter of Cîteaux's secular patrons; she was at Jully before being sent circa 1123 with a group of nuns to establish Tart.[25] Soon Tart had a congregation of daughter houses attached to it, creating a virtual women's filiation within the developing order.[26] Adelaide, the mother of Matthew, Duke of Lorraine, entered Tart in 1148, going from there to the new house founded by her son at Étanche; she died there in 1153.[27] The nuns at Poulagny were attached to Tart circa 1149, and Tart gained other daughter houses in the diocese of Langres at Belmont, Coulonges, and Vauxbons.[28] In the diocese of Autun, a house of nuns associated with Tart was established at Lieu-Dieu, and in the diocese of Toul there were nuns associated with Tart at Benoîtevaux and Droiteval.[29] In the diocese of Besançon, a nuns' abbey at Montarlot was founded in 1174 and another at Corcelles in 1179.[30] In the diocese of Laon, the abbey of Montreuil-les-Dames appeared in 1136 and Montreuil's daughter house at Fontsomme appeared in 1140; it was later moved to Fervaques.[31] Nearly a century later, in 1228, the bishop of Laon moved an overflow of recruits at Montreuil to Saint-Sauvoir-sous-Laon.[32] Tart's fame throughout greater France was also apparent by 1172 when the powerful lord William of Montpellier left money in his will for his daughter's entrance into that abbey.[33]

There were other twelfth-century foundations for Cistercian nuns that were not attached to Tart, for instance, those of Coyroux and Nonenque (see Chapter 3). Still the relative openness to women that is seen from the time of Bernard's appearance at Cîteaux was suddenly overturned after the new "Cistercian" pope, Eugenius III (1145–53), placed Jully and its daughter houses firmly under the control of Molesme and severed any ties between Bernard and Jully.[34] Perhaps a side effect was that these and the foundations at Jully and Tart were given almost no attention by Cistercian historians until 1953, when Father Jean de la Croix Bouton presented "L'établissement des moniales cisterciennes."[35] Why was this?

A History of Denying Cistercian Nuns

The expansion and economic success of what would become the premier reform order in western Europe, that of the Cistercians, had by the mid- to late twelfth century meant that there were more than five hundred houses of Cistercian monks. For many of the order's monks, their successes must have been seen as the result of God's favor for their austerities and from the dispatching of contingents of leaders with twelve followers across Europe in a process that might be called "apostolic gestation."[36] In reality such expansion stemmed less from sending out monks to found new communities than from the affiliation of existing reform communities into the Cistercian network, as well as from secular economic growth at the time that favored Cistercian economic practices. Cistercian expansion thus often involved the incorporation of such groups, their endowment, and their locally trained recruits, This is the most viable explanation for how a single foundation at Cîteaux in Burgundy expanded to more than five hundred houses of Cistercian monks by the end of the twelfth century. Although houses of nuns emerged from the double communities of the twelfth century and most existing abbeys of nuns associated with the communities and congregations of the twelfth century had already been incorporated, abbeys of Cistercian nuns continued to appear de novo in the thirteenth century (see Part II).

With power and prosperity, moreover, Cistercian monks and abbots became increasingly unpopular, and by the end of the twelfth century they had begun to be described as land-grabbing and profiting from privileges that had been granted to them because they were poor, but which they still utilized after they had become rich. Increasingly hegemonic, riding a wave of appointments of their abbots to be bishops, Cistercian leaders had become pompous, complacent, and arrogant. Then in the first decade of the thirteenth century abbots and monks found themselves preaching against heresy in southern France. The heretics they encountered there lived lives of obvious poverty that challenged Cistercian claims to purity and asceticism. Cistercian preaching against them was ineffective and frustrating. The abbots were soon demonizing the practices and beliefs of those poor "good men" and "good women."[37] The heretics' supposed openness to women as religious practitioners (at the same time that they eschewed procreation) may have considerably confused the discussion. Given this bad publicity, some Cistercian monks may have encouraged the foundation of new abbeys for Cistercian nuns, and northern French knights embarking on crusades against the Albigensians are seen founding and supporting houses of Cistercian nuns rather than houses of Cistercian monks (see Chapter 4).

Already by the mid-twelfth century monastic association with women was becoming a hallmark of heresy. Catholic preachers tried to eschew women's company, but chroniclers of the Crusade like Peter of Vaux-de-Cernay may have exaggerated the difficulties in converting heretical women back to Catholicism as in his description of the northern French Catholic woman Matilda of Garlande and her efforts to convert Cathar women. Dominican writers too were soon retrospectively describing the association of Dominic of Osma to the nuns of Prouille, as if that relationship had been the "conversion" of Cathar nuns, when in fact those supporters of Dominic had always been Catholic nuns.[38]

In the face of a new propensity for patrons to support Cistercian nuns and of such bad reports, the discourse was seized back by one of the order's abbots in the first decade of the thirteenth century. Abbot Conrad of Eberbach, who had been trained at Clairvaux, composed the *Exordium Magnum Cisterciense*; in later centuries it became the Cistercian proof text, the standard account of Cistercian origins.[39] Conrad's opening draws heavily on earlier reports composed by the Cistercians themselves, such as the *Exordium Parvum*, which had attempted to legitimize the monks' departure from Molesme.[40] Like many such foundation narratives, Conrad's was highly rhetorical, self-promoting, and with a very questionable truth status; it had no discussion of the order's nuns.[41]

While stressing the institutional and economic successes of Clairvaux and other Cistercian abbeys of monks, Conrad also maligned earlier monastic groups like the Cluniacs, describing the Cistercians and Bernard of Clairvaux as appearing just in time to save monasticism from disastrous crisis. Historians like John Van Engen, Giles Constable, Barbara Rosenwein, and Dominique Iogna-Prat have all made clear that Cluny remained nevertheless the center of the twelfth-century Western monastic world. Van Engen, indeed, pointed out that the "monastic crisis" of the twelfth century was nothing more than an illusion created by Conrad's exaggerated, self-promoting rhetoric.[42] Despite such findings about Conrad's distortions with regard to Cluny, many readers of Conrad's and earlier Cistercian *exordia* have used the absence of any discussion of Cistercian women as proof that there were no Cistercian nuns or that they forced their way into the order only after Conrad's time. This was only one way that they have argued that there were no Cistercian nuns.[43]

In addition to citing Conrad, such naysayers on the subject of Cistercian nuns have cited the Cistercian *Statuta* to support their arguments that there were no such nuns, or only a few houses briefly in the thirteenth century, but this is to wholly misunderstand the content of the *Statuta* as published in 1933 by Joseph-Marie Canivez.[44] As Canivez noted in his opening volume, the *Statuta* were a compilation of notes brought back by abbots from General Chapter meetings, rather than a transcript of proceedings. Moreover there are no such notes surviving from before the 1150s. It is true that the earliest reference to nuns in these volumes is that regarding Huelgas dated 1191, but to see this as the earliest instance in which Cistercian nuns are documented wholly explodes the notion of a very early twelfth-century Cistercian Order. Indeed to argue that there were no Cistercian nuns because they are not found in the order's surviving statutes any earlier than the 1190s is to argue that there were no early houses of Cistercian monks for the same reasons.

Moreover, the *statuta* from 1191 do mention Cistercian nuns at Huelgas.[45] Attempts to explain away that reference have been undone by the 1985 publication of early charters for that royal abbey.[46] The charters confirm that the abbey of nuns at Huelgas was founded in 1187 by King Alphonso VIII of Castile and his wife, Queen Eleanor of England (the daughter of Eleanor of Aquitaine and Henry II). The founders' request for a general chapter of abbesses to be held there was most likely inspired by the annual chapters of all prioresses at Fontevraud dating to at least 1149.[47]

Canivez's edition of the *Statuta* and the earlier compilations on which it was based contain many references to thirteenth-century Cistercian nuns. They showed, according to German historian Herbert Grundmann in his 1935 text *Religiöse Bewegungen im Mittelalter: Untersuchungen über die geschichtlichen Zusammenhänge zwischen der Ketzerei, den Bettelorden, und der religiösen Frauenbewegung im 12. und 13. Jahrhundert*, that such Cistercian nuns had appeared only circa 1200.[48] His work also insisted that women's devotional concerns were real and that the entrances of prosperous women into beguinages revealed them making their own choices not a lack of alternatives. While Grundmann's contributions had broken new ground in discarding an argument that had attributed late medieval women's religious foundations to demographic tendencies, described as the *Frauenfrage* (too many unmarried and underemployed women), he was working from limited data when it came to Cistercian nuns.[49] He concluded that thirteenth-century communities of Cistercian nuns were few because he had found almost no documentation for them in 1935 when he was completing this study. In fact, this was an artifact of his imperfect access to evidence at the time. Moreover, the notion of a separate "women's religious movement" found in his title itself has led to the exaggeration of a women's movement divorced from the larger reform one.[50] His contentions about the appearance of Cistercian nuns only in the thirteenth century along with mendicant nuns and about the tiny number of houses of Cistercian nuns or those "imitating" the order's practices would be reversed by later historians like Micheline de Fontette.

Grundmann cited Jacques de Vitry's characterization of Cistercian nuns in the *Historia Occidentalis*, "*On the increase in Cistercian women*": "The reverend religious men of the Premonstratensian Order, wisely attending to the assertions of experts within their own family, that it was burdensome and dangerous to guard such charges, decided that they should henceforth not receive women into the houses of their Order. Thereafter abbeys of nuns of the Cistercian Order multiplied like the stars of heaven and increased enormously, blessed by God as it is said: 'Increase and be multiplied and replenish the sky.'"[51] Grundmann's reading of this specific passage ignores the larger tenor of Jacques de Vitry's work, which might be described as providing a series of caricatures of the monks and nuns of various religious groups, which reflect little of the Cistercian or Premonstratensian reality.

Grundmann does conclude that between 1200 and 1228 the Cistercian General Chapter accepted a few abbeys of nuns. He lists evidence for them in Germany, but he also concludes that those nuns were not really worth the effort. In his view "the trouble and responsibility which went with the organizational leadership and pastoral care for new women's communities" soon led to the General Chapter's refusal to accept any more: "As early as 1220 the decision was made not to incorporate any more women's houses into the order . . . [and] in 1228 . . . the general chapter decided not to accept any more women's houses into the order, neither existing houses nor new establishments. [Thus] while it was impossible to forbid women's houses to follow Cistercian customs, the order refused to provide them with pastoral care or visitation."[52] Grundmann concedes the existence of communities of nuns "imitating" Cistercian practices. He also recognizes other communities of nuns, which the abbots were forced to accept because of papal provision. For instance, as he saw it, the ambition and greed of certain abbots in southern Germany in the 1240s led them to transform wealthy beguinages into abbeys of Cistercian nuns.[53]

Grundmann's 1935 conclusions about Cistercian nuns were influential over the next few years as seen in a 1953 dissertation for the University of Würzburg written by Ernst Günther Krenig, "Mittelalterliche Frauenklöster nach den Konstitutionen von Cîteaux."[54] Krenig's use of Canivez's *Statuta* as a definitive record of all General Chapter actions, however, led him to conclude: "Only in 1213 were there nuns who were also incorporated by the order."[55] Counting only nuns' houses referenced in Canivez's edition, Krenig found four houses of nuns added between 1213 and 1220 and five more before 1228—a total of nine before what he regarded as the cessation of those nuns' acceptances by the abbots.[56] Any houses of nuns accepted by the abbots after 1228 had been added only because of the intervention of the papacy, a practice that was ended (in Krenig's view) by 1251.[57]

Krenig does discuss some late twelfth-century houses of nuns, but contends that they were "only imitating" the order's practices and were not really Cistercian. This was his view of the nuns at Schönau who in 1190 received documents from Pope Clement III (1187–91), describing them as following the Rule of Saint Benedict and the Cistercian constitution. He concluded likewise that the nuns of Kloster St. Maria and St. Theodor in Bamberg, whom the bishop of Bamberg in 1157 described as following the Rule of Benedict and the Cistercian customs, were not Cistercian.[58] In Krenig's view such papal and episcopal confirmations for houses of Cistercian nuns evidenced only their "imitation" of the order.

Krenig similarly dismisses the foundation of the abbey of nuns made by Stephen Harding at Tart: "[It was] not the action of a founder of orders [or of] a founder of a daughter house; it was more a personal intervention. . . . Because there was nothing about it in the statutes, Tart was not a daughter house of Cîteaux."[59] Having denied that such references to houses of nuns were about real Cistercians, Krenig then analyzes the rest of the evidence in Canivez's volumes about those "pseudo-Cistercian" nuns.

Moreover, just as Krenig's study appeared in 1953, its conclusions were challenged by evidence about twelfth-century abbeys of Cistercian nuns in France, which was presented by Father Jean de la Croix Bouton at the eighth centenary of the death of Bernard of Clairvaux.[60] The reaction among traditional historians of the order was immediate. If they accepted Bouton's contentions at all, they treated the incorporation of such nuns into the order as a disaster. They employed vivid imagery, imagining an overwhelming tidal wave of Cistercian abbesses pushing their communities into the order against the fierce resistance of its abbots, who were, despite all efforts, unable to prevent those women from forcing open the floodgates. Such images of the order's abbots resisting those nuns drew on reports and early television footage from 1953 showing heroic Flemish and Dutch men resisting the brutal storms that had overwhelmed the dikes and flooded much of the coastline of the North Sea.[61]

In describing the onslaught of those nuns against the resistance of the thirteenth-century General Chapter's abbots, modern historians portrayed those Cistercian women as irrational, natural forces poised against the rationality of the order's abbots attempting to contain them.[62] It seems likely that modern monastic writers described those monks resisting the nuns in such terms because, in a modern world in which fewer men were being ordained as priests, those monastic writers found themselves overwhelmed by the *cura animarum*, the care of souls, but the evidence that thirteenth-century monks found the *cura monialium*, the care of nuns and their souls, burdensome is limited, seemingly deriving entirely from the description of a sainted abbot at Villers who feared diluting the spirituality of his own community and therefore gave back control of four houses of nuns to the abbot of Clairvaux.[63] Recent work by scholars like Sharon K. Elkins and Fiona Griffiths suggests instead that twelfth-century advisers to nuns saw in the *cura monialium* a route to their own salvation.[64] Would this not also have been the case for Cistercian monks?

Such images of medieval Cistercian abbots objecting to the care of the order's women, moreover, distract us from a different question, that of whether nuns always sought Cistercian affiliation. Some communities of nuns resisted the order's governance: abbeys at Poulagny and Rifreddo successfully left the order, while those at Nonenque were unsuccessful in an attempt to do so.[65] Still the tendency of the historiography has been to view medieval nuns seeking the aid of monks but posing a burden on them. The pressure for affiliation has been seen, without question, as coming from the women. This may or may not have been true.

That religious women were a burden to religious men is clearly how a 1967 study on the nuns' juridical status by Micheline de Fontette saw them. She describes it as a central issue:

Women's piety posed complex and arduous problems for the medieval church. . . . That in the twelfth century thousands of women flocked into the monasteries, while not easily explicable . . . certainly caused political troubles and economic issues that almost immediately gave birth to difficulties about juridical status and material needs. It was difficult to establish how the nuns fit into the masculine orders, but even more burdensome were the material demands that so many female recruits imposed on the male houses, material demands that were not sustainable [*insupportable*]. . . . In such a situation the masculine orders attempted to stop admissions. This only contributed to the battle for their very existence by these communities of nuns, who could not live, in fact, without the support of those men. . . . For over 150 years [from the early twelfth to mid-thirteenth centuries] the orders sought solutions to the problem of women's vocations. This study is a limited presentation of how several of such groups coped.[66]

Fontette's assumptions about medieval nuns' dependence on medieval monks suggest her ambivalence about the religious women she studied, whether they were Premonstratensian, Dominican, Clarissan sisters, or those of Fontevraud. Her chapter on Cistercian nuns is no less judgmental.[67]

Most influential of Fontette's pronouncements on Cistercian nuns was probably on the vexed issue of abbeys versus priories. She opined that "all houses in the [Cistercian] Order were abbeys," whereas priories could not be Cistercian.[68] This led to the circular reasoning that although the foundation of Jully had served the vocations of women associated with Bernard of Clairvaux, "Because Jully was a priory it could not be a house of Cistercians."[69] Similarly, when Jully became overcrowded, the decision to send nuns to found a new abbey at Tart in 1123 had, according to Fontette, nothing to do with Bernard of Clairvaux: "Stephen Harding gave the new abbey of Tart the customs of Cîteaux, but he should not be thought to have intended any consequence for the order. Tart existed and its existence was tolerated only as a type of personal possession of Stephen Harding."[70] Nonetheless, by the

fourteenth century abbots and abbesses had come to be treated without dif-
ferentiation by the order's General Chapter, and Fontette concludes that
Cistercian nuns had often been successful in their efforts to become part of
the order: "They were small abbeys generally, with small numbers of nuns
holding a limited endowment, but there were some more important ones:
Flines, Maubuisson, Lys, Huelgas, and Herkenrode (Liège).[71] Indeed Fontette's census of houses of Cistercian nuns described as *incorporatio pleno jure*
totaled 837, including 320 houses in Germany.[72] On this, see Appendix 5,
"Numbers of Cistercian Nuns' Houses According to Selected Historians."
Thus on numbers Fontette reversed Grundmann. Moreover, for nearly a
decade this appeared to be the last word on Cistercian nuns.

After 1975

Soon after 1975 a flurry of publications began to appear and historians began
to contest the conclusion that there were few Cistercian nuns, for instance,
in Britain. In 1976 at a Cistercian Studies conference in Kalamazoo, Michigan, Dr. Elizabeth Hyde from the University of Manitoba presented a paper
entitled "The Cistercian Priory of Nun Cotton."[73] She argued that the nuns
of Nun Coton, whether or not those nuns constituted an abbey, were indeed
part of the Cistercian Order, because the surviving documents said so. When
challenged on this point, she picked up her transcription of the abbey's cartulary and read aloud the papal and episcopal confirmations describing them as
following the practices and customs of the *ordo cisterciensis*. Such an
approach, using the administrative records as evidence, was seen as well in
1979 when Janet Burton published a study on Yorkshire nunneries in which
Cistercian nuns were unabashedly treated as Cistercian nuns.[74]

Influenced by the pronouncements of Fontette, an American scholar,
Coburn Graves, published "English Cistercian Nuns in Lincolnshire" in 1979
in *Speculum*.[75] Graves presented evidence that seemed to confirm Fontette's
assertion that a priory could not be part of the Cistercian Order and that
those nuns in priories who claimed to be Cistercians were "only imitating"
its practices. In an attempt to allow those nuns to be discussed, he proposed
that those nuns be called "English Cistercian nuns." Such terminology
allowed Graves to discuss a case about crusader tithes and Cistercian exemption for 1268–70, documented by an entry in Henry III's Close Rolls. The
question had arisen as to whether six houses of nuns in Lincolnshire, claiming

to be Cistercian—Stixwould, Greenfield, Nun Cotham, Legbourne, Goke-well, and Saint-Michael's Stamford—were indeed Cistercian and hence exempt from payment of a crusader tithe. The query itself does not survive, but the General Chapter's response was enrolled on Henry III's Close Rolls for 1270 by the Lincolnshire archdeacon William of Lexington.

That officious archdeacon appears to have been stirring up trouble. King Henry III and two bishops, as well as the nuns themselves, had already stated that those communities were of Cistercian nuns and were exempt. Moreover, it is likely that Cistercian abbots at the time were not happy to be queried on this issue, for they appear to have made a gracious payment in support of the Crusade for the entire order to preserve its tithe exemption.[76]

We have only the abbots' response to a question recorded in the Close Rolls: "In this letter in response to your inquiry, we understand that the abbesses of the monasteries of Stixwould, Greenfield, Nun Cotham, Leg-bourne, Gokewell, and Saint-Michael's Stamford, have been seen to wear the clothing of our order. But [if?] they are not [*non tamen sunt*] part of our order, nor have been incorporated by it, then as a consequence [*propter quod*] they should neither enjoy the privileges and freedoms of our order, nor be reputed to be part of our order."[77] Graves, in assuming that the General Chapter could have answered anything but a hypothetical question, attributes an administrative apparatus at Cîteaux that did not exist. The abbots could only have sent out other abbots to inquire, and there is no indication that they did so. Instead the abbots must have treated the query as a hypothetical one. If so, at issue is how to translate the words *non tamen sunt* in the abbots' response. Graves reads them as a simple negative "they are not," but it is possible that the abbots had answered the more hypothetical question: "If they are Cistercians, do they share the Cistercian tithe exemption?" with an explanation of "if they are not," or "their not being so." In the end, Graves's view of the situation is based on his acceptance of Fontette's statement that there were no Cistercian priories as much as on the argument from the Close Rolls.

At almost the same time that Graves's article appeared, Sally Thompson's "The Problem of the Cistercian Nuns in the Twelfth and Early Thirteenth Centuries" was published in 1978 by the Ecclesiastical History Society in a volume in honor of Rosalind Hill; Thompson, in the middle of writing a book on the founding of English nunneries, asserted that there were few documents, but it remains without saying that her sample was limited to Britain.[78] In a second article from 1986, Thompson would go on to explain that the fragmentary condition of documents for early Cistercian nuns was a result of the nuns' poverty, their lack of Latinity, and their inability to find chaplains.[79]

Changes in the approach to medieval nuns came in a volume on Cistercian nuns edited by John A. Nichols and Lillian Thomas Shank in 1995. Most notable was the English version of earlier arguments by Brigitte Degler-Spengler that many nuns calling themselves Cistercian were indeed part of the *ordo cisterciensis*; it appeared as "The Incorporation of Cistercian Nuns in the Order in the Twelfth and Thirteenth Centuries."[80] Degler-Spengler argued for several criteria that could be used to show that a house of nuns was indeed part of the Cistercian Order: having documents in their archives describing them as Cistercian; having foundation documents announcing a foundation of Cistercian nuns to be made; or having been mentioned in the *Statuta* edited by Canivez. Degler-Spengler thought the most solid documentation for such houses of nuns being abbeys of Cistercian nuns was when all these criteria were available, but she opined that given the considerable possibility that such documents had been lost, even one such proof showed a house of nuns to be part of the order.

The arguments elaborated by Degler-Spengler and made so easily available by Nichols and Shank suddenly allowed historians to consider many more houses of nuns as Cistercian and provided an enormous improvement over earlier pronouncements that these nuns had only been "imitating the order." Still, as I argued in *Church History* only slightly later (1999), given that houses of monks were treated without question as part of the order, requiring such proof for their status as Cistercian nuns, as advocated by Degler-Spengler, appeared excessive. As proof, it constituted a gendered double standard for status as Cistercians for houses of nuns that was not applied to monks.[81] Moreover, establishing that women were part of the Cistercian Order did not prevent the repetition of long-held misogynous tropes about those nuns.[82]

CHAPTER 2

Visitation of Nuns
and Their Regularization

One of the hallmarks of the Cistercian Order has been its universal tithe exemption and exemption from episcopal visitation, both of which appeared throughout the order, at least for the order's monks, in the late twelfth century, although Clairvaux and its daughters had acquired tithe privileges earlier.[1] Such visitation was organized according to filiation lines so that founding abbots of houses of monks visited daughter abbeys once a year and vice versa. As Louis Lekai has pointed out, the actual practice of such annual visitation even among houses of monks was probably not possible given the number of visitations that would have been required, particularly for heads of filiations.[2] Moreover, the lines of filiation for houses of monks were still being established circa 1200 when disputes were still seen about how many filiations there should be and how the incorporated groups of houses of monks fit onto those filiation trees, for instance with regard to Cadouin.[3] Only in the 1210s did abbots in the Cistercian General Chapter begin to consider the order's nuns on any issues, at least as is evidenced in the surviving *Statuta* or in the *Codifications* of the order's practices from 1237 and 1257.[4] Once the presence of nuns begins to be mentioned in the General Chapter's *Statuta*, references to them appear contradictory, varying and repeating themselves from year to year. This should not be surprising, but it means that Cistercian historians should not interpret the statutes about women, whether about visitation or other issues, as if they were rigid, enforceable laws or norms.

Who Visited Abbeys of Cistercian Nuns?

From the time of foundation, houses of nuns were sometimes visited by bishops, most often when they had been episcopal foundations. Such episcopal visitation, where it appeared, probably reflected the close association between a bishop and the original foundation of a house of nuns as at Voisins where the founding bishop had encouraged lay holders to return tithes to the church by gifts to its nuns.[5] Episcopal visitation may have been preferred by communities of nuns, because visitation by neighboring abbots disrupted earlier ties between those nuns and their patrons or between houses of nuns, like those between Acre and Cyprus discussed below. Until the 1240s episcopal visitation of Cistercian nuns had been acceptable to the order. Only in 1249 did the order's abbots and Pope Innocent IV come to agree that women's houses should be visited by abbots rather than bishops.[6]

Some bishops commended abbeys of nuns to the visitation of the abbot of one of the order's founding abbeys. Thus, the bishop of Paris recommended both Saint-Antoine-des-Champs and Port-Royal to the General Chapter in 1204, to be visited by Cîteaux's abbot.[7] The archbishop of Sens circa 1226 requested that the abbot of Cîteaux be visitor for the nuns of Cour-Notre-Dame. Blanche of Castile similarly appears to have placed her own foundations at Maubuisson and Lys under the oversight of Cîteaux's abbot, who had oversight over the community at Saint-Antoine that had sent nuns to Maubuisson.[8]

Certainly some early thirteenth-century abbesses expected that they would visit the communities of nuns that they had founded. Presumably such visitation among abbesses had been part of what had constituted the filiation of Tart, although there is no clear evidence on that point. Beyond Tart's daughters, visitation by abbesses was practiced elsewhere. Thus in 1222 the abbess of the house of Cistercian nuns at Saint Mary Magdalene at Acre regularized the situation of a cell or group of nuns at Nicosia in Cyprus. Speaking about the relationships between herself, the mother abbess, and the daughter house: "M., abbess, and the community of Saint Mary Magdalene of Acre of the Cistercian Order, following the advice and admonition of our Lord and Reverend Father, Archbishop Eustorgius of Nicosia, and with the counsel and will of the Venerable Father, Lord L., abbot of Belmont, with whom we are in unanimous accord, have decided that the house that we own on the island of Cyprus in Nicosia should be given an abbess [that is, elevated into an independent abbey]." The abbess of Acre explained that Nicosia's first abbess would be elected in Acre and that Nicosia's nuns, like those at Acre, owed obedience to their respective episcopal authorities. Still, mother abbesses would have authority: "This new abbess at Nicosia ought to have the same relationship to the Lord Archbishop of Nicosia that we have to our Lord, the Bishop of Acre, saving only the obedience which any daughter house owes to its mother house according to the practices of the Cistercian Order."[9] By 1237, however, limits had begun to be placed on abbesses' visitation as stated in the order's codifications:

> Abbesses who have daughter [houses] may not undertake [official] visitations, which are to be done by abbots. Instead, those abbots should themselves visit those houses of nuns, correcting what needs correction, and establishing what is necessary following the practices of our order. Abbesses or abbess mothers if they arrive later [i.e., after the abbots' visitations] can correct with love what they find needs correction, but taking care against presuming to diminish or change what the abbot visitor had established or to establish anything contrary to that which the abbot visitor had established in writing.[10]

Abbesses could visit, but they were not to undermine what the abbot visitor had established; moreover, abbesses were not to constitute part of the General Chapter at Cîteaux.[11]

Still such a mother abbess, who was effectively the patron of this new abbey, was not easily reduced to a solely advisory role. An abbess's close supervision is asserted in the 1267 foundation charter issued by Agnes, abbess of Nonenque, for her new abbey of nuns at Saint-Sulpice near Albi: "By this contract she and her community would have in perpetuity the rights of patronage and visitation of this convent of Saint-Antoine at Saint-Sulpice."[12] In this and many other cases the diminution of the authority of a visiting abbess in favor of a neighboring abbot could challenge social hierarchies, for this was a time when Cistercian nuns were often of considerably higher social status than were the monks and abbots who visited or provided them with care of souls.[13]

Then there was the issue of double houses. By mid-twelfth century, Cistercian monks had persuaded others that there were no such Cistercian double houses. Thus, Herman of Tournay, the chronicler of the life and times of Bishop Barthélemy of Laon, mentions Cistercian concern with maintaining gender separation. He asserted that, "while Norbert of Xanten [founder of the Premonstratensians] founded double houses, Bernard of Clairvaux [often treated as the founder of the Cistercians] promoted separate communities of monks and nuns."[14] But there were double communities that had been incorporated and that had other visitation practices. For instance, Coyroux, an abbey of nuns that had its origins in a double house, was visited by the abbot of Obazine, the neighboring house of Cistercian monks, from which it had separated; in this case, like that at Jully, the monks were to have provided for all the nuns' material needs.[15] Ironically, this visitation by neighboring abbots eventually became the norm, but without those abbots admitting any responsibility for the nuns' needs like that seen at Obazine.

Indeed, among various efforts on the part of thirteenth-century Cistercian abbots to regularize and control the order's nuns, perhaps most drastic was their insistence in the 1240s on the visitation of houses of nuns by abbot visitors, usually abbots of neighboring houses of Cistercian monks. Resistance to this idea among houses of nuns across Europe is suggested by entries in the Cistercian *Statuta* for 1243, which record upheavals at houses of Cistercian nuns from Britain to Germany: at Droiteval, Saint-Antoine-des-Champs, Beaufays, Goujon, Salzinnes, Hocht, Tarrant-Keynes, Notre-Dame de l'Isle at Auxerre, Moncey, Marquette, Heiligenkreuz, Parc-aux-Dames, and Lieu-Notre-Dame at Romorantin. The nuns were described as insubordinate: some for having locked out their newly appointed visitors and denying their authority, others for shouting and clapping their hands to drown out the new visitors' decrees. Only in 1249 was there papal agreement to such abbatial visitation; see below.[16]

But was this visitation by neighboring abbots good for the nuns? The abbots of neighboring houses of Cistercian monks could be rivals for property rights, as is suggested by disputes between the abbots of Mazan and Silvanès in southern France over which of them was father visitor for the abbey of Cistercian nuns at Nonenque.[17] Complaints were made to the General Chapter by the nuns at Garrigues (probably Saint-Félix-de-Gigean near Montpellier) about the encroachments on the nuns' properties by nearby monks.[18] This rivalry may have been one reason that Poulagny's Cistercian nuns became a house of canonesses.[19] Similarly, the nuns of Rifreddo became Dominican after a long period of disputes with abbot visitors from the neighboring house of Cistercian monks at Staffarda, who were casting envious eyes on Rifreddo's endowment in tithes and who did not, as the nuns complained, conform to papal decrees that they provide Rifreddo with lay brothers.[20]

Only occasionally were nuns living according to Cistercian practices but without benefit of the order's governance, as is mentioned by Alexis Grélois about the nuns of Yerres near Paris.[21]

Two Accounts of Visitation of Cistercian Nuns

The actual practice of visitation for houses of nuns in the early thirteenth century is revealed in surviving visitation reports from a bishop and an abbot. They are similar in their concerns about the good management of resources and avoiding "scandal," which was more than the appearance of sexual irregularities; scandal included things like wandering outside the abbey or having friends visit or gossiping with outsiders.

A visit by Hugh of Wells, bishop of Lincoln (1209–35), to the Cistercian nuns at Nun Coton in Lincolnshire is undated but probably should be assigned to circa 1230. Bishop Hugh showed concern about population size. Given the abbey's current endowment, he established that the number of nuns and other sisters ought not to exceed thirty, although they could also have twelve lay brothers to do the work on their rural properties and three chaplains. To maintain the seclusion of the religious life, no one wearing secular garb was to be received within the enclosure. The nuns should not talk without supervision to anyone from outside the cloister. Bishop Hugh decreed that neither sisters nor nuns were to live at the granges to supervise animal husbandry or for any other reason. They should avoid wandering outside the enclosure and were not to be sent outside on errands. Nuns were not to have private property. There should be no privileges in terms of food, but all nuns, chaplains, lay brothers, and lay sisters, as well as guests, were to be served the same daily bread and drink. Finally, the monastic seal should be kept under lock and key with three individuals in charge of it: the master chaplain, the prioress, and a wise elderly nun. By limiting population size, avoiding simony in admissions, personal property, and food privileges, Bishop Hugh sought to ensure regular practice in all aspects of the religious life of this small community of nuns with its limited endowment.[22]

Similar concerns are found in the reports by Stephen of Lexington, an English abbot who visited a series of houses of nuns in northern France in the 1230s after he became abbot of Savigny in Normandy in 1229 and before he became abbot of Clairvaux in 1243.[23] Stephen's visits to houses of Cistercian nuns in Normandy and in the diocese of Paris between 1229 and 1233 reveal concerns very similar to those of Bishop Hugh. In his *Ordinatio status monialium Moretoniensium*, the visitation report on the nuns at Mortain, or Blanches-Abbaye, Abbot Stephen addressed the issue of scandal. He decreed that to avoid scandal and danger to souls, the men who accompanied a noble lady or secular woman to the abbey should not enter the nuns' enclosure. A nun should not speak to anyone at the visitor's window, except with a mature companion beside her, nor should any nun have long conversations with men, whether those men wore religious garb or not. Also the nuns were to receive no one under twelve years of age as postulant or novice, and children were not to enter the monastic enclosure.[24]

In 1232 in another visitation of Blanches-Abbaye and Villers-Canivet, Stephen further specified that it was forbidden for noblewomen or their servants to stay overnight at the abbey and that the nuns should not provide any care (medical?) to secular women, because of the possibility of scandal; indeed, the nuns should be extremely circumspect in allowing entrance to visitors: the elderly, young girls, and particularly the sick or pregnant were not to enter unless they were pious.[25]

In visits to the Cistercian priory of nuns at Moncey near Tours, Stephen underlined how essential the community's porteress was to the prevention of scandal. She should neither allow any unauthorized person to tend the gate (whether secular or religious men, including relatives), nor let nuns speak to anyone there without witnesses. No men were to be provided shelter; only women and their children under age four were allowed to enter the hospice for the poor. Because of the possible appearance of scandal, no woman nearing childbirth was to be welcomed at the nunnery's guesthouse. Similarly, alms should not be given to "ribald or suspect" women, but only to paupers and the truly indigent. Indeed, while Stephen lauds the custom of distributing alms at the gate several times a week, he reiterates that the porteress should avoid giving housing or food to those clerics called "goliards" or "trouvères." Monastic men, even from within the order, should not seek hospitality at Moncey but instead seek food and shelter from abbeys of monks and their granges. Offering such hospitality was incompatible with the lives of religious women.[26]

Concerns About the Size of Nuns' Communities

Generally, Abbot Stephen's visitations reveal fears among the abbots that communities of nuns might become financially dependent on the monks, but so had that of Bishop Hugh.[27] Already in the 1230s Stephen set maximum sizes for some communities of nuns. The Blanches-Abbey's community should not exceed fifty nuns unless their assets increased.[28] At first Moncey was limited to forty-two inhabitants: thirty nuns, six lay sisters, four priests and two conversi (that is lay brothers), with two of those priests assigned to the celebration of special masses for a specific donor's soul; later Moncey's total size was increased to forty-four, but with fewer nuns (twenty-eight, not thirty).[29] For Port-Royal, Abbot Stephen established a maximum of sixty nuns.[30] Even at Saint-Antoine, as discussed further in Chapter 7, Stephen was concerned about community size and forbade admission of new nuns without the permission of the regular father visitor, the abbot of Cîteaux, "unless it was someone of such reverence that refusal would be scandalous."[31] Slightly later, in the 1260s, the order's abbots followed papal initiatives in imposing official maxima for all houses of nuns. For Blanche of Castile's foundation at Maubuisson, for instance, Pope Urban IV established a maximum of 140 nuns in 1262, but his successor Clement IV in 1267 and 1268 lowered that to 120 nuns.[32]

Yet all this concern about excessive numbers and sufficiency of endowment runs counter to the narrative of miraculous expansion told in the story of twelfth-century Cistercians. Clairvaux and other daughter houses of Cistercian monks were extolled for their rapid expansion. Under the leadership of its charismatic abbot Bernard, Clairvaux was celebrated for attracting recruits, for sending out daughter colonies and in attaching whole filiations of houses of monks; such abbots were praised when they were forced to send out new colonies of monks.[33] Indeed, early Cistercian hagiography—see, for instance, *The Life of Pons de Léras*—described it as an occasion for miraculous intervention when food supplies ran out.[34]

But expanding numbers of Cistercian women were never met with such praise. This was obviously gender linked. As is seen in the visitation reports just discussed, Cistercian abbesses were scolded in the 1230s for having population numbers that might exceed the capacity of their endowment. Abbots' and other visitors' concerns about the growing populations of houses of Cistercian nuns and their need to be self-supporting suggest a considerable shift from attitudes about equality and charity once central to the order's appeal. When it came to nuns, the abbots had moved away from the Charter of Charity, which had established that, "if any of our monasteries shall become extremely indigent, the abbot shall give notice to the General Chapter; then all the abbots assembled, animated by a lively charity, shall contribute to its relief, according to the means with which God may have blessed them."[35] Whereas early houses of monks were treated with such charity, women in the order were subject to censure if they became impoverished. A clear double standard was present.

Such concern about the adequacy of endowment found in the visitation records came to be applied as well to the adequacy of the physical facilities provided for new houses of nuns. Inspection of the site and buildings for a house of nuns was to be done before its incorporation: as seen for instance, in the 1226 record of an inspection at Cour-Notre-Dame near Sens.[36] A decade later it is also seen in the slow process by which Queen Blanche of Castile's abbey of Cistercian nuns received its foundation charter (see Chapter 6). The notion of site inspection was included in the order's Codification of Statutes of 1237: "No house of nuns ought to be constructed or associated with us under the name or jurisdiction of our order except by command of the lord pope. If it is decided to receive such nuns for any other reason, this should await verification that there are buildings, possessions and the property needed to endow those nuns, so that they may live enclosed according to our practices [ordo] and without any need to beg."[37] Such concern about mendicancy among Cistercian nuns may have reflected a more universal issue, arising with the increased numbers of women among the mendicant orders seeking to live by begging.[38]

Also of concern for abbots of the Cistercian Order was that adequate distances be maintained between abbeys of nuns and their neighbors; presumably this was in part a means of preventing competition for endowment and patronage.[39] Abbots asserted in 1218: "Abbeys of nuns should not be constructed within six leagues of our [men's] abbeys . . . [and] . . . should be distanced from other houses of nuns by ten leagues."[40] Also associated with this concern for patronage was a concerted effort to turn all nuns' communities into abbeys (rather than priories), which would preclude houses of monks having to take responsibility for the nuns' material lives, but would also allow abbesses to be elected canonically from within their own communities (on this see discussion of Port-Royal in Chapter 4). Such concerns about visitation, size of endowment, physical plant, distance between houses, and what women's communities were to be called all reflect moves toward regularization of communities of nuns, rather than necessarily any "ending of their admission."

Regularization of Nuns' Enclosure

Added to concerns about size, abbot visitors wanted nuns to live a life according to the Benedictine Rule and Cistercian customs: that is, a communal life
without private property or individual privileges but also maintaining enclosure and limiting interaction with outsiders. Such concerns are seen in surviving early thirteenth-century *Statuta*—most notably those from 1213, 1218,
1220, 1228, and 1251—and have been cited by many scholars.[41] While these
references suggest that the abbots had begun to grapple with issues regarding
the nuns in their midst, the constant repetition of some injunctions may
suggest that in fact they had met with little success in their application. One
such issue centered on enclosure and larger issues about "scandal" associated
with the order's nuns having free egress from their communities, but it was
more than that, for it was also about the separation of men and women who
were members of the order. It began with the insistence, found in Canivez's
edition of the *Statuta*, 1213, no. 3, that "incorporated houses of nuns must be
strictly enclosed."[42] The enclosure of Cistercian nuns had been cited already
in 1184 when Lucius III issued the bull "Prudentibus virginibus" to the nuns
of Tart, decreeing that its professed nuns should not leave their enclosure
without an abbess's permission.[43]

By 1218, an abbess's permission was no longer sufficient for such egress.
Thus in *Statuta*, 1218, no. 84, the abbots asserted: "Any nuns that are incorporated by the order are enjoined to be enclosed, and to own no [personal]
property. It is allowed for abbesses, with the license of the father visitor, to
leave the enclosure when necessary but only rarely and for legitimate reasons
and if accompanied by two other nuns. Moreover, the abbot visitor should
establish the number of inhabitants for each community, which should not
be exceeded." Moreover, even the order's abbesses could depart from enclosure only with the permission of the father visitor and when accompanied by
two other nuns.[44] Concerns about enclosure are again central in *Statuta*, 1220,
no. 4: "It is prohibited by the authority of the Chapter General that henceforth any abbey of nuns be incorporated into the order. The nuns of our
order shall be cloistered, and those who should not wish to be cloistered
shall find themselves removed from the care of the order. Nevertheless, it is
permitted for abbesses (or cellaresses) to leave the house with two nuns for
the purpose of handling the affairs of the house."[45] More ambiguous is *Statuta*, 1228, no. 16, which has been read as if the General Chapter were trying
to halt the addition of new abbeys of nuns altogether: "No nunnery of any

sort ought to be constructed or associated under the name or the jurisdiction of our order. If a nunnery that has not yet been incorporated into our order or has not yet been constructed wishes to copy our practices, we expect that these nuns will be visited by he who has recommended them."[46] Whether this statute from 1228 is read as an attempt to avoid imposing the duty of visitation on neighboring abbots willy-nilly or something more, it had little effect on the addition of new communities of nuns.

Whereas the abbots in the 1230s may have backed away somewhat from the issue of enclosure, they were becoming more adamant on the separation of nuns from monks, abbots, confessors, and lay brothers. Thus *Statuta* 1231, no. 6 was not so much about enclosure as about gender separation: "Nuns' confessions should be made through a window or grill, except when the father abbot visited the nuns' chapter house, or in the case of grave illnesses."[47] This concern that nuns be separated from confessors, father abbots and celebrants of the mass would lead to changes in the layout of nuns' abbeys, giving the priest access to the altar, often by a door to the exterior on the north side of the church, but eventually by wholly separating the nuns from the altar, in some cases so completely that the nuns could not have seen the altar or the elevation of the host.[48]

As for interactions with secular individuals, the case of the queen of France, Blanche of Castile, who in 1244 seems to have brought the entire family to the General Chapter meeting at Cîteaux, was unusual.[49] Still, after she died, her son Louis IX continued to visit the abbey of Maubuisson and issued a number of royal charters from there.[50] The abbots' concerns about interactions between the order's nuns and secular women was again stated in the 1257 *Codifications*: "No visitor should come into the nuns' cloister, even if a revered or honest woman, lest such access make it impossible to deny grave accusations of scandal. Nor should schoolboys be taught within the nuns' enclosure. Moreover, secular women ought not to stay overnight in the enclosure of the nuns, nor in the infirmary."[51] Thus concerns about enclosure led to the exclusion of secular women from women's monastic space. It also precluded any women, including abbesses, from the Cistercian General Chapter, as seen in the codification of Cistercian legislation for 1257.[52] More than anything else such codifications must be seen as intending that abbesses, even those with elite backgrounds, like Alice of Mâcon at Lys, had no part in the order's governance.[53]

Indeed the experiments after mid-thirteenth century with a general chapter of abbesses meeting at Tart were short-lived. The chapter was the occasion only for the abbot of Cîteaux to report to the abbesses on the abbots' deliberations in their General Chapter; the abbesses soon dropped such meetings as an unnecessary expense.[54]

Abbesses' Powers and Papal Evidence

Nowhere was the threatening power of Cistercian abbesses clearer than in complaints about the "scandalous" assertion of power by the abbess of Huelgas, once attributed to the year 1210 and to Innocent III, but now correctly tied to a letter of Innocent IV (for 1244). It was described by Lekai in 1970: "The strange custom that the abbess of Las Huelgas arrogated priestly privileges, such as blessing novices, preaching homilies and hearing nuns' confessions. The abuse was stopped only by the energetic invention of Innocent III in 1210."[55] Long attributed to Innocent III (1198–1216), probably by Manrique in the seventeenth century, the papal letter (which contained no year, as is common for such shorter papal letters in this period) must be identified as being from Innocent IV (1243–54). Indeed, the papal registers of Innocent IV for 1244 describe the incident: "Concerning the mad temerity of that most arrogant abbess of the monastery of Huelgas of the Cistercian Order, where Berengaria is a nun, [that abbess] who has indeed defiled the sacrament [of ordination] by presuming to place veils on nuns, although forbidden to do so by the bishop of Burgos, should be reprimanded and disciplined appropriately by the abbot of Cîteaux. Moreover, he should forbid such actions by all the order's abbesses in Spain, lest others later try to do the same."[56] In addition to the identification of this in a papal register for 1244, it is unlikely that the abbesses of the new royal abbey, founded only in 1187, could have expanded their power so much by 1210; also the reference to Berengaria, or Berenguela, relates to the mid- and not the early thirteenth century.[57]

The incident of 1244 may have shaken Innocent IV's confidence in and favor for Cistercian nuns. Certainly the next two agreements between the pope and the order, those for 1249 and 1251, appear to support the abbots' efforts to regularize the nuns. That in 1249, one which is not discussed by Lekai, appears to be the papal confirmation of the General Chapter's determination that nuns be visited by father abbots, not by bishops—the newly introduced practice that seems to have led to rebellions of nuns in 1243. An item in Innocent IV's registers, as published by Élie Berger, refers to a letter sent by the pope from Lyons on April 27, 1249, to the General Chapter of

Cîteaux, agreeing that the Cistercian abbots could require that all houses of nuns be visited by members of the order: "In the General Chapter of the Cistercians it is said to have been established that nuns of the order will no longer be placed under any authority other than a father abbot or a representative assigned by him, and that no other kind of religious or secular priests will hear nuns' confessions or be allowed to absolve their sins. The pope provides that no other practice be allowed."[58]

Still whereas the abbots in the General Chapter may have asserted abbots' oversight in visitation, it is not clear how seriously those abbots took their responsibilities as is seen in examples from Part II of this study. Saint-Antoine's nuns in Paris were exceptional in having important charters witnessed or co-issued with the abbot of Cîteaux, but these concerned extremely large amounts of cash; otherwise even at Saint-Antoine, benign neglect was probably the norm. In contrast when papal commissioners in Sens called the abbess of Cour-Notre-Dame to testify about why she had not paid a crusader tithe, it was the abbess, not her father visitor or even a representative of her father visitor, who appeared. Even when the nuns of Blanche of Castile's foundation at Lys discovered that royal officials were trying to pay them in cash rather than making the grain deliveries promised by royal donations, those nuns appear to have complained directly to King Philip IV without any support from a father abbot (for all these examples, see below). Indeed, Bondéelle-Souchier has suggested that abbot visitors' failure of oversight, rather than any poor management by the nuns, explains those nuns' difficulties in the fifteenth century.[59]

A second item of papal business with the order is dated to 1251 by the General Chapter records and by Lekai (but not found in the published papal records, which are notoriously incomplete). Thus, in the Cistercian *Statuta* of 1251, no. 4 reports: "As has been granted by the highest pontiff to our order, lest we be held to the incorporation of abbeys of nuns by apostolic letters, the General Chapter establishes and commands that no more abbeys of nuns for whatever reason be incorporated into our order."[60] Lekai comments on it: "After a number of forced admissions [that is, forced on it], the Chapter of 1251 finally obtained from Innocent IV the ultimate guarantee: the Order was free to ignore future papal briefs in the matter and to enforce a total halt to [nuns' communities'] incorporation."[61] This is an overstatement. While political pressure on the order, like that from Queen Blanche of Castile (d. 1252) and Pope Innocent IV (1243–54) may have kept the doors of the order open wide until midcentury, the Pope now agreed not to expect houses of Cistercian nuns to be admitted by papal recommendation. Nevertheless, the incorporation of houses of Cistercian nuns did not halt; such incorporations, albeit at a slower rate, continued up to and beyond the end of the thirteenth century. This is revealed even in the *Statuta*, and is now attested by many historians because it is clear in the archival evidence.[62]

Cistercian nuns were part of the order, and what the charters for this study show is that they were rarely poor or ephemeral. Instead, the documents show the effectiveness of Cistercian abbesses in amassing the considerable property that supported their communities. Those abbesses were competent leaders and skilled managers of estates and other properties. Their communities were highly respected by thirteenth-century patrons who sought association and prayers from those nuns.[63] Indeed, although it is no excuse for having denied women power over the sacraments, the fact that abbesses were denied priestly roles may have actually given them more time to devote to the administration of property and oversight of their communities of nuns.[64]

CHAPTER 3

Cistercian Nuns and the Order's Economic Practices

In the 1940s historians Francesco Gosso and David Knowles asserted that there was a distinctive Cistercian grange or estate, consisting of large expanses of land managed by monks and worked by lay brothers. Those imagined Cistercian estates were contrasted to traditional Benedictine ones based on peasant family farms producing rents, taxes, and tithes, and perhaps labor services. Such assertions that Cistercian communities had different economic practices from Benedictine ones were challenged by Catherine E. Boyd in 1943, when she published a study of Rifreddo, the thirteenth-century abbey of Cistercian nuns in the "Valle del Po" in the Italian Piedmont near Saluzzo.[1] Rifreddo could not be characterized as either Benedictine or Cistercian, for it was located in a mountainous environment, occupying an economic niche that fit neither idealized description, and this worried Boyd. There is little reason to worry, however, as Boyd once did, about whether nuns' management of property could define them as Cistercian or not. More recent studies have shown much more diversity than was once thought in the economic practices between Cistercian or Benedictine abbeys of monks and between those of nuns and monks. The properties of Cistercians cannot always be starkly contrasted to those of the Benedictines.[2]

This chapter rejects myths about "Cistercians and the forest," once applied to the order's monks and the sites they settled in, showing that the sites they came to occupy can no longer be assumed to have been in the "deserts" of western Europe.[3] The economic success associated with the order's abbeys of monks was not based on "frontiering" activities. Cistercian monks and nuns arriving at abbey sites found little wilderness remaining and they were rarely involved in the pioneering activities once attributed to them. Instead, both monks and nuns among the Cistercians acquired endowments of long-cultivated properties.[4]

This chapter, which considers abbeys of Cistercian nuns in a number of parts of Europe beyond the more focused area of Part II, suggests just how much our understanding of twelfth and thirteenth-century monastic economies, especially those of the Cistercians, has advanced since the 1940s.[5] Yet our explanations for Cistercian successes that have posited a transformation of uncultivated places into cultivated ones are largely unfounded. Indeed it turns out that clearance and reclamation were nearly complete when those early twelfth century reformers arrived.[6] Whatever cutting down and uprooting of trees had been done in the recent past had been done by their predecessors—possibly a few hermits, but most often anonymous peasants clearing plots at the edge of villages or draining areas on the banks of streams and rivers. "Cistercian grange agriculture" had little to do with the reclamation once attributed to monastic communities and explanations derived from the narratives that Cistercians used to describe themselves or to justify their exemption from such levies as tithes. While tithe exemption was important, the order's considerable economic success derived from the reorganization of long-cultivated properties and its rationalized agricultural approaches. It appears, moreover, that within the reform movement more generally there was considerable rethinking about medieval monastic resource management. For the Cistercians, that discussion is only imperfectly reflected in such declarations as their *prima collectio*, or *instituta*.[7] Whatever the date of those lists of principles, the fact that rethinking about monastic labor and resources was being attempted is too easily lost in a modern and often legalistic discourse about "forbidden resources" or "ideals and reality."

Much of the land acquired by Cistercians for abbey sites, but also for their granges, had been cultivated for generations. Cistercian success was found not in frontiersmen-like activities but in an austere lifestyle, revised liturgies that allowed monks and nuns time to abide by Benedictine injunctions about manual labor and self-support, and other efficiencies created by the consolidation of long-fragmented holdings, investment in new tools and practices, increased pastoralism, and access to growing markets for meat and animal products in the growing towns of twelfth-century Europe. The order's early abbots and abbesses soon acquired exemptions from tithes, passage tolls, and market taxes in nearby cities, which provided them with favored conditions for selling. The cash income from such sales was invested not in elaborate buildings or impressive liturgical celebrations but in more land, new and better iron tools, mills, forges, and barns, as well as better breeding stock, all of which contributed to the effectiveness of what has often been called "Cistercian grange agriculture."[8]

Cistercian Sites

Nevertheless early Cistercian narratives that had depicted those monks as heroic ascetics creating sites in the "new deserts" of the medieval West have long held sway. They do so in part because glances at modern-day Cistercian sites seem to confirm them. The author of the life of Pons de Léras, describing the foundation of a southern French hermitage that became Cistercian, stated that its founders chose to live "in the wilderness in the company of beasts."[9] Ellen F. Arnold, however, has shown in a study of early monasticism in the Ardennes that such descriptions of monks and lay brothers in the forest had been used in monastic narratives and hagiography long before the twelfth century and should not be taken literally.[10]

Often too we have misinterpreted the evidence of manuscript painting. Cistercian manuscript illuminations show monks and conversi cutting branches and splitting logs, but in fact those manuscripts do not document monks and lay brothers transforming forested wilderness that had never before seen human occupation into agricultural expanses. Instead they document Cistercian practices of forest management through regular coppicing and pollarding, which were widespread in medieval Europe (Figure 1).[11] Cistercian monks and conversi climbing into trees were cutting back branches or attacking the new growth on stumps; in such situations, moreover, their arduous labor was limited.[12]

Still new monastic communities of the twelfth century appear to have been founded "far from cities, castles, and human habitations," and the sites on which Cistercians and other reformers established their communities give the impression of being isolated in the uninhabited "deserts" on the fringes of existing settlements.[13] Those "deserts," however, were of very recent date, created by the purchase and consolidation of land and the removal of earlier tenants by a process of village creation or consolidation. Such village nucleation, the process of *incastellamento*, has been described by Pierre Toubert for Italy, by Monique Bourin for southern France, and by Robert Fossier for Picardy.[14] In it peasants who had been responsible for recent settlement and cultivation on the

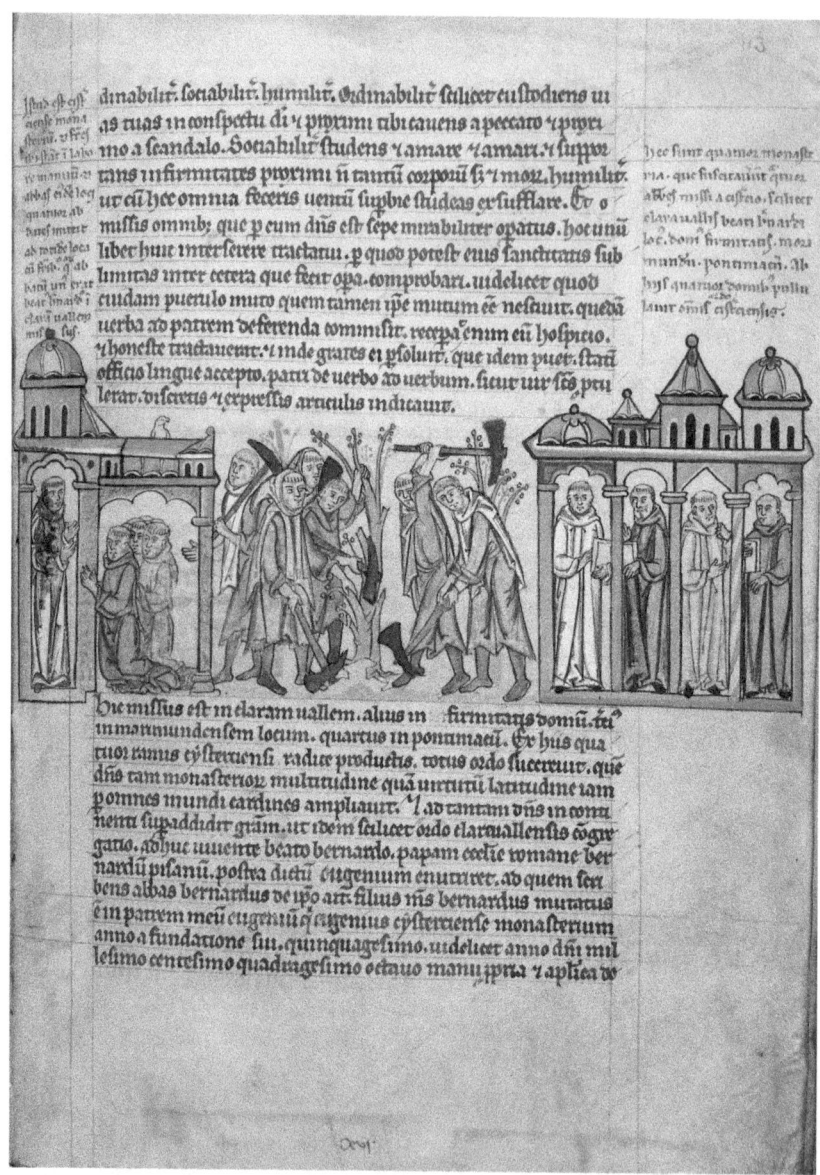

boundaries of parishes were moved into newly centralized villages in the vicinity of churches and castles and offered new amenities such as mills, wine presses, and communal ovens. As peasants moved, or were moved, into new villages, recently cultivated locations on the edges of settlement became available and were given or sold to monks and nuns (often to the monastic reformers).

Thus establishment of monastic settlements in isolation on the boundaries of parishes and far distant from the new villages was at least partly a result of this larger secular trend of village creation. Sites farthest from the new villages were those that earlier owners and cultivators were most anxious to give up, not only because of travel costs, but because they may have involved more risk. Particularly for peasants who had drained rich river bottoms, their flooding every dozen years or so could be disastrous and not absorbed as easily as it could be by monastic communities. Owners were eager to give and sell those holdings to someone else. This is seen north of Toulouse in the marshy river bottom of the middle Garonne where peasant cultivators had drained swamps after 1100 but eventually sold their riverine holdings to the Cistercian monks of Grandselve. The monastic community could better absorb the risk of flooding, and its tithe exemption may have made the difference between losses or profits from those lands (as is seen for nuns in the region of the Sologne, as discussed in Chapter 5).[15] Occasionally it was Cistercian monks and nuns in agreements with earlier lords who created some of these new villages to which peasants were moved; this is seen, for instance, at Villelongue east of Carcassonne or at Villeveyrac near Valmagne, but also in an extensive history of founding bastides (planned towns on what had earlier been granges) by Cistercians in concert with civil authorities.[16] There was sometimes resistance to such removals, as in Gascony when peasants murdered a servant attempting to establish the boundaries for a new grange at Cuelas, but as far as the record reveals this was unusual.[17]

Whereas it was once assumed that nuns could not have managed the hard and arduous labor undertaken by the monks of this new "pioneering" Cistercian Order, there may have been very little arduous work to be undertaken by either monks or nuns when their settlements were made on the edges of existing parishes that had been consolidated in nucleated villages. Moreover, if this is a reliable explanation for Cistercian monks, it is probably also true for Cistercian nuns. Thus an oft-cited description of Cistercian nuns at Montreuil-les-Dames near Laon, written circa 1150 by Herman of Tournay, a canon of the cathedral of Laon, must be reassessed. He said: "Those nuns lived in accord with the *ordo* or practices of Cîteaux, which is difficult even for men . . . working hard, not at spinning and weaving (the usual work of women), but also at harvesting the fields, pulling up brush, uprooting the forest, and cultivating their fields, living with only wild beasts as their neighbors. Indeed, seeking their food in silence, these women imitated in all things the lives of the monks of Clairvaux, a clear sign from the Lord that all is possible for those who believe."[18]

While this description attests to the presence of Cistercian nuns in the diocese of Laon from the mid-twelfth century, its portrayal of nuns "uprooting trees and brush" is unlikely. Like Cistercian monks at the time, Montreuil's nuns were not established at an isolated site that required arduous reclamation, but probably one from which peasants had withdrawn into newly created villages like those described for this region by Fossier.[19] Herman's comments about pioneering and his dismissive remarks about the spinning and weaving that were women's work and the miraculous feats accomplished by those nuns "only with the Lord's aid" draw from the same tropes that Ellen Arnold has described about monks in the forest, but also from a stock of long-held misogynous assumptions about women's work.[20]

Cistercian Expansion and Grange Agriculture

Cistercian monks and nuns alike had considerable success in their rural activities. While Cistercian injunctions about manual labor and self-support meant that agricultural work was to be undertaken by the entire community of monks or nuns, this was a successful plan only when fields were close to the abbey. New abbeys of Cistercian monks and nuns were characterized by their accumulation of grange properties—satellite holdings at some distance from abbey centers, acquired both through gifts and purchases. The abstemious lifestyle of these reformers provided savings of cash that could be reinvested in land purchases that were systematically aimed at optimal production by reintegration of what had become fragmented holdings into larger, more compact estates. On these granges it was lay sisters (for the nuns) and lay brothers (for both) who were dispatched to the more distant granges; they were peasant converts to the religious life from families once living on lands that became Cistercian granges.[21] Monks and nuns, however, continued to join lay brothers and lay sisters at more distant granges during labor-intensive seasons, for instance, when the entire community of Cistercian monks of the abbey of Grandselve near Toulouse was dispatched for the olive harvest at Elne near Perpignan.[22]

Very important in the rapid expansion of Cistercian abbeys for monks in the twelfth century was the order's incorporation of independent eremitical and monastic groups. Such independent reformers, among them wandering preachers and hermits, came to be settled like the Cistercians on the fringes of settled villages. They eventually sought rules and regulations for the full-fledged monasteries they were becoming. Many found affiliation with the early Cistercians to be an attractive prospect because of Cistercian espousal of austerity and because early Cistercian texts provided practical guidance on the practice of animal husbandry using lay brothers.[23] Often these groups ended up adopting Cistercian liturgical and economic practices. In this process of incorporation, the use of written documents was becoming central, although reading aloud and discussion would have created the "textual communities" coming to be found around such documents.[24] For nuns there is evidence of the use of written documents for active management, as we see in Chapter 6 for the abbey of Maubuisson and in Chapter 7 for Saint-Antoine.

Beyond the benefits of more consolidated agricultural holdings, Cistercian monks and nuns alike introduced labor savings associated with pastoralism and animal husbandry, sometimes even turning into pasture the marginal agricultural lands that earlier peasants had attempted to cultivate. Generous twelfth- and thirteenth-century lords and ladies who often gave the order's monks and nuns access to "pasture in all our lands" encouraged such pastoralism.[25] Often this pastoralism incorporated transhumance, a practice in which animals were moved seasonally from higher to lower elevations and back again. The labor savings of pastoralism were particularly attractive to communities of nuns, as discussed below.

Cistercian monks and nuns alike acquired extensive agricultural expanses that served as granges, but they also acquired mills and increased viticulture. Water-powered mills were among the most important assets for Cistercian nuns at Cañas in the Riojas region of Spain, as described by Ghislain Baury; those nuns owned at least a dozen mills by the mid-thirteenth century, but whether or not such numerous mills reflected the cereal output of their granges is less clear.[26] It may be that they were instead used simply as sources of revenue, as Georges Duby has suggested for early Cistercian monks at la Ferté in Burgundy[27] Such water- and, later, wind-powered mills saved labor, producing flour for bread and other materials that had once been processed by human or animal power; that labor could then be put to more productive tasks.[28] Viticulture and wine production, at least for internal purposes, had been practiced by the Cistercians from an early date. Indeed, among

Cîteaux's earliest properties was the famous Burgundian vineyard of the Clos de Vougeot.[29] Baury's study underlines the activities of Cistercian nuns at Cañas in the Riojas purchasing vineyards, trellises, and appropriate lands for wine production.[30] There and elsewhere contracts *ad medium* for planting vineyards were used by many houses of nuns, including those in the province of Sens that are considered in Part II of this study.[31]

Diverse Adaptations: Rifreddo's Cistercian Nuns

Rifreddo's founders were a mother and daughter, both acting in their widowhood. The elder was Alice of Montferrat, the widow of Manfred II, Marquis of Saluzzo; she was regent in the early thirteenth century for her underage grandson, Manfred of Montferrat. The younger, Alice's daughter, Agnes, was the childless widow of Comita II (he who had ruled the Sardinian judgeship of Torres). After Comita II's death in 1217 Agnes had returned to the Piedmont and joined her mother, Alice, in founding Rifreddo in the next years, probably using the funds that had come from Agnes's marriage portion. The holdings purchased for the abbey site had belonged to the young Manfred of Monferrat, the grandson for whom Alice was regent. Both Agnes and Alice soon retired to Rifreddo. The daughter, Agnes, died first, in 1223.[32] Her mother, Alice, acted in several subsequent contracts for Rifreddo, entering the abbey before her death in 1233.[33]

The abbey was not at first Cistercian, for Alice's relationship with the nearby Cistercian monks at Staffarda was not cordial.[34] There is some evidence that in 1221 Pope Honorius III had confirmed Rifreddo as a house of nuns following the Rule of Saint Benedict, exempt from local episcopal control, answering directly to the pope, and paying a nominal annual fee in recognition of that papal overlordship, but the evidence is embedded in a mid-thirteenth-century document.[35] In 1249, a papal confirmation of its properties included the typical Cistercian tithe exemption of the thirteenth century that begins "Sane novalium" and recognized Rifreddo's nuns as Cistercian.[36] In the next two years Rifreddo's nuns admitted into their community two recluses from the village of Moncalieri just outside the city of Turin; in so doing, they incorporated urban penitent women, probably proto-mendicants.[37]

Nearly all Rifreddo's property was purchased immediately. The two founders spent more than 1,500 Genovesan pounds for Rifreddo's endowment and site in the early 1220s. Some of the new abbey's holdings must have looked more like those of a Benedictine estate than a Cistercian one (if one wanted to make such a distinction), because in 1224, Alice purchased an entire Benedictine priory of nuns at Saint Hilary in nearby Revello for 300 pounds, "with all the lands of Saint Hilary: its fields, cultivated or fallow, grasses, pasture, meadows, vineyards, and woods in the territories of Revello and of Henuis, both in the mountains and in the plain, including alpine pastures at Calveto, rents, produce, claims, annuities, contracts, and debts."[38] Still Rifreddo's economic practices were more like those of the Cistercians. A list of its properties dated ca. 1250 recalls that the abbey was founded in an existing village, some of it adjoining the abbey itself: "The lands and meadows beyond the Po River that belong to the monastery of Rifreddo, [and.] a field that was once Jacob of Rifreddo's, a meadow belonging to the *furnicarius* [baker or smith?], a cow barn, the millrace, and the field adjoining the *battendario* [threshing floor?]."[39] That list from the 1250s included sixty-three journaux of arable land scattered over twenty-four holdings, as well as eighteen pieces of meadow and woodland beyond the Po (at this point a mere brook) and above the village of Rifreddo, including "five journaux of land, which Warner Martini had uprooted [*runchavit*]."[40] The surviving documents suggest a carefully managed mountain economy, located much closer to the margins of settlement than was generally the case for either Cistercian monks or Cistercian nuns.[41]

To practice its agriculture tithe-free, Rifreddo's nuns, like other Cistercians, acquired tithes that had fallen into lay hands over land that the nuns eventually cultivated in demesne by buying out rights from earlier lay or monastic owners and with agreements from the bishops of Turin for the nuns to hold those repurchased tithes.[42] The charters are filled with disputes over tithes, particularly with the monks of Staffarda, perhaps because as a revenue source tithes, if they remained a percentage of the harvest, were more inflation-proof than other income.[43] Rifreddo's nuns believed, probably correctly given the many disputes over tithes, that the abbots of Staffarda, assigned as their abbot visitor, were envious of the nuns' rights. Their complaints about Staffarda eventually led Rifreddo to be assigned to the visitation of the abbot of Lucedio. Eventually Rifreddo withdrew from the Cistercian Order and attached itself to the Dominicans instead.[44]

Diverse Adaptations: A Double House of Cistercians at Obazine and Coyroux

Obazine was founded in the 1130s, and what became the two communities of Obazine and Coyroux developed in unusual circumstances. In 1134 the bishop of Tulle recognized that the hermitage founded by Stephen at Obazine had become the monastery of Obazine.[45] By the 1140s it was documented as a "double community," eventually incorporated by the Cistercians, and probably transformed into two abbeys in the 1160s when the property at Coyroux was acquired and the nuns were established there.[46] At that point the assets of both, of nuns at Coyroux and of monks still at Obazine, were placed in the hands of the monks of Obazine, who were to provide for all the material needs of Coyroux's nuns.[47] It was apparently the nuns themselves who insisted on living an even more austere lifestyle than that of the monks; their church was located in a steep valley that flooded several times, and the entire physical plant would always be less substantial than that of Obazine.[48]

The community had attracted men and women from an early date. Indeed entire families entered to join the religious life.[49] Some of them were probably married priests and their wives who had chosen to live chaste lives together; often they came with considerable property, as if an entire village had entered. For instance, circa 1160, Peter of Veyrières, his brother Bernard, and Petronilla, their sister, as well as Peter's wife and their sons and daughters, "left the world to enter the abbey of Obazine . . . and gave the abbey their fortified house or estate of Veyrières with its lands, meadows, waters, mills, woodlands, and appurtenances, including three *mansi* (family farms) and a long list of rents on lands there."[50] Veyrières would become a grange. Similarly, Peter William of Albussac and his wife Aalmas, "renouncing the world in exchange for the celestial lands," gave Obazine a village at Albussac (that also became a grange) with its church, mill, tenants, and fief holders, when they "gave themselves" as "*dévotées*" to enter Obazine with their sons "to serve the poor of that place."[51] Another entrance of several entire families is documented in the form of a will: "This is the testament that Ademar Berengarii made when he, his wife and all their children relinquished the world and gave themselves for the religious life at the monastery of Obazine, giving all their possessions to that monastery . . . their houses at Saint-Palavy, the gardens they hold there, a meadow, a vineyard, and a field adjoining the mill dam . . . and rents by cultivators there."[52] They were joined by Gausbert of Sarrazac and his two daughters and by Hugh of Saint-Michael, his wife, Berniarz, and their two daughters, all of whom entered the abbey; this resulted in the grange of Saint-Palavy.[53]

When Obazine had acquired a priory or monastic cell around which settlers had already established themselves it might be maintained as a separate monastic cell, as was the case for "the paupers of Obazine" who were living at the church of Baudrun. They so impressed Boso, Viscount of Turenne (1142–53) that he vowed to give them "whatever they needed from his lands"; his widow, the viscountess, fulfilled that vow after his death.[54]

Gifts of fields already under cultivation and their income, tithes, mills, barns, and fortified buildings were often made when someone entered the community, but the contracts might also concern the return of tithes to the church or the recognition of Cistercian tithe exemption. Thus, in 1162 Obazine acquired tithes in the parish of Graulière when Peter the Judge granted rights to a *mansus* to Obazine and to tithes "over whatever was worked by Obazine in that parish." In 1164, the tithes at Graulière were granted by Raymond of Bouchiat, and in 1170 Bartholomew of Saint Clement gave tithes there when his son was received into Obazine, presumably as a monk.[55] After various tenants had transferred rights to Obazine for the grange of Montagne in 1159, Brunisenz, the Viscountess of Comborn, along with William de Vitrac and his wife, granted lordship and tithes at Montagne in 1162.[56] Such women could be prominent as patrons. When they entered the community of Coyroux after the deaths of their respective fathers, four women, two daughters of Gerald Geoffrey, and their two first cousins, daughters of Peter Geoffrey, brought rights to what became the grange of Ramière near Meymac, including rights over their tenants there.[57] Another woman involved with that grange at Ramière was Berniarz, the wife of Gerald Pistor (baker) of Turenne.[58] Among previously unaffiliated groups, Obazine and Coyroux also incorporated the nuns at Sallac and the *reclusae* at Damnach.[59]

In the 1190s a gift was made to fund a pittance meal for the nuns of Coyroux, when they celebrated an anniversary mass once established at the failed abbey of Cistercian monks at Sourdain.[60] Monks and nuns at Obazine and Coyroux practiced pastoralism based on gifts of pasture rights from local elites, as in 1168 when Garin of Castelnau granted pasture in all his uncultivated lands, passage rights, and exemption from tolls for all of Obazine's animals.[61] They also practiced transhumance between various granges near the abbey and those near the high summer pastures.

Cistercian Nuns and Pastoralism

Such pastoralism was particularly attractive for communities of nuns, because it was much less labor intensive than cereal cultivation. Often it was practiced in cooperative arrangements among several monastic communities. Thus the

nuns at Nonenque, in the Rouergue, appear to have been part of a congregation of reform monks and nuns who had been moving animals in early June
up into the high summer pastures of the Central Massif, then bringing them
back in the fall to the winter pastures in the marshes of the Rhône delta and
Languedoc.[62] The abbey of Nonenque had been founded in the 1130s by nuns
coming from Bellecombe in the Auvergne and probably arriving earlier in
the vicinity than the nearby hermit/monks of Silvanès.[63] A list from 1170 of
parishes in the highlands of the eastern Rouergue in which the nuns held
freedom from ecclesiastical tithes included Saint-Paul-de-la-Fos, Saint-Jean
of Olcas, Saint-Jean of Alcapiès, and Notre-Dame of Cassanuéjouls.[64] This
practice of transhumance predated the affiliation of many of the local religious houses with the Cistercians, and such a practice is still seen at places
like Saint-Rémy-de-Provence, where on the first Sunday of June animals are
decorated and paraded through the streets to be blessed before they begin
their ascent to the *montagnes*. In areas around Arles the animals may be seen
in the fields in the winter months.

Given its location in the region long known for its production of Roque-
fort cheese, the Cistercian nuns at Nonenque probably focused their sheep
pasturing on the production of milk.[65] Some details about their tithe-exempt
sheep raising are documented in the account of a dispute over tithe exemption that arose in 1177 when the Benedictine monks of Saint-Sauveur in
Lodève made claims against Nonenque. The monks disputed Nonenque's
claim to tithe exemption for its grange of Mas Andraud located in the parish
of Saint-Beaulize, citing their own papal privileges there. Eventually Nonenque's tithe privilege was given priority, because it had been granted earlier. It
was agreed that Saint-Sauveur's monks were not to exact tithes from the
nuns' grange of Mas Andraud, but as owners of the church of Saint-Beaulize
they were owed small dues: "one sheepskin, one cheese, and one lamb—
neither the best nor the worst," and "first fruits" for all *mansi* in the parish,
including those owned by the nuns. Any dispute about whether an individual
animal belonged to the nuns or not was to be resolved by the testimony of
the nuns' lay brothers and lay sisters at Mas Andraud.[66]

In contrast, for Cistercian nuns in Britain, it was wool production that
was paramount, as seen at the priories of Cistercian nuns at Stixwould in
Lincolnshire and Coldstream in Scotland. The first, Stixwould, had been
founded between 1129 and 1135 by Lucy, Countess of Chester, a royal vassal
holding directly from King Henry I, and is discussed by Coburn Graves.[67]
He describes its nuns' emphasis on sheep raising:

Sheepfolds (*bercariae*) were maintained outside grange limits at Horsington, Winelle, Hungerton, Stoke, and Edmesthorpe. Pasture rights for flocks ranging from fifty to two hundred sheep were distributed even more widely over the countryside at Ferriby, Hundelby, Barkston, Panton, Winelle, Hungerton, Stoke, Wymondham, and Edmesthorpe. . . . In some instances the lands attached to sheepfolds were taken from arable, and on occasion the reduction of arable to pastoral use seems to indicate an economic sensitivity to where the greater profit lay.[68]

Stixwould's emphasis on commercial wool production is confirmed by the nuns' properties and privileges in Boston, the major port at the time for export of English wool to the continent.[69] Graves also comments on the balance between pasture and arable in its holdings: "By maintaining some sort of balance between commitments to crops and sheep, the nuns avoided the potential disasters attendant on a commitment to a one-crop economy. In this sector of their economy the nuns gave clear proof of managerial prudence and competence."[70]

The balanced economy seen at Stixwould was less apparent for the Cistercian nuns at Coldstream in the diocese of Saint Andrews in Scotland, where the emphasis was very much on pastoralism. Coldstream probably dates to circa 1165, when Gospatrick II, Earl of Dunbar, granted a foundation charter for its new community of nuns whatever he had in the territories of Laynal and Hersil.[71] His son Patrick gave whatever was "within the villa and outside it, that is in moors and marshes in meadows and pasture, in water, in ponds, in fishing and in mills, and all else, without any subtraction."[72] Although they had some mills, some fishing rights, and apple orchards, animal husbandry provided the nuns' major source of income; pasture rights were granted to them in large expanses where boundaries were described by peaks and valleys, as in this grant from Patrick: "Located on one side of the ridge or fell between Whitcester and Otterburn that stretched up to a spring or water source and then extended across the moor to a peak to the north, [where pasture was acquired] from the crossing at the top of Whielhope outside the woods, then extending up into the vale to Selbuckley, before descending between Fermley and Strikesly."[73] Particularly explicit are pasture rights for various animals granted in the common pasturelands at Thornditch or Thorndike: "The nuns could send forty mares and their foals of up to three years old, eighty cows or oxen, eighty pigs, and two hundred sheep.

Sheep there could enjoy access [*gaudebunt*] without payment in the common pasture of Gordon when necessary, although the nuns were not to construct a sheepfold there."[74] Coldstream's nuns also acquired rights in the port of Berwick, which became a rival to Boston for wool exports.[75] Coldstream appears to be similar to some of the important border abbeys for monks recently studied by Emilia Jamroziak.[76]

Extensive pastureland was also granted to Cistercian nuns in Spain, for instance by King Alphonso VIII in his foundation document of 1187 for Huelgas. The king granted "to the monastery and its granges anywhere in the kingdom the freedom to buy, sell, transport without tolls, and to have free pasture for its animals in all the woods and other places where the king held pasture for his own animals. Also he [granted] passage rights without tax for the nuns' animals going up to or coming down from the mountain pastures. The nuns' shepherds and shepherds' huts would have the same."[77] Such concern about pasture is also seen for abbeys of nuns in the Riojas. Baury shows founders of the abbey of Cistercian nuns at Herce there, Alfons Lopez and Maria Alvarez, giving an "inherited estate" with its tenants, and one thousand sheep, one hundred cattle, and two hundred pigs in 1246.[78] From at least the second half of the thirteenth century, moreover, the nuns of Cañas participated in the great transhumance of central Castile as documented by an exemption dated 1281 about its nuns' participation in itinerant pastoralism there and the conversion of a grinding mill into one for fulling cloth in 1272, which likewise suggests their production of wool and woolen cloth.[79]

Conclusions

The many recent studies of abbeys of Cistercian nuns across Europe (a number of them cited in the bibliography but not mentioned here) are now beginning to allow historians to count the number of communities of Cistercian nuns. Given such data as that found in Appendix 5, "Numbers of Cistercian Nuns' Houses According to Selected Historians," it is then possible to chart the pattern of their expansion. This is shown in Figure 2.[80]

This brief survey of some of the resources acquired by houses of Cistercian nuns across Europe shows that for nuns as well as for monks, there was considerable diversity in patterns of land use and asset acquisition across Europe. This has forced us to think anew just what it is, if anything, that characterizes the Cistercian economy. There is no single type of Cistercian

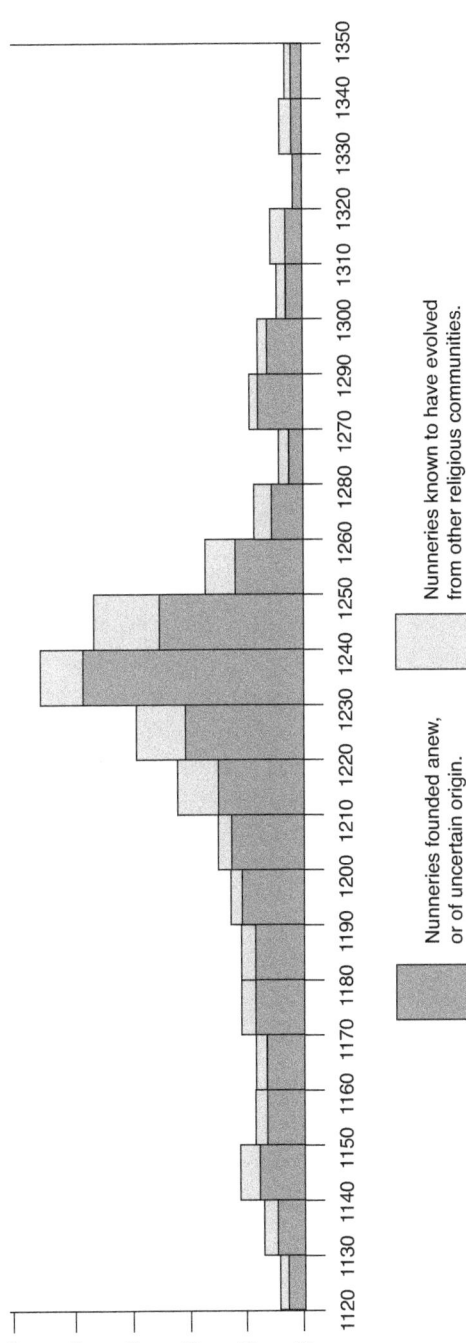

FIGURE 2. The growth of the early Cistercian nunneries in ten-yearly cycles, 1120–1350. Original drawing by David Williams.

Nunneries known to have evolved from other religious communities.

Nunneries founded anew, or of uncertain origin.

grange or grange agriculture. There is no one signifier among the economic resources of the order's houses of monks or nuns that would indicate which were or were not part of the order. There is no consistency in our understanding of the incorporation of earlier groups by Cistercian monks or nuns or of the consequences of such incorporation. We can no longer assume that the incorporation of entire congregations of monks and nuns or that the appearance in the order of double houses that would eventually be divided into one house of monks and one of nuns signaled an end to the pristine unanimity of an order.[81]

A serious reassessment in the late eleventh and early twelfth century of how monastic economies should be operated is probably reflected in lists of "forbidden assets or practices," but the point here is that these should not be taken in too legalistic a way.[82] Instead, such lists reflected discussions of how spiritual communities could live that looked back at earlier texts and models—the primitive Rule of Benedict, the lives of the desert fathers, and in particular to the lives of the apostles. They reveal monastic reformers' experimentation with new styles of living, but their specifics were not as important as the rethinking behind them. Unanimous only in being opposed to the old ways of a monumental Benedictine lifestyle, the new reformers, monks and nuns alike, Cistercian and others, welcomed and embraced a new diversity and eschewed uniformity in details of economic life. Such freedom to rethink was essential to the actual success of the practitioners of the Cistercian grange economy. This is seen in Part II of this study as well.

PART II

Cistercian Nuns in the Ecclesiastical
Province of Sens

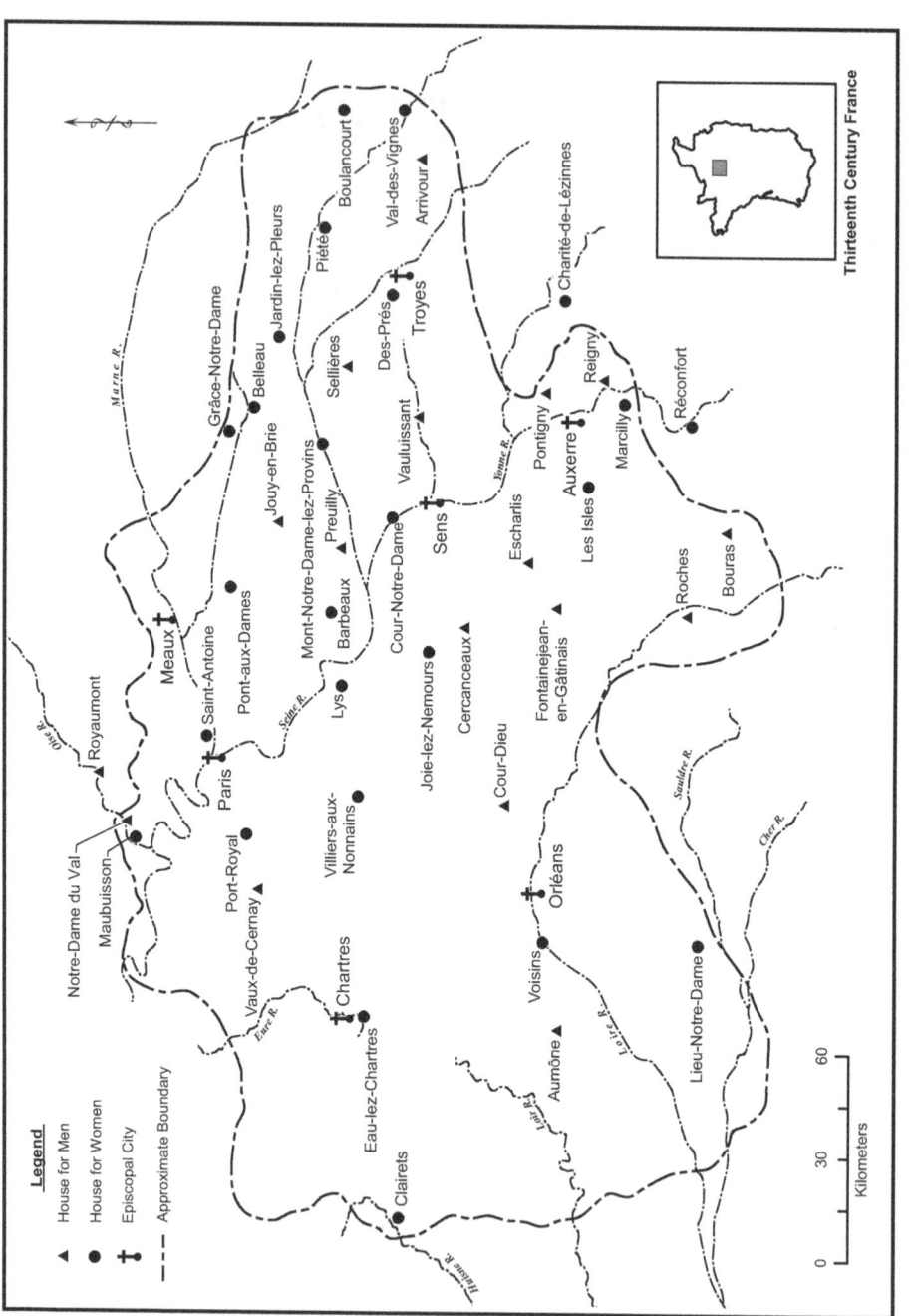

MAP I. Abbeys of Cistercian monks and women in the environs of Sens, Meaux, and Sées (see Appendices).

Legend
▲ House for Men
● House for Women
✝ Episcopal City
– – – Approximate Boundary

Thirteenth Century France

Notre-Dame du Val
Maubuisson
Royaumont
Meaux
Saint-Antoine
Pont-aux-Dames
Paris
Port-Royal
Vaux-de-Cernay
Villiers-aux-Nonnains
Chartres
Eau-lez-Chartres
Clairets
Aumône
Voisins
Orléans
Lieu-Notre-Dame
Cour-Dieu
Joie-lez-Nemours
Cercanceaux
Fontainejean-en-Gâtinais
Lys
Barbeaux
Cour-Notre-Dame
Mont-Notre-Dame-lez-Provins
Preuilly
Vauluissant
Sens
Escharlis
Les Isles
Auxerre
Pontigny
Reigny
Réconfort
Marcilly
Roches
Bouras
Chanté-de-Lézinnes
Des-Prés
Troyes
Sellières
Piété
Jardin-lez-Pleurs
Boulancourt
Val-des-Vignes
Arrivour
Jouy-en-Brie
Belleau
Grâce-Notre-Dame

Marne R.
Seine R.
Oise R.
Eure R.
Loire R.
Loir R.
Cher R.
Sauldre R.
Yonne R.
Huisne R.

0   30   60
Kilometers

CHAPTER 4

Women Regents, Cistercian Nuns, and Feudal Crisis: Clairets, Villiers, Voisins, and Port-Royal

There were over twenty houses of Cistercian nuns founded in early thirteenth-century France in the ecclesiastical province of Sens; there had been earlier houses of Cistercian monks there as well, so that in the end the numbers were about equal. See Map 1 for all the houses in this study and the earlier foundations for men's houses as well. The evidence for abbeys of Cistercian nuns founded in the province of Sens shows that they were often founded by *dominae*, or lady lords, elite women of some power and standing.[1] Those women were acting in one of two possible capacities. Some acted on behalf of husbands who had just died, often using income from dower properties. Others were heiresses who came to power after the death of all male heirs in their families. The latter sometimes had husbands for part of their rule but had few limits on their power to disperse land and revenues to religious foundations, particularly if they had no direct descendants. Chapter 4 discusses three abbeys of Cistercian nuns, Clairets, Villiers, and Port-Royal, all founded by regents and widows who were not heiresses in their own right; a fourth abbey, at Voisins, was founded in 1215 by a group of widows on behalf of husbands' souls.[2] Foundations by the other group of abbeys, made by heiresses in their own right, but like the founders in this chapter making foundations in western France, are discussed in Chapter 5. These foundations discussed here as well as those for the houses of nuns discussed in Chapter 5 along with some of their major properties are included in Map 2.

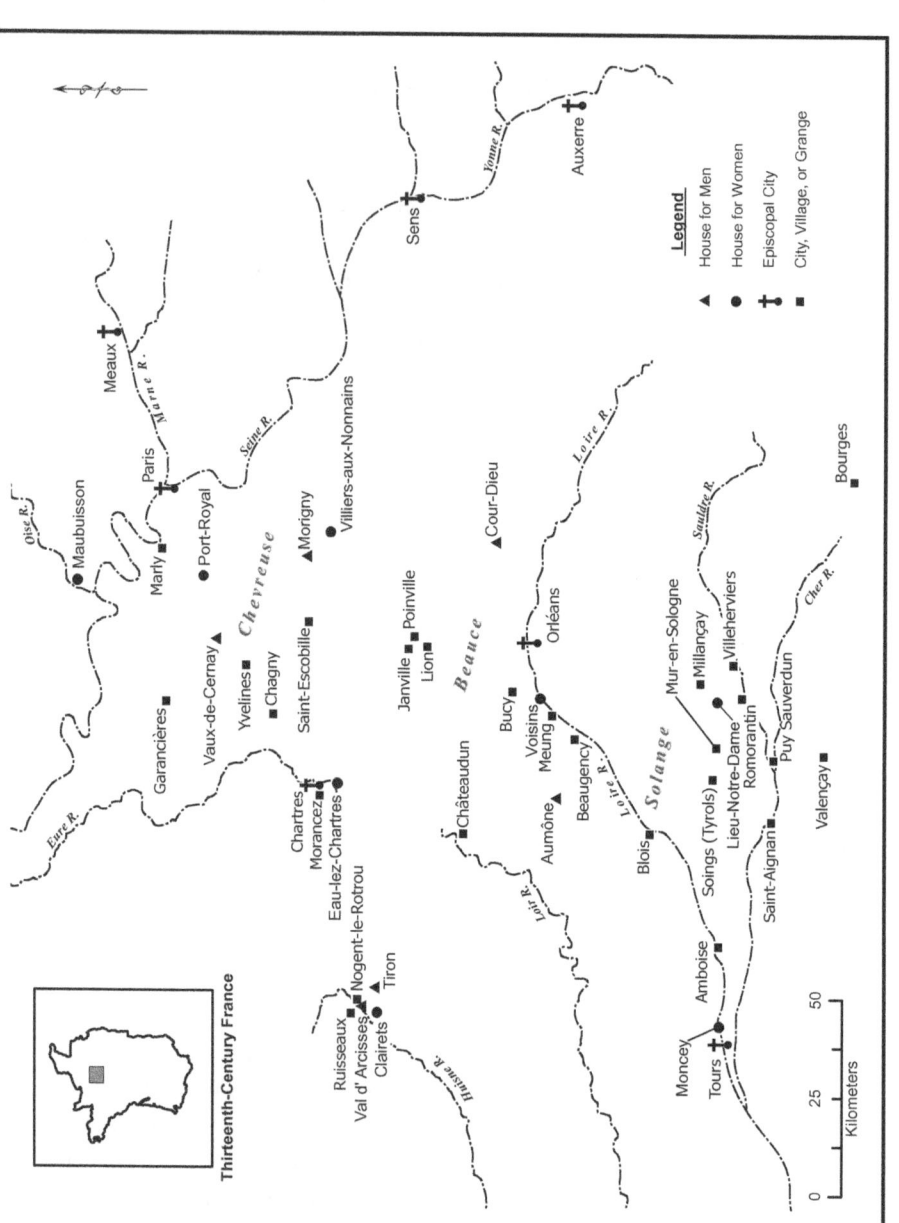

Map 2. Early foundations for Cistercian nuns west of Paris and their properties. Map created by Gordon Thompson

Cistercian Nuns at Clairets

The abbey of Cistercian nuns of Clairets was founded by an important person. She was Matilda of Brunswick, Countess of Perche, daughter of Matilda of England, Duchess of Saxony, and thus granddaughter of Eleanor of Aquitaine and King Henry II of England (see Figure 3). Countess Matilda's foundation at Clairets in 1202 was made after her husband, Geoffrey, Count of Perche, died before fulfilling a crusader vow.[3] She gave extensive rights in the forest of Clairets, including rights over two *métairies* (working farms within the forest boundaries) at Bavaria and Pont, as well as two arpents of meadow at Tillium, half the ownership of a mill at Saint-Victoire and ten marks of annual rent from her English manor of Hagenet. She allowed the nuns to have an agent for their business in the town of Nogent-le-Rotrou and usage rights (except in the forest of Perche) in all her woodlands (for building materials, firewood, and pasture for animals, including pigs).[4] Yet she is virtually erased from the history of the abbey.

In 1213, a decade after the foundation and probably shortly after Matilda's death, her son, Thomas, the new count of Perche, confirmed his mother's gifts. He granted for her soul the other half of the mill at Saint-Victoire and established boundaries for the woods of Clairets where the abbey was sited; indeed, his confirmation referred to the abbey as that of "Bois des Clairets." Later Thomas added twenty more acres of woodlands and again usage rights for construction and heating.[5] In 1216, having had repairs made on the mills of the Bourg in Nogent-le-Rotrou, Thomas conveyed his share of those mills to the nuns, guaranteeing that neither he nor his heirs would build other mills that would interfere with the operation of those belonging to the nuns of Clairets.[6] In 1217 Thomas died at the siege of Lincoln and was succeeded as count by his father's younger brother, William, bishop of Châlons, who resigned that bishopric to become Count of Perche. William succeeded in having Pope Honorius III (1216–27) lift any threat of excommunication because of Thomas's participation in the invasion of England.[7] This secured Thomas's earlier gifts for Clairets.

The new count and former bishop William celebrated a refoundation in June 1218, issuing a new foundation document in the form of a *pancarte*.[8] It attested that Clairets had been founded for the souls of his dearest brother, the late count Geoffrey of Perche, and of his nephew, the late count Thomas. William confirmed his own and their earlier gifts and granted an additional annual rent of sixty sous to the nuns. In this document William listed gifts

Henry II (1133–89) m. 1154 Eleanor of Aquitaine (1121–1204)

Children of Eleanor and Henry:

Henry (1155–83)

Richard I (1157–99) m. Berenguela of Navarre in 1191—no children

Geoffrey II (1158–86) m. Constance, Duchess of Brittany—two children, Eleanor and Arthur I

Eleanor (1162–1214) married m. Alfonso VIII of Castile

Children of Eleanor and Alfonso:

Urraca, Berengaria, Eleanor, Henry, and Blanche of Castile

This Blanche of Castile (d. 1252) m. 1200 Louis VIII, king of France (r. 1223–26)

Children of Blanche and Louis who outlived their father:

Louis IX, king of France (r. 1226–70)

Robert of Artois (d. 1250)

Alphonse of Poitiers (d. 1271)

Isabelle of France (d. 1270)

Charles of Anjou (d. 1285)

Three sons died after Louis VIII: Stephen, 1227, John and Philip Dagobert, both in 1232.

The first five children had died earlier.

Matilda (ca. 1164–89) m. Henry the Lion, Duke of Bavaria and Saxony

Children included three sons and a daughter:

That daughter, Matilda, Countess of Perche (d. 1213?), m. Geoffrey of Perche (d. 1202)

Their son was Thomas, Count of Perche (d. 1217 at Lincoln)

Joan (ca. 1166–99) m. Raymond VI of Toulouse in 1196

Children of Joan and Raymond:

Raymond VII of Toulouse (1197–1249)

Jeanne (1220–71), Countess of Toulouse, m. Louis VIII's son, Alphonse of Poitiers (d. 1271)

John (1166–1216), king of England, m. 1200 Isabelle of Angouleme (ca. 1188–1246)

Son: King Henry III (b. 1207; r. 1216–72)

FIGURE 3. Genealogy: Eleanor of Aquitaine and Henry II of England.

by forty-eight donors, some of whom were probably present. Notable were conveyances of two types of income for Clairets' nuns, tithes and rents from mills: "Guy of Mondoucet and Peter of Beauregard who gave tithes held jointly; Girard Capreolus who gave five sous at Ceton; Geoffrey Gaudi who gave some deniers in the *métairie* of Burolis in the parish of Vichères; and Lancelin of Faiet who gave a sestier of wheat in the tithes of Prés-Nouvel. . . . Gascon gave two sestiers of grain in the mill of Amauri, Rotrud of Maugatel five sous in that of Choissent, William of Foliet two sestiers of wheat in those of Mausagii, and Rotrud of Blainville a sestier of wheat in the mill of Orgères to be paid at Christmas."[9] The document confirmed a total of 130 sous (6.5 livres) in annual cash income and rents in kind totaling twenty-eight sestiers and six mines of grain. Tithes, presumably also paid in kind, were given at three places, with rents and tithes from twelve different mills: at Cortresol, Mellart, Nogent, Clinchamp, Chesnaie, Grillon, Capella Gastinelli, and Pont, the last from Heloise, widow of Raoul Viarii. Yet there is no mention of Matilda of Brunswick, who had in fact founded the abbey, here or in any subsequent documents.

William's patronage emphasized income from mills and tithes. In 1220 he granted Clairets additional mills for both grinding grain and fulling cloth at Moulins du Comte on the Huisne River below Nogent. In 1221, in addition to what his nephew Thomas had given, William gave an additional eight livres in annual rents over those mills. He granted rights for all the nuns' animals (except goats) to graze in the woods of Clairets and also rights in the woods called Morasilva, including pasture without charge for up to fifty pigs.[10] William's gifts to Clairets of mills and tithes may have been more inspired by the economic ideals of reformers associated with the abbey of nearby Tiron than by those that had inspired the Cistercians. This is suggested by there being so many conveyances of mills and income from tithes.[11] Tironist monks at nearby Val d'Arcisses were William's beneficiaries in 1226 and in 1233; he appears to have retired and died there.[12]

After William's death the county of Perche escheated to the king, and thereafter Clairets was considered a royal abbey, although not one that had been founded by the crown. Shortly afterward, Thibaut IV, Count of Champagne, acting on behalf of Blanche of Castile, who was regent for the young Louis IX, confirmed to its nuns the *feodum* over their holdings at Clairets, which was worth at least twenty-five livres annually.[13] In 1280, Heloise of Orville, to fund a priest for a chapel for her soul and that of her late husband Reginald, gave Clairets land, rents, produce, and tenants in the lordships of Feulard and Richebourg.[14]

For the nuns of Clairets, access to the nearby town of Nogent-le-Rotrou and rights in its water-powered mills were important. Clairets received rights in mills for grinding flour and payments in grain, but its mills for fulling cloth also attest to a growing regional textile industry, as well as possible artisanal activities within the abbey enclosure (again a possible tie to Tiron). In May 1222 Raoul Asini had granted the nuns the mills at Ruisseaux near Margon and to the land on which those mills were built, rights to take millstones from a nearby quarry and to income from *multura* for grinding grain and from *fullagium* for fulling cloth.[15] A dispute arose in 1248 with the neighboring Tironist monks at Val d'Arcisses, a dispute that turned on who was responsible for making repairs on the jointly owned and managed milling complex at Ruisseaux. The Cistercian nuns owned the mills as well as fields there; the Tironist monks had a pond, fishing rights, and meadows. Those monks needed regular access to water to flood those meadows to produce multiple cuttings of hay each summer. This meant diverting water from the nuns' millrace into those meadows by opening four channels or culverts cut beneath the surface of the milldam. This could reduce the millrace to a trickle, and so such flooding of the meadows needed to be scheduled at a time when the nuns had no need for the waterpower for their mills.

An agreement was reached that the monks could open the culverts to flood the meadow no more than once a week. This was to be from the first call to Vespers on Saturday evening until whenever on Sunday those meadows had been sufficiently watered. The culverts were then to be closed off again so that the water in the millrace would build up and regain its force by Monday. Clearly the nuns did not use this mill on Sundays. If the water in the millrace was too low to flow into those culverts, the monks could block the millrace temporarily to raise the water level. If an excess of water threatened to flood those meadows and the monks had to break open the banks of the millrace to drain them, they would be responsible for repairing any damages after the flood had receded; they were also to pay for any damage suffered by the nuns because of their delay, defect, or negligence in such repairs. The same applied to the nuns if they opened the millrace for whatever reason. Since both parties needed access, while excluding everyone else, the nuns were to construct a gate to the complex, a gate to which both monks and nuns would have a key. This allowed the nuns to "observe, repair, care for and remake" the milldam and the millrace, while allowing the monks to access the culverts and irrigate their meadows.[16]

In 1276 the nuns of Clairets were given rights to build yet another mill at Ruisseaux, to be located slightly below the existing one; for that mill they were to pay thirty sous in annual rent, but they were also to have additional rents and fishing rights there.[17] The complexity of such mill arrangements in this case probably reflects practices elsewhere in the region that were never so explicitly discussed. In addition to their mills, among the nuns' earliest acquisitions were a winepress and vineyards, which suggest that the nuns of Clairets were producing their own wine.[18] Such resources as these, allowed Clairets' nuns to survive until the French Revolution.[19]

The Abbey of Villiers

The story of the abbey of Cistercian nuns at Villiers or Villiers-aux-Nonnains is not as well documented; almost all the information comes only from the abbey's surviving obituary book.[20] The abbey is first mentioned in May 1220 when Peter of Corbeil, archbishop of Sens (1200–1222), confirmed the request of Lady Amicia of Breteuil to found an abbey of Cistercian nuns at Villiers and endow it with the tithes from Cernay, tithes earlier given for his soul by Amicia's late husband, Jean of Briard.[21] At about the same time the Cistercian General Chapter approved the foundation.[22] Additional donations were made in 1227, when with the assent of his wife Agnes "so that an anniversary mass be made annually in that church," Herloin of Meulan, royal chamberlain, gave Villiers three hundred arpents of arable land in the villa of Mespuits and the right to pasture animals in all his lands; the rents paid to the nuns amounted to thirteen and a half livres annually.[23] In June 1228 Jacquelinus of Ardennes and his wife Garlande gave Villiers one and a half muids of oats in annual rent with the king's approval. Also in June 1228, Hesmes Brice with the consent of his wife gave the nuns three and a half arpents of vines in the *métairie* of Beauvais.[24] In 1229 the nuns acquired rights to eight arpents of land in three separate holdings, all near their granges. In 1230/31 they got four arpents at Courdemanche. In 1243 they got two pieces of arable land at Isle-Dudon and Longueville for the foundation of an anniversary mass for Bourguignelus and his wife Sancelina, and in 1247 the nuns received a gift from Philip of Montfort and his wife, including rights over justice at Garancières and a fourth of the tithes at Sarmonville and Garancières.[25]

The nuns also made purchases. In 1235 they bought fifty arpents of arable land, a dwelling, a vineyard, and a garden at Audeville; each tenant would owe seven sous annually at the feast of Saint-Rémy; in 1237/38 Robert, abbot of Morigny, confirmed the nuns' purchase for 260 livres of the fishpond, meadow, and watercourse adjoining the abbey of Villiers from Simon, prior of Morigny's dependency at Ferté-Alais.[26] Gift conveyances also continued. In 1249 the brothers Jean and Pierre of Mésnil-Girault gave six livres of annual income to discharge rents earlier owed; in December 1250 Petronilla with the assent of her children gave tithes, vineyards, and a house at Neuville; probably she entered the abbey of Villiers as a nun. In 1251 Ascelin of Voisins gave the nuns a fifth of everything he owned at Sarmonville; in 1252/53 Jean of Fromont, cleric, sold Villiers four arpents of arable land at Mauvoisin; in 1254 the *métairie* of Neuville was augmented by a purchase of land from Pierre de Courbevoie and his wife Beatrice of Chartres; in 1254 Renault, lord of Sana, gave tithes in the parishes of Saint-Germain of Dourdan, Granges-du-Roi, and Rouillon. In 1265 Jeanne de Montsuperb gave rights at Leude-ville and two years later added the rights to hold that property in mortmain.[27]

Villiers also had rights in nearby towns: in 1255 a house in Étampes near Saint-Basil was exchanged with Jean Bourguigne, the king's chamberlain, for an arpent and a half of meadow; in 1259 the nuns received a house and other rights at Vitry, four arpents of land near Fontaines-de-Villiers, a vineyard and garden at Étampes, and a second and third garden in Étampes. In 1266 the nuns rented out a house on the Rue de la Vannerie (Tannerie) in Étampes to Jean Hudebert, weaver, along with an arpent of meadow adjoining the river-bank, probably for drying cloth. By 1280 Villiers was renting out land: the nuns granted two pieces totaling ten arpents in Guillerville to Guillaume Micheland, ferryman at Chartres, for eight deniers annual rent per arpent; they also rented out a *métairie* containing one hundred arpents to Jean Bouv-ard of Mespuits.[28]

Louis IX and his mother Blanche of Castile, the ultimate lords of the region in which Villiers was founded intervened on its behalf on at least five occasions.[29] In 1232, they appointed arbitrators to resolve a dispute between the nuns at Villiers and the knight Jean of Briard, and in 1234 the king confirmed that knight's concession to the nuns.[30] In 1247 Louis IX gave them firewood in one of the royal forests; Blanche of Castile gave an annual rent of forty livres drawn from her dower income in the *prévôté* of Étampes.[31] Villiers was remembered in Louis IX's 1270 will and his widow Marguerite of Provence founded a chapel there for his soul in 1272.[32]

A number of conveyances by widows entering Villiers are found. Agnes of Briard, the founder, had entered Villiers in 1233 bringing a house in

Corbeil. Conveyances were made at Neuville in the 1250s: by Eremburge of Chantinonville, widow of Robert of Forêt, squire; by Lady Marie of Ferté-Alais, widow of William, lord of Mont-Saint-Jean; by Marguerite of Borne, widow of Renaud of Garancières; by Odeline, widow of William of Neuville; and by Aceline, widow of Matthew Guymon.[33] While the documentary evidence is limited, the abbey of Villiers survived up to the French Revolution.[34]

Voisins, Tithes, and the Bishop of Orléans

The Cistercian nuns of the abbey at Voisins, referred to by Manasses II, bishop of Orléans (1207–21), as "his dear daughters," became recipients of ecclesiastical tithes conveyed back to the church at the urging of that bishop.[35] The earliest transfers of tithes that came into those women's hands had been given several years earlier to hermit/monks in the forest of Bucy. In 1215 the bishop replaced those religious men with Cistercian nuns. A number of local lady/lords appear in the early charters for Voisins. Many of them were widows of knights or had husbands going off on crusade; some had daughters who entered the new abbey. It appears that no single woman can be identified as the secular founder, but instead there was a group of women founders, many of them widows, who chose to found a house of Cistercian nuns. (See Table 1.) In 1217 the bishop moved the nuns to a more clement site at Voisins from which they took their name. Indeed, a 1219 document described it as the house of Cistercian nuns at Notre-Dame-de-Voisins; the nuns continued commemorations that had been promised to earlier donors at Bucy.[36]

Along with religious obligations at Bucy, the nuns also acquired religious obligations and the properties of a failed canonry at Janville given to them in 1218 or 1219.[37] The nuns of Voisins also acquired other property at Janville that had been given to the Cistercian nuns of Moncey, but which they sold to Voisins.[38] These holdings in the rich grain-producing agricultural lands of the Beauce between Orléans and Paris would form the nuns' granges at Lion, Tillay, and Poinville; they were confirmed in the 1234 privilege from Gregory IX, which also mentions the nuns' status as Cistercians and their tithe exemption.[39]

Among the conveyances to Voisins was that made in 1233 by the priest John, who lived in a house adjoining the nuns' church; in a postmortem gift he granted them his house and various liturgical objects and manuscripts: "A missal in two parts, a book of letters, the great breviary, a new antiphonary

Table 1. Voisins: Widows as Donors, ca. 1217–26

Date	Donor	Gift	Reference
	Knightly widows and wives		
1210	For soul of Alice, late wife, Simon of Baugency		Pibrac, p. 318
1215	John Desroes (fief-holder) with wife Elina		Pibrac, p. 319
1216/17	Herveus Chesneaux and wife Isabelle	New site	*Voisins*, nos. 2–4
1218/19/1220	Margaret Butler on deathbed	Janville	*Voisins*, nos. 173–77
1220	Lady Agnes, dying wife of William Prunelé, confirmed by daughter Elizabeth	Gross tithes	*Voisins*, no. 56
1220	Andreas of Joiac, knight and wife, with daughter Ysavia entered	Gross tithes	*Voisins*, no. 168
1220	Garinus and his wife Elizabeth; daughter Jacquelina entered	Half of tithes	Pibrac, pp. 322–23.
1220	Gila Laterie, widow, husband died on pilgrimage to Jerusalem; two daughters entered		*Voisins*, no. 116
1221	Lady Matilda, widow of Peter of Longueto	Tithes	*Voisins*, no. 75
1222	Petronilla, late wife of knight Hugh of Bucy	Tithes	*Voisins*, no. 61
1224	Albina, sister of William Manasse, *crucesignatus*		*Voisins*, p. 192
1225	Elizabeth of Pateio, widow of knight, Simon of Pateio, on her deathbed	Rent	*Voisins*, no. 118
1226	Aaliz, confirmed gift by husband Geoffrey of Soligniac, knight, *crucesignatus*	Land	*Voisins*, no. 63
1215	John of Freez with wife Hedelina	Bucy Tithes	*Voisins*, no. 44
1222	Lebertus, original founder of hermitage, anniversary for his sister		*Voisins*, nos. 46–47
	Citizens or others		
1217	Floria, wife of John Pasquerius, citizens of Orléans, a joint postmortem gift; he was leaving on pilgrimage to Jerusalem	House	*Voisins*, no.124
1218	Maria, daughter of Hervy Viy, citizen of Orléans, postmortem gift	Vineyards	*Voisins*, no. 84

(con't.)

Donor	Gift	Reference
Citizens or others		
Bertier of Fossatis, citizen of Orléans,with wife Marie, and two daughters who entered	Land	*Voisins,* no. 154
Luca, widow of Peter of Corvey with confirmation by Templars	Land at Theniac	*Voisins,* nos. 155–56
Edelina, widow of John of Viridario	Vineyards	*Voisins,* no. 79
Hugh of Martres, citizen of Orléans, with consent of Cassina, his wife		*Voisins,* no. 91

s: *Cartulaire de Notre-Dame de Voisins de l'Ordre de Cîteaux,* ed. Jules Doinel (Orléans: Herluison, and A. du Faur, comte de Pibrac, "Histoire de l'abbaye de Voisins," *Mémoires de la Société d'agriculture,* , belles-lettres et arts d'Orléans* 22 (1881): 177–348.

in two parts, a great sequenciary, a large psalter, two passionaries, a new book of homilies and the lives of the Fathers."[40] Also interesting was a transaction from 1234 in which Margarita, prioress of a convent of nuns who ran the Hospital of Orléans, sold a rent in kind to the nuns of Voisins.[41] In 1246 before his departure on crusade, Louis IX granted the nuns of Voisins a daily wagonload of dead wood from the royal forest; in 1289, Jeanne, Countess of Alençon and Blois, gave rents to those nuns; in 1300 Philip IV granted them a "tithe" of all the food consumed by his court whenever he visited his hunting lodges near Orléans.[42]

Vineyards were important assets in this region, especially in the suburbs of Orléans where a number were acquired along with winepresses, wine cellars and vats, and also rents on grinding mills.[43] The nuns acquired houses and urban rents by gifts or purchases from citizens of Orléans; they acquired properties in Beaugency and in the town of Meung, including the *jambage*, a tithe of all the hams produced by its butchers on Martinmas (November 11, the traditional date for butchering).[44] Rents in 1229 totaled fifteen muids and six mines (half a sestier) of winter wheat, twenty-one barrels of wine, and twenty-five sous in cash. The fact that grain payments were made to Voisins in winter wheat is probably indicative of the rich soil for grain production of the region (on this, see discussion for Port-Royal as well). By 1275 cash income had increased to nearly 350 sous (17.5 livres) per year, and deliveries of grain had increased to thirty-three muids annually; that last is an enormous amount—nearly four hundred large sacks of grain per year. Overall the nuns had paid 1,162 livres over the years for such property and income.[45]

Still the charters indicate that such income could be fragile. In 1248 there were difficulties in collecting a rent in wine; records from 1312 and later show that poor harvests had allowed the nuns to collect only a portion of their grain rents and the nuns ended up forgiving the arrears.[46] Nonetheless, with its mixed endowment of income from tithes, granges on which it could practice the order's tithe-free agriculture, and extensive vineyards not far from Orléans, with houses to be rented out near the abbey, the nuns had sufficient assets to survive until the French Revolution.[47]

Port-Royal and the Albigensian Crusade

The community of Cistercian nuns at Port-Royal was founded by Matilda of Garlande circa 1204.[48] She had been authorized to do so by her husband Matthew of Marly, who directed that if he did not fulfill his crusading vow for Jerusalem, she should use fifteen livres of annual rents for his soul. He died at Constantinople in 1204, and Matilda, with the assistance of Eudes de Sully, bishop of Paris, founded Port-Royal in the Chevreuse Valley west of Paris. In 1204 Matilda acquired the abbey's site, the fief of Porrois in the parish of Magny from Milo of Voisins. Her sons, Bouchard of Marly and Matthew of Marly confirmed their mother's conveyance to Port-Royal, as did Paganus of Ursine and his wife (probably the tenants there).[49] Port-Royal's site was in the diocese of Paris and in 1206 Bishop Eudes de Sully of Paris recommended that the nuns of Port-Royal and those of Saint-Antoine-des-Champs outside Paris be accepted by the abbot of Cîteaux.[50] In 1209 Bouchard confirmed the site to the nuns and the original fifteen livres at Meulan designated by his father for the foundation. He also confirmed ten muids of wheat (each roughly a cartload) that his mother had assigned to the nuns from her mills at Richebourg and Herchenout. Bouchard himself granted the nuns thirty-six arpents of woods at Moleretz, a gift that involved his repurchase of the twenty sous annual rent that his parents had once promised to the canons of Falaise.

At first Port-Royal was designated as a priory dependent on the nearby abbey of Cistercian monks of Vaux-de-Cernay, famous for their preaching against the Albigensian heretics, and Port-Royal's nuns received early support from the bishop of Chartres in whose diocese the abbey of Vaux-de-Cernay was located.[51] So it is not surprising that early supporters of Port-Royal included knights who participated in the Albigensian Crusade. Thus, in 1208, probably at the instigation of the bishop of Chartres and just before their departure in 1209 for the first campaign against those heretics, the knights, Reginald of Prunet and Simon Rossegni, returned to the bishop of Chartres those ecclesiastical tithes they had owned at Gourville, so that he could transfer them to the nuns of Port-Royal.[52] The lords of Marly and their family also made gifts just before departures on campaigns against the Albigensians in both 1209 and 1226.[53]

Matilda of Garlande's two older sons, Bouchard and Matthew, married two sisters, Matilda of Châteaufort and her younger sister Mabilia, both of whom also came to be associated with gifts to the abbey. Bouchard departed in 1209 for the initial campaign against the Albigensians accompanied by his mother Matilda of Garlande, who is said to have dramatically rescued Cathar women from a fire; Bouchard was captured and held for more than a year.[54] Was it during this time that his sister Marguerite married a viscount of Narbonne? Having returned from the Midi, in 1214 Bouchard and his wife Matilda of Châteaufort confirmed an earlier conveyance at Moleretz and granted Port-Royal rights to acquire an additional ten arpents of vineyards there; Matthew and Mabilia gave Port-Royal vineyards at Pruniac and one hundred sous income in the cens of Marly at the same time.[55]

Such gifts as well as their activities on the Albigensian Crusade must have impressed the bishop of Paris, who soon elevated the priory into an abbey. It undoubtedly helped that Matilda and Matthew's fourth child, William of Marly (d. 1229/30), was a cathedral canon in Paris. A refoundation was enacted in the presence of the bishop of Paris's archdeacons and recorded in the bishop's cartulary for 1215.[56] That bishop, Peter of Nemours, recognizing the generosity of the lords of Marly, in 1215 elevated Port-Royal into an abbey of Cistercian nuns, free to elect its own abbess and independent of Vaux-de-Cernay: "Note that at the site of Porrois, the Lord God has intended there to be an abbey of white nuns and that its abbesses be elected by its community."[57] In 1217 the son Bouchard and his wife Matilda gave Port-Royal additional income amounting to forty sous, nine deniers, and one obol (half-denier) from the woods of Moleretz as well as twenty sous annually from an oven held in the Jewish quarter of Paris.[58]

Although Port-Royal became an independent abbey only in 1215, the nuns had already begun purchasing endowment from neighboring lords. In 1207 and 1208 the nuns paid 160 livres to Guy of Chevreuse for his mill at

Germainville and nearby lands. Guy granted them rights to graze their animals (except goats) in all the common pasturelands of his lordship, but added that the nuns should not complain if he or his heirs later decided to make assarts (clearances) in those woodlands. The nuns would also have the right to make whatever acquisitions they wished between the abbey's site and Champgarnier.[59] In May 1220, it was probably another Guy of Chevreuse, the previous Guy's son, who granted Port-Royal ten arpents of land in the forest of Champgarnier.[60] The younger Guy's arrangements with the nuns were complicated, but in 1239 they paid him 185 livres for his cancellation of an annual rent of five muids of oats that they had owed him.[61] Two years later an annual rent of four sestiers of winter wheat from the mill of Corcelles was given to the nuns as an outright gift.[62]

The elder Guy's sister, Cecilia of Chevreuse, included Port-Royal in her will of 1221. Her husband, Robert of Mauvoisin, another Albigensian crusader, had made an even earlier gift to Port-Royal, one in 1216 of rights at Aulnay north of Paris; those rights would eventually be exchanged between the abbess of Port-Royal and that of Saint-Antoine-des-Champs.[63] In 1242 the nuns again purchased a rent of two muids of grain (one of wheat, one of oats) at the grange of Beauvoir for one hundred livres from Peter of Beauvoir. He had held this rent from the king, who confirmed and sealed it. That Blanche of Castile also confirmed and sealed the document suggests the conveyance came from her dower lands. Clearly part of what was being sought was provisioning for the community.[64]

Matilda of Garlande died in 1223/24 having confirmed her own conveyance of the original fifteen livres of rent at Meulan; the elder son Bouchard also confirmed his mother's final gift of land at Chagny, property that had once belonged to his bride, Matilda of Châteaufort.[65] Matthew, the younger son, established a chapel at Port-Royal "to celebrate the holy dead," granting an additional ten livres annually from the *prévôté* of Meulan, as well as lordship rights (mills, meadows, land, and tenants) at Aulnay and Germainville. In 1224 he gave the nuns another one hundred sous annually and the tithe at Réaus, describing this gift as having been purchased with his own funds.[66] Bouchard and Matthew's sister, Marguerite, who had married Aimery III, Viscount of Narbonne, had given Port-Royal one hundred sous at Marly and a vineyard called Cripta at the time of their mother's death in 1223/24; then in 1226, Marguerite and her husband granted the nuns another one hundred sous in annual rents.[67]

In May 1226 additional gifts to Port-Royal were made just before Bouchard set off on another campaign against the Albigensians, one led by Louis VIII. He granted Port-Royal an additional one hundred sous in annual income; Matthew, Bouchard's brother gave one hundred sous from his own income at Meulan to fund his own anniversary at Port-Royal.[68] At the time of Bouchard's departure, his own eldest son, Thibaut, had entered Vaux-de-Cernay as a monk; Thibaut later became abbot there, dying in 1247.[69] Bouchard died at the siege of Avignon in fall 1226. The way was being prepared for Bouchard to be recognized as the real founder of Port-Royal, given that his widow Matilda of Châteaufort (d. 1260) lived another thirty-four years and was probably still alive when the nuns were having the cartulary made.[70]

Before the 1220s Port-Royal began to acquire tithes from lay owners (although often by purchase) and used those tithe acquisitions as the stepping-stones to their creation of granges. For example, in 1215 the bishop of Chartres transferred to them a fourth of the tithes, great and small, at Saint-Escobille. Those tithes had just been returned to the bishop by Peter of Favereuse and his wife Eremburgis who wanted them to go to the nuns. In 1217 Peter of Richeville, their feudal lord, consented to their conveyance and allowed a grange to be established there.[71] Then, in 1220, Port-Royal paid forty livres for a pledge (mortgage) over the tithes on a large farm of recently cleared land at Saint-Escobille; its size is reflected in the report that it had already been planted with what the document says were twelve muids of seed (each muid about a cartload); more likely this is a copying error for twelve sestiers (one muid), still already a substantial amount.[72] In 1231 and 1233 the nuns paid fifty-five livres and then sixty-five livres for additional tithes at Saint-Escobille.[73] Such transactions would soon make the nuns' grange at Saint-Escobille free of tithes.[74]

Another tithe-free grange was created by Port-Royal at Villeray-en-Saclay. The nuns first acquired claims over tithes there in 1216 by paying five livres for a mortgage over some of those tithes.[75] Then in 1224 they purchased tithes from previous secular owners, engaging in an elaborate charade in which Hugh of Joiac and his wife Margaret granted tithes at Saclay to the bishop of Paris, who then granted them to Port-Royal; only the confirmation by Bouchard of Marly mentions that the nuns had paid 170 livres to those "donors."[76] In 1234 the nuns got eleven arpents at Saclay, for ten livres per arpent.[77] In 1241 and 1242 the nuns paid 195 livres for thirty-six arpents of land at Villeray (more than five livres per arpent), including the right to hold

Table 2. Port Royal: Acquisitions at Villeray-en-Saclay

Date	(ref.)	Acquisition	Cost
1216	(no. 29)	pledge over tithes	5 livres
1224	(nos. 79–80)	tithes purchased	170 livres
Total cost for tithes:			175 livres
1234	(no. 150)	11 arpents of land	110 livres
1241	(nos. 205–6, 2120	36 arpents in *la main morte*	195 livres
1241	(no. 209)	4 arpents of land	exchange
1262/63	(no. 294–95)	45 arpents of arable land	700 livres
		40 arpents of woods	
		7 arpents in *champart*	
		27 sous annual cens	
		8 livres annual rent	160 livres*
Totals (land and woods):		133 arpents	1165 livres
Censier (fol. 117v)	63.5 arpents at Villeray		
	61.5 arpents at Villars		
	6.5 arpents at Billet		
Total:	131.5 arpents owned by the nuns at Villeray, Villars (Villers), and Billet		

Source: *Cartulaire de Port-Royal*, pp. 13ff., *censier* dated by contents of charter no. 294 (1262/63) and list above from *censier* fol. 117v, printed on p. 22 of the edition.

* 160 livres to purchase 8 livres annual rent, or 20 livres invested for one livre of income is high in comparison to other numbers found for this study; see, for instance, the discussion of Queen Marguerite's funding of a chapel for Saint-Louis's soul, in Chapter 6.

that land permanently in *la main morte* (the land would no longer owe feudal relief, but see more discussion in Appendix 1). An additional four arpents of land were acquired by a property exchange; then another forty arpents at Villeray were purchased for 180 livres (here 4.5 livres per arpent) from Katherine, widow of Gervais of Valautre, knight.[78] In 1263 the nuns purchased another 45 arpents of arable land, 40 arpents of woods, 20 arpents in the village, 7 arpents in *champart* (rights in the common fields), rents or cens of thirty sous annually, and an annual rent of 8 livres from William of Meudon and his wife Isabelle for 700 livres; another 160 livres went to William's brother, and in 1263 Louis IX confirmed this conveyance, allowing it to fall into *la main morte* (see Table 2).[79] Note that the entry on fol. 117v of the original *censier*, reproduced at the bottom of Table 2, suggests that the *censier* (or at least this part of it), dates to circa 1263.

Port-Royal's nuns were clearly moving from simple tithe acquisition to the creation of granges on lands over which they had acquired tithes—creating tithe-free holdings presumably to be cultivated under their own management. These developments are also found for Chagny, where land was conveyed to Port-Royal by Matilda of Garlande in her last charter in 1223/24 and confirmed by her son Bouchard.[80] In 1230, soon after both of their deaths, a dispute over the nuns' claim to tithe exemption at Chagny arose with the parish priest of Escrones, the parish in which Chagny was located. The nuns asserted that, "because they were Cistercians, they had the right to tithes on noval lands created and cultivated at their own expense."[81] Whereas the nuns were claiming Cistercian tithe exemption because those lands were *novales*, the parish priest asserted that it had been Bouchard of Marly, not the nuns, who had done this reclamation.[82] That was perhaps beside the case, but the nuns ended up granting seven arpents of land to the parish priest in lieu of his claims to the tithe.[83]

The overall mixture of gifts and sales to Port-Royal is striking in that its nuns acquired not just tithes and arable land but vineyards, land on which to plant more vines, mills, and rights to forest usage for firewood and pasture. All this is seen in a *censier* for the abbey from circa 1255. See Table 3, which shows that the nuns' total annual cash income amounted to nearly 161 livres, including rents of nearly 20 livres each given by half a dozen donors, all payable on the feast of Saint-Rémy at the single site in the diocese of Rouen at Karrerias (Quarrerias). Many rents were paid to the nuns at four terms, but in one case twelve sous and six deniers were to be paid at the Châtelet in Paris at three terms; such payments at the Châtelet were granted by a variety of patrons who had acquired them, not just the king. This opening section of that *censier* lists some of the most important of Port-Royal's supporters and their gifts: thirty-eight livres annually at Meulan from the Marly family; income from Lord Philip of Montfort for his wife or mother Petronilla; gifts from Master Simon of Gif, Lady Clemencia of Plessy, Lord Milo of Plessy, Lord Hugh of Plessy for his daughter, and so on. The *censier* lists deliveries of wine or grain to the nuns. What is striking there is not just the total amounts, which were substantial, but the numbers of payments by lords who promised both winter wheat (*hibernagium*) planted in the fall and spring-planted crops like oats and in one case barley. The fact that such rents in

Table 3. Port-Royal: Samples from *Censier* (1262/63)

Annual payments to nuns in cash

Amount	Source
45 livres, 12 sous, 6 deniers	Drawn on Châtelet in Paris
38 livres	Meulan from Sedilia of Noisy
30 livres	Meulan from Matthew of Montmorency, lord of Marly
20 livres	Romerville from Lady Clemencia of Plessy
15 livres	Ferté by Lord Philip of Montfort, for Petronilla
12 livres	Paris, Sainte-Geneviève, by Marguerite, Lady of Narbonne and others

Total is 160 livres, 6 sous, 6 deniers

Annual payments to nuns in grain

Paid by or from	Amount of Grain	Type
Lady of Bussières	24 sestiers	winter wheat (*hibernagium*)
Andreas Polin	12 sestiers	oats
	12 sestiers	winter wheat
Peter of Beauvais	12 sestiers	oats
	12 sestiers	wheat
Joiac	12 sestiers	oats
	12 sestiers	winter wheat
Tithes at Coupières	9 sestiers	oats
	9 sestiers	wheat
William of Chaponval	5 sestiers	oats
	5 sestiers	winter wheat
	1 trousse	straw
William of Voisins	3 sestiers	oats
	3 sestiers	wheat
	1 mine	winter wheat
William of Erunville	12 sestiers	winter wheat
Lady Cecilia of Beaumont	10 sestiers	winter wheat
Raoul of Bendeville's *champart*	6 sestiers	winter wheat
Peter of Corcelles	4 sestiers	winter wheat
Milo of Corcelles	4 sestiers	winter wheat
Matthew of Meudon	3 sestiers	winter wheat
	3 sestiers	barley
Hauteville, *champart*	2 sestiers	winter wheat
Ferricus, armiger, of Saint-Rémy	3 mines	winter wheat or oats

Total is 176 sestiers of grain plus one trousse of straw

Table 3 (con't.)

"We owe these rents annually": Payments made by the nuns

TO PENSIONERS	(GRAIN PAYMENTS)
Priest of Saint-Lambert	6 sestiers of wheat
Priest of Magny	3 sestiers of wheat
Prior of Chèvres, mill of Germerville	2 sestiers of wheat
Wife of Lord Amalric of Meudon	1 mine of wheat
Leprosarium of Chèvres, priest	1 mine of wheat

FOR VINEYARDS AT MALLIAC (THAT IS, CASH PAYMENTS TO LABORERS OR OVERLORD)

Laborer	Property in question	Amount annually
Michael Cleric	(replanting) vacant vineyard at Voisins	6 deniers
Walter Gaudio	vines at Longueville	4 deniers
Prior of Malliac	vines at Longueville	4 deniers
Peter of Val-de-sel	vines at Longueville	4 deniers
Adam Lovell	Rive Fulcrod	4 deniers
Adam Lovell	vines at Cripta	3 obols
Hugh Boudri	*quartier* of vines at Saint-Germain	3 deniers
William of Font	vines at Cripta	3 obols
John of Voisins	vines at Clos and Cripta	3 obols
Overlords		
canons of Sainte-Geneviève	for house of William of Cripta	3 deniers
canons of Sainte-Geneviève	for vines at Cripta	3 obols

Source: *Cartulaire de Port-Royal*, pp. 13ff., *censier* dated by contents of charter no. 294 (1262/ 63) and list found in Table 2 from *censier* fol. 117v, printed on p. 22 of the edition.

kind from both fall and spring crops were coming to the nuns from lords in the vicinity suggests that in this region west of Paris where Port-Royal and its granges were located, an advanced alternation of fall and spring crops was being practiced.[84]

A list of the nuns' obligations to make payments to others is also found in Table 3. The payments in cash concerning vineyards appear to be made by the nuns to viticultural workers or overlords of lands being cultivated for Port-Royal; while the names may have changed over time, the numbers probably remained similar. In the case of deliveries in grain it appears that the nuns had promised annuities to several dependents (priests, lepers, a widow?). Some of these may have been promised for a lifetime and this list would have changed over time. The evidence of the *censier* suggests how much Port-Royal's management of income and property was part of a larger web of agricultural obligations, with the nuns both receiving and owing money and kind at the time of the harvest.

Several royal mediations in Port-Royal's affairs occurred just before Louis IX's 1248 departure on crusade. In 1244 the king exempted Port-Royal from paying passage tolls in the royal domain and confirmed an earlier gift by his father, Louis VIII.[85] In 1247 Louis IX confirmed the gifts made by the Marly family, and in 1248 he granted the nuns annual rents of fifty livres *tournois* over the villa of "Mont-Martin" (could this be Montmartre?).[86] In July 1248, just as Louis IX was about to embark on crusade from the new port of Aigues-Mortes, John, Count of Montfort, who accompanied the king, gave a large holding that would come to be called "the Petit-Port-Royal"—an expanse of 240 arpents of land, along with usage rights in the forest of Yvelines and an annual muid of wheat at Mériac. Louis IX confirmed this at Aigues-Mortes. He would return from this first Crusade, but John of Montfort would be among those who did not survive, dead by 1249.[87]

Port-Royal quickly developed rights in Paris. Already in 1220 Petronilla of Auvergne had granted its nuns an annual rent of ten sous over a Parisian *fenestra* (shop window) on the Grand Pont.[88] In 1220 Port-Royal also got rights from Emelina, widow of Adam of Drancy, in the little square across from the Halles.[89] In 1262, Herric of Naves gave an augmented cens or rent over another house on that same square, and in 1263 additional urban rights came from the Montfort family.[90] This property in Paris was increased over the centuries.

Recruiting Nuns and Feudal Crisis

The Port-Royal cartularies, like other charters employed in this chapter, begin to document the popularity of becoming a Cistercian nun in this period, not just in new abbeys being founded but also in the recruiting of nuns. Donors and patrons made property gifts to Cistercian nuns for their own souls and the souls of loved ones, but also made such gifts when women entered those communities to become nuns. Such contracts must have been worded carefully so as to avoid any impression of simony, but such "gifts" still generated charters when they concerned real estate or rents; cash gifts less often did so.[91] Sometimes conveyances were for both commemoration and entrance into a community. Thus, in 1214 Geoffrey of Saint-Quentin had given the nuns of Clairets the *feudum* that he held from Geoffrey of

Vendome at Saint-Rémy of Lavardin; his sister Agatha became a nun at Clairets and the nuns promised anniversary masses to be celebrated in their church for the donor, his father, his mother, and other relatives.[92] In 1228 Odeline, the widow of Ingorrent of Sèvres gave Port-Royal four arpents of vineyards at Sèvres for the soul of her late husband; their daughter had become a nun there.[93] Some documents record more than one daughter entering a single abbey. Two sisters entered Port-Royal in 1231; in 1245 the nuns received land at Vaumurier from a father citing "devotion to that house where my two daughters are nuns"; in 1264 the four daughters of the late knight John of Coupières all entered Port-Royal "with all their earthly goods."[94] Somewhat later, Port-Royal received the four daughters of Guy de Lévis, lord of Mirepoix in the Ariège, which he had acquired during the Albigensian Crusade. The abbey's necrology records a gift of five thousand livres upon the entrance of one of them, Philippa de Lévis, who became abbess in 1275; this was sufficient to build the refectory. At her death circa 1280, she granted a silver cross, a silver reliquary, a pyx of gold, and a chalice for the main altar of Port-Royal.[95] In contrast in 1259 it had been only with difficulty that Port-Royal's nuns obtained the shares of Guy of Montfort's holdings "from lands that he had acquired in the conquest of the Albigensians," which were promised for Guy's daughters, Alice and Agnes, when they entered the abbey.[96]

Charters used in this study that record the entrance of multiple daughters from a single family into abbeys of Cistercian nuns suggest something about demographic growth in the region, and confirmations by all members of a generation also speak to the importance of the *laudatio parentum*, the individual confirmations to a familial conveyance by as many claimants as possible.[97] Such growth in family size and increased fertility allowed more women to choose to become Cistercian nuns, to enter religious communities as young girls, or to retire to such communities as widows after children were grown.[98] While there is no reason to conclude that thirteenth-century women entered Cistercian houses of nuns for any other reason than because they could and did choose to do so, the large size of noble families at the time suggests the beginnings of financial stress at the level of knightly families.[99] Indeed among the many Port-Royal charters is reference to William, squire, called by the sobriquet "Sans Avoir"—"Without Anything."[100]

Often seen are combined gifts and sales. This may be the case when in 1251 Garin Haran and his wife Eremburgis, with their sons Adam, Garin, Stephen, and Philipot, granted property to Voisins at the moment when the daughters of that family, Agnes and Jeannette, entered that abbey as nuns. The parents and the eldest son had already sold land located near Voisins' grange of Lion to the nuns for fifty-six livres in 1249. Even earlier, in 1244, they had made a typical gift in alms of 20 percent of a holding at Lion, and then had sold the rest of it (the 80 percent) to the nuns for forty-five livres.[101] Similarly, in the early 1270s William of Boisvilliers gave the nuns of Villiers nine livres and eleven sous payable at Étampes on the feast of Saint-Rémy; it was the inheritance portion of his two daughters, Eustache and Isabelle, who had become nuns at Villiers.[102] In 1237 four sisters became Cistercian nuns at Lieu-Notre-Dame and brought their shares in a new milling complex at Villeherviers on the Sauldre River; their conveyance was confirmed by their brother, Hervy of Trecy (squire, later knight), and two more sisters.[103]

Something similar is seen in a combination of land sale and donation made at Savigny north of Paris. A fifth of a property, described in 1230/31 as containing forty-six arpents of land at Luat and held in fief from Adam of Beaumont, was given to the nuns of Saint-Antoine by the knight Dreux of Montfermiel and his two brothers. Then in 1234 all three brothers sold the remainder of that property to Saint-Antoine for three hundred livres "ad usus et consuetudines francie ecclesie," an act done with the consent of their four sisters and the husbands of two of those sisters—both husbands were identified as knights.[104] A large family like this might face a gradual but substantial loss of rural properties as is suggested when charters for Port-Royal show women entering the community with gifts of income rather than land. In April 1217/18, the abbey received Asceline, daughter of the knight Hugh of Marchaise; her father confirmed the conveyance of her inheritance share: annual income of ten sous, a muid of wheat, and three muids of wine.[105] Ten years later in 1227 the knight Simon of Bordes gave the nuns of Port-Royal a muid of wine and five sous annually from the Clos of Verneuil and a vineyard at Bordes when his mother Eustachia entered that abbey.[106] In 1228 Peter of Voisins confirmed his sister Sibilia's gift of tithes at Maule when she entered Port-Royal.[107] In 1237 another donor similarly gave his sister's inheritance share when she became a nun there.[108] Sometimes these rents were only for a nun's lifetime.[109] Particularly striking is a conveyance made by the knight Raoul Potet and his wife Maria when two of their daughters became nuns at Voisins; their gift of six muids of good mixed grain was only for the lifetimes of their daughters; only one muid was to be held by Voisins in perpetuity.[110]

Such evidence of multiple daughters of feudal elites entering thirteenth-century religious houses, although they probably made positive choices to do so, reflects changing ownership patterns in the countryside. For bourgeois it may have been different. When in the 1260s Port-Royal's abbesses agreed to bring up two underage daughters, Marie and Agnes, sent there for their upbringing by their father, John of Lagny, a Parisian goldsmith, what is suggested is a lack of other alternatives for the education of his daughters and thus the very real social services provided by new houses of nuns.[111] Such bourgeois women's entrances into abbeys of Cistercian nuns, unlike those in the countryside, whether they were temporary or permanent, do not begin to suggest familial financial failure or feudal crisis.

Conclusions

The evidence of the charters discussed in this chapter is that Cistercian nuns' houses in thirteenth-century northern France were acquiring substantial land-holdings from knightly families based in the countryside around Paris. Certainly the penury of some of the arrangements made for the entrances of mothers or sisters suggests that those families were encountering financial problems, possibly what Guy Bois once described as a "feudal crisis."[112] But the evidence is difficult to parse. The documents discussed here suggest not a failure of the land, as sometimes has been suggested, but the transfer of that land from settled knights and other authorities toward new parties, like the abbeys of Cistercian nuns newly founded in the region. The latter had the cash to buy new lands and to invest in agricultural inputs (such as labor, fertilizers, or fallowing) or to convert land from cereal production to more market-driven production of wine or animal products. This change in ownership was not a decline in the productivity of the land; indeed the "feudal crisis" was very much in the eyes of those "beholders."[113] Some fought back. For instance, as this "feudal crisis" extended to the king and his highest feudatories, they attempted to prevent more land from falling out of feudal ownership into *la morte main* of the church by insisting on getting grants of *amortissement* before such land could fall into the "dead hand" of the church, as is discussed in Appendix 1.

But there was a different and much larger crisis of the time—an increasing failure of male heirs, which must be acknowledged as one of the reasons that so many elite women came to power and authority as heiresses. In the thirteenth century Capetian warfare had exposed the kingdom to enormous cost in treasure and the lives of its most glorious knights. Scions of the greatest feudal families of the realm were brought up with notions of chivalry and masculinity found in the romantic literature of the time as well as Christian preaching about crusade. They appear to have developed an insatiable appetite for religious warfare. Those warriors frequently departed on religious campaigns, leaving womenfolk at home to care for their affairs, and many of those knights died on such ventures.[114]

The fervor for crusading also led knights to depart on such ventures as the Albigensian Crusade and upon their departures they often made gifts to such new houses of Cistercian nuns to assure prayers for their own souls. A number of those donors to Cistercian nuns ended up dying on such ventures. The Albigensian Crusade claimed Bouchard of Marly, who had helped his mother found Port-Royal and who died in fall 1226 at the siege of Avignon, as did Guy of Châtillon, who had helped found Pont-aux-Dames for the soul of his late wife (as discussed in Chapter 5). Queen Blanche of Castile and her young son, Louis IX, founded a house of Cistercian monks for the soul of her husband and his father, King Louis VIII, who died in November 1226 returning from that same campaign against the Albigensians. Blanche's second foundation of Cistercian nuns at Lys, nearly completed by 1248, had probably been spurred on by anticipation of Louis IX's departure on crusade. The outcome was that mothers, sisters, wives, and daughters who had been left at home to mind the estates and the castle found themselves ruling as regents for young heirs, or inheriting castles, counties, and provinces in default of male heirs. It is those heiresses as patrons for Cistercian nuns and the foundations they made that are discussed in the next chapter.[115]

CHAPTER 5

Cistercian Nuns and the Great Heiresses
of Chartres, Blois, and Auxerre

This chapter turns to foundations for Cistercian nuns made by a different category of patrons, those who became heiresses in their own right. It considers two complex instances: that of Isabelle of Chartres and her daughter, Matilda of Amboise, who founded a series of houses of Cistercian nuns west of Paris, and that of Matilda of Courtenay, Countess of Auxerre, Nevers, and Tonnerre, known as Matilda the Great. This chapter shows that heiresses could differ in their approach to such monastic foundations from the women regents described in Chapter 4. The heiresses discussed here were less hindered in making property alienations than were widows, dowagers, and regents (all of the latter were expected to be prudent caretakers of property, but which they administered only for life). Such heiresses were active rulers of their estates and provinces, who used their religious patronage as part of their rule and could be very responsive to the desires of other women to enter religious communities, making foundations for those other women as surrogates in prayer, rather than entering religious communities, at least until their deaths.[1] Locations for some of the holdings for the houses in western France discussed in this chapter are indicated in Map 2, above.

Great families at the time trained and knighted sons with the expectation that they would inherit castles, counties, and family property, but those men's primary duty was to fight. Some women did accompany their sons or husbands on crusades, but the more normal division of labor was for noblewomen to produce children, to make decisions about commemoration of souls, and to remain at home to keep properties in order when men went off to fight.[2] Thus, while sons perfected their military skills, daughters were trained to raise children, establish anniversary masses, manage estates, and even on occasion defend the castles under their command. Like their sisters and cousins who had acted as regents or those who had entered religious life to become abbesses, the heiresses discussed in this chapter, heiresses in their own right, handled the reins of power with great competence. As abbesses they could not have risen to their positions without careful scrutiny by the nuns who had elected them; knightly families too had some choice about who was left with the keys of the castle. Thus, traditional assumptions about inept or profligate women in charge, whether secular or religious, do not accord with the evidence that survives in the archives for Cistercian women.

These women often managed property by using written documents to replace the claims to power based on "custom" enforced by the brute force that men had used. Indeed it was because such women used written documents to aid in management that we know about them and the abbeys of Cistercian nuns they founded.[3] Whether religious or secular and whether or not those women themselves were doing the copying, they were instigating the making of written records and probably doing the reading and referencing of such documents.[4]

Isabelle, Countess of Chartres, as Heiress

In 1218 two sisters, Marguerite (ca. 1175–1230) and Isabelle (ca. 1180–1248/49), inherited the counties of Blois and Chartres after the death of their nephew, Thibaut VI (r. 1205–18). He was the last male among the descendants of Countess Alix of Blois and Thibaut V, Count of Blois. His grandmother, Alix, was the younger daughter of Eleanor of Aquitaine and Louis VII; Marguerite and Isabelle were Alix's daughters and, as Thibaut of Blois's aunts, inherited the counties, which were divided.[5] In 1218 after their respective husbands had paid feudal relief, King Philip confirmed Marguerite in the county of Blois with her husband Gautier of Avesnes, and Isabelle in the county of Chartres and various castellanies with her husband, John of Oisy.[6] Marguerite of Blois's grandson Jean of Châtillon would reunite the counties of Chartres and Blois in 1256.[7] (See Figure 4.)

The fact that such heiresses were allowed to inherit, rather than having their inheritance escheat to the crown is notable. In England at the time fiefs and heiresses attached to them were sold to the highest bidder, but Philip

Alix of Blois (d. 1197/98) m. Thibaut V, Count of Blois/Chartres (d. 1191)

Children included:

Alice, abbess of Fontevraud (1209–18)

Louis, Count of Blois/Chartres (d. 1205)
   His son Thibaut VI, Count of Blois/Chartres (d. 1218)
      His aunts Marguerite and Isabelle inherited in 1218

Marguerite, Countess of Blois (1218–30/31), m. second husband Gautier of Avesnes
   Their daughter Marie, Countess of Blois (d. 1240/41), m. ca. 1230 Hugh of Châtillon (d. 1248)
      Marie and Hugh's son Jean of Châtillon inherited Blois in 1248 and Chartres in 1256

Isabelle, Countess of Chartres (1218–48/49)
   m. 1190 Sulpice of Amboise (d. 1216); six children*
   m. 1218 John of Oisy (d. ca. 1238/39); no children

* Two children from first marriage inherited Amboise (the others—John, William, Alice (?), and Dionysia—disappear from the record).

   Hugh, lord of Amboise (d. ca. 1237)

   Matilda, lady of Amboise, m. Richard of Beaumont (d. 1239); no children
     She also became Countess of Chartres (1248–56)
     Her heir, a cousin, Jean of Châtillon, reunited the counties

FIGURE 4. Genealogy: Alix of Blois, daughter of Eleanor of Aquitaine and Louis VII of France.

Augustus seems to have been subtler in his actions, sometimes granting counties and combinations of counties to such heiresses and their husbands—in effect allowing women to act as his subordinates in rule of parts of the realm and preventing their properties from becoming allied to the provinces of his greatest feudatories.

The elder sister, Marguerite of Blois, appears to have continued familial preference for Fontevraud, whereas Isabelle turned to the support of Cistercian nuns. It is primarily the younger sister, Isabelle, Countess of Chartres, who is considered here. This Isabelle acquired an interest in Cistercian nuns even before becoming countess and possibly from her royal cousin Blanche of Castile (1188–1252). Isabelle was as much as a decade older than Blanche, but the two probably had come to know one another after Blanche arrived in France in 1200.[8] In her 1247 will, reiterating her gifts to the house of Cistercian nuns at Lieu-Notre-Dame, Isabelle also endowed a chapel there for daily masses for her family and "for her own soul and that of her dear cousin, Queen Blanche."[9]

Isabelle's interest in Cistercian nuns is documented for the years just before her inheritance of Chartres in 1218. With her first husband, Sulpice of Amboise, Isabelle founded a priory of Cistercian nuns at Moncey, or Moncé, near Tours on the Loire River. Its first appearance is in a report of four women living the evangelical life there in 1209.[10] In 1214, Isabelle appeared in a charter with her husband Sulpice, when he granted rights at the Île-Barbe to the nuns of Moncey with her consent and that of their children: their son Hugh, their daughter Matilda, and their four younger children: John, William, Alice (?), and Dionysia.[11] After Sulpice's death (sometime between that gift in 1214 and her remarriage by 1218), Isabelle made gifts for his soul to Moncey, endowing a priest there to say daily mass, granting the nuns an annual twenty-four sestiers of grain and two muids of wine from the tithes of Amboise to be paid on the feast of Saint Rémy in the fall, and seven livres *tournois* on the feast of the birth of Saint John the Baptist in June. Moncey's prioress, Ermengarde, is found in the charters for Voisins for 1220 when she sold to Voisins for fifteen livres what had been a gift from the deceased Margaret Butler, who had given a fifth part of all her inheritance near Janville at Lion: this amounted to eleven muids of wheat and nearly six sous in cens, but Prioress Ermengarde stated that the income was too far away for Moncey's nuns to collect.[12]

By 1218 when she became Countess of Chartres, Isabelle had married John of Oisy, but if there were children from that second marriage, there is no record of them. Her first husband Sulpice is mentioned in the Lieu-Notre-Dame cartulary from which it is possible to infer that their eldest son, Hugh of Amboise, ruled as lord of Amboise from Sulpice's death in the mid-1210s until his own death circa 1237. Hugh was followed in that rule of Amboise by his sister Matilda; as lady of Amboise Matilda ruled with her husband, Richard of Beaumont, until his death in 1239 and then ruled in her own right there until her own death in 1256.[13] At her mother Isabelle's death in 1248/49, Matilda became Countess of Chartres herself, ruling both Chartres and Amboise until 1256. Matilda and her mother Isabelle had been widowed at about the same time, for John of Oisy also died circa 1238/39, but definitely slightly before Richard.[14] Isabelle ruled in her own right for another decade. Thus for nearly a decade Isabelle of Chartres and her daughter Matilda, as widowed heiresses, and without any expectation of direct heirs, continued their active support of Cistercian nuns and encouraged that of others in their territories. Their religious bequests represent those of a specific type of great heiress at the time, with few limits on her religious patronage.

In the 1220s Isabelle and John of Oisy in their enthusiasm for Cistercian nuns founded two more abbeys for those nuns. (See Map 2.) The earlier foundation was that made in 1222 at Lieu-Notre-Dame in Isabelle's holdings in the castellany of Romorantin—a territory south of Blois between the Loire and Cher Rivers, the very marshy parts of which are called the Sologne. The second abbey was closer to the city of Chartres: at Aqua, or Eau, founded with the cooperation of the bishop of Chartres and the abbot of the great Benedictine abbey Saint-Père-de-Chartres in the more long-settled grain-producing fields that surround that great cathedral town. The abbey of Eau-lez-Chartres is first documented in 1226.

The sources of support for these two abbeys, like their locations, differed considerably. So did the ways in which their documents did or did not survive. A fire destroyed many of the documents for Eau, including the medieval charters, during the Wars of Religion; what remains are the charters or copies of charters found in other archives, such as those for the Benedictine monks of Saint-Père.[15] For Lieu-Notre-Dame the opposite is the case. There is a charter book, or cartulary, identified in its opening colophon as having been completed in 1269/70 by a notary from Orléans; its contents are rich in conveyances, lists of holdings, and so on, but only for the half century up to that date.[16] This means that we have a very incomplete picture of what properties and sources of income had been acquired by the nuns of Eau in those early decades, whereas for Lieu the record is more exhaustive until it stops.

Table 4. Charters for Eau (Founded 1226) and Lieu (Founded 1222)

Decade	Ruler of Chartres	Eau	(Est.)	Lieu	Both Actual	Both Estimate
1220s	Isabelle, countess	14	(14)	5	19	(19)
1230s	Isabelle, countess	12	(36)	36	48	(72)
1240s	Isabelle, countes	9	(51)	51	60	(102)
1250s	Matilda and John	21	(41)	41	62	(82)
1260s	John of Châtillon	14	(27)	27	41	(54)
1270s	John of Châtillon	16	(16)	1	17	(17)
1220s–1270s		86	(185)	161	247	(346)

Sources: *Cartulaire de l'abbaye royale du Lieu-N.-D.-lès-Romorantin*, ed. Ernest Plat (Romorantin, 1892); and *Cartulaire de l'abbaye de Notre-Dame de l'Eau*, ed. Charles Métais (Chartres: Ch. Métais, 1908).
Note: This table includes an estimate for the numbers of lost charters for Eau. Assuming a similar distribution of charters for the two abbeys of Eau and Lieu, the decade totals for Lieu, when larger than those for Eau, have been used as an estimate for Eau.

The comparison is seen in Table 4, which suggests that there may have been about one hundred charters for Eau that are now lost.

At first, the founders' attention may have been divided equally between the two new abbeys, although documents for Lieu suggest that its nuns may have arrived slightly before the date of its earliest charter in 1222. The earliest document for Eau from 1226 probably reflects quite closely the foundation events. Given its location near Chartres, the abbey of Eau was similar in terms of assets acquired to the abbey of nuns at Port-Royal as seen in Chapter 4. For instance, Eau's land rights and tithes had been dispersed into many hands and had to be purchased and consolidated into granges for the new abbey and there was a certain amount of resistance to the nuns' acquisitions.[17] The more limited surviving evidence for Eau-lez-Chartres is considered first.

Cistercian Nuns at Eau-lez-Chartres

In 1226 the bishop of Chartres granted permission to Isabelle of Chartres and her husband John of Oisy to found a house for Cistercian nuns at Aqua, or Eau-Notre-Dame, in the parish of Saint-Victoire-de-Ver not far from the city of Chartres.[18] They purchased a site for the abbey at a place called Pentoise in that parish in 1226 from Lady Adeline of Ver and her sons William, Evrard, Reginald, and Robert, and her (unnamed) daughters, who made the conveyance for the soul of Robert of Chartres, Adeline's late husband.[19] Some of the earliest concessions to Eau were made in 1227 when the knight Garin of Fresia, vîdame of Chartres, and his wife, Margaret, granted the nuns ten livres annual income at Châteaudun; that income had been granted to Garin by Louis of Blois, Isabelle's brother who had died in 1205.[20] In August 1228 Isabelle and John gave Eau's nuns income from the fulling mills of Chartres and from other rights in that city, as well as promising provisions from Isabelle's flour mills and winepresses near the abbey. By summer 1228 the community of Eau had been established in temporary buildings at Pentoise.[21] Additional rights there came to the nuns in 1229 from a priest and his mother, Ersendis of Pentoise. The son, the cleric Perry, had been associated with the early nuns there; perhaps he had been their first confessor.[22]

Eau's foundation was made with the support of the bishop and of the abbot of the Benedictine monastery at Saint-Père, but obstacles soon arose. The thirteenth-century mayors for the abbot of Saint-Père had acquired claims to be fief holders for Pentoise from Saint-Père and only in December 1229 did Nicholas, mayor, acknowledge that the abbot of Saint-Père had granted Pentoise for the foundation of the abbey of nuns. Nicholas conceded those rights to Isabelle and her husband but only in return for a promise to pay those mayors eight barrels of wine annually from the winepress there.[23] Later, just to acquire a mortgage over Pentoise's tithes, this same Nicholas required that the nuns pay him another fifty livres.[24]

By 1228 purchases of nearby properties that would become Eau's first granges had begun, when the nuns of Eau paid two hundred livres to a different Nicholas, Nicholas of Ivry and his wife Amelina, for land, grange, and pasture rights at Morancez, or Morencez (both spellings are used).[25] That the property at Morancez had belonged to Amelina rather than to Nicholas is revealed in later disputes over its ownership.[26] Documents from 1241 and 1248 reveal that her father, Raoul of Moulin, had purchased Morancez from Robert of Torel, a citizen of Chartres. By 1248 Amelina, presumably by then a widow, had become an important personage at Eau; she lived at the abbey, perhaps as a boarder, but in one charter noting that she wanted to endow an anniversary for her own soul. In return for another four pieces of land adjoining the grange of Morancez she established for herself a formal annuity for life of half a muid of wheat to be paid to her on All Saints' Day; after her death that annuity would fund a pittance (a celebratory meal for the nuns) on her anniversary.[27] In the early 1250s Amelina appears to have been acting on behalf of the nuns when she purchased land just outside the abbey gates for seventy sous.[28] Then in 1257 just before her death she gave another piece of land and two butchers' stalls in Chartres to support the abbey's infirmary and promised another four arpents of land at Ermenonville next to the nuns' grange at Montes, requesting that she be buried as a nun.[29]

Surviving charters record other conveyances to Eau's nuns in the vicinity of the abbey and its granges at Morancez and Montes (Moinz) in the 1240s. In 1243 William of Rèteville and his wife Agnes sold three arpents of land at Montes in the *censive* of the Countess of Chartres to Eau for four livres; John Peri, citizen of Chartres, and his wife, Isabelle, donated a meadow at Font-de-la-Varenne in the *censive* of the lords of Ver; in 1244 the nuns were given two more pieces of land, already sown, located between the church of Ver and the elm of Morancez and held from the lords of Ver.[30]

The nuns of Eau acquired mills and income from mills; often such mills were conveyed in shares, for they were becoming expensive investments. In 1237 the nuns of Eau purchased half the rights over two mills at Fosse from the knight Aimeric of Loches for 240 livres. This entitled them to half the rights over that milling complex (later described as two mill wheels under one roof at a single site, with water, meadows, land, and millrace), allowing them to use the mills every other day. By 1274 they paid another eighty livres for the rest of the rights there.[31] A sixth of another such mill, one in Chartres itself, was granted in 1247 by the knight William Gode and his son, the squire Geoffrey, along with half of three sous in annual rent over a house in Chartres.[32]

Isabelle of Chartres had granted revenues from her mills in Chartres to Eau's nuns. Her last surviving enumeration of gifts to Eau, a charter of 1241/ 42, emphasized the importance of that income. She began by saying that she had founded the abbey of Eau "de novo," then she listed all her earlier gifts to its nuns: four muids of grain at her mill at Coudray and five arpents of meadow at Valféry, to which she added another five arpents of meadow. She then explained that although at first she had granted the nuns twenty-two livres of annual income from the fulling mills at Chartres, she had increased the amount to forty livres per year. This was because at his death (circa 1233) her *consanguineus* William, bishop of Châlons, Count of Perche, had asked her to distribute his own eighteen livres of income over those mills "in sup-port of the poor" (ad erogandum pauperibus). Isabelle then stated that she had fulfilled his wish that the income be given to support the poor by giving those eighteen livres to the nuns at Eau, making their total holdings in the mills of Chartres worth forty livres per annum.[33]

All this seems straightforward, but it also provides a tantalizing glimpse of attitudes about almsgiving and the identity of the poor at the time. What is striking is that for Isabelle it appears that the poor for whom she was fulfilling this charitable bequest were the monastic poor, a house of nuns that she had founded. Possibly the nuns of Eau set aside this portion of their -income for almsgiving, but more likely their almsgiving consisted of distributions of excess food from their own table.[34] Such an attitude is probably not unusual for the time but it is reflective of Isabelle's personal views on poverty and charity.[35] Indeed, Isabelle may have done her almsgiving earlier. She had granted cash income for alms for his soul after John of Oisy's death in 1238/39, as was recorded by her daughter Matilda, lady of Amboise, and her son-in-law Richard, viscount of Beaumont and lord of Amboise.[36] In 1239 Matilda and Richard recorded that their dear mother Isabelle had granted 330 livres from her annual income at Chartres and its vicinity, and another 105 livres from her annual income at Romorantin and Millençay for almsgiving. The nuns of Eau would receive additional bequests after Isabelle's death in 1248/49.[37]

Lieu-Notre-Dame-lès-Romorantin

Early foundation events for Lieu replicated to some extent those at Eau, but for Lieu more details survive. In 1222 Isabelle of Chartres and John of Oisy issued a foundation charter for the religious women of the abbey of Lieu-Notre-Dame near Romorantin "newly planted there," where its nuns were to live "under the rule and practices of the Cistercian Order"; this was done so that the nuns there would establish a chapel to pray daily for the souls of the dead, including those of Isabelle and John. Included in the foundation gift were the abbey site, income from an oven in Romorantin, firewood in the woods of Briode for the nuns' heating, and the tithe on wine produced at Reuilly.[38] These were the usual types of appurtenances given by a founder for a new foundation. Isabelle reiterated these gifts at the end of her life and attempted to dictate the nuns' use of income, specifying that fifty of the sixty livres of income from the hearth tax (*festagium*) of Romorantin were to be spent on wheat to make the nuns' bread.[39]

But something else is found in the foundation charter from 1222 that reflects the landscape in which Lieu was founded—a landscape that looked very different from that around Chartres. Lieu-Notre-Dame was founded south of Orléans and Blois in the castellany of Romorantin, an area between the Loire and Cher Rivers that was not contiguous with the territory of

Chartres (the territory of Blois being in between).[40] In this area of marsh, scrub, woods, and waste, the new community of nuns at Lieu was given thirty-six arpents of uncultivated land adjoining the abbey site with the expectation that reclamation would take place under the aegis of the nuns. That expectation was clarified in a charter from 1232 in which Isabelle's daughter, Matilda of Amboise and Matilda's husband, Richard of Beaumont, granted the nuns up to one hundred additional arpents of uncultivated land in the forest of Calmont, north of Romorantin, to be brought under cultivation and to be held free of rent. That charter also granted the nuns the right to bring even more land under cultivation there, if they paid rent at the usual rate on the additions.[41] One other early property granted to Lieu in 1224 seems to have come from those of John of Oisy, the new count. It is described as a grange and its property-holdings at Lande in the parish of Lanthenay not far west of the abbey; it was given with the tithes and all rights and lordship in John's *censive* there.[42]

Other early acquisitions by Lieu were in the more developed regions east of Lanthenay and Romorantin. In 1232 the nuns paid fifty livres for tithes over vineyards at Landonière in the parish of Villeherviers and in 1234 they were promised additional tithes there.[43] In 1237 rights in that same parish at Villeherviers over new mills on the river Sauldre came to the nuns in 1237 when the four sisters of Hervy of Trecy entered the abbey.[44] Included were mill or mills, mill house, adjoining land, access to materials from Hervy's lands for mill repair or construction, *multura* (payment for mill use), fishing at the mill and in the millpond, and rights for the nuns to do as they pleased with the island below that mill. Hervy kept the woodlands and water rights, but promised not to dig ditches to divert the water that fed the mill or to do anything else that might prevent the millstones from grinding.[45]

In 1245 and again in 1254 the nuns acquired additional rights at Coudray, next to Villeherviers.[46] In 1246 they purchased back from Hervy of Trecy an earlier obligation to pay two sestiers of rye to him annually; they also paid eighty livres for additional water rights at Villeherviers.[47] By 1254 Hervy had become a knight and with the agreement of his wife Alice and his brother Urseius sold to Lieu, for another twenty livres, "the mill that I had over the Sauldre River with land, waste, islands, marsh, meadows, and whatever rights and lordship he had had from the nuns' new mill on the Sauldre up to the road that leads to Romorantin."[48] He also promised neither to increase or decrease the amount of water in the nuns' stretch of the river nor to do anything that might harm or reduce the fishing there.[49] Eventually this complex had at least two separate mills—one held outright by the nuns.

At the same time the nuns of Lieu began acquiring urban rights. In 1237 they were given eight acres of gardens at Ferté-Hubert.[50] In Romorantin, in addition to the oven given by the founders, they acquired houses.[51] In 1245 when Sister Lucie entered Lieu to become a nun, she brought a rent of forty sous on a house in Romorantin at the Paris gate.[52] In 1262 the priest John Chauvet sold them his stone house located next to the countess's oven, along with rights over a winepress (and cellar?) for seventy livres.[53] Perhaps donors were inspired to make such gifts by the royal favor expressed when in 1242 Louis IX, acting on behalf of his sister Isabelle of France, gave a yearly rent of two sestiers of salt from the royal storehouses at Romorantin; the nuns promised anniversary masses for them both.[54]

Lieu-Notre-Dame's earliest documents were copied into a cartulary in 1269/70. Its opening twenty-five acts describe money rents acquired from a variety of sources, and the scribe totaled those rents per annum in 1269: 228 livres and sixteen sous.[55] In addition, the last fifteen entries in the cartulary are identified by a rubrication as "acquisitions of rents" in kind of wheat or rye (see Table 5). What is noteworthy is how little wheat was received from such rents before the 1260s, while rents paid in rye suggest something of the poor character of the local soils.[56]

The charters include abundant descriptions of the landscape west of Romorantin and Lanthenay where the nuns' tenants were involved in reclamation. Thus, a charter from 1238 issued by Countess Isabelle and her husband John described conveyances of another forty arpents in those woodlands in which the nuns could do as they wished, eight arpents of vineyards next to the nuns' lands at Roulaiz (adjoining the great pond and a small pond next to the abbey), and rents called *terrages* in the parish of Millençay: at Pin, Pleinbois, and Combren. The charter specified that those who currently owed *terrage* to the count and countess should thereafter "make their payments of *terrage* to the nuns."[57] Similarly, in 1246 the nuns paid forty livres for the tithes of wheat, wine, and other income from Reginald Legros, bourgeois of Valençay: "Whatever [he] had in the great vineyard and in the little forest in the territories of Lanthenay and Romorantin, from where the road extends from Blois to the place called Rangeroulx and stretching from another marker beside the marsh and pond belonging to the knight William of Furnum and so on."[58] This region full of game birds and other wildlife, of marshes and

Table 5. Lieu-Notre-Dame: Annual Payments in Kind

	Measures of Grain*		
Date	Rye	Wheat	Source of payment
1236	3 sestiers		terrages† of Cormain
1239	1 sestier		tithes at Mur
1240		2/3 sestier	paid at Lieu
1243	2 sestiers		tithes of Fontanes
1247	1 sestier		tithes of Billy
1251	12 sestiers		terrages at Soemio
1252	2 sestiers		tithes at Marcelliac
1255	12 sestiers		tithes at Veillens
1260	38 sestiers		paid at Pruniers
1263	18 sestiers		mills of Calciata
		6 sestiers	paid at Blois
1268		14 sestiers	tithes of Genilleyo
1269	2 sestiers		paid at Goscherière
1270	12 sestiers	28 sestiers	tithes and mill of Sazeyo
1236–1270	103 sestiers	4854.67 sestiers	Total of both: 151.67

Source: Cartulaire de Lieu, nos. 142–45, 147–56 (no. 146 is not actually a conveyance).
*With 12 sestiers = 1 muid. (A sestier is about a 100-pound sack, a muid a cartload.)
†On terrages, see below.

ponds in which to fish, was coming to be known as the Sologne. Despite such efforts at reclamation as were attempted in the thirteenth century, it would eventually be virtually abandoned for agricultural production, becoming instead an area of royal forests and hunting lodges.

That this was marginal land is indicated by the lack of the traditional nomenclature for medieval landholdings found elsewhere, of mansi and villas. The charters suggest how much the tenants of the nuns of Lieu were being encouraged to undertake the reclamation of marshy lands, riverbeds, and streams, creating noval and tithe-exempt lands on which terrage rents were to be paid. Following the charters for the grain rents found in Table 5, the last folios of the manuscript cartulary, fols. 46r–52r, list tenants and income called terrages, the rent paid on recently cultivated lands often expressed in amounts of grain, as well as of those who were diggers and what they paid in kind, and a list of those who paid a tax for animals used to plow, called mestine.[59] (See Table 6.)

This made Lieu's nuns very unusual insofar as having a mixed endowment coming both from established sources of revenues and from terrages

Table 6. Lieu-Notre-Dame: *Terrages, Rapinax,* and *Mestines*

Terrages *(examples)*
"Hec sunt terragia de Morays [Morais] ("uprooted" or "adjoining the marsh")
Owed by fourteen individuals, mostly men, but also two widows and one mother,
over twenty-seven separate pieces:
> Michael Petit Leu pays at the *métairie* of Vallinières more than three muids
> (thirty-six sestiers) for *terrage* over land surrounding the *métairie*, up to the
> lands of Reginald Boisin, the men of Bruyères and Alice of Haie . . .
> Odet of Bruyères had two sestierades that adjoin a grove (*tosca*) of Boys (Bois)
> Adjoining were three sestierades belonging to the widow of John of Bruyères
> One sestierade of land adjoining the road to Vallinières held by another widow
> One sestierade "in rupturam" (cleared/dug up land), etc.

At Tyrols *terrage* owed by thirteen individuals and often described as bounded by
roads:
> Along the great road leading from Mur to Soings
> Adjoining the road to the marsh of Juech and to Benedict's land
> Up to the road of Beraudière
> From the little street that divided the lands of Petite Haie
> From the road of Lardière leading to Tyrols and the road to Blois
> Up to the road to Blois at Tyrols next to the road of Giraudières
> Land enclosed with ditches belonging to Gerard Coroneau, etc.

Rapinax
"Ci sunt les hommes qui sunt noz Rapinax" (who dig land and drainage ditches)
Four men each pay nine *boysseaux*/bushels and nine deniers:
> Andreas Grison, Andreas Voisin, Ratier, Reginald le Grand

Two men each pay four *boysseaux*:
> Paquille, Paquille's son

Eleven men or parties each pay one sestier and twelve deniers:
> Benedict Brocart, Bernard Terri, Girard Bodin, John de Haie, the children of
> Haie, Peter Bruerart, Peter Bruerart's son, Reginald Bodin, Reginald de Haie,
> Reginald Terri, Roseroles' merchant

Five men each pay one mine (half a sestier):
> Girard Angebaut, Angebaut's son Martin, Hernault le Gendre au Pin, Peter
> Naquet, Stephanus de Noa

Two(?) men each pay one quart:
> Le gendre (son-in-law) de Nione, Vitus (is this referring to two people?)

Twenty-three or twenty-four men or parties each paid on average seven deniers and
about two *boysseaux* of grain per year.
Total payments annually: 168 deniers, 44 boysseaux, 11 sestiers, 5 mines, 2 quarts.

Mestines (payments for plow animals?)
"Ci est la mestine" de Bosco, de Bueria; de Bray; de Chevremort; de Guerroet; de la
Châtre; de la Corbelière et dou Mesfloy; de la Forgeterie; de la Minerie et de la
Pinardière; de Tyroles; de Voy; and dou Pozat.

Source: *Cartulaire de Lieu,* pp. 107–20 (from fols. 46r–52v of the manuscript).

levied on reclamation. However, it is likely that such land being brought under cultivation in the thirteenth century may have been profitable only when it was newly cultivated and cultivated tithe free, and hence that the tithe exemption claimed by Cistercian nuns on noval lands (although it had often to be repurchased) was essential to such production. This is suggested by an accord regarding noval tithes between Lieu and the priory of Saint-Cosme of Insula near Tours made in the 1270s; for any noval tithes there the nuns agreed to pay a lump sum of two sestiers of rye per year but no more.[60] Concerns over tithes in the parish of Mur-en-Sologne west of the abbey also arose. At Mur half of the tithes had been mortgaged for 120 livres in 1234 to the church of Saint-Sauveur in Blois by one of Isabelle's feudatories, the knight Roger Bugle. A decade later, in 1244, acting on behalf of the nuns, Isabelle redeemed those pledged tithes by repaying the mortgage principal to Saint-Sauveur. In 1247 she purchased the other half of those tithes from Roger Bugle for 180 livres.[61] Two years later in August 1249 dispute over tithes at Mur arose again. Arbitrators concluded that the nuns of Lieu should hold rights to both new and old tithes at Mur, but that they also owed the parish priest of Mur an annual six sestiers of rye in lieu of noval tithes and seven sestiers in lieu of ancient ones; they should also relinquish to him all the minute tithes (on smaller items, like gardens).[62] But established tithes could also be at issue. In 1249 the nuns purchased half the tithes over vineyards at Landonière from Petronilla, widow of Philip Ternerii, for eighty livres *tournois*.[63]

In her will of 1247 Isabelle of Chartres listed those lands that could be brought under cultivation (or not) in a wide swath of territory given to the nuns: "My entire woods called Druillay, located next to the road that goes from Millençay to Romorantin . . . those nuns could preserve, sell, give away, uproot, and reduce to agriculture as they pleased."[64] But Lieu's nuns were also told what was not to be cleared; she identified places where the nuns had only usage rights and those where they simply were not to make clearances. Still pasture was available even in the latter for all the nuns' animals of whatever type, including mast for one hundred pigs. The nuns could hunt or trap small game such as rabbits and could build another mill at a designated site. Elsewhere the nuns could continue to oversee reclamation, and Isabelle granted them rights over all the *terrages* made or to be made there—*in terragia facta et facienda*. She allowed them to collect rent from those men who had recently done the digging to uproot lands, confirmed the nuns' new income at Mur and Pin, and announced that the *terrages* at Morais should produce twelve muids of rye annually.[65]

In 1249, soon after her mother's death, the new countess Matilda of Amboise granted Lieu's nuns a rent of twelve livres annually from the exchange tables at Chartres, a rent that had been promised to the Cistercian monks at Vaucelles in 1227 as a postmortem gift to fund an anniversary for Isabelle and John. The promise came due with Isabelle's death, and her daughter Matilda reacquired it for the nuns of Lieu by convincing the monks to take in exchange ten livres in annual rent from a vineyard at Marquises that John of Oisy had given to Lieu.[66] In 1249 Matilda also confirmed to the nuns of Lieu their rights in the woods near the abbey and its great pond where they could make ditches to limit access, have rabbit warrens and rights to hunt small animals for feeding the sick.[67] She gave them rights to new property "in all her woods near the grange of Hagueville, in the castellany of Romorantin," where the nuns could "guard, sell, give, uproot and reduce to agriculture." This was to fund anniversaries for herself and for the souls of her father, Sulpice of Amboise, her mother, Isabelle of Chartres, and her husband, Richard of Beaumont.[68]

In 1248 just before she died, Countess Isabelle had begun to purchase rights for the nuns of Lieu in an additional area of reclamation at what became the grange of Puy Sauverdun, or Saugirard. That property had been transferred at the beginning of the century by Isabelle's brother, Louis of Blois (d. 1205) to the Cistercian monks at Barzelles in the diocese of Bourges.[69] (Again, see Map 2.) Isabelle and her daughter Matilda proposed repurchasing that grange for the nuns of Lieu for five hundred livres, but the document of transfer from 1248, written in the voice of the monks of Barzelles, makes it impossible to know whether Isabelle had lived long enough to see this happen: "May all recognize that we have sold to the abbess and community of nuns at Lieu-Notre-Dame that grange of ours at Puy Sauverdun sited in the castellany of Romorantin in the diocese of Orléans, with all its appurtenances, whether in houses or vineyards, meadows, pastures, lands, woods, water, tithes, *terrages*, and whatever other income we have in the parishes of Gy [Giacho], of Soings [Soemio] and of Auberière with all the appurtenances of those properties"[70] The nuns of Lieu had already begun acquiring rights there, for instance in the parish of Gy, where they had purchased tithes in 1239 at a place called Bâtarde for sixty livres; in 1248 they were given a rent over tithes in the parish of Gy that amounted to six sestiers of wheat per year.[71] Countess Matilda oversaw the sale to Lieu of tithes in the parish of Soings en Sologne in 1251 made by the squire William of Cormain for 145 livres. Again a dispute over noval tithes arose with the parish priest, and it was eventually agreed that the priest and his successors were owed one muid of rye from the noval lands, but that the nuns could keep all the tithes over wheat there. As seen in Table 5, production of wheat was being supplemented or supplanted by rye on the more marginal, noval lands.

What Lieu's founders, Isabelle of Chartres and Matilda of Amboise, accomplished at Lieu was unusual. They enabled its nuns to oversee considerable reclamation in the Sologne. The examples of *terrages* paid, noted in Table above, reflect only a small number of the recently reclaimed holdings that would come to pay those rents to the nuns of Lieu. Such reclamation, both clearance and drainage of marshy, waterlogged lands, was unusual for almost all thirteenth-century houses of Cistercian nuns and for many houses of Cistercian monks as well.[72]

Matilda of Amboise and Perray-aux-Nonnains

Slightly earlier, in the 1240s, Matilda of Amboise became associated with yet another community of nuns that became Cistercian. Those nuns were originally settled at Coudray near Angers and were associated with the Cistercian monks at Loroux in the diocese of Angers. They were then moved in 1249 to a site called Perray that become the abbey of Cistercian nuns of Perray-aux-Nonnains where they replaced an earlier community of monks at Perray founded circa 1190. The surviving record suggests that an inquiry by Gregory IX about the earlier monks at Perray was instigated circa 1229. Report was that there were only three monks left at Perray, that the community was slowly declining, and that it had become encumbered with debt. In 1249 it was decided that the monks could not continue to fulfill their monastic vows and Marguerite de Séez and Matilda of Amboise (Beaumont) received approval to replace the monks at Perray with the holy women who had been living at Coudray, where numbers had increased.[73] But just how reliable is the record that avows the need to replace the monks at Perray? Was such a tale of laxity, poor management, and abrogation of vows overemphasized by ambitious female supporters of a new community of Cistercian nuns at Perray?[74] Was this a familiar trope about the need for suppression more often directed at the suppression of women's houses? (See Chapter 8.)

There is no additional evidence for Matilda's continued support of nuns at Perray and little more for her support for nuns at Lieu and Eau. Abbeys of Cistercian nuns would no longer have the single-minded patronage they had received from Matilda and her mother Isabelle in the 1240s. Particularly in that decade, however, mother and daughter had acted together not just as heiresses in their own rights, but also as heiresses having no direct heirs. Once it was clear that Matilda would have no direct heirs, they became exceptionally generous patrons to Cistercian nuns. This would change after Matilda's death in 1256.

Jean of Châtillon and the Reuniting of Chartres and Blois

Upon Matilda of Amboise's death in 1256, her cousin Jean of Châtillon reunited the counties of Blois and Chartres (see Figure 4). Upon becoming Count of Chartres in 1256, he and his wife Alice of Brittany confirmed the ten livres of annual income from the *prévôté* of Chartres that had been given to the nuns of Eau-lez-Chartres by his *consanguinea*, the previous countess, Matilda.[75] He and his wife also gave Eau an annual rent of twenty-six livres to be paid at the rate of half a livre per week by the *argentarius* of Chartres; this was probably in lieu of earlier gifts made by Isabelle and Matilda.[76] Three years later in 1259 the couple gave income from Chartres to the nuns of Grâce-Notre-Dame in Champagne, which was closer to the area where he had grown up; in 1280, that bequest was repurchased by Eau's nuns for 120 livres.[77]

Local families continued to make gifts to the Cistercian nuns of Eau and Lieu. In 1257 Jean of Châtillon granted an *amortissement* over all the land and pasture rights at Villegallon that had been given to Eau by Alipdis, lady of Neuville, who had become a nun there.[78] In 1260 Thibaut of Aulnay granted Eau's nuns two muids of grain annually from his grange of Bretigny for his sister Isabelle, a nun there, and for an anniversary for their mother.[79] Circa 1263 the knight Girard of Chartres and his wife Blanche gave those nuns substantial rights for their grange of Montes: thirty-two arpents of land (three of them planted with vines), pasture rights, and eighteen sestiers of wheat and oats paid at Bonneville; in return the nuns were to fund a priest to celebrate daily mass for the relief of the souls of Girard and his wife Blanche, and for those of Girard's two earlier wives, Isabelle and Beatrix.[80]

Jean of Châtillon, the new count, and his wife Alice appear to have focused more on Lieu-Notre-Dame, perhaps because its nuns' location near the castle of Romorantin was closer to his base in Blois. In 1261 they granted Lieu's nuns forty livres per annum from the *prévôté* of Romorantin and the *festagium* (hearth tax) of Millençay, instructing the nuns that twenty-six livres were for their infirmary and fourteen livres for the clothing of the nuns. Such a specific bequest suggests personal ties between Alice and Lieu's nuns; perhaps they had cared for her in their infirmary.[81] Her death was marked by Jean of Châtillon's confirmation to Lieu-Notre-Dame in 1268 of one hundred sous in annual rent for celebrating anniversaries for his own soul and that of Alice, his late wife.[82]

Other donations to Lieu in this period included one in 1261 of eleven deniers in cens from an inheritance and twenty sous cash given by Hugh of Bois-Simon when his sister Petronilla entered Lieu as a novice. He promised another eight livres for her clothing when she became a nun.[83] In 1266, when Alexaudis and Amelina became nuns at Lieu, their brothers John and Geoffrey of Bruyères and their other sisters, Petronilla, Alice, and Isabelle, granted a third of the tithes in the parish of Millençay and twenty sous annually from the passage tolls at Romorantin.[84] In 1270 the knight John of Saint-Brice gave Lieu sixty sous in annual income when his two nieces, Agatha and Mathia, became nuns there, but also so that after his death this gift would fund an anniversary for his soul.[85]

In 1279 Jean of Châtillon, Count of Blois and Chartres, died. His successor was his daughter Jeanne of Châtillon. Shortly before his death, her father had confessed to having fallen into arrears for three years in his payments of ninety livres per year owed to Eau's nuns; he persuaded them to agree to a permanent reduction from ninety to sixty livres per annum and to give up claims to the arrears.[86] The difficulties at this point underline how fragile such rents could be. After her father's death, Jeanne and her husband Peter of Alençon, one of Louis IX's sons, attempted to redress some of this. With Peter, she restored to both Eau and Lieu rents on the fulling mills of Chartres that had been given by Isabelle and Matilda, granted Eau rights to twenty-five livres of income derived from cutting wood at Champrond, gave Eau twelve arpents of vineyards at Luisant, and granted its nuns rights to acquire up to one hundred livres of rents in Peter's properties.[87]

Still the thirty-some years of support for the nuns at Eau and Lieu by Isabelle of Chartres and her daughter Matilda, which had occurred in part because they had no direct heirs, had been an extraordinary boon for the growth of both abbeys. Jean of Châtillon, Matilda's heir, may have been less pleased with some of their alienations of what he must have seen as his

rightful inheritance. Once Jeanne of Châtillon, the heiress of Blois and Chartres, had married a royal prince, the crown would probably not continue to
turn quite such a blind eye on alienations to the church. Earlier in 1218 when
Philip Augustus had put the two heiresses and their husbands in charge of
the counties of Blois and Chartres, although he had divided the two counties,
he had prevented more powerful vassals from attempting to take over those
territories. He and his son Louis VIII and his grandson Louis IX also saw it
in the royal interest to allow a great heiress to rule in her own right in the
region of Auxerre, Nevers, and Tonnerre.

Matilda of Courtenay, Countess of Nevers, Auxerre, and Tonnerre

In the thirteenth century the French king also found it useful to have the
great feudal heiress Matilda of Courtenay rule as his vassal for the counties
of Nevers, Auxerre, and Tonnerre. Often called Matilda the Great, this
daughter of the king's cousin Peter of Courtenay was born circa 1180 and
ruled until 1256.[88] Although there is a relative dearth of records about her
religious patronage, Countess Matilda founded or supported at least three
houses for Cistercian nuns in her realms.[89] A fourth abbey at Pont-aux-
Dames was founded for the soul of Matilda's daughter, Agnes, and it did
receive patronage from Matilda's grandson, the famous knight Gaucher of
Châtillon.

Matilda was one of a remarkable succession of female rulers of Auxerre
and Nevers. Her mother, Agnes (d. 1192), was the sole surviving child of
William V, Count of Nevers (1175–81), and had ruled as Countess of Nevers
and Auxerre following her father's death in 1181. In 1184 Agnes married King
Philip's first cousin Peter of Courtenay. After Agnes's death in 1192, their sole
heir, Matilda of Courtenay, inherited the counties, which were ruled until
1199 by her father, Peter of Courtenay. In 1199 Peter of Courtenay was
defeated in a military skirmish and taken prisoner by Hervé of Donzy, who
asked for Matilda's hand in marriage as the price of her father's release. In
1199 when they married, Matilda and Hervé were immediately vested in the
county of Auxerre, but only after her father's death in Constantinople in
1216/17 did they receive the counties of Nevers and Tonnerre.[90] (See Figure 5.)

Matilda and Hervé appear to have been a devoted couple, both of them
interested in the Cistercians; her religious foundations were all made for his
soul.[91] They had faced charges that their marriage was consanguineous and

William of Nevers (d. 1181), Matilda's grandfather
Sole heir Agnes of Nevers (d. 1192) m. 1184 Peter of Courtenay (d. 1216)
Sole heir Matilda of Courtenay (d. 1256) m. 1199 Hervé of Donzy (d. 1222);
m. 1226 second husband Guy of Forez (d. 1241), no issue
From first marriage sole child Agnes:

Agnes of Nevers (d. 1225) m. ca. 1220 Guy of Châtillon (d. 1226)*
Two children from this marriage:
Gaucher of Châtillon (d. 1251), no issue
Yolande of Châtillon (d. 1254) m. Archambaud of Bourbon (d. 1249)
Their two daughters marry two brothers:
Agnes m. Robert of Burgundy
Matilda II (inherits in 1256; d. 1262) m. Eudes of Burgundy
Their daughters: Yolande, Marguerite, Adelaide inherit Auxerre, Nevers and Tonnerre

* His brother is Hugh of Châtillon; see Figure 4

Figure 5. Genealogy: Matilda of Courtenay.

were declared legally married only in 1220 by Pope Honorius III; this secured the rights to their counties and the legitimacy of their daughter Agnes, their only child. This daughter Agnes was born around the beginning of the century, for in 1221 she married Guy of Châtillon, Count of Saint-Pol; the legality of their marriage too was challenged but declared legitimate by the pope.[92] Agnes and Guy of Châtillon produced two living children, Yolande and Gaucher. Their mother, Agnes, died in 1225, possibly in a third childbirth. In 1226 her husband, Guy of Châtillon, made a foundation for Cistercian nuns at Pont-aux-Dames, for Agnes's soul and his own.[93]

Agnes's death in 1225 was foreshadowed by an earlier one in 1222 when Matilda's husband Hervé of Donzy died at his castle of Saint-Aignan in Berry, said to have been poisoned by supporters of the Albigensian heretics. Then in August 1226, shortly after the foundation of Pont-aux-Dames, Guy of Châtillon also died, felled by a stone during the siege of Avignon.[94] Countess Matilda of Courtenay was left to protect her two orphaned grandchildren, Yolande and Gaucher of Châtillon; probably it was to do so that she quickly remarried—a marriage to Guy, Count of Forez, that appears to have been one of convenience. Matilda settled Guy's debts and they agreed that his son from a previous marriage would be heir to his county of Forez but be excluded from any claims to her lands. There were no children. Guy of Forez soon returned to the East where he died in 1241. By then Matilda's grandson, Gaucher of Châtillon, born circa 1220, was old enough to serve as her proxy knight; he departed on crusade with Louis IX in 1249. In the seven following years, until her death in 1256, Matilda ruled in her own right, having made religious foundations for the soul of her first husband, issuing charters to protect and promote the growth of her towns, minting coinage bearing her own name: Matilda, Countess of Nevers.[95] Like other women at the time, she too ruled in part by the issuance of written documents—although many fewer of these have survived than for Countess Matilda of Chartres, who also died in 1256.

Matilda the Great, Countess of Auxerre, Nevers, and Tonnerre, had buried her first husband, Hervé of Donzy, at the Cistercian abbey for monks at Pontigny and then began founding or reestablishing houses of Cistercian nuns to pray for his soul and to establish a burial place for herself. In 1229/30 she converted an existing community of women at Celles near Auxerre into an abbey of Cistercian nuns, moving them to a new site on the Yonne River, granting them rights to collect firewood in her forests and changing the abbey's name to Isles-Notre-Dame. Its nuns became part of the Cistercian Order under the guidance of the nuns of Saint-Antoine-des-Champs in Paris

and may have followed the customs that Stephen of Lexington had established for Saint-Antoine circa 1235.[96] In 1239 a colony was sent from Isles to
found a daughter house at Marcilly where Matilda would be buried.[97] Her
influence also led in 1237 to the attachment to the Cistercians of a house of
nuns at Charité-lès-Lézinnes, which had been founded in 1184 by William of
Lézinnes.[98]

While Countess Matilda appears to have made no property transfers to
Pont-aux-Dames, which had been founded for the soul of her daughter
Agnes, her grandson Gaucher of Châtillon made gifts to those nuns both in
1240 and in 1248 before departing on Louis IX's crusade. He died in Egypt
in 1251, a glorious knight in defense of his king, but with no offspring.[99] His
sister Yolande of Châtillon had married Archambaud IX of Bourbon, probably in the 1240s, but Archambaud died in 1249 en route to that same crusade.
Yolande appears to have died in 1254 before her grandmother Matilda of
Courtenay in 1256.

Matilda of Courtenay continued to rule until her death in 1256. Her survivors were the two daughters of Yolande of Châtillon and Archambald. These
two great granddaughters, Matilda II and Agnes, married two sons of Hugh
IV, Duke of Burgundy. The elder, Matilda II, inherited the counties of Nevers,
Auxerre, and Tonnerre in 1256 with her husband Eudes of Burgundy. After
Matilda II died in 1262 their three daughters Yolande, Margaret, and Adelaide
inherited the three counties, which were split among them. It was these three
granddaughters whose maternal great-grandmother Agnes had been commem-
orated in the founding of Pont-aux-Dames. Even given the death of so many
of the men of this family on crusades, the propensity for female births in this
family over male ones seems unusual. (See again Figure 5.)

Pont-aux-Dames

In April 1226, Matilda the Great's son-in-law, Guy of Châtillon, had founded
a community of Cistercian nuns at Pont-aux-Dames for the soul of his late
wife Agnes, Countess Matilda of Courtenay's daughter.[100] The abbey was
located east of Paris and not far from Meaux in the village of Pont-de-
Couilly. Religious communities from both Meaux and Paris had acquired
properties there, and they must have found the village an attractive retreat
with its bridge over the Grand Morin, a swift-flowing left tributary of the
Marne River, and access to the considerable forests nearby.

Table 7. Pont-aux-Dames: Hugh of Châtillon's Early Interventions for Its Nuns

Date	Results of Hugh of Châtillon's Actions
1226	Part of tithes acquired at Bouleurs and Montaudier from cleric of Meaux
1226/27	Bishop of Meaux approved the new community Bishop and canons of Meaux transferred Couilly buildings to nuns Saint-Germain-des-Prés gave up claims to a rent at Pont-de-Couilly Hugh confirmed the nuns' water rights between mills of Talemer and Quintejoie, up to the mill at Liary, with fishing rights on that stretch of the Grand Morin River, promising that the nuns would not hinder Saint-Germain's mills
1227/28	Tithes at Bouleurs acquired from Fontevraud's abbess and prioress at Collinances Tithes granted by Hugh's provost of Crécy, Stephen Bocel
1228	Nuns were granted rights to an oven at Villeneuve-le-Comte, the new town to which earlier inhabitants of Pont-de-Couilly had been moved Bishop of Meaux was asked to arbitrate dispute with parish priest over tithes
1229	Nuns got rights in a mill at Prémol and tithes from Robert of Villeneuve Nuns got rights to tithes at Pont-de-Couilly
1229/30	Hugh granted thirty arpents of woodland to Hospitallers at La Celle to replace tithes the nuns had received at Bouleurs and Montaudier
1231	Hugh arbitrated with canons of Saint-Martin of La Chapelle, a priory of Saint-Martin-des-Champs, Paris, over tithes at Bouleurs

Source: Berthaut's edition of *Cartulaire de Pont-aux-Dames*, nos. 9–39.

In a ceremony before the bishop of Meaux, by whom the nuns would be visited, the bereaved husband Guy gave an annual rent of ten muids of wheat from the mills of Claye and ten livres annually from the territory of Montgé. But Guy soon died at the siege of Avignon in 1226, and it was his younger brother, Hugh of Châtillon, lord of Crécy, who took over the foundation at Pont-aux-Dames.[101] Hugh of Châtillon's swift intervention in support of the abbey founded by his elder brother followed his concession of wine to the nuns at the foundation in 1226.[102] By 1231 Hugh and his new wife Marie d'Avesnes (who had just inherited the county of Blois upon the death of her mother Marguerite) confirmed "all they had given since he became lord of Châtillon upon the death of his brother Guy in late 1226 and all the fiefs and holdings they had confirmed in their censives."[103] Hugh established the rights of the nuns of Pont-aux-Dames in a series of interventions (see Table 7). But it is important to note that among all the surviving charters for Pont, there is no evidence that an earlier group of sisters or a *domus Dei* had been there before the Cistercian nuns were established in 1226.

Once having encouraged or purchased concessions from other groups, Hugh continued in encouraging conveyances by others. Thus in 1230 Robert of Moulignon and his wife Matilda made a gift of two sestiers of wheat annually with approval of their overlord (Hugh).[104] In April 1232 Jean Leroy of Crécy and his wife Ada gave all their vineyards and vines at Champfauçon; Hugh approved, and he himself gave one arpent of vineyards at Froid Monceau.[105] With or without Hugh's explicit approval, such conveyances continued. In 1231 Jean of La Voute, cleric, sold and gave to the nuns "a large number of pieces of land, meadow, and vineyards."[106] In 1232 Fromentin and Adeline, his wife, gave an arpent of land with vines that they had purchased and another half arpent of vineyard that came from Adeline's dowry; it was her three brothers who confirmed this gift from her family lands.[107]

By 1237 it may have been concern for the reliability of the nuns' food supply that led Hugh and Marie to grant them the rights to grind grain at any of their mills, without paying *multura* (for mill use). Hugh and Marie also promised that if the eight and a half muids of wheat usually drawn from the mill at Saule were not available there, the wheat would be supplemented from their other mills.[108] In 1239, Hugh and Marie added deliveries of ten thousand herring and three containers of butter to be delivered to the nuns by the Cistercian monks of Cercamp (diocese of Amiens).[109] In 1242 Hugh approved the gift of ten muids of wine given by John of Reims and his wife Agnes.[110] Additional provisions in grain and wine were the tithes at Sancy and those of the nuns' new grange of Bouleurs; there in 1232 arbitrators declared that the nuns held tithes "on the production of all new and old vines and those planted recently and even on those that were not yet planted."[111] Eventually the newly acquired grange at Bouleurs would be granted the right to have mass celebrated there.[112] In 1233/34, the knight John Lemoine and his wife Elisabeth gave their entire holding at Vaucourtis and then sold the nuns all their rights over old tithes at Sancy, over a tithe barn, a house, and a meadow.[113]

The nuns eventually moved from Pont-de-Couilly but kept the same name, Pont-aux-Dames. Their acquisitions at the new site began in earnest in 1233/34 when one of Hugh of Châtillon's knights, Guy du Port, gave ownership to his daughter Elisabeth of the mill of Arnold located at Rus and other rights there held from Hugh; this daughter then granted those rights to the nuns.[114] In 1239/40 Hugh of Châtillon and his wife Marie confirmed the nuns' site change from Pont-de-Couilly to the hamlet of Rus, describing the improved situation of the abbey and its enclosure there, bordered by the road to Crécy, with a stone bridge, pastures, and mill at Arnold and roads on the other two sides. The priest of Couilly approved of the move at first, but soon made claims.[115] In 1240 Hugh and Marie confirmed a donation made by the father of John Bocel for his own soul: ten livres of income to build a chapel at the nuns' new site. It was presumably this John's son, Stephen Bocel, and Stephen's wife Heloise who gave another two and a half muids of grain from the tithes of Bouleurs, which they had earlier held in fief from Hugh of Châtillon.[116] Hugh and Marie had given permission in 1239 to build a bridge for pedestrians, horses, or carts near the mill of Arnold and confirmed the nuns' ownership of the little street that crossed through the nuns' enclosure.[117] A charter from 1263 describes a winepress, oven, and wooden bridge near the mill of Arnold.[118]

Once the nuns moved to their new site at Rus there were additional acquisitions of tithes. In 1240 John Bische of Crécy, described as a cleric, with his wife Clemence sold for eighty livres their tithes over wheat and wine at three places: Saint-Martin near Crécy, Berbonne, and Genevray. The knight Peter of Cornillon, lord of Quincy, gave them half the tithes from the vineyard of Saint-Georges of Couilly. Gaucher of Châtillon, the founder Guy's son, gave tithes at Fresne also in 1240.[119] At Rus the nuns were located near the newly founded villages of Villeneuve-le-Comte and Villeneuve-Saint-Denis and just south of the Forest of Jariel, where they eventually acquired forest rights specifically for cutting wood.[120] They had acquired forest rights earlier in the late 1230s when Hugh of Châtillon and his wife Marie made an outright gift to them of three hundred arpents of woodlands in the forest of Crécy, near Lubeton, but they forbade the nuns from cutting down any part of those woods.[121] Such rights to forests and firewood could be particularly important if, as seems likely, the nuns of Pont were involved in grinding flour at their mills and baking bread in the ovens they owned.[122] They also acquired a series of urban properties in Meaux and others in Paris.[123]

Conclusions, as the Two Families Merge

Matilda of Amboise, Countess of Chartres, died in 1256. So did Countess Matilda of Courtenay, and at this point their stories merge. Hugh of Châtillon, Guy's brother, had taken over the foundation at Pont-aux-Dames made by Guy of Châtillon in 1226 for the soul of Matilda of Courtenay's daughter Agnes. Circa 1230 this Hugh had married Marie of Avesnes, the daughter of Marguerite, Countess of Blois. When Marguerite (Isabelle of Chartres's sister) died in 1230/31, Marie and her husband Hugh of Châtillon became Countess and Count of Blois. After Marie died circa 1240/41, Hugh continued as Count of Blois, but also began arrangements for their oldest son, Jean of Châtillon, to inherit that county. Hugh of Châtillon himself died in 1248 during a skirmish as he departed for Louis IX's first crusade.[124] Jean of Châtillon then became Count of Blois at almost the same time that his cousin Matilda of Amboise became Countess of Chartres.

Gradually the outlying counties were being reintegrated into the kingdom and the ability for some women as heiresses to rule unchecked was disappearing. Countesses Isabelle and Matilda of Chartres and Countess Matilda the Great in Auxerre (the heiresses discussed in this chapter) had few restrictions on their alienations of property and their rule had been encouraged by French kings who may have thought to prevent the rise of powerful rivals. When Matilda of Amboise died in 1256, Jean of Châtillon, already Count of Blois, inherited Chartres and reunited the two counties (see Figure 4). Jean's daughter, Jeanne of Châtillon, inherited the reunited counties of Blois and Chartres from her father in 1279; she was married to Peter of Alençon, one of Louis IX's sons.

What Chapters 4 and 5 have shown thus far about the abbeys of Cistercian nuns in the province of Sens is the variety of sites and assets acquired. The nuns appear to have created for themselves consolidated landholdings that had access to water-powered mills to grind their grain and had begun to create extensive vineyards. Such assets were not unlike those of their noble neighbors or of the neighboring houses of Cistercian monks. A generation ago the existence of those medieval Cistercian nuns was often denied and no one had any idea that there were so many foundations of Cistercian women in medieval France and beyond, or how many of them would be thriving communities that survived up to the French Revolution.[125] More surprising perhaps are the numbers of independent thirteenth-century elite women who founded, populated, and ruled these new houses of nuns. Population growth and an expanding economy allowed women in this period to choose to become nuns, but such evidence also documents the considerable access to power and authority of the women who founded and supported those nuns. This is a slightly changed story of dowagers and heiresses ruling because the men of their families went off on religious military campaigns, often not to return. The excessive practice of chivalrous ideals in some families led to so many male deaths that women often ended up ruling.[126] That this was a wider trend was probably not recognized at the time, when families would probably have considered using women as rulers or inheritors through whom more men could inherit a stopgap measure. That in the thirteenth century, as bureaucracies and written records came to be the norm, this rule by women became easier, again, was probably not recognized at the time. Certainly, however, the written documents generated by those women who ruled as well as by those who ruled communities of religious women are the materials on which such a study as this is based. In all this the many examples of women's power and authority can no longer be viewed as exceptional examples.

Most women who founded abbeys of Cistercian nuns did so to support other women as their surrogates in prayer; founders of such abbeys usually entered them only on their deathbeds or for burial after death, with only a few entering these abbeys to rule them for a number of years. The most impressive example of such a widow becoming an abbess is Alice of Mâcon, a cousin of Blanche of Castile, but from the Champagne branch of the family; see Chapter 8, Figure 11. Alice of Mâcon (the heiress and her husband who was to depart and die on Crusade shortly afterward) sold her county to the king in 1239. She used nearly all her income from that sale to enter Maubuisson and then to endow the abbey of Lys after she became abbess there in 1248 (see Chapter 6).

Like the dowagers seen in Chapter 4 who often had to be prudent overseers for the families into which they had married, some of the heiresses who were their contemporaries were less free to make religious benefactions, even if they were great heiresses. Eleanor of Vermandois, the heiress of that great county, was limited by her own heir, who was Philip Augustus, although she lived long enough to overcome some of his strictures.[127] Queen Blanche of Castile, who encouraged much of the support of Cistercian nuns, was not herself an heiress, but as Louis IX's queen and regent, she, like Eleanor of Vermandois, had to use income rather than landed assets to support Cistercian nuns, as seen in Chapter 6.

CHAPTER 6

Blanche of Castile (1188–1252) and Cistercian Abbeys for Nuns

Blanche of Castile's interest in Cistercian nuns began before her arrival in northern France to marry the future King Louis VIII (r. 1223–26) in 1200.[1] Her parents, Alphonso VIII of Castile and Eleanor of England, had founded the abbey of Cistercian nuns at Huelgas in 1187, and Blanche and her sisters are reputed to have played in its cloisters as children.[2] Blanche's maternal grandmother, Eleanor of Aquitaine (1122–1204), traveled to Castile on behalf of her son, King Richard of England, and chose Blanche from among her sisters to become the future queen of France. Soon after her arrival in Paris as a young bride, Blanche seems to have begun encouraging foundations for Cistercian nuns by the women who were her friends and relatives. Throughout her life she advocated for houses of Cistercian nuns before the Cistercian General Chapter.[3] Yet only in 1236 did Blanche begin the foundation of Maubuisson, which would be dedicated in 1242. Only in 1244 did she begin that of Lys, which was dedicated in 1248. Blanche's foundations were thus among the last in the great expansion of Cistercian nuns' foundations in thirteenth-century France. (See Figure 6 and Table 8.)

The Young Blanche and Her Associates at Court

After their marriage in 1200, Blanche and the future Louis VIII were brought up at the royal court in Paris under the eye of Philip Augustus's mother, Adele of Champagne. Adele was an important force in Paris, and until her

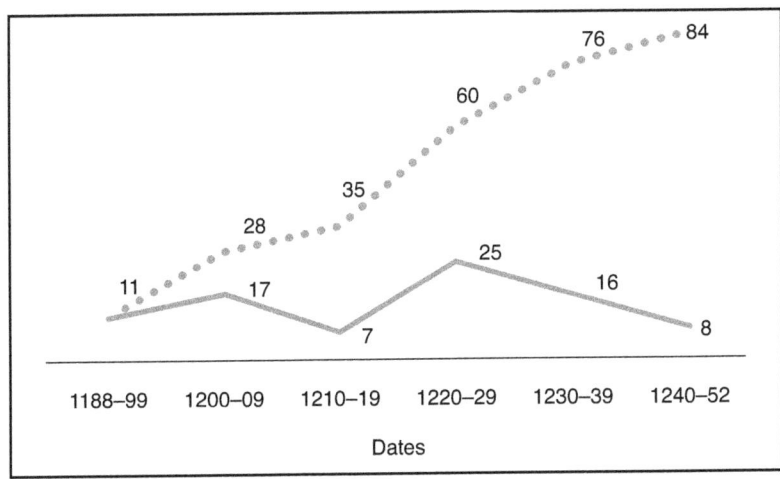

FIGURE 6. Foundations for Cistercian nuns in Blanche's lifetime. The solid line represents decade totals, and the dotted line represents the cumulative total. Based on Anne Bondéelle-Souchier, "Les moniales cisterciennes et leurs livres manuscrits dans la France d'Ancien Régime," *Cîteaux* 45 (1994): 193–337. Drawn by author.

death in 1206 had supervised the newly married couple along with other children who were wards of the king. Among the latter were probably Jeanne and Marguerite of Constantinople, Blanche's cousins and eventually successive countesses of Flanders, orphans at court from sometime after the deaths of their parents in the Levant in 1204 and 1205; as countesses they would be particularly supportive of foundations for Cistercian nuns.[4] Also present in Paris was Adele's good friend, who was also Blanche of Castile's great-aunt, Eleanor of Vermandois (1146?–1213), the daughter of Petronilla, Eleanor of Aquitaine's sister. Eleanor of Vermandois, besides founding a priory of nuns associated with Fontevraud circa 1180, founded an abbey of Cistercian nuns at Parc-aux-Dames in 1205, probably at the behest of the young Blanche. This Eleanor appears to have lived at court until her own death in 1213/14, but particularly after that of her husband Matthew of Beaumont in 1208; with Matthew, she founded a chapel for Adele of Champagne's soul soon after Adele's death in 1206.[5] Others at court in Paris were probably the young Marie and Thibaut IV of Champagne (1201–22 minority; 1222–53 majority), the children of the celebrated marriage in 1199 between Thibaut III, Count of Champagne (r. 1197–1201) and Blanche of Navarre, who ruled as regent of Champagne for her son until 1222. Queen

Table 8. Cistercian Abbeys for Nuns Founded During Blanche of Castille's Life

Date	House (Diocese)	Date	House (Diocese)
	1188–99		
1188	Angostrines (Uzès)	1190c	Koenigsbruck (Strasbourg)
1190c	Vassin (Clermont)	1191	Ravensberghe (Thérouanne)
1194	Benoîtevaux (Toul)	1195	Netlieu (Agde)
1195	Woestine (Thérouanne)	1196/1217	Brayelle (Arras)
1198	Saint-Antoine-des-Champs (Paris)	1199	Bonlieu (Lyon)
1199	Willencourt (Amiens)		
	1200–1209		
1200	Les Plans (Orange)	1200	Oraison-Dieu (Toulouse)
1200	Saint-Aubin-de-Gournay (Rouen)	1200c	Olieux (Narbonne)
1202	Abbaye-aux-Bois (Noyon)	1204	Clairets (Chartres)
1204	Beaupré-sur-Lys (Thérouanne)	1204	Port-Royal (Paris)
1205	Saint-Pons-de-Gémenos (Marseille)	1205	Parc-aux-Dames (Senlis)
1206	Mégemont (Clermont)	1206/9	Valnègre (Rieux)
1207	Mercoire (Mende)	1208/18	Mollégès (Arles)
1209	Gomerfontaine (Rouen)	1209	Moncé (Tours)
	1210–19		
1211	Beaulieu (Maguelone)	1212	Fontenelle (Cambrai)
1215	Voisins (Orléans)	1217	Pentemont (Beauvais)
1217	Valsauve (Uzès)	1217/18	Douai (Cambrai)
1219	Paraclet-des-Champs (Amiens)	1219/20	Isles (Auxerre)
	1220–29		
1220	Almanarre (Toulon)		
1220	Costejean (Rodez)	1220	Virginité (Mans)
1220	Leyme (Cahors)	1220	Villiers-aux-Nonnains (Sens)
1222	Clairmarais (Reims)	1222	Lieu-Notre-Dame (Orléans)
1223	Bonhan (Thérouanne)	1223	Grâce-Notre-Dame (Troyes)
1224	Argensolles (Soissons)	1224	Marquette (Tournai)
1225/29	Sainte-Hoilde (Toul)	1226	Battant (Besançon)
1226	Eau-lez-Chartres (Chartres)	1226	Cour-Notre-Dame (Sens)
1226	Pont-Notre-Dame (Meaux)	1227	Verger (Cambrai)
1227	Vivier (Arras)	1227	Saint-Dizier (Châlons)
1227/28	Saint-Catherine (Geneva)	1228	Trésor (Rouen)

Table 8 (con't.)

Date	House (Diocese)	Date	House (Diocese)
		1220–29	
1228	Séauve-Bénite (Puy)	1229	Font-les-Alès (Uzès)
1229	Jardin-lez-Pleurs (Troyes)	1229	Piété-Dieu (Troyes)
		1230–39	
1230	Félipré (Liège)	1230	Joie-lès-Nemours (Meaux)
1230/31	Notre-Dame-des-Prés (Troyes)	1231	Val-des-Vignes (Sens/Langres)
1234	Beauvoir (Bourges)	1234	Châteauvieux (Fréjus)
1234	Flines (Tournai)	1234	Amour-Dieu (Soissons)
1234	Joie Notre Dame (Soissons)	1235	Biaches en Peronne (Noyon)
1235	Mont-Notre-Dame (Sens)	1235	Réconfort (Autun)
1236	Maubuisson (Paris/Rouen)	1238/42	Marienfloss (Trêves)
1239	Mazures (Reims)	1239	Marcilly (Autun)
1239	Monchy les Perreux (Beauvais)		
		1240–52	
1240	Rosiers (Reims)	1242	Belleau (Troyes)
1243	Florimont (Besançon)	1244	Lys (Sens)
1247	Perray-aux-Nonnains (Séez)	1250	Joie Notre Dame (Vannes)
1251	Avignon (Avignon)		

Source: Anne Bondéelle-Souchier, "Les moniales cisterciennes et leurs livres manuscrits dans la France d'Ancien Régime," *Cîteaux* 45 (1994): 193–337.

Adele had been at that great wedding and so had the sister of the bride, Queen Berenguela of Navarre, the childless widow of Richard I.[6] The king's support of Blanche of Navarre's regency over Champagne for Count Thibaut IV, the son born several weeks after his father's death, meant that Thibaut and his slightly older sister Marie were virtual hostages at court. Their mother, Blanche of Navarre, must have visited the children there and possibly so did her sister Berenguela. Both sisters eventually founded Cistercian abbeys—that for nuns at Argensolles founded by Blanche of Navarre (d. 1229) using her dower income in her years of retirement after her son's coming of age in 1222.[7]

Other visits to court by such elite women were probably occasioned by plans for Prince Louis to launch an invasion of England circa 1216. Among

those who accompanied him was Matilda of Courtenay's first husband,
Hervé of Donzy, who went to England to pursue his wife's claims there.[8]
Perhaps it was also in this period that Blanche of Castile came to know her
half cousin Isabelle who became Countess of Chartres in 1218, for Isabelle's
future second husband, John of Oisy, had participated in that 1216 invasion
as well; in 1247 Isabelle would found a chapel for her own soul and that of
her dear cousin Queen Blanche.[9] Matilda of Brunswick's son, Thomas of
Perche, the sole knight to have died on that 1216 invasion, had probably also
been at court during the preparations for that campaign; likely too his
mother, Matilda, Countess of Perche (d. ca. 1213), another of Blanche's cousins, would have had occasion to meet the young princess Blanche at about
that time, if not earlier.[10]

It was during this period that the Capetians came to exercise direct control over much of what is today's France. Although expansion of the realm
did generate new resources that could be used for religious foundations, religious patronage probably took second place to conquest and state building.
Normandy had already fallen to the Capetians, and in 1212 Philip Augustus
won the battle of Bouvines and gained influence in Flanders and parts of the
Empire. Prince Louis's raid on Lincoln was a failure, but as King Louis VIII
(1223–26), he annexed the counties of Anjou and Poitou in 1225. His premature death in 1226 meant that it was his queen, Blanche of Castile, who
secured the kingdom for the young Louis IX (1226–70), and negotiated the
treaty of Meaux/Paris in 1229 that would eventually bring back much of the
Midi to Capetian control. Blanche secured the Toulousan heiress for one of
her younger sons, Alphonse of Poitiers, and made marriages to daughters of
the count of Provence, for her eldest son, the king and the youngest, Charles
of Anjou. It was probably with his marriage in 1234 that Louis IX took over
control of the realm from his mother. During this period the county of
Perche fell to the crown by the mid 1230s and in 1239 Louis IX purchased the
county of Mâcon. When he left for his first crusade in 1248, Louis IX was
accompanied by his wife, Marguerite of Provence; he placed the regency in
the hands of his mother, Blanche of Castile. Blanche died in 1252, and the
regency then fell to the king's younger brother Alphonse of Poitiers, whose
wife Jeanne of Toulouse had inherited Toulouse in 1249; her entire realm fell
to France when both Jeanne and Alphonse died in 1271 while on Louis IX's
second crusade, that in which Louis IX died in 1270. The next king, Philip
III (1270–85), consolidated the kingdom and arranged the marriage in 1284

of his son Philip who became Philip IV (1285–1314) to Jeanne of Navarre, heiress of Champagne. When Jeanne's father died in 1295, Philip IV annexed Champagne. He also gained Lyons for France in 1312.[11]

For Blanche and Prince Louis at court in the early decades of the century, access to cash was probably limited, particularly for Blanche. At the outset her marriage settlement was an affair of state, not particularly concerned with her personal use. It was part of the Treaty of Goulet, a truce between Philip Augustus, king of France, and Kings Richard and John of England. It left Blanche's dowry in the Berry to Philip Augustus for life.[12] If it were Blanche who was expected to undertake religious gifts for their young family, this meant that Blanche had little cash for almsgiving in those years.[13] Moreover, not long after becoming king, Louis VIII died in 1226 during his return from a crusade against the Albigensians. He had begun a resettlement of Blanche's rights in 1224/25, but his will of 1225 was not made in anticipation of his own immediate death. He promised his wife 30,000 livres plus 4500 livres per annum income and his daughter Isabelle 20,000 livres for her marriage. He also made a long list of cash alms to be distributed at his death to various religious foundations. He promised parts of the realm (including Artois, where Blanche's dower lands were located) to a younger son and specified that the crown and royal jewels would fund a Victorine foundation for his soul—probably in imitation of bequests made by his father and grandmother Adele of Champagne.[14] Particularly given that Ingebourg of Denmark, Philip Augustus's queen, would live until the summer of 1236, it was Blanche's interests that were most compromised by Louis VIII's premature death. Only after the young king's marriage in 1234 and probably only in the spring of 1236 did Louis IX begin to resettle dower and dowry properties for his mother, Blanche. (See Table 9.)

Blanche and her son, the new king Louis IX, fulfilled the bequests of his father's will and set out to make a monastic foundation for Louis VIII's soul. Otherwise, during that first decade of his reign, Louis IX's gifts to other religious houses were very limited and tended to be conveyances that would not diminish crown resources: usage rights in the forest of Retz given in 1227 to the Cistercian nuns of Parc-aux-Dames, confirmations of others' gifts, or ceremonial gifts made to new foundations, like those for the abbey of Cistercian nuns founded in 1228 at Trésor near Rouen or those for a new abbey for the order's monks founded by Berenguela of Navarre at Piété-de-l'Épau near Mans in 1229.[15]

Table 9. Blanche of Castile's Dower and Dowry Settlements

Year	Event	Change in Circumstances	Source
1200	Marriage to Louis	Treaty of Goulet[1]	
		Dowry, Berry properties held for life by Philip II	Listed when given back in *Layettes*, 2, no. 2885 (1240)
		Dower, in three towns in Artois from Philip II	Listed when given to Robert in *Layettes*, 5 no. 400 (1237)
1223	King Philip dies	Louis VIII becomes king and Blanche queen	
1224/ 25	Louis VIII	Resettles some of Blanche's dower lands	Petit-Dutaillis, *Étude sur la vie et le règne de Louis VIII*, no. 219
1225	Louis VIII's will	Promises Artois to second son; Blanche to get 30,000 livres plus 4500 livres/year; Isabelle gets 20,000 livres	*Layettes*, 2, no. 1710 (1225)
1226	Louis VIII dies	Blanche begins Louis IX regency	
1228		Royaumont begun	Paris, BnF, Latin 9166–69, *Cartulaire de Royaumont*, fol. 1157
1229	Blanche negotiates	Treaty of Meaux/Paris	Richard, *Saint-Louis*, pp. 99–109
1236	Maubuisson begun	Pontoise given to Blanche	*Achatz d'héritages*, fol. 5r
1236	Queen Ingebourg dies[2]	Lands in Orleanais/Vermandois become available?	*Layettes*, 5, no. 540 (1237)
1237	Robert knighted	Gets Artois	*Layettes*, 5, nos. 400, 401 (1237); also in *Layettes*, 2, no. 2562 (1237)
1240	Louis IX issues	"Pro dotalitia Blanchae Reginae ampliando"; Blanche's dowry and dower merged; she gets Meulan, Pontoise, Étampes, Dourdon, Corbeil, and Melun, and holdings in the Vermandois: at Crépy, Ferté-Milon, and Pierrefonds; 4,500 livres in annual income; he limits alienations of lands to 800 livres' worth of annual income	*Layettes*, 2, no. 2885 (1240)

Table 9 (con't.)

Year	Event	Change in Circumstances	Source
1244	Blanche begins Lys	First purchases noted	Paris, BnF, Latin MS 13892, *Cartulaire du Lys*
1248	Louis IX departs on crusade	Dower/dowry resettlement adds right to alienate another 300 livres income, to give life income to "her [Blanche's] people," to give alms worth two more years' income from lands	*Layettes*, 5, no. 514 (1248)
1252	Blanche dies	Buried at Maubuisson; heart to Lys	On heart burial, Erlande-Brandenburg (2000)

1. On Treaty of Goulet, see Turner, *King John*, pp. 53–54.
2. Orleanais and Vermandois lands both were likely held by Philip II's long-lived and once repudiated queen Ingebourg until her death in 1236; see Jean Richard, *Saint-Louis: Le justicier sans faiblesse* (Paris: Fayard, 1983), p. 55. On the heart burial, see Alain Erlande-Brandenburg, "Le tombeau de coeur de Blanche de Castille à l'abbaye du Lys," in *Art et architecture à Melun au Moyen Age*, edited by Yves Gallet, pp. 255–57 (Paris: Picard, 2000).

Louis IX, Royaumont, and the Cistercians

In 1225 Louis VIII updated what had probably been an earlier version of his will, but probably also maintained earlier parts in declaring that a Victorine foundation was to be made for his soul.[16] This interest in the Victorines probably did not continue for Louis VIII for several reasons. Not least of these was the recent construction of the abbey of Victoire near Senlis, founded for the Victorines by Philip Augustus after his victory at Bouvines in 1212; even the Victorines themselves may have had little interest in a competing Victorine foundation only a decade or so later. The dying king had turned to the Cistercians around him and he charged Cistercian bishops Gautier of Chartres and Fulk of Toulouse with his last wishes: for aiding Blanche in making arrangements for his funeral, the coronation of their son, and fulfilling the provisions of his will. Queen Blanche, having quickly fulfilled the bequests for prayers in Louis VIII's will, in September 1227 requested that the Cistercian General Chapter establish an anniversary mass on November 7 for Louis VIII's soul.[17] She then turned to the new foundation for his soul. It became the abbey of Cistercian monks at Royaumont.

The foundation of Louis IX's new abbey for the soul of his father, sited in what had been a contested region on the edge of Normandy, asserted the crown's control not only over that region but over the entire realm. Given the king's young age and the precarious early years of her regency for Louis IX, the Dowager Queen Blanche acted with considerable political skill in allying herself with the Cistercians. Most likely, however, the decision to found a house of Cistercian monks for his own soul was the dying Louis VIII's own. Cistercians were very much in the ascendant at the time of his death. They had been closely involved in the campaign against the Albigensians from which the king was returning in 1226 when he died. Louis IX concurred in his father's apparent choice, describing himself as fulfilling his father's wish to make a Cistercian foundation "with the advice of wise men and the executors of his father's last testament."[18] Louis IX supported Cistercians throughout his life.[19]

The Cistercian abbey for monks at Royaumont has been studied by Caroline A. Bruzelius, who describes it in comparison to twelfth-century Cistercian buildings like Fontenay as a "great innovation" in Cistercian style, an impressive monastic version of the new and highly fashionable "court style" of High Gothic architecture, an example of "Cistercian High Gothic."[20] As she explains, the remains of Royaumont's triforium exemplify the new construction technique of using bar tracery to replace punched-out window openings like those found in the earlier choir at Saint-Denis.[21] Bruzelius argues that the presence of such bar tracery characterized the new style at Royaumont, establishing what she described as its light, intricate, jewel-like character in its construction. With the weight of window frames decreased, their openings could be larger, allowing more natural light to pass through the glass. For an example, see Figure 7.

Such a construction technique, incorporating precut stone for door and window framing, also considerably decreased the total amount of stone used and the cost of its carving and transport. It would be used at Blanche of Castile's two foundations for Cistercian nuns and is documented in the Maubuisson account book. If using this stone tracery cut costs somewhat, nonetheless, it was still said that 100,000 livres were spent for building the impressive abbey church at Royaumont.[22] The large sums spent at Royaumont were well spent for the young King; they asserted Louis IX's wealth, power, and authority at the beginning of his reign and underlined his ties to the Cistercians, still one of the most powerful religious orders. Royaumont also inspired acts of patronage by those who were supporters of the young King's rule.[23]

FIGURE 7. Lys, abbey with bar tracery from a distance.
Photograph by the author.

Royaumont was begun expeditiously. Large initial expenditures were
made to acquire an abbey site and the initial array of granges. The documents show that in June 1228 Louis IX paid six hundred livres to Saint-
Vincent of Senlis to purchase a grange called Lys, a vineyard at Wruis held
by Odeline la Bavarde *ad medium vestum*, and a half muid of wine, which
had once been delivered annually to Saint-Vincent of Senlis by John Carnifex
of Asnières; all was conveyed in perpetual possession and lordship.[24] In
August 1228 the king purchased the actual site for the abbey—one that had
existing buildings:

> The place called Cuimont, but now to be called Royaumont after
> the abbey the king is building there, including eighty journaux of
> land next to the grange, two arpents of land at Saint-Martin of
> Colle, *champart* [income over the common fields] over what

Table 10. Royaumont Cartulary: Payments for Site and Endowment

Intervals	Amount Spent (length of interval)	Yearly Average
1228–29	1,440 livres (2 years)	720 livres
1230–39	1,955 livres (10 years)	196 livres
1240–49	1,985 livres (10 years)	199 livres
1228–49	5,380 livres (22 years)	245 livres

Source: Paris, BnF, Latin MSS 9166–9169, *Cartulaire de Royaumont.*

amounted to four arpents (three at Buloi and one at Saint-Martin), five other arpents of land, half an arpent of meadow, three arpents of woods at Boisnières, three and a half muids of wheat in the measure of Beaumont in the mill there, half a *quartier* of vineyards at Asnières *ad medium,* one *mansura* next to the monastery of Asnières, rights to pasture like those given to the nuns of Parc, etc.[25]

For this grange the king paid eight hundred livres to the priory of nuns at Saint-Martin of Borenc, a priory that answered to Heloise's abbey of the Paraclete in Champagne; the king also promised to build a new grange elsewhere for those nuns.[26]

In September 1229, Louis IX issued a foundation charter for Royaumont, transferring the properties at Lys and Cuimont to his new foundation. Cistercian monks were settled in existing buildings at Cuimont.[27] There were many generous conveyances made by the king and his followers to the Cistercian monks at Royaumont. In June 1231 the knight Thibaut of Beaumont, lord of Luzarches, and his wife Ermengarde, sold and gave annual rents of seven livres in cash and three muids of oats from the villa of Belle-Église along with "whatever other rights they had over that villa and its tenancies, including vineyards and two winepresses, fifty arpents of land, the farmstead and its appurtenances, a water mill, watercourses, marshland, rights to *champart* and pasture shared with villagers."[28] The tenants there and in nearby villages, "who were accustomed to grind their grain at the village mill," could continue to do so. The previous owners gave a fifth of all those rights to Royaumont; then the king paid them 1,050 livres for the rest.[29] Similarly in December 1230, Eudes of Vaugier and his wife Alix sold rights in the diocese of Beauvais to Royaumont for three hundred livres *parisis,* but in this case they were also granted a life rent of forty livres *tournois* annually to compensate them for other rights there.[30] (See Table 10.)

Overall, Royaumont's foundation by Louis IX and his mother Blanche of Castile was a great political success, reinforcing the power and authority of the crown early in the regency. In October 1235, within a decade of Louis VIII's death, Royaumont was consecrated. In May 1239, Pope Gregory IX issued a bull of confirmation to it as a house of Cistercian monks, including the standard thirteenth-century papal exemption, "Sane novalium," from tithes on "noval" lands and on their gardens, vineyards, fishing, and animal husbandry. The list of properties and holdings in the papal confirmation included the abbey site and woods at Burvesium, vineyards of Wruis and Nootel, vineyards and winepress at Pompoing, as well as at Belle-Église, what was acquired from the cleric Hugh of Borenc at Lampoing, and a manor at Pont-Sainte-Maxence with its houses, mill, water, lands, meadows, pastures, vineyards, woodlands, rents, and all appurtenances. (See Map 3.)

The 1239 papal confirmation also listed annual income coming to Royaumont from royal sources: fourteen muids and two and a half sestiers of wheat at Compiègne; ten muids of oats at Gestium; ten muids and seven sestiers of wheat at Gerberoy; six muids, two and a half sestiers of wheat and ten muids of oats at Gonesse; fourteen muids of wheat and fifty livres in cash to be paid by the king's chamberlain. This amounts to an annual thirty-five muids (cartloads) of various cereals (at twelve sestiers per muid) as well as fifty livres of yearly cash income (in coin that would be 12,000 deniers).[31] There would be a doubling of those royal conveyances five or six years later after Louis IX doubled the size of the Royaumont community when he made a crusader vow. That the king countenanced no limits in his funding of its monks is suggested by his letter from Damietta of September 1249, in which he granted Royaumont another eighteen arpents of land from the royal grange at Valpendant and pasture rights in the royal lands for up to four hundred sheep.[32] Royaumont's acquisitions are found in their own specific realm of the Parisian countryside, hardly at all overlapping with those of the new abbeys for Cistercian nuns that were being founded nearby.

Blanche's Income

By the time of the consecration of Royaumont in 1235, Louis IX was married to Marguerite of Provence, Blanche was a widow in her late forties, her youngest child was about nine, and her youngest son was soon to be knighted. Marriage arrangements had been made for her children. The time

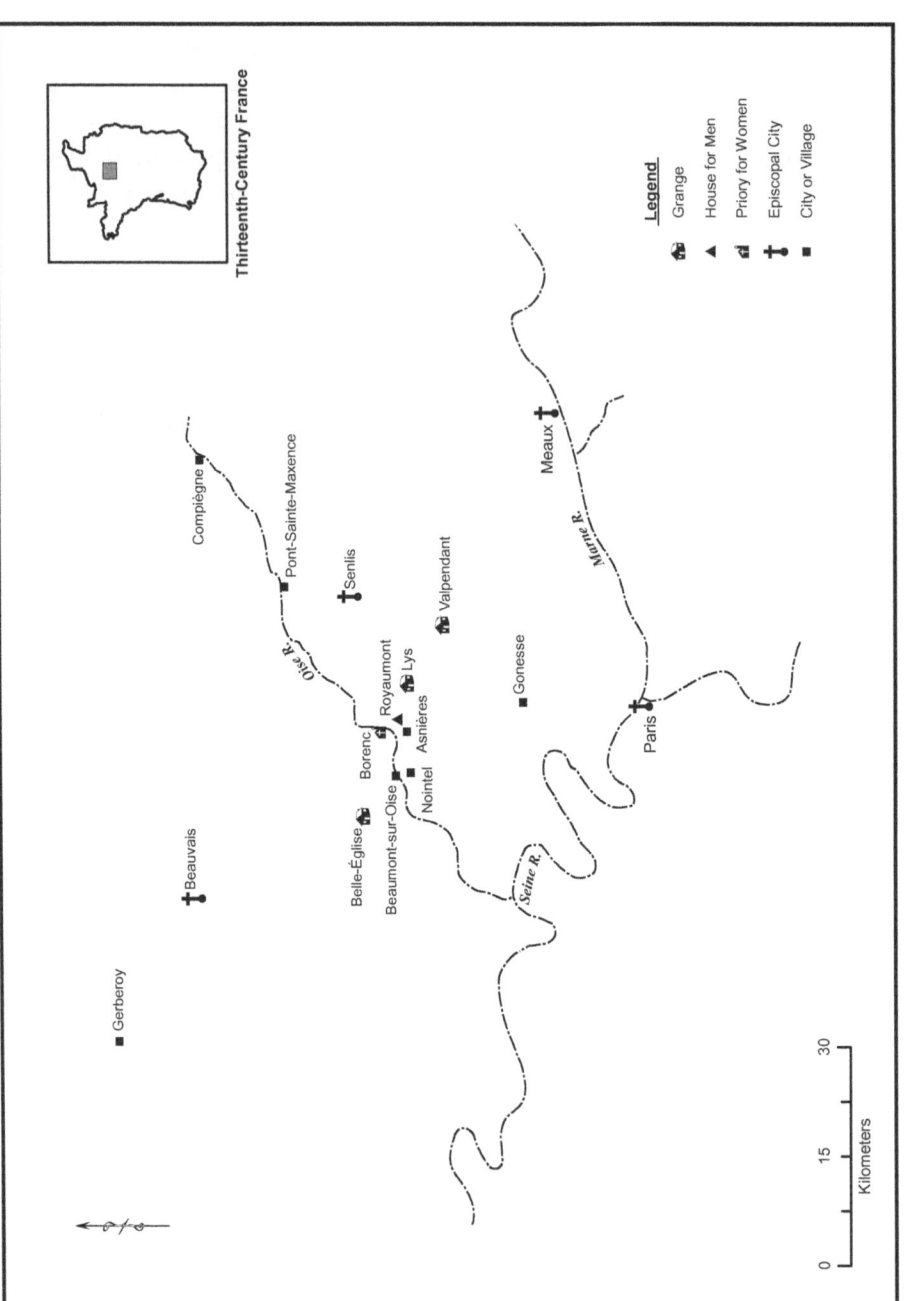

MAP 2. Royaumont abbey for Cistercian monks and its granges and priories. Map created by the Center for

was ripe for beginning her long-anticipated foundations for Cistercian nuns. However, Blanche's foundations for Cistercian nuns still hinged on the resettlement of her combined dower and dowry rights, which did not begin until 1236 and was not finalized until 1240.[33]

Although the royal documents do not mention it, the settlement began ca. 1236, for it must have been then that Louis IX granted his mother Blanche an abbey site in Pontoise in the parish of Saint-Ouen at Aulnay, the royal villa called Maubuisson, along with rights to take building materials from the nearby royal forest of Cergy, as discussed below. He then turned to other things. In 1236 he began to sort out property rights held as dower until her death in that year by Ingebourg of Denmark. In 1237 he settled the Artois on his youngest brother Robert at the time the latter was knighted. Louis also took on new and expensive religious projects: acquiring the Crown of Thorns and associated relics in 1238/39 for 135,000 livres; building a chapel to house them first at the royal palace at Saint-Germain-en-Laye; beginning the construction of the Sainte Chapelle in Paris, and commissioning a grand reliquary to house the relics there permanently.[34] But it was also during this time that Louis IX in his formal resettlement of Blanche's dower/dowry rights began to put limits on his mother's alienations from crown properties, having apparently come to realize that the royal treasury was not limitless. A new type of pious gift, the *amortissement*, seems to have been developing at this time and could be used to make gifts that avoided immediate loss of crown holding: these grants made to religious corporations allowed the latter's acquisition without fine of a certain amount of annual income in land held from the king; those holdings thus fell into the "dead hand" (*la main morte*) of the church; the insistence that amortissements be obtained appears to have been aimed at limiting alienation of Crown lands. (See Appendix 1.)

In his 1240 resettlement document, "Pro dotalitia Blanchae Reginae ampliando,"Louis IX granted Blanche 4,500 livres parisis in annual income from the royal treasury.[35] He granted her six towns (Meulan, Pontoise, Étampes, Dourdan, Corbeil, and Melun) and properties from the Vermandois (Crépy-en-Valois, Ferté-Milon, and Pierrefonds) that had once belonged to Eleanor of Vermandois and probably after her were held by Ingebourg of Denmark). In return Blanche gave up claims to Hesdin, Bapaume, and Lens (her dower towns in the Artois) and those from her dowry in Berry at Issoudun, Craçay, and the fiefs of Andrew of Chauvigny. Louis IX also established that his mother, Blanche of Castile, could alienate from crown properties no more than eight hundred livres in property and rents over the rest of her life, including the one hundred livres she had already given to Maubuisson.[36]

Thus, even before the king began amassing treasure for his crusade, Blanche's almsgiving was being considerably restrained. The king relented somewhat in 1248 before his departure for the crusade, when he increased the total amount his mother could alienate on her religious projects over her lifetime from 800 to 1,100 livres (property producing that much annual income). He also allowed her to make life grants "to her people" and to designate two years' worth of income from her lands in her postmortem almsgiving.[37] Still the limits on her alienations from dower properties made formal in 1240 meant that Blanche's foundations of abbeys for Cistercian nuns required a careful deployment of assets. In this Blanche acted like other dowagers in her acquaintance (Blanche of Navarre for instance)—spending income from those dower lands, but not excessively alienating the dower lands themselves.

Blanche's attitude about her son's crusade was a positive one, although some historians have argued otherwise.[38] She may have worried about losing her son to death during that expedition, but she assisted him considerably, founding Lys expeditiously so that its nuns could pray for the venture's success and agreeing to act as regent while he was away. Indeed there is much to show that Blanche and Louis were on cordial terms when he departed in 1248 for his first crusade. Blanche died in 1252 before his return, but his affection for his mother is clear in a letter he sent to Maubuisson from Sidon in July 1253 shortly after hearing of his mother's death: "Louis by the grace of God King of the Franks, let it be noted that we founded with Our Dearest Lady Mother of pious memory Blanche, once Queen of the Franks, the abbey of the Blessed Mary Queen of Heaven at Pontoise [that is, Maubuisson]."[39] The letter also confirmed her gift to Maubuisson of a house at Étampes.

The Abbey for Nuns at Maubuisson and Its Account Book

Blanche's first abbey for Cistercian nuns at Maubuisson was located downstream from Paris near the confluence of the Seine and Oise Rivers at Pontoise and not far from the boundaries of the ecclesiastical province of Rouen. Maubuisson's site, like that of Royaumont, thus guarded what had once been a border region, but was also close to river transport, to resources like the forest of Cergy and to a royal palace in Pontoise from which construction could be overseen. The abbey's endowment was accomplished by a painstaking repurchase of fragmented properties by the queen and by the first abbess. (See Map 4.)

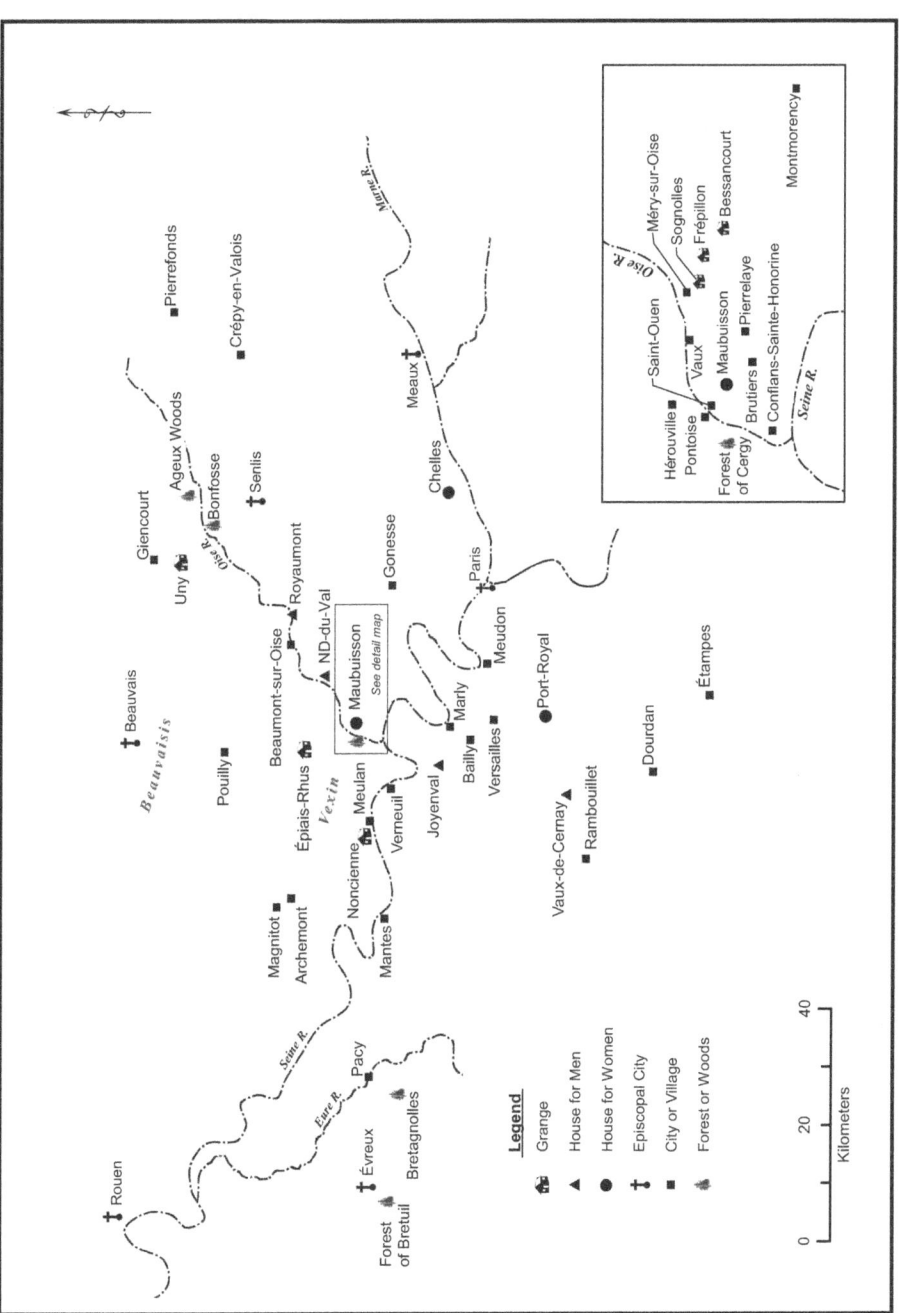

MAP 4. Maubuisson's granges and properties. Map created by Gordon Thompson.

Blanche managed this and the construction at Maubuisson by a careful tracking of expenses with her overseer, the Templar master Richard of Tourny. This is revealed in a surviving account book for Maubuisson, *Achatz d'héritages pour Maubuisson*, which states at the top of its original opening page, folio 5 recto: "In the year of the Lord 1236 a new abbey near Pontoise was founded by Blanche, by the grace of God, Queen of the Franks. And these are the receipts for the work on that abbey, which began to be built in the first week after Pentecost, 1236."[40] These accounts were to be presented to the queen three times a year by the Templar master.

The opening sections of the account book record delivery of cash from Paris, but also receipts from the queen's other assets paid directly into the abbey account: for instance, the four hundred livres paid in the winter of 1238/39 by Philip Concièrge of Senlis, the sale of the tolls at Lyencourt for five hundred livres for the work of the abbey, and the receipt of fifteen muids of wheat negotiated for the queen by one of her knights.[41] The volume tracks the sums expended in intervals that mark the presentation of the accounts to the queen, right up to the completion of construction. (See Table 11 for a complete description of the volume.)

There is a list of construction materials from the summer of 1236 up to November 30, 1237, totaling 733 livres.[42] For that year and a half, everything from ironwork and rope, to nails, floor tiles, and wine for the laborers was included. There were payments to subcontractors for constructing the fountain, for rafters and roof beams for the dormitory and chapel, for ironwork for doors and windows, for the masonry of the dormitory and chapel, and for the precut stone for doors and window frames used for its bar tracery.[43] There are extensive records of payments to construction workers and purchases of endowment ranging from a few sous to many livres. *Achatz d'héritages* thus records the total sums sent to Maubuisson from the beginning of the project up to when the nuns arrived around Easter 1242: "From the start of construction [*a principio operis*] at Pentecost 1236 up to Easter 1242, there had been received from the Temple in Paris [from Blanche's funds], a total of 24,431 livres, 15 sous, and 4 deniers."[44] Even though some of this income came from her dower lands, this total would have amounted to a large part of the 30,000 livres left to Blanche by Louis VIII. Her coffers must have been depleted by 1240 when she began to receive the annual 4,500 livres granted by her son Louis IX in the resettlement of that year when her dower/dowry lands were acknowledged to be in Meulan, Pontoise, Étampes, Dourdan, Corbeil, Melun and the Vermandois (Crépy-en-Valois, Ferté, and Pierrefonds).

The accounts show that these were not buildings put up by volunteers, as myths about the Cistercians once asserted. A section described as "Payments" reveals that total wages for laborers up to 1242 were 17,269 livres, 14 sous, and 10 deniers, something over two-thirds (71 percent) of total costs.[45] That such wages were tallied up each week in the building season, but less often in the winter, contributes to our understanding of how seasonal was construction work. For instance, for the building season, the twenty-six weeks between Pentecost 1237 and Martinmas in November of that year, total amounts paid to laborers came to 1,380 livres, 75 sous, and 7 deniers. This was nearly three times what was paid over the next six months, from November 1237 to early June 1238, when such labor costs totaled 480 livres and 6 sous.[46]

The account book documents the sending of materials from sources like the forest of Cergy, which was part of Blanche's dower lands. Its details of activities at Cergy cover the year 1238/39, when Maubuisson was under construction, and it lists payments made by the queen's overseer, Master Richard, to two woodsmen: "Peter of Marinus and Master Michael of Villerii [who received] one hundred sous [five livres] from Master Richard for their work when the forest of Cergy was measured, and when Peter also received ten livres for surveying or laying out the boundaries."[47] There were other payments to these two men for forest work, but also entries for transporting materials, three payments to Jacob of Soissons and one to Robert of Gonesse. Total payments listed here for forest labor or hauling were 803 livres, 15 sous, and 10 deniers, a sum possibly not included in earlier wage payments, but this may have almost been balanced out with forest income, described on folio 21r as "cash coming in from the woods of Cergy totaling 987 livres and 11 sous."[48] The evidence suggests that lumber or boards (*merrengi*) and other building materials were being partially finished in the forest before being transported by boat to the abbey site. This partial processing of lumber paralleled the partial finishing that would have been happening at the quarries before shipping stone for bar tracery. Once taken out of the woods, the materials were guarded at the river landing and then transported to the abbey by water.[49]

Welcoming, Provisioning, and Endowing Maubuisson's Nuns

In 1237 the queen asked the Cistercian General Chapter to send nuns to her new abbey; they apparently did not do so at first, instead awaiting the completion of the buildings. This delay may reflect General Chapter strictures

Table 11. Account Book, *Achatz d'héritages*

Pontoise, AD Val d'Oise, 72H12, "Achatz d'héritages pour Maubuisson," a limp parchment register into which earlier accounts were copied, began to be redacted by 1242; its last major entries were done by circa 1250. The volume measures 26 cm x 18.5 cm on the outside. There are no illuminations or colored initials. Most of it is written in single columns, but where double columns appear, they follow the same system of page ruling. There are two distinct hands: one associated with the original Templar master's accounts, the other with additions made at the time of Abbess Guillelma (1241/42–75).

The volume has eight quires. All eight quires (except possibly the third) once consisted of four bifolia. Quires 4, 5, 6, and 8 are intact. There is currently no folio 14, but folio 47 is followed by folio 47bis. Folios 58 and 59 are sewn-in inserts, badly damaged, with nearly illegible writing and written on only one side.

Folios are numbered from 1 to 59, but the opening of Quire 1 (fols. 1–4) appears to be a later insert. Thus fols. 5–8 mark the original opening of the redaction of accounts.

Partial contents:

Fols. 1r–4v: Miscellaneous (includes 1224 gift by Louis VIII to abbot of Lyre)

Fols. 5r–8r: "Anno Domini millesimo ducentesimo tricesimo sexto [1236] fundata fuit nova abbatia iuxta Ponthisarium ab illustri Blancha Dei gratia Regina Francorum. . . . Item summa summarum a principio operis usque Pascha anno XL° II° [1242] recepta de Templo XXIIII^M IIII^CC XXXI livres, XV sous, IIII deniers." (Receipts in cash from the Temple in Paris)

Fol. 8r–8v contains entries on purchase of forest rights dated 1257, 1259, and 1260

Fol. 9r–9v is blank

Fols. 10ra–13rb: "Anno Domini MCCXXX° sexto [1236]. Prima paga prime ebdomine post Penthecostem . . ." (payments to workmen)

Fols. 13v and 14r–v are blank

Fols. 15r–17v: "Hec accomodavit magister extra pagam . . ." (records for expenditures for other materials, not wages)

Fol. 18r: "Anno Domini M° CC° XLII° emptio facta apud edictum per[?] manu[m] Domini Viviani et Gauguelini . . ."

Fols. 18v, 19r–v are blank

Fols. 20r–22r: "Hec receperunt Petrus de Marinus et Magister Michealus de Vilencii . . ." (receipts for the forest of Cergy, until All Saints' Day 1239)

Fol. 22v: "Emptiones fecit apud Moellum per manum Domini Gaulteri presbiterii fratris abbatie nove Beate Marie Regalis iuxta Pontisarum anno Domini M° CC° quinquagesimo tercio . . ." (purchases of endowment, 1253)

Fols. 23r–26v: "Hec est emptiones que fecerint pro nova abbacia Pontisare . . ." (purchases of endowment for the abbey of Maubuisson, up to November 30, 1237)

Fols. 26v–29r: "Hec pagavit Magister post compotum . . ." (purchases of endowment with dates in 1237 and 1238)

Table 11 (con't)

Partial contents:
    Fols. 29r–29v: "Anno Domini M° CC° XXX° nono [1239] emptiones . . ."
(nails for building, metal for wagons, lead for plumbing, nails for
horseshoes)
    Fols. 29v–38r: "Item Anno Domini M° CC° XXX° nono [1239] in crastino
Beati Michaelis Hyemalis . . ." (purchases of endowment by Queen Blanche
between 1239 and 1242)
    Fols. 38v–41r: "Theobaldus de Frepellione vendidit abbatisse et conventui Beate
Marie Regalis iuxta Pontisarium quamdam terram quam habebat et quamdam
domum sitam apud Frepellionum . . ." (sales to the abbess and nuns in 1244)
    Fol. 41r: "Ad Pascha Anno Domini M CC L quarto [1254] emimus . . ."
(purchases by the abbey of Maubuisson in 1254 and 1255)
    Fols. 41v–46r: "Tales sunt redditus abbacie Beate Marie Regalis et ad tales
terminus . . ." (rents owed to the abbey. On fol. 43v there is a sale to the abbey
that was paid for in November 1258 and February 1259)
    Fols. 46r–47r: "Anno Domini M° CC° L° octavo [1258] in Pascha
vendiderunt . . ." (various sales to the abbey dated 1256, 1258, and 1259)
    Fol. 47v: Rents with homages, undated
    Fol. 48r is blank
    Fols. 48v–59r: Rents or cens owed to the abbey with dates of 1241, 1242, 1245,
1246, 1247

Source: Pontoise, AD Val d'Oise, 72H12 parchment register, *Achatz d'héritages pour Maubuisson*
(1224–60).

about foundations for nuns: for abbeys of women, everything had to be in
place before they arrived.[50] The first abbess, Guillelma (r. 1241/42–75) and a
group of nuns appear to have been sent from the Parisian abbey of Saint-
Antoine in 1241/42.[51] But it may be that some nuns were there earlier, for
instance Alice of Mâcon whose entry gift had been approved by the King in
1240.[52] They found a completed church and a furnished abbey, annual deliveries of provisions established, and the beginnings of an endowment. Unlike
for Royaumont, for which the foundation charter was issued in 1229 but the
church dedicated only in 1235, work for Maubuisson had begun in 1236, but
its foundation charter was not issued until 1241/42, the year of the nuns'
arrival.

    The accounts show that the queen had paid for everything: construction
of Maubuisson's church, cloister, conventual buildings, and cloister walls.
This is just as she stated in her foundation charter of 1241/42, when she
framed her actions as those of a dutiful daughter of the church:

The doctors of the most holy mother church assert that the blessed
angels are filled with joy at the baptism of the reborn [newly con-
verted] Christian, but to do this is difficult in our present time. . . .
Therefore to increase the affection of those heavenly friends and for
the honor of the omnipotent Deity and especially his most glorious,
ever-virgin Mother, and everyone in that heavenly city . . . we
[Blanche] with the approval of our dear son, Louis [IX], king of the
Franks, . . . for the health of our souls, and those of the late Alphonso, illustrious and well-renowned king of Castile, our father, and
Queen Eleanor, his wife, our mother, and for our dearest lord and
beloved husband of great renown, Louis VIII, the late king of the
Franks, and for our dear son Louis IX, and for all our children . . .
have founded this abbey of nuns of the Cistercian Order . . . on the
estate of Aulnay next to Pontoise. And we shall call it Notre-Dame-
la-Royale, because it is to be founded in honor of the Celestial
Queen. We concede to it in perpetuity . . . the place itself and the
land on which it is sited, the monastery and its church, the dormitory, the refectory, the cellar, and all the necessary buildings contained within its walls, those buildings and walls and whatever is
within them, from their length and breadth, right and left. All this
was acquired with our own personal funds.[53]

As is seen in the account book, although construction of the church, abbey,
and the nuns' enclosure had been completed, the first abbess would continue
the process of acquiring endowment begun by the queen.

In 1239 Blanche began assigning income for the community's support,
including two annual payments of fifty livres each from the *prévôté* of Meulan, a conveyance confirmed by Louis IX; the king himself granted another
one hundred livres annually at Mantes. In 1239 Blanche granted Maubuisson
the tithes of wine and grain she held at Étampes, at nearby Châtelliers, and
at Dourdan, and an annual rent of eight muids (cartloads) of wheat at Pontoise, once held from her by Dreux of Beaumont.[54] The queen also purchased
tithes in grain from Archemont, Magnitot, and Hérouville, eventually paying
nearly one thousand livres for twenty-two and a half muids of grain annually;
her Templar manager held off making the last payments for those tithes until
he had verified the amount of grain actually coming from them.[55]

Louis IX also continued to make concessions to Maubuisson's nuns. For instance after making his crusader vow in 1244 the king provided Maubuisson with an annual rent of thirty livres for the purchase of herring at Arques (near the coast).[56] In 1248 he granted an additional twelve muids of grain annually from the tithes of Bailly, Marly-le-Roi, and Versailles (he had purchased these for the nuns for 540 livres) and he granted them an *amortissement,* allowing its nuns to acquire up to 500 livres' worth of additional holdings in royal lands. He also confirmed Blanche's grant of thirty muids of oats from the granaries of Crépy-en-Valois in the Vermandois.[57] Such initial efforts assured the nuns' subsistence during the years before they had consolidated and made productive their food-producing granges. (See Table 15.)

As is described for the 1240s in the Preface of this volume, the process of such acquisition was slow. Only in the summer of 1241 was Robert of Maubuisson paid more than four hundred livres for his claims to the fief at Maubuisson: "Two houses near the monastery, fifteen arpents of land, vineyards, meadows and their woodland of Noue [*nauda,* or marsh, rather than *nova*] for the work of the new abbey."[58] The situation was more complicated because Robert of Maubuisson did not hold directly from the queen or her son. Instead the intermediary was a community of Premonstratensian canons at Joyenval, south of Maubuisson, whose abbot confirmed the sale by Robert of all his rights at Maubuisson in August 1241.[59] The parish priest of Saint-Ouen also gave up claims to minor tithes, oblations, and burial payments in return for a lump sum of fifty livres; major tithes once held by the abbey of Saint-Martin of Pontoise had been conceded already.[60] Soon thereafter that priest ceded rights and was paid twenty-four sous for the fourteen deniers annually he had been owed for a half arpent of land already in the queen's hands, as well as for three obols owed for another piece of land and meadow there. That such claims existed even so close to the site of the new abbey suggests that, in common with most houses of Cistercians, the foundation was being made on already cultivated land, land on which tithes had been collected for some time.[61]

As she assembled endowment for her nuns, Blanche also sought the support of neighboring feudatories like Dreux of Beaumont and the Tyrels there at Pontoise. In 1237 Hugh Tyrel granted four arpents of woodland near Maubuisson, eight arpents of land, and an arpent of vines adjoining the bridge at Pontoise and the road to Beaumont.[62] As seen in Table 12, Hugh gave the nuns income from the assarts there as well. Where such terms as *assarts* or

Table 12. Maubuisson Accounts: Cens from Assarts and Vineyards

Hugh Tyrel granted cens paid by tenants for newly cleared land at Sognoles to the nuns (1240s)

Tenant	Deniers Paid
Andreas de Curia	44
Radius de Curia	39.5
Petrus de Curia	27.5
Galterus de Curia and Arnulphus de Puteo	26 each
Lanfredus Auvergne	25.5
Robertus Coullart	24
Dreux de Puteo	18
Petrus de Puteo and Richard the Mason	9 each
Arnulph Gibellan, Dyel, Robert Gibellan, and Robert Loufegrue	6 each.
Domina Richendis	4
Theopania de Channeris	3

Cens over vineyards transferred by Guiard of Frépillon in the 1250s*

Tenant	Vineyard Location	Deniers Paid
Robert of Cergy	Évragny	8
Heloysus, Chef de Ville	Fougières	2
Eudes Alent	Larraz	10
Raoul of Frépillon	Passage	12
Robert Blancha	Passage and Plastières	9
Children of late Milo Rufi	Pencherol and its house	24
Richard Boschet	Pencherol	6
Girardus Furnarius (baker), Richard of Teulense	Pencherol	3 each
John of Chambly	Plastières	32
Robert Creste	Plastières	12
Walter of Valles and Morel of Muides	Plastières	3 each
John of Hérouville	Plastières	1.5
Richard the Mason and Bernard	Plastières	1 each
Nicholas Carpenter, Walter of Bonneville	Prato	1 each
Guiard Bandet	Three *quartiers* at Rubea Terra	6
William of Cruce	One arpent at Viart	7

Source: Pontoise, AD Val d'Oise, 72H12 parchment register, *Achatz d'héritages*, fols. 53v, col. b (Tyrel), and 45r (Guiard).
*Some artisans, perhaps construction workers, are included in this list.

essarts are found, however, it must be recalled that the very fact of their being called clearances means that the cutting had already occurred. Acquisition was often of such very fragmented holdings paying very small amounts to the nuns.

In January 1239/40 John of Montmorency and his wife Maria Tyrel granted a third of the woods at Rosières, which they had held from Hugh Tyrel, but which they now granted to the queen "for the abbey she had begun building at Pontoise."[63] In late 1239 a fief at Pontoise, attested to provide a minimum of thirty-three sous and four deniers of minute cens each year, was sold to Blanche by Dreux le Mallier (of Beaumont?) and his associates for twenty-five livres and three sous; that group also returned the land adjoining the bridge at Pontoise and a meadow on the island of Teulense in the Oise River, which they had held from her for military service.[64] Somewhat later, in 1247, another knight, William Gouffier and his wife Petronilla similarly sold for thirty-eight livres holdings in the fief of Tyrel described as held from the king.[65] Merchants and artisans from neighboring towns, including Pontoise, joined such lords in their conveyances to Maubuisson. In 1239 the queen paid sixty-five livres to Sibille, widow of Marcel Ragis, bourgeois of Paris, for everything that widow had at Pontoise.[66] In 1244 the abbess paid six livres to the daughter of Aubert the Draper for two pieces of land; another draper in Pontoise was paid ten livres for an arpent of vineyards; John the Vintner of Pontoise got sixteen livres for seven arpents of land; other purchases of land and vineyards from artisans in Pontoise and a bourgeois of Paris cost respectively twelve livres, eighteen livres, and thirty-two livres.[67]

It was the rich witness of the early charters used by Armelle Bonis that led her to conclude that by the time the church of Maubuisson was consecrated on June 26, 1244, "The nuns held a demesne of more than 100 arpents of woods, meadows, vineyards, gardens, fishponds and mill at the abbey itself, a seigneurie at Bessancourt, and other land near Pontoise at Frépillon, and Méry-sur-Oise."[68] The church would be consecrated in 1244.[69] Still considerable endowment remained to be acquired at places like Cergy, Aulnay, and Mateigne, as is clear from the middle quires of the account book, *Achatz d'héritages*, in which the acquisition of endowment for the abbey begins on folio 23r, which opens quire four: "Here are the purchases that were made for the new abbey at Pontoise."[70] Such acquisitions continued through the end of quire 6 (fol. 47v) and up to the year 1245.

The creation of granges in the vicinity of Pontoise was through the consolidation of many fragments of arable land mixed with woodland, meadows, and vineyards. Included in the three quires just mentioned are acquisitions at more than seventy places (often with more than a single transaction at any one of them). Such purchases often involved considerable sums of cash with prices ranging from one or two livres up to twenty-five, thirty, or fifty livres— once more than 180 livres. It varied. In 1239 the queen paid sixty livres to Philip of Hérouville for various rents and five *quartiers* of vineyards associated with the lordship of Sognolles in Méry.[71] But in the next year, in 1240, the queen paid the knight William only nine sous for a *quartier* of vineyard that he held from the church of Sainte-Honorine in Conflans.[72] Lacking some of the verbiage found in the equivalent charters still extant, but also recording payments not found in the surviving charters, the entries provide evidence of payment for confirmations by fief holders, parish priests, and the like. For instance, in 1246, the abbess purchased woodland rights for 140 livres from the knight Thibaut of Frépillon, but the immediately following entry tells us that Heluyus de la Truie (or d'Atrio) and his associates together received fourteen livres, thirteen sous, and four deniers for their confirmations. That more than 10 percent of the original purchase price was paid to them is unusual, but smaller amounts were not; yet this is something often not seen in the charters themselves.[73]

The queen began the process of acquisition in the villa or village of Bessancourt in January 1239/40, when she paid thirty livres for rights of lordship over vineyards to Peter of Pouilly, who sold them with the consent of his mother, Lady Isabelle, and brothers, John and William Clerc.[74] In June 1240 Blanche paid 110 livres to Gautier Roussel and his wife Emelina for a *mansus* (family farm) and two pieces of vineyard at Bessancourt.[75] Some of these vineyards would pay such very small rents to the nuns (as seen in Table 12) that one can imagine the pennies paid over each year. In 1242 Louis IX confirmed all Maubuisson's acquisitions in the villa of Bessancourt, as well as those near Sognolles and Frépillon and near the bridge at Pontoise, all of which appear to have been part of the royal holdings at Pontoise.[76]

Abbess Guillelma continued purchases at Bessancourt begun by the queen: in November 1244 paying thirty livres to John of Pontoise and his associates for vineyards; in 1246 paying for another arpent of vineyards on which the nuns would still owe a rent; in 1247 again paying thirty livres to Peter of Pouilly for the minute cens he was owed at Bessancourt; in 1257 paying forty livres for half the rights over the winepress and in 1258 paying forty livres to John of Saint-Cyr and his wife Isabelle for all the tithes the

latter held there. In September 1261 conflict arose with the Premonstratensians of Ressons over a tenant in the village of Bessancourt and over the rent
of five livres from a *mansus*, bread oven, and other rights to rents once paid
to Robert of La Truie (Atrio) and Helvidis, his wife.[77] In fact, including a
purchase of meadows at Bois-Daniel, the abbess had expended 860 livres for
rights at Bessancourt between 1242 and 1271.[78]

At nearby Frépillon the abbess Guillelma paid almost 130 livres for vineyards, other holdings, and a winepress between 1244 and 1271. Some of the
contracts were for relatively minor sums: six livres paid in 1246 for a house
located on the street of Frépillon; it owed rents of oats, bread, chickens, eggs,
and twenty deniers.[79] She paid thirty-four livres in 1244 to Thibaut of Frépillon for a house and land at Frépillon; in 1254 she paid fourteen livres to John
of Agout and his wife Theophania for vineyards at Perruchel; in 1255 she paid
thirty livres to Guy of Frépillon for rents and a third of a winepress there; in
1258, she paid five and a half livres for another piece of land.[80] Gifts for souls
could accompany such sales: in April 1248 the squire Eudes and his wife
Aelis gave twenty-four deniers of annual rent for Maubuisson to celebrate
anniversaries for his late lord Auberic of Frépillon and the latter's widow,
Lady Matilda; in July 1248, the abbess paid that same Eudes a total of fourteen and a half livres for a rent over the house and vineyard of Robert Cotil-
lart at Frépillon; in 1271, in one of her last acts, Abbess Guillelma paid thirty-
five livres to Bernard of Frépillon for a house, vineyard, woodland, and garden in Frépillon, property that Bernard had purchased earlier from the
widow Agnes.[81]

Rights to vineyards at Verneuil, Mateigne, and Aulnay were also conveyed by a diversity of owners.[82] Thus, shortly after Queen Blanche's death
in 1252, Abbess Guillelma paid the knight John of Villiers nearly nine livres
for his rights, lordship, and justice at Aulnay (near Pontoise), including a
meadow and vineyards in the fief of Mateigne. In 1257 Guillelma paid 332
livres to John of Cléry and his wife, Lady Margaret, for the entire fief of
Mateigne, and then smaller sums were paid for vineyards at Mateigne, some
of them adjoining those of the nuns.[83] That Maubuisson's nuns and their
neighbors were transforming suitable land into vineyards is also implied by a
contract from August 1263 in which the tithes at Étampes, mentioned as
being collected on both old and new vineyards (*vieilles vignes et novelles
plantes*), were sold to Maubuisson for fourteen livres by the Cistercian monks
of Vaux-de-Cernay.[84] These acquisitions of vineyards suggest that the nuns

produced wine not only for internal use but for sale as well. There were also payments by tenants for assarts near Frépillon. (See Table 12.)

Expansion Beyond Pontoise

The new abbey, Notre-Dame-la-Royale, or Maubuisson, would eventually have an array of granges, many of them associated with viticulture, stretching from north of Paris toward Normandy and of cereal-producing lands in the open fields of the Île-de-France north of Paris. Beyond the immediate ambit of Pontoise, many of Maubuisson's granges with vineyards were in the French Vexin and the Beauvaisis. Between 1247 and 1258, Abbess Guillelma used considerable cash to acquire them, spending 440 livres in three contracts for the major part of the villa, or estate, at Épiais, or Épiais-Rhus, in the French Vexin.[85] The same purchase pattern is seen for Nonciennes. In 1262 the abbess paid 100 livres for rights over land and vineyards in what had been a fief held from the king. She also paid another 163 livres for rights over vineyards located along the road from Nonciennes to Vaux and for a wine-press and cellar at Nonciennes. In one case, the agreement stated that rents due would differ according to whether lands were cultivated in grain, as opposed to being planted in vines.[86]

Acquisitions in the Beauvaisis were less successful.[87] In a contract dated 1255 the nuns agreed to pay Aleaume d'Uny and his wife 2,800 livres for all their rights in the villas of Uny and Giencourt-sous-Clermont. That charter listed rents, cens, *champart*, water, fisheries, and winepresses, all to be con-veyed to the nuns in *la main morte*. The contract would take effect in 1256 on the day when Aleaume's wife, Margaret, consented, and the nuns paid them 2,800 livres in cash.[88] Although Louis IX had confirmed this sale to the nuns during a visit to Maubuisson in 1269, the contract itself was soon chal-lenged by other powerful religious communities: Benedictine nuns at Chelles argued that the sellers held that land from them and not directly from the king, and the canons of Saint-Quentin of Beauvais claimed rents over the vineyards there.[89]

Still there was considerable revenue derived from the region west and north of Paris as is seen in Table 13. It extracts some of the more important payments found in the account book in comparison to Table 12, which lists small sums collected from many individuals.

Table 13. Selected Extracts from Maubuisson Rent Roll, 1248–56

At Christmas, in cens and caponage: 17 sous, 1 denier; and 76 hens worth 40 sous
Also on that feast, 57 loaves worth 57 sous . . .
At Easter, from cens at Frépillon, Bessancourt, etc., 33 sous, 2.5 deniers, and 222 eggs
For *moutonage* in May, 3 sous, 11.5 deniers at abbey and at Vaccaria[1] . . .
On Ascension Day [May] and All Saints' Day [November 1] from Meulan, 100 livres
Also on the same feasts at Mantes, 100 livres
For wheat at Pierrefonds, 100 livres . . .
On the Feast of John the Baptist's Birth [June 21], 7 livres from the oven at Bessancourt
For *taxamentum* [head tax?] for a year at Bessancourt, about 8 livres, 16 sous
For the tithes at Étampes, about 120 livres, including the oats
At Michaelmas, from the gift from the Countess of Mâcon, once our sister, 80 livres[2]
Also on that feast, from Arques, 24 livres[3]
Also from the woods of Rosières, 100 livres . . .
Also in rents from Normandy, 400 livres *tournois*[4]
Also for the woods of Bonfosse, 50 livres . . .
On All Saints' Day, for the house of Emily Rose, 20 sous in cens
In the meadow of Verneuil, the twenty arpents are worth 10 livres [fol. 42r] . . .
Also in the tithes of Hérouville, 4 muids of wheat and 4 of oats from the Lady Queen
Also in the tithes of Archemont, 7 muids of wheat and 7 of oats . . .
At Bretagnolles, 120 livres in wheat or oats from the mill (at Pacy?), arable land and cens[5]
At Pontoise, 8 muids of wheat, also 8 muids of oats . . .
Also at Bessancourt, twenty arpents of vines worth about 20 livres
Also near the abbey, twenty arpents of vines worth about 20 livres
Arable land worth 100 sous
Also seventeen arpents of meadow worth 9 livres
Also 3 sestiers of chestnuts worth about 12 sous . . .
At Crépy, 30 muids of oats, in the measure of Paris
For the vines at Éspeis from the Lady Queen, 20 livres
At Cergy, 30 sous
At Rouray, 18 sous

Source: Pontoise, AD Val d'Oise 72H12, *Achats d'héritages*, fols. 41v–42r.
1. *Moutonage*, payment for new lambs [?].
2. It reads IIII^XX. Alice had gotten permission from Louis IX in 1240 to give Maubuisson one hundred livres *tournois* from her annual income. That amounts only to eighty livres suggests that the king took 20 percent as a fine in lieu of *amortissement*.
3. *Cartulaire de Maubuisson*, no. 112 (1244). The king gave thirty livres for herring there.
4. This is the rent from the forest of Breteuil granted in 1248; it had not yet been reduced by a transfer of more than half of it in a concession to the nuns of Saint-Sauveur in 1256. See *Cartulaire de Maubuisson* no. 285 [1256].) This helps date this list to before 1256.
5. See *Cartulaire de Maubuisson*, no. 252 (1246).

Table 14. Maubuisson: Nuns' Purchases at Gonesse, 1257–66

Year	Number of Contracts	Total Spent
1257	29	961.7 livres
1258	10	324.3 livres
1259	9	253.5 livres
1260	2	44.0 livres
1263	1	1.0 livre
1264	4	59.0 livres
1265	2	121.0 livres
1266	11	570.4 livres
Total contracts	68	2,334.9 livres

The 2,335 livres spent here would produce about 233 livres annual income.

Source: Pontoise, AD Val d'Oise, 72H10, 1668 cartulary, vol. 2, fols. 393ff: liasse 72H110, and summaries in the published *Cartulaire de Maubuisson,* nos. 367–438. There are additional, later transactions concerning Gonesse in Pontoise, AD Val d'Oise, 72H110.

Maubuisson also acquired *champart* shares in the great open fields of the Île-de-France north of Paris. This included considerable holdings at Gonesse where the nuns are seen spending 2,335 livres in sixty-nine contracts dated between 1257 and 1266 to create a sizable grange there. (See Table 14.) Such consolidation of the nuns' endowment at Gonesse had been made possible by Louis IX's 1248 grant of *amortissement* to Maubuisson for up to 500 livres of income from his holdings.[90] Although this *amortissement* was not confined to lands at Gonesse, at Gonesse the nuns had exercised its possibilities up to its limit by the late 1260s. In 1269 the concession to Maubuisson by Louis IX of a *métairie* of forty-six arpents at Gonesse had to include an additional grant of *amortissement* by the king, as did a second such grant of a *métairie* of twenty arpents there in 1270.[91] Maubuisson's holdings at Gonesse were rounded out in 1274 when the nuns paid sixty livres to the monks of Vaux-de-Cernay for a house, its site, and two arpents of land at Gonesse, which had owed a cens of thirty-one deniers to the king; it probably became the nuns' grange center.[92]

Maubuisson's Urban Acquisitions and Social Services

Although in his grant of *amortissement* in 1248 Louis IX attempted to limit the properties owned by Maubuisson to no more than two houses in any town, the nuns soon had a number of Parisian properties. Already in 1240, the abbey's nuns had paid five and a half livres for a house in Paris in the *censive*, or lordship of the lord king.[93] In 1252 William the Cahorsin and his wife Heloise granted them a house in the weavers' district in exchange for one on the street of the old mint.[94] In 1289 Maubuisson bought for ten livres a house near the cemetery of Saint-Gervais occupied by Peter the Norman, a seller of dye-stuffs (*pastillarius*); it produced annual income of 47 sous.[95] In 1294 the priest/scholar William of Anjou gave Maubuisson a house near the Seine in Paris and various personal goods, including a volume of the *Decretals*; he was to be buried at Maubuisson. In 1302 the nuns paid 60 livres for a house in Paris; in 1304 they paid 140 livres for another; and they paid 400 livres for a third in 1310.[96]

Finally, regarding Paris, in 1256 Jeanne, widow of Philip of Metz, made her testament before a Parisian official and granted annual rents of six livres annually over a house in Paris to her three daughters who were nuns at Maubuisson. As they died, the residue would be shared by the survivors. After all three died, income would revert to their heirs in exchange for payment of 80 livres for memorials at the abbey. In 1279 Petronilla a fourth daughter of the late Philip of Metz, gave income to the nuns over Parisian houses amounting to 8 livres 4 sous each. After Petronilla's death in 1289, the two remaining sisters, the nuns, Jeanne and Marie of Metz sued for their rights against her surviving husband, Jean Bourdon, bourgeois of Paris and again began to receive the 16 livres 10 sous granted them.[97] Petronilla had outlived the woman who was presumably her mother (it could possibly be a step-mother) by 33 years, Jeanne and Marie of Metz, two of the three nuns, were still living in 1289. What is most striking here is that this Parisian family had in 1256 established personal, private income for the three daughters who became nuns at Maubuisson.[98] The issue is discussed further in Chapter 7.

Maubuisson provided a burial place for Blanche of Castile and a place of retreat for her son Louis IX.[99] Together they had assured its annual income in money and kind (see Table 15). The nuns also granted spiritual services for other elites, including some who endowed chapels for their souls. In the 1250s, Alesia of Noyon left 240 livres for the construction of a chapel in the parish church at Cormellion, where masses were to be celebrated for her own and her family's souls; in 1262 her executors decided instead to build a chapel in the cemetery at Maubuisson, so that one of the nuns' chaplains could celebrate mass there.[100] After Louis IX's death in 1270, Queen Marguerite of Provence assigned funds for chapels for Louis IX's soul at Maubuisson as well as at Saint-Antoine and Villiers.[101] Later in 1310 an anniversary mass was funded at Maubuisson for a father and son.[102] In 1326 Matilda of Artois gave eleven arpents of land at Gonesse and a *mansus* at Uny for the burial of her father at Maubuisson, making the gift to Isabelle of Montmorency, Maubuisson's fourth abbess (1309/10–45).[103]

Maubuisson also housed pensioners and underage girls, probably from an early date, but they remain largely undocumented. A document from 1292 mentions a thirteen-year-old Breton girl who eventually became a nun there.[104] One from 1294 mentions the nearby property of Emeline the Beguine, possibly a dependent of the nuns.[105] A charter from 1309 mentions a married couple living in one of Maubuisson's houses as corrodians, or pensioners.[106] In 1324 "in order to be fed and housed like a lay brother at Maubuisson for the rest of his life," Martin of Vaux from Bessancourt gave the nuns a postmortem gift of his properties and fief at Vaux.[107] In 1323, Margaret of Beaumont, once princess of Antioch and Countess of Tripoli, gave her properties at Plessy and Franqueville to Maubuisson, where she was living and where she wished to be buried; those properties were reserved for her own use for life, for that of Lucy of Vaugour thereafter, and only after Lucy's death were they to come to the nuns when they were to be used to celebrate an anniversary mass and a pittance meal for Margaret.[108]

Blanche's Foundation of Lys and Louis IX's 1248 Crusade

Only after Maubuisson was well established did Blanche of Castile begin to devote funds to a second foundation for Cistercian nuns at Lys. In 1244, only shortly after Maubuisson's church had been consecrated, first her daughter Isabelle and then Louis IX fell ill. Isabelle recovered that summer; Louis recovered in late 1244 and made a crusader vow. Between those two events, in September 1244 the royal family attended the meeting of the Cistercian General Chapter; Blanche of Castile, Louis IX, Robert of Artois, and Alphonse of Poitiers all made bequests in support of the order's annual General Chapter, totaling 240 livres in annual rents. Blanche was granted the right to have public prayers said for herself, her parents, and other family members throughout the order, and she probably also discussed plans for another abbey of Cistercian nuns near Melun, for she had already begun making purchases there in the summer of 1244.[109] Later that year when Louis IX fell ill and in despair for his life made his crusader vow, he would double the size of the abbey of Royaumont and of its endowment in support of that crusade. Although plans for Blanche's second abbey at Lys had begun before Louis IX's crusader vow, the urgency with which the construction of Lys and the establishment of its community was undertaken suggests that it too soon became associated in the minds of Blanche and her son with prayers for the success of the crusade.[110]

Lys was located on the outskirts of Melun, on the Seine upstream from Paris. The abbey's access to the Seine (indeed it had its own port on the river) allowed the nuns to transport wine to markets in Paris. A large royal gift in nearby forests allowed the nuns' construction of barrels and vessels. The site of Lys and most particularly its grange at Mâlay were located, like Maubuisson, close to a border, in this case the frontier with Champagne, marked by the forest of Othe, a massive woodland south of the Vanne River and east of Sens. As at Maubuisson, Blanche's first priority was to assure the nuns' provisioning once they arrived. In less than four years, the queen, with the assistance of Louis IX, accomplished much of the massive project (which had taken six years at Maubuisson), of construction, provisioning, and the beginnings of endowment in the four years from the summer of 1244 to the consecration of the church of Lys in the spring of 1248 before Louis IX's departure on his first crusade. (See Tables 15 and 16.)

In the summer of 1244 Blanche of Castile had made the first purchases of a site at Lys in the seigneurie of Dammarie for a second abbey of Cistercian nuns to be located near her dower lands of Melun. There were a number of reasons for Blanche to found another abbey at this time. She had suffered a series of personal losses: Louis IX's eldest daughter, Blanche (the dowager queen's granddaughter and namesake), had died in April 1243; news came in 1244 of the deaths of Eleanor of Castile, Blanche's sister, of their sister Berenguela's daughter Constance, and in December of that year of their half cousin Jeanne, Countess of Flanders. The foundation also allowed Blanche to provide a suitable position for her half cousin Alice of Mâcon, who would become the first abbess of Notre-Dame of Lys (1248–59).

Alice was Queen Blanche of Castile's *consanguinea*; unlike Blanche, who was a granddaughter of Eleanor of Aquitaine and Henry II, Alice was a great-granddaughter of Eleanor and Louis IX, granddaughter of Marie of Champagne, and heiress in her own right to the county of Mâcon.[111]

Table 15. Maubuisson: Gifts from Blanche of Castile and Louis IX

Cash	Other
Gifts from Blanche of Castile	
1239 100, not 150* livres (Meulan)	
1239 100 livres (Pierrefonds)	
	8 muids of wheat (Pontoise)
	10 mines of oats (Pontoise)
	100 mines of oats, (Crépy)
	Terrages (Marolles)
	16 muids (Archemont tithes)
	4 muids (Hérouville tithes)
1239	1.5 muids (tithes of Magnitot)
	Tithes, Étampes, Dourdan, Châtelliers
Gifts from Louis IX	
1239 100 livres at Mantes†	100 livres from Royal Exchequer from
	Alice of Mâcon confirmed
1242	Confirmed conveyances at Pontoise,
	Bessancourt, Sognolles, Frépillon
1244 30 livres to purchase herring at	
Arques	
1245	Pasture/300 pigs Retz and Guise
1245	Woodland at Ageux
1245	100 arpents woods, Bonfosse
1246 400 livres (from Breteuil assarts)	
Later Gifts from Blanche of Castile	
1246–48	Bretagnolles woods and half mill,
	purchased by her for 1,500 livres
1248	30 muids oats (at Crépy)
	(Louis confirmed)
Later Gifts from Louis IX	
1248	11 arpents meadow, Verneuil
1248	12 muids grain (Bailly, Marly,
	Verneuil)
1248	*Amortissement* for 500 livres' worth of
	income-producing land
1257	*Gruage‡* at Bonfosse, Châtelliers
1257	12 muids (Pontoise mill)
1259	*Métairie* of Gonesse, 46 arpents with
	amortisssement
1260	*Métairie* at Gonesse, 20 arpents with
	amortissement

Table 15 (con't)

Cash	Other
	Later Gifts from Louis IX
1268/69	Amortissement, meadow at Bonfosse
1270	Daily carts of firewood at Halatte

*The king did not add more income at Meulan, but only confirmed it.
†Alice of Mâcon in 1240 gave 100 livres of her income from the Royal Exchequer.
‡Gruage is a customary payment to the forest officials.
Sources: *Cartulaire de Maubuisson*, nos. 300 (1239), 304 (December 1259), and 305 (1263);
Pontoise, AD Val d'Oise, 72H10 Cartulaire de Maubuisson 1668; Bonis, *Maubuisson*, table 2,
p. 33.

According to the latest history of the Baron's Crusade of 1239, Alice and her husband had sold her county to Louis IX in 1239 when he embarked for the East using the immediate cash settlement to finance his crusading, but he soon died there.[112] Part of the settlement for Alice's sale of her inheritance of Mâcon was an annual pension of 1000 livres *tournois* payable to her for life from the Norman exchequer. In 1240 she became a Cistercian nun and got royal permission to give one hundred livres of that pension to Maubuisson as her entrance gift.[113] In 1248 it was she who brought nuns from Maubuisson to the new community at Lys. after the departure of the king on his first crusade and following Blanche's death in 1252, it was Abbess Alice (1248–59) who oversaw the endowment of the abbey. She subsequently secured the burial of Blanche's heart at Lys.[114]

Unfortunately, the documentation for Lys is considerably less satisfactory than what survives for Maubuisson and much of it is post-medieval. There is an inventory dated 1675 apparently made for the commendatory abbess of Lys, Claire-Cécile Colbert. It provides a listing of properties acquired and transaction dates, but few other details of what was in the charters; for instance, it usually does not provide any purchase prices and it is not really clear if only substantial purchases and gifts were included in the inventory.[115] There is also a small early fourteenth-century cartulary for Lys, Paris, BnF, Latin MS 13892, *Cartulaire du Lys,* but it was copied for the purposes of a complaint made at the royal court and consists almost entirely of royal charters. Of the original parchments, only a few have survived: those from the grange of Mâlay, which had ended up in Auxerre at the time of the Revolution; those stored in Melun have disappeared.[116]

Table 16.   Lys: Gifts from Blanche of Castile and Louis IX

Date	Cash Income	Income in Kind and Other
	From Blanche of Castile	
1248	80 livres in *prévôté* of Melun	
1248		Tithes and land at Syriac
1248		160 arpents, rents at Chaintreaux
1248	60 livres in *prévôté* of Paris*	
1250		15 muids of wheat from mill at Poignet
1250		Rents in Melun
1250	50 livres at *prévôté* in Étampes	
1252	60 livres at *prévôté* in Étampes	
1252		100 arpents of forest*
	From Louis IX	
1248		25 muids of wheat at Sens
1248		45 muids of grain at Melun
1248	50 livres at Corbeil	
1248		54 muids of oats at Chapelle-la-Reine
1248	60 livres in *prévôté* of Paris	
1248		Life rent (wheat/wine) in Sens
1248		Tithes at Sivry and Malbranche
1248	100 livres in *prévôté* of Sens	
1248		200 arpents in forest of Bièvre
1248	45 livres in *prévôté* of Melun	
1248		*Amortissement* for 600 livres
1255		Forest rights at Mâlay
1260		Forest rights at Mâlay
1268		Forest rights at Mâlay
1269	20 livres rent, from Jean of Châtelet*	
1270	300 livres in his will	

Source: Paris, BnF, Latin MS 13892, *Cartulaire du Lys* and Dimier, *Saint Louis et Cîteaux.*
*Confirmed by Louis IX.

Royal Provisioning and the Lys Cartulary

The queen's first two purchases for the abbey of Lys, made in summer 1244, were of vineyards and associated properties at Dammarie, which would become the abbey site. Blanche's acquisitions there would continue right up to March 1248 when Adam of Dammarie and his wife conveyed what they held in fief or demesne "in houses, laborers, hay meadows, and vineyards" in the parishes of Dammarie and Chailly. Blanche of Castile and Louis IX made generous gifts of annual deliveries of wheat and wine, as well as of cash to provision the nuns who arrived in 1248. Louis IX would continue to do so after his mother's death. These royal conveyances to Lys were recorded in the early fourteenth-century *Cartulaire du Lys*, and it is only from the cartulary's copies that it is possible to reconstruct what Blanche and Louis provided; see Table 16, which is drawn from the evidence of that cartulary.

The early fourteenth-century cartulary preserves the text of an April 1252 confirmation by Blanche of Castile, her final statement (for she died in November 1252) of her intentions in making this second foundation for Cistercian nuns:

Blanche, by the grace of God, Queen of the Franks, sends greetings to all reading the present words. We make known that our dearest son, the King, has taken the road to transmarine parts for the service of Jesus Christ. Before leaving he conceded to us the power to make additional gifts in alms for the remedy of our soul, those of our sons, and our ancestors, up to the value of three hundred livres in annual rents from the properties that we hold in dower. After the departure of our son, the King, we gave additional annual rents worth one hundred livres to the abbey of the Blessed Mary and the nuns serving God at Lys near Melun of the Cistercian Order, which was founded by our son and ourselves. We gave fifty livres in money to be paid every year by the provost in Étampes on the feast of All Saints and fifteen muids of grain to be paid annually from our mill at Poignet near Melun. Wishing to increase our concession of rents to that abbey of Lys and the nuns serving God there, we now give and concede in pure and perpetual alms for our soul and the souls of our son, the King, and those of all our ancestors, an additional fifty livres to be paid annually by the provost of Étampes on the feast of the Ascension. Furthermore, we wish and establish that the provost of Étampes should make the two annual payments of fifty livres in money without any delay or postponement, and that for every day late, the nuns shall be owed an additional five sous. In witness of these things we have fortified this charter with our seal. This was done at the abbey of Notre-Dame-la-Royale [Maubuisson] near Pontoise, in the year of the Lord, 1252, in the month of April.[117]

This final act by Blanche underlines the cooperation between mother and son in founding Lys, but that cooperation between Blanche and her son has been called into question by modern historians.

Those historians, perhaps convinced for other reasons of a breach between Louis IX and his mother, have over-interpreted what must be regarded as copying errors that crept into the early fourteenth-century volume, *Cartulaire du Lys*, where the exact wording of royal donations was much less important than their promises of delivery of grain from the royal granaries. The Paris manuscript *Cartulaire du Lys* was compiled on the occasion of a dispute between the nuns of Lys and royal agents who were attempting to pay the nuns in cash rather than by the deliveries of grain from royal granaries, although such payments in kind were what had been promised to the nuns. The nuns' response was to present their royal charters to Philip IV, arguing that the fluctuation of grain prices (and the general inflation of the time?) made it disadvantageous for them to receive cash payments rather than actual grain deliveries. King Philip, agreeing with the nuns, issued charters guaranteeing them the continued payment in kind. His acts are the last ones in the *Cartulaire du Lys*. Such copies of royal charters found in that cartulary are all that remain of the original charters and any discrepancies in them should be read as copying errors and not as reflecting any dispute between mother and son at the time of his first crusade.[118]

Lys's Other Properties

Only for the grange of Mâlay, located east of Sens on the edge of the forest of Othe, do some original charters survive for the abbey of Lys.[119] These are important for recording details of acquisitions there made by Alice and her successors. The grange of Mâlay was established by the nuns of Lys in an area of newly established towns or villages established by rival kings and counts at Mâlay-le-Roi and Mâlay-le-Comte. The documents suggest recent reclamation along the Vanne River where peasant settlers appear to have been willing to take up new contracts with the nuns to plant vineyards *ad medium vestum*, but also sometimes just sold their rights to established vineyards to the nuns. Viticulture would be important to the abbey's economy. To promote wine-production Abbess Alice seems to have given particular attention to this area for planting and acquiring plots of vines, enclosed vineyards, and the presses and cellars needed for processing and storing that wine.[120]

The first recorded acquisition by Abbess Alice associated with the grange at Mâlay was of a site in nearby Sens where wine could be stored; it was acquired in 1252 when Abbess Alice paid 194 livres *tournois* to Felix of Pontarlier and his wife Isabelle, for rights in a house, cellar, and its appurtenances in the parish of Saint-Hilaire of Sens.[121] Then in 1253 another large acquisition was made at Mâlay itself when Alice paid 665 livres *tournois* to the bourgeois Peter of Châteauvieux of Sens and his wife Felicia for a house, barn, barnyard, vineyards, and other rights in the *censive* and lordship of the lord king at Mâlay-le-Roi. That acquisition included one and a half arpents of willow groves (*saulsaie*) in front of the seller's house, fourteen *quartiers* of vineyards on the banks of the Vanne River, a meadow, and twenty pieces of land containing twenty-four and a half arpents at Épinette de Pasqui, rights at Île-Pêche-Verte, and so on.[122]

Some of the later documents suggest that the grange of Mâlay had a more complex origin than most. A certain Guy Legaigneur (sometimes identified as Guy Lucrator) had taken up rights from the king to forest exploitation there, which may have included lumbering as well as rights to firewood and usage.[123] At his death Guy Legaigneur gave his rights at Mâlay to support a *domus Dei* there; according to Théophile Lhuillier, the editor of the Auxerre charters for Lys, that *domus Dei* had been given to the brothers of the priory of Clairlieu. These were not Cistercians, but the Caulite (Val-des-Choux) brothers at Clairlieu, who had a priory near Nemours and who in 1247/48 conveyed those rights to the Cistercian nuns of Notre-Dame of Nemours; those nuns in turn conveyed them to those of Lys for the latter's grange of Mâlay.[124] In 1253 Abbess Alice also paid 100 livres *tournois* to the Caulite monks of Clairlieu for half a vineyard at La Garenne in Mâlay-le-Roi, rights over a mill, a winepress, wine sheds, and a fourth part of the stand of willows adjoining the pond of Mâlay; she eventually had to pay much more—an additional 268.5 livres *tournois* to various claimants to Guy's rights.[125] (See Table 17.)

Other charters indicate Alice's consolidation of Lys's rights at Mâlay. In 1254 she paid twenty-two and a half livres *tournois* to Stephen Juignes and his wife Agnes for a house at Mâlay "across from that owned by the nuns."[126] Also in 1254 she paid forty livres *tournois* to William of Dimion and his wife Isabelle for their rights along the river Vanne in the parish of Mâlay.[127] Later Alice paid eighty-four livres to the executors of the estate of the late Gilles

Table 17. Lys: Expenditures and Contracts for Mâlay and Sens from 1252

Expenditures

Year	Gifts	Purchases	Average Expenditures	Total Expenditures
1252	1	1	194 livres	194 livres
1253	0	2	383 livres	765 livres
1254	1	6	70 livres	419.25 livres
1255	1	1	20.25 livres	20.25 livres
Total	3	10	140 livres	1,398.5 livres

Contracts per (approximate) decade (without prices after 1255)

Date range	Number of contracts
1248–59 (Alice of Mâcon is abbess)	13
1260–70	14
1271–85	18
1286–96	12
Total contracts, 1248–96	57

Source: Th. Lhuillier, "Inventaire des titres concernant la seigneurie que les religieuses de l'abbaye royale de N.-D. du Lys, près Melun, possédaient à Mâlay-le-Roi," *Bulletin de la Société archéologique de Sens* 10 (1872): 347–57.

Herman of Mâlay for six pieces of land totaling eighteen and a half arpents, including a vineyard in the parish of Mâlay in the territory of the lord king (presumably Mâlay-le-Roi); the abbess Alice paid another forty livres to Gilles's widow for other claims (and these all appear to have been *tournois,* suggesting that Alice was using her income from the Exchequer for these purchases). Among those giving up claims was a priest described as the "nephew and chaplain of the late Guy Legaigneur."[128]

Such acquisitions continued even after Alice's death in 1259. In January 1260/61 Hugh of Mâlay and his wife transferred to Lys a house located across from another house in Mâlay already owned by its nuns. The nuns paid eleven livres, fifteen sous to Herman of Mâlay and his wife for a field at Mâlay adjoining land belonging to Hugh Charmiau and the *champart* of the lord king.[129] In 1263 Lys got six and a half arpents scattered over six parcels, near their ditch and woods from William Cimetico and his associates. In 1264 William himself gave the nuns another six and a quarter arpents at Val Licée. In 1264 Sicard of Villers gave land at Mâlay near the nuns' oven. In

1265 they acquired a vineyard near Chapelle-des-Guillelmas as well as properties on the major street adjoining the nuns' oven and those at Champfroid
near the Garenne, again facing the nuns' oven. In 1266 they acquired land at
Goule and Galley and two additional parcels adjoining that oven. In 1269,
1270, and 1271, the nuns got land at Mâlay-le-Roi adjoining their fields and
woodlands at a place called Sannière that extended toward Mâlay-le-Comte.
Such acquisitions continued right up to the nuns' purchase in 1296 from
Isabelle, widow of Geoffrey, of a house at Mâlay-le-Roi with its own courtyard and other buildings.[130]
     Something of the total expenditures made by Alice during her years as
abbess (1248–59) may be inferred from the total number of acts during those
years that are found in the 1675 inventory made for the commendatory abbess
of Lys, Claire-Cécile Colbert (see Table 18).[131] What this summary of the
inventory shows is that sixteen of the thirty-five acquisitions made during
Alice's rule (46 percent) concerned Mâlay and Sens—those are the extant
original charters in Auxerre. This suggests that archival losses for Lys in its
early years were not as drastic as they might have been, because Alice seems
to have devoted most of her attention to the complicated acquisitions at
Mâlay. This does not mean that more money was spent there than elsewhere.
Although the inventory rarely cites amounts spent, it does mention 600 livres
spent in a single contract for Orsonville, while only a little more than twice
that amount (1,398 livres) was spent at Mâlay and Sens. Many of the granges
described in the later inventory were acquired after Alice's abbacy; only after
her death did the nuns make additional acquisitions at Chaintreaux, Boiss-
ises, Dammarie, and Farcy, as well as those at Mâlay (see Map 5).

Maubuisson and Lys: Size and Architecture

Blanche's two foundations for Cistercian nuns at Maubuisson and Lys were
built like Royaumont in the new Cistercian High Gothic style, employing
the new bar tracery technology, which appears to have been less expensive
than earlier methods in terms of stone, labor, and transport costs.[132] Vestiges
of the abbey church of Lys remain; it was one of remarkable elegance, but
considerably smaller than those of Maubuisson and Royaumont. Perhaps
Blanche of Castile had scaled back, having been told by the abbots at Cîteaux
of their increasing concern about the lavishness of abbeys like Royaumont
and Maubuisson.[133] Lys's church was simpler than that at Maubuisson, with

Table 18. Lys: Properties Purchased by Abbess Alice of Mâcon (1248–59)

Boissises-le-Roi	
1250	Lawrence sold vineyards there.
	John sold what he held from king: 6 sous, house, arpent of vines and land.
1251	*Amortissement* there.
Rubella	
1251	Two purchases of vineyards.
Dammarie	
1251	*Amortissement* and three more houses close to the abbey.
1252	*Amortissement* of earlier acquisitions.
1254	*Amortissement* of rights given by Hugh of la Grange.
1255	Confirmation of sale by Stephen of la Grange.
1259	Purchase of one piece of land.
Fontaine-le-Port	
1252	Watermill, vines, meadows, and press from William Messier, Robert Porq.
	Quarter of fief of village.
Sens/Mâlay	
1253	Sixteen contracts for Alice's lifetime.
Orsonville	
1254	Six hundred livres paid for 260 arpents of woodland in Tillières and 65 arpents of arable land at grange of Orsonville.
Croix-en-Brie	
1253	Two purchases of rents in wheat and cash from 240 arpents of land near winepress, from Jean Britauld, lord of Nangis. including 120 arpents of woods.
1256	Another 106 arpents of woods, etc., near grange of Villers-en-Brie.

Source: Melun, AD Seine-et-Marne H566, Inventaire du Lys, 1685, made for the commendatory abbess of Lys, Claire-Cécile Colbert, sections 15 (Dammarie), 20 (Boissises-le-Roi), 25 (Orsonville), 30 (Rubella), 31 (Fontaine le Port), 34 (Croix-en-Brie), 35 (Sens/Mâlay).

a two-story elevation rather than a three-story one and with a simple cruciform plan and a flat east end. Still the remains of the window frames have elegant bar tracery that shows considerable refinement. (See Figures 7 and 8.) Lys's endowment also may have been slightly less than that of Maubuisson, but the only real comparison that can be made is that between what Blanche and Louis IX themselves gave to the two abbeys (see Tables 15 and 16). The result in each case was an impressive although smaller church than Royaumont. Whereas Louis IX raised the size of Royaumont to 160 monks, Maubuisson and Lys were to have 120 nuns each.[134]

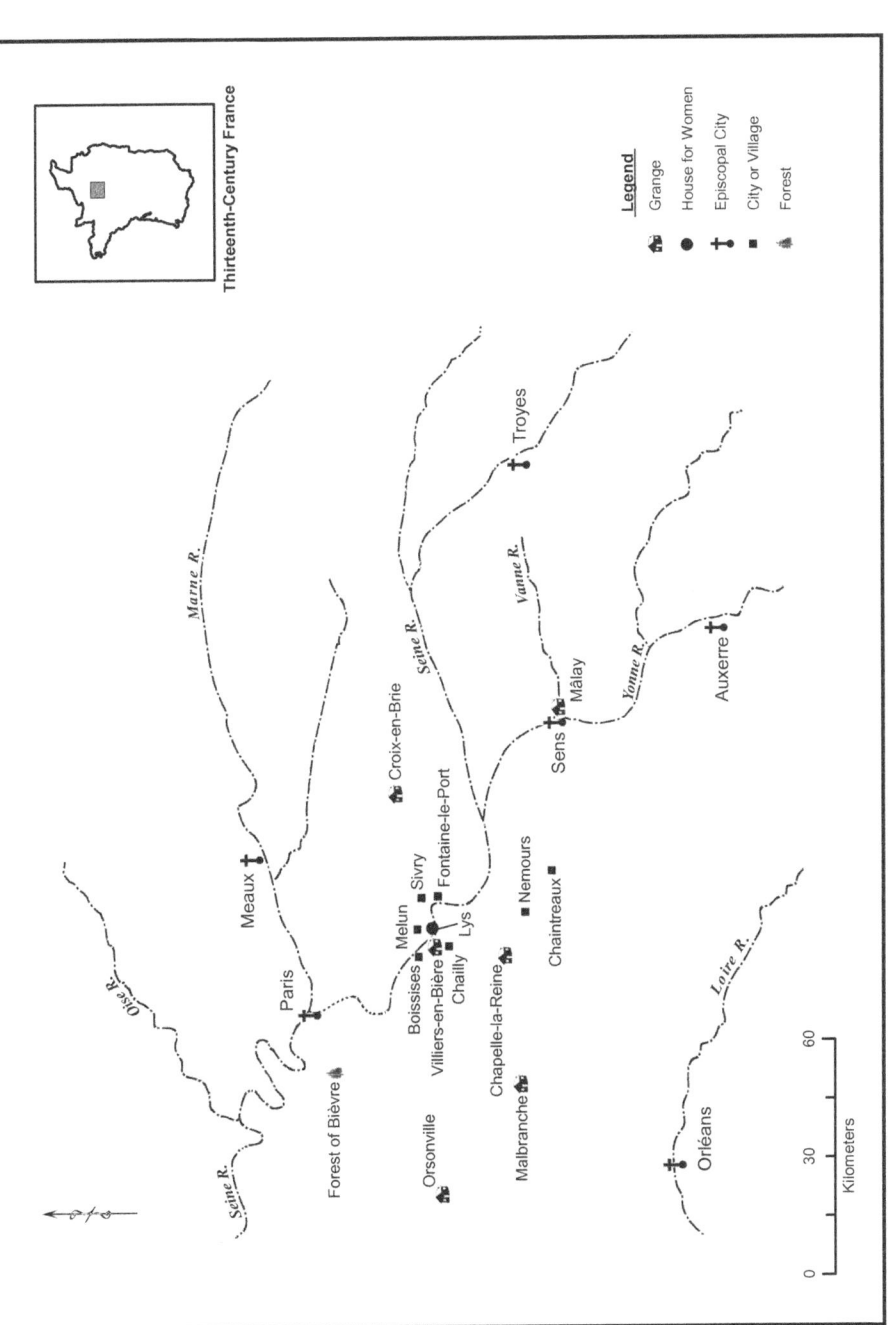

MAP 5. Lys and its granges and properties. Map created by Gordon Thompson.

FIGURE 8. Lys, bar tracery, detail.
Photograph by the author.

The implication of the remains of these two abbeys is that constructing, provisioning, and endowment for either Maubuisson or Lys was a massive administrative task for the queen and for the first abbesses, Abbess Guillelma (r. 1241/2–75) at Maubuisson and Abbess Alice (1248–59) at Lys. The accomplishments of both the founder, Blanche of Castile, and those two very competent first abbesses is impressive. Such records, moreover, contradict what were once the standard descriptions of medieval women—of frivolous, inept, or flighty nuns and illiterate founders and patrons. This chapter clearly shows how untrue such descriptions are.

Forest Rights at Maubuisson and Lys

Many abbeys of Cistercian nuns acquired some rights in royal forests—often the concession from a king or queen to collect a certain number of cartloads of firewood per week or to allow pigs to feed on nuts and acorns during the fall. In regions east of Paris, as discussed in Chapter 9, several houses of nuns acquired forest rights in the forest of Jariel. For other abbeys a count or countess may have conveyed forest access, as had, for instance, Countess Matilda of Brunswick and her son Thomas for Clairets.[135] Forest rights are prominent among concessions by Blanche and Louis IX to both Maubuisson and Lys. They set Maubuisson and Lys apart from other Cistercian abbeys of nuns in terms of their access to royal forest and possibly too to the ability to organize a cycle of cuttings within them.[136]

Maubuisson's acquisition of forest rights beyond those used in the abbey's construction began as the traditional usage rights in woodlands like those acquired by other religious communities for taking firewood and allowing pigs to feed on mast in the fall. From early dates Blanche of Castile is seen seeking out such woodland rights for Maubuisson near the new abbey site and the account book shows the nuns acquiring rents over newly cleared holdings, or assarts, in the vicinity of the abbey (see Table 12). Such woodland acquisitions are striking insofar as the account book for Maubuisson suggests that these were the only acquisitions for which the abbey used agents. In 1240 and 1241 Brother John of Longpence spent 196 livres on behalf of Maubuisson for land, woodland, and meadows in the nearby "nemus Moelli."[137] Later, in 1253, Lord Walter, "priest and brother of the new abbey of the Blessed-Mary-la-Royale [Maubuisson] at Pontoise," made woodland acquisitions for the nuns elsewhere.[138]

Other rights were paid for directly by the queen or abbess. In 1241 Robert of Meudun and Mathias de Wautel, mayor of Pierrelatte, were paid twenty-seven livres by the queen for seven and a half arpents of woods at Noua next to Bessancourt; Lord Peter of Poissy, from whom Robert and Mathias held their rights, was paid more than his dependents: thirty livres for rights that had been held from the queen.[139] The queen also spent 200 livres for the 200 arpents at Rosières and Brutiers, and in 1246 the abbess paid 140 livres for such rights to Thibaut of Frépillon.[140] The abbey's nuns, however, soon came up against the claims of other new religious groups. In May 1255 following an earlier dispute over tithes, conflict arose with the Cistercian monks of nearby Val-Notre-Dame when the latter attempted to establish a grange in the woods of Rosières, near the pond and sheepfold at Montargis, all of which belonged to the nuns. Maubuisson's acquisitions there had been made earlier and arbitrators ruled in its favor.

Usage rights came to Maubuisson in May 1245 when the king granted it rights to feed three hundred pigs on mast in the woods of Retz and Guise.[141] In October 1245, while visiting the abbey of Maubuisson, the king also gave rights in the "Ageux woods" (north and upstream on the Oise River from Pontoise) and one hundred arpents of woods at Bonfosse between Verneuil and Pont-Sainte-Maxence: the latter adjoining Royaumont's woods and those of the knight Peter Cook.[142] These woods at Bonfosse became central to the nuns' acquisitions as seen when the knight Peter Cook gave them twenty arpents of additional woods at Bonfosse in October 1250; this gift was followed in November 1250 by Peter Cook's sale to Maubuisson of another 150 arpents at Bonfosse for six hundred livres.[143] Then in 1255 the nuns paid Peter Cook sixty livres for "woods located between those belonging to the lords of Montmorency, those of Jacob Lombardi, and those of the Lord King."[144] Such combinations of gifts and sales were frequent.

Later Maubuisson also acquired woods in installment contracts at Bonfosse, possibly from Saint-Rémy of Reims. This happened twice, in 1248/49 and in 1257, 1258, 1259. In 1248/49 the nuns made two payments of $56^2/_3$ livres each, making a total of a little more than 113 livres for about fifty arpents at Bonfosse. At Christmas 1257 they acquired another one hundred arpents of those woods at Bonfosse, for which they paid a total of 214 livres, paying each year (1257, 1258, and 1259) the sum of $71^1/_3$ livres; not much different per arpent from that paid a decade earlier.[145]

Not recorded in the account book, but in surviving charters, is Blanche of Castile's 1246 payment of fifteen hundred livres to Bouchard of Marly (grandson of the founder of Port-Royal) for forest rights at Bretagnolles near

Évreux and for half a mill at Pacy on the Eure River; the queen then gave those forest rights and the half mill to Maubuisson in 1248 and Louis IX confirmed.[146] In 1251, at the queen's recommendation Maubuisson's nuns purchased the other half of the mill at Pacy and fishing rights there for 180 livres.[147] Also not recorded in the Maubuisson account book was Louis IX's 1246 grant, made as he prepared for his first crusade, of four hundred livres per annum of rents from the new assarts at Breteuil in that forest near Évreux.[148] Ceding such rents to Maubuisson, Louis IX garnered prayers for his crusade's success but perhaps also tried to prevent usurpations in the royal forests of Normandy by placing them in the hands of the nuns. Following a dispute over the tithes there in 1256, Maubuisson sold some of its rights in Breteuil, creating for itself a windfall in cash that would allow extensive purchases at placed like Gonesse in the next years.[149] While it is unlikely that the nuns were responsible for overseeing any of the assarts at Breteuil, the account book does record a list of assarts at Sognolles paying a total of twenty-five sous to the nuns. See again Table 12 and Table 13; in the latter, the rights in forests at Breteuil and Bretagnolles are among extracts from the account book.

Management of Endowment

How was property management, its *gestion*, accomplished by Maubuisson and Lys? An earlier chapter mentioned that Port-Royal's nuns claimed tithe exemption because they had introduced direct cultivation on noval lands. For Maubuisson such direct cultivation was probably found as well. The Maubuisson account book lists sales of produce from the royal estate and forest—pigs, dyestuffs, and leeks—that suggest what crops could be produced there.[150] Lists of minor tithes like those conceded by the parish priest of Saint-Ouen to Maubuisson also suggest what products were produced: "Products from gardens, orchards, and wasteland including flax, hemp, mushrooms [but *cepis* could also refer to vine cuttings, perhaps newly rooted], and scallions or leeks, tithes on lambs, pigs, and calves, trees, meadows, or the nuts from the beech grove above the mill pond and in the sheepfolds [*becceriae*]."[151] Even more important were the fields and granges that produced grain, but about whose cultivation little evidence is given. Sometimes it appears that lands were under *champart* and what was given was a share in that production. There was evidence of grain and wine production when

FIGURE 9. Maubuisson Abbey barn.
Photograph by the author.

disputes arose over tithes. There is also indirect evidence of cereal cultivation seen in the great medieval tithe barns like that at Maubuisson (see Figure 9). There were also hay meadows as seen in such contracts as that from 1268 when Raoul of Verneuil, son of the knight John of Villiers, conveyed eight arpents of hay meadows adjoining the woods of Bonfosse to Maubuisson.[152] In 1272 the widow Johanna of Méry and her son granted Maubuisson rights to have its goods ferried across the Oise at Méry-sur-Oise, but they also granted fifteen arpents of meadows there.[153] Hay from such meadows would allow cattle to be fed and kept under cover in the winter.

One charter suggests how those meadows were managed. Maubuisson had a dispute with a cowherd from Neuilly because he had allowed his cows to graze in a hay meadow belonging to Maubuisson before the nuns had made a second cutting of hay; the complaint was to be resolved by six good men.[154] The nuns' smaller and often invisible investments in improved tools, stock, and rationalized agriculture may be inferred from larger investments in tithe barns, wind or water-powered mills, or the grange center at Gonesse.[155] Maubuisson and Lys both also took advantage of their access to a ready market in Paris and nearby towns to sell surpluses they produced. Indeed the considerable emphasis on vineyards in the contracts for both abbeys suggests wine production aimed at an expanding urban market.

The exercise of seigneurial rights by the Cistercian nuns at Maubuisson and Lys is clear. For Maubuisson, typical lordship over village ovens is seen at Bessancourt, but two other ovens are found in a list from 1263 of assets sold to the nuns by Matthew of Montmorency: a communal, or banal, oven, vineyards, a quarter *mansus* near the house of Alberic, the mason, tithes over a number of properties, a garden next to the priest's house and that house, as well as at least three other houses—one with an oven. Another property included a mill, half a winepress, many pieces of vineyard, including those in the walled vineyard, or *clos,* of Fermel; there the nuns acquired control of half the mayorship and access rights to that seigneurial property.[156]

Over the passage of time Cistercian nuns at Maubuisson profited even more from the revenues of lordship. Thus one account described Maubuisson's holdings at Bessancourt as having "a lordly mansion, another smaller estate house and grange or barn, along with rents, tithes, 112 arpents of arable land, 280 arpents of woodland, 150 livres of rent from the oak forest *bois de chêne,* four winepresses, a banal oven, and a windmill with a house and 6 arpents of land attached to it."[157]

As for Lys, by the second half of the seventeenth century, according to Armande Prieur's assessment of its 1675 inventory, "its holdings numbered 1,750 arpents with 34–35 arpents in the monastic enclosure including conventual buildings, cloister, church, farm, and dovecote; the abbey's mill was located north of the enclosure wall and the abbey farm of 180 arpents was bounded by the Seine, the road from Melun to Dammarie and a line from Dammarie to Farcy; in those lordships at Dammarie and Farcy, the nuns had banal winepresses, tithes and cens on wine grapes, grain and vegetables, and rights to fish on the Seine from the bridge at Samois up to Saint-Assise."[158] The abbesses had the power of command and rights of lordship over their properties as *dominae* (lady/lords). While we have no evidence about the background of Lady Guillelma, Maubuisson's first abbess, the first abbess at Lys was the former countess Lady Alice of Mâcon and among the very elite, having ruled an entire county before retirement; this would probably have counted for little if she had also not been, like Guillelma, an able administrator.

Conclusions and Remembering Blanche of Castile

Maubuisson and Lys may be seen as the outcome of Blanche of Castile's lifetime enthusiasm for Cistercian nuns. The benefit of discussing Royaumont along with them, as this chapter has done, is that it reveals something about the financial limits on a foreign queen. Unlike her son Louis IX who was drawing without limit on the royal fisc for Royaumont and for other projects, Blanche had no inherited property for supporting her foundations of Cistercian nuns. Her access to properties settled on her at her marriage was blocked from an early date. So she was forced to exercise patience and prudence. Blanche spent more than a decade in widowhood before she could begin the abbey of Maubuisson, and Louis IX's limitations on her alienation of crown properties were strict. Those limits made it particularly important for her to keep careful accounts. Hence her actions in founding first one and then a second house of Cistercian nuns were separated in time; the abbeys were introduced serially and only late in her life. This must be seen in comparison to the rapid establishment of Royaumont with her son, or the actions of her cousin Isabelle of Chartres, who had founded two new houses of Cistercian nuns in a single decade, as seen in Chapter 5.

Blanche's sons, particularly Louis IX and Alphonse of Poitiers continued supporting the communities of nuns she had founded, but they also did more. They endowed the Cistercian college, or Collège de Saint-Bernard, in Paris, with funds surely intended to pray for Blanche's soul—a large gift (180 livres per annum) was granted to it by Alphonse of Poitiers, who had been acting as sole regent of France on behalf of Louis IX since Blanche's death in 1252. Located on the left bank in the Latin quarter of Paris where "twenty student monks would live and study, among them thirteen priests," this college of priests took on a commemorative function with the gift from Alphonse of Poitiers. In that, it was similar to such foundations for souls as Clare College, Cambridge, England, founded by Elizabeth de Burgh, Countess of Clare, to pray for her own soul.[159] The cooperation of Pope Innocent IV in a series of bulls in 1254, many aimed at protecting Cistercian students in a hostile atmosphere, as Daniel LaCorte has explained, would have supported that commemoration as well, for Innocent IV had been Blanche's longtime supporter.[160] Undoubtedly the conditions of endowment by Alphonse of Poitiers for the College of Saint Bernard in Paris in 1253 suggest that the more important motivation was the commemoration of the Blanche of Castile. Today it is yet another medieval monument to Blanche and to Cistercian Gothic, and one that has only recently emerged from the damage of the Haussmann era to become a cultural center in the middle of Paris.[161]

Blanche's son Robert of Artois died on crusade soon after a gift of rights in Artois had been made in 1248 to the Cistercian nuns at Saint-Antoine.[162] Another son, the youngest, Charles of Anjou, also continued Blanche's support of the Cistercians. After his successful 1266 "crusade" that won for him the crown of Naples, he founded houses of Cistercian monks in 1277 at Santa Maria di Realvalle and at Santa Maria della Vittoria, both near his battlefields in southern Italy. At these "victory foundations" Cistercian Gothic architecture made its first appearance in that region.[163] Only Blanche's saintly daughter, Isabelle, would move away from the Cistercians. Shortly after her mother's death in 1252, Isabelle began the foundation of a house of Franciscan nuns at Longchamp in 1253.[164] While exercising her independence in disdaining her mother's close association with Cistercian nuns, Isabelle, neither marrying nor becoming a nun herself, nevertheless followed in her mother's footsteps in supporting a new group of religious women and a foundation for them.

CHAPTER 7

Saint-Antoine-des-Champs Outside Paris

Among the most successful houses of Cistercian nuns in the ecclesiastical province of Sens was Saint-Antoine-des Champs, an abbey of nuns founded just outside the eastern walls of Paris that were being built just before 1200 by Philip Augustus.[1] The new abbey of nuns at Saint-Antoine, although outside the walls, had many properties within them, including some near the older city gate at Porte Baudéer. The nuns of Saint-Antoine also acquired granges near the city that produced considerable supplies of grain, often in shares of communal production called *champart*. The nuns were developing vineyards. Even in suburban areas just outside the city walls, those vineyards would begin to meet some of the growing demand for wine in the city. The city of Paris was also becoming a textile production center, and rising numbers of water-powered mills were established for grinding grain and for preparing, or fulling, cloth, much of it woolen, so the nuns may have complemented their cereal production with a certain amount of sheep-raising. The evidence for their acquisition of pasture, however, is very limited. By the early modern period Saint-Antoine had exceeded in wealth many other religious foundations in Paris, and its properties had become concentrated in what became the Faubourg-Saint-Antoine, where its abbesses ruled as great royal feudatories.[2]

Saint-Antoine was described by the famous churchman Jacques de Vitry as being founded circa 1198 by a group of male and female penitents inspired by the reformer Fulk of Neuilly's preaching against usury and prostitution. Those penitents settled at a chapel dedicated to the hermit Saint Anthony just outside the walls of the city.[3] By 1204 the community was beginning to emerge as one of nuns, and Eudes de Sully, bishop of Paris, requested that the Cistercians incorporate the nuns of Saint-Antoine and those of Port-Royal (discussed in Chapter 4). A Cistercian document dated 1206 established the two as houses of Cistercian nuns, and both Saint-Antoine and Port-Royal would come to be under the direct authority of the abbot of Cîteaux.[4] In 1208 soon after the incorporation of Saint-Antoine's nuns, the Cistercian General Chapter promised its abbess that when the priests and lay brothers serving Saint-Antoine visited other abbeys of the order they would be treated just as if they were representing an abbey of monks.[5] The General Chapter also agreed in 1213, presumably in response to a petition from the abbess, that male Cistercians (abbots, monks, and lay brothers) visiting Paris were not to request food or lodging at Saint-Antoine.[6]

Saint-Antoine appears to have become the head of a small group of Cistercian houses for nuns following its customs.[7] Those customs were probably those established for the abbey in the 1230s by Stephen of Lexington, abbot of Savigny, who was acting on behalf of the abbot of Cîteaux when he conducted a visitation of that abbey, probably on the occasion of the consecration of its church in 1233. These customs recognized that Saint-Antoine's location so close to the Parisian capital meant that its nuns would be subjected to the demands of the rich and powerful. Saint-Antoine's abbesses were to preserve the nuns' enclosure and not admit sick or elderly seculars, unless they were found by four mature nuns to be honest and reverent. The abbess was to limit conversations between her nuns and seculars, and such interactions, when they occurred, were to be overseen by two other nuns. The nuns were not to stay out overnight in Paris or in any establishments there or even dine outside the abbey, unless with the lady queen and her entourage, or if it were for the community's "utility." The entrance of girls less than eight years old was forbidden, and those who then entered could not take their final vows until past adolescence. Except for the abbess, nuns were not to ride horses.[8]

Still the charters show that in 1243 Saint-Antoine's nuns took on the guardianship and education of two underage girls, Isabelle and Margaret, daughters of the late John Vicarius, a citizen of Paris. His two executors, themselves citizens, fulfilled his deathbed request in making the arrangement, assigning for those girls for as long as they were under the nuns' care a number of rents in the city of Paris: over a house on the street of the oven of Saint-Médard, over a stone house in the fish market in the *censive*, or lordship, of the abbess of Montmartre, over a house adjoining the cemetery of Saint-Honoré, over the house of Adam of Meulan located in the *censive* of the king, over the house of the students (*matriculariorum*) of Notre Dame adjoining a house belonging to the community of Val Profund, and so on.[9]

The young Louis IX and his mother, Blanche of Castile, attended the consecration of the church of Saint-Antoine in 1233. It was from Saint-Antoine that nuns would be sent to Queen Blanche's new foundation at Maubuisson in 1241/42, and Saint-Antoine was a staging place for various processions.[10] Located as it was just outside the city's eastern gates, the abbey was the first place at which King Louis IX displayed the Crown of Thorns in 1238; it was also the departure point for his 1248 crusade. The nuns of Saint-Antoine, in common with the religious of Royaumont, Maubuisson, Lys, and Port-Royal, received royal grants of *amortissement* (see Appendix 1) at the time of Louis IX's departure for his first crusade.

Although it came to resemble Maubuisson and Lys in wealth and size, Saint-Antoine was not a royal foundation. Often acquiring land within the king's *censive*, the area under royal lordship in the city of Paris, the nuns of Saint-Antoine tended to receive royal confirmations rather than royal gifts, that is, confirmations of the faits accomplis of his inferiors by the king in his capacity as a royal overlord. This is seen in 1261/62 in royal confirmations of its acquisitions in the countryside near Beaumont-sur-Oise; in the same document Louis IX confirmed to Saint-Antoine the Parisian rents granted by John Flament, citizen and agent of the Parisian cathedral chapter, and conveyances of income drawn on the royal Châtelet by Petronilla, widow of Jean Matthew, citizen of Paris.[11] She designated that those funds be used to provide the furs from which to make the nuns' cloaks.[12]

The Religious Community at Saint-Antoine and Its Documents

The nuns at Saint-Antoine-des-Champs were Cistercians. They performed the Divine Office, the weekly repetition in praise of God of the entire book of Psalms, and they organized the anniversaries celebrated at their abbey. Saint-Antoine's church had chapels that provided employment for priests who celebrated masses for patrons and provided the *cura monialium*. But it was the nuns' prayers with which donors wished to be associated, and young Parisian clerics who included Saint-Antoine on regular thirteenth-century preaching circuits asserted as much.[13] Thus one such preacher, Nicolas du Mans, preaching at Saint-Antoine in May 1273, told the nuns. "Surely, such donors made gifts to you *not* for your beautiful eyes, but in order to have a part in your prayers."[14] Many Parisian clergy, including members of the university, made bequests for anniversaries, confirming clerical faith in the value of Saint-Antoine's activities. The abbey also attracted the almsgiving of widows and other women from city and countryside; some of them became nuns there. The nuns provided security in retirement and a place of burial to such donors. Their primary mission, however, was prayer.

Saint-Antoine's nuns were often highly educated. Documents consulted for this study show the working Latinity of Saint-Antoine's nuns as well as their careful management of acquisitions using written records. Most original charters for Saint-Antoine are described as having been registered before the bishop's chancery or by the clerk of the *prévôté* at the king's palace at the Châtelet: a few of the latter were in some version of Old French, possibly Picard. Some may have been dictated to a scribe by the abbess herself.

Surviving documents include a medieval cartulary, Paris, AN LL1595, a parchment quarto volume of ninety-nine folios containing records of the abbey's Parisian property acquisitions from 1208 to 1303. Only some of the urban charters are included in full in this cartulary, suggesting a selection, possibly by a community member, but also an awareness of the cost of parchment, ink, and copying. The nuns selected 140 charters to be copied *in extenso*, although not always *in toto*, but they also referenced an additional 140 to 150 charters that were not copied. This means that a total of about 300 charters once existed, although some of the missing ones are found as loose charters in the archives. Charters that were left out were described, for instance when the text on folio 6r says: "cum ista invenientur confirmationem abbatis et conventus sancti Mauri Fossatensis" and "nota alia littera . . . quam sic incipiet"; on folio 38v, "cum istis duabus litteris precedentibus insimul" and "undecim alie littere in pluribus baculis posite que locuntur de eadem materia."[15] The text reveals that the archives had been organized by the nuns in cupboards or presses in the upper reaches of the church, on shelves where they were stored in small cloth bags. Eventually most of the seals dangling from those charters would also be placed inside cloth bags to protect them from damage.

A second, early modern volume, Paris, AN S*4386, remains more cartulary than inventory and concerns the abbey's rural holdings. While including dates, descriptions of land and donors, it may have omitted no longer current references about women entering the abbey. Its rubrication, added by the early modern copyist, has a tendency to misidentify some places: for instance, on folio 60r, where the rubricator identifies Saint-Antoine's properties at

Savigny (a holding at Aulnay today only indicated by a street name) as if at Savigny-le-Temple, still seen in the eastern Parisian suburbs near Montreuil-sur-Vincennes.[16]

Chapels were endowed at Saint-Antoine to commemorate souls. One was founded by Simon of Montfort in 1223 for the soul of the knight Robert of Mauvoisin, Simon's companion in arms.[17] More often it was widows who endowed chapels at Saint-Antoine. Lady Alice of Venisiac founded one in 1219.[18] Another chapel is documented for 1243 when the widow Isabelle gave an annual rent of thirty livres to support a chapel at Saint-Antoine where a priest would celebrate three anniversary masses accompanied by pittance meals—for her soul and for those of her two late husbands, Hugh Cuillier and Tybond of Grève.[19] In 1246 the widow Aalysia Preposita, in order to found a chapel at Saint-Antoine, left the abbey a house in the *censive* of the bishop of Paris that owed two livres in annual rent, as well as an eighth of a mill at Planche Mibray, later the site of the Pont-Notre-Dame that connected the right bank to the cathedral.[20] Likewise, in 1272 the recently widowed queen Marguerite of Provence founded a chapel for Louis IX's soul at Saint-Antoine.[21] There were men too who made gifts to Saint-Antoine, some of them clerics. In 1260 Humbert Tochard, a canon of Beauvais, gave a house behind the royal palace of the Châtelet and rents from three other houses in Paris to support a chapel at Saint-Antoine.[22] Such chapels for donors' souls undoubtedly affected the architecture of Saint-Antoine's church, although little is known for sure. Its church remains were built over in the 1950s.[23]

A number of urban conveyances to Saint-Antoine came from clerics, a fact that underlines the respect in which the nuns were held. Such clerical gifts were often postmortem ones, made to establish annuities for themselves or relatives for what remained of a lifetime. For example, in 1210 Sagan, *matricularius* of the cathedral of Notre-Dame gave Saint-Antoine's nuns half a house in the Clos Brunel (a well-known clerical enclave in the Latin quarter) in a postmortem gift "so that the nuns would celebrate a perpetual anniversary for his soul."[24] A substantial house in which Thibaut of Bray currently lived, located in the *censive* of Saint-Magloire and across from the house of the king, was granted to Saint-Antoine in 1213 by Peter of Nemours, bishop of Paris, who described it as a house he had purchased for seventy livres; it was confirmed to the nuns by the abbot of Saint-Magloire.[25]

Such clerical donors thus sometimes stated explicitly that they were not diverting church assets, but had purchased the property with their own funds. For example, Eudes, chaplain of the King's Chapel at Beaumont-sur-Oise, had purchased two parcels of vineyards at Champagnes near Beaumont and granted them to Saint-Antoine in 1248, "in pure and perpetual alms for his parents' souls and his own, for celebrating an anniversary annually in the church of those nuns."[26] An annuity was funded in 1289/90 by Master Martin, canon of Compiègne, who granted Saint-Antoine substantial vineyards at Montreuil for his soul and for an annual life rent of six muids of wine.[27]

Less generous was the conveyance by John of Paris, master of the scholars from Soissons, acknowledging that he was responsible for distributing thirty livres in alms for the souls of Hugh of Provins, late prior of the canons of Saint-Germain, John of Septmons, bourgeois of Soissons, and Daniel Pelliparius, citizen of Paris. As executor he avoided paying out cash for those thirty livres, instead granting in 1229 an income source to the nuns of Saint-Antoine, "because of their poverty, devotion, and religiosity." This was apparently an existing "increased rent" of forty sous (two livres) owed annually over a house in Paris not far from the Halles on the rue de la Ferronérie. He noted that this was half of the sum owed to himself and his sister by the tenants there. One can only speculate about why he did not give the more appropriate rent of three livres in return for the thirty livres bequest, as well as about whether his sister, Petronilla of Champs, was indeed a nun at Saint-Antoine-des-Champs or who the tenants might be. On the face of it, this is the action of a rather churlish executor, but it may be that he had been made executor precisely in order to make him pay cash owed to those seeking commemoration.[28]

Other gifts for remembrance came from knights from outside the city, the class from which the abbey's early abbesses were drawn. It was out of concern for his own soul that in 1209 the knight William of Galande gave Saint-Antoine an annual rent of two livres from the passage tolls at Tournan-en-Brie east of Paris.[29] In 1226 and again in 1239, members of the Marly family, the feudal lords who had founded Port-Royal, made gifts for anniversary masses at Saint-Antoine.[30] In 1238 Lord Philip of Montfort made gifts for "an anniversary for the soul of my late wife, the most dear Eleanor, who was buried in the church of Saint-Antoine."[31] Gifts made for anniversary masses by the counts of Beaumont and their wives in 1248 were probably occasioned by the departure of Louis IX and his followers on his first crusade; later gifts came from the counts of Beaumont in 1274/75 and 1290.[32] In 1256 Raoul and Margaret of Villenovette gave three arpents of arable land to Saint-Antoine for their anniversary masses.[33] In 1261 the knight Lord Simon *dictus Monachus* of Ville Guiraud also made a gift to

Saint-Antoine for an anniversary to be celebrated in its church.[34] In 1285 there would be a grant made for an anniversary mass to be celebrated for the soul of the Duke of Brabant.[35]

Recruiting Widows and an Important Donor of Cash

The nuns provided essential social services, not just for young orphaned girls in the city, but for aged men and women, perhaps particularly for aged widows, who as donors often became pensioners bringing Parisian properties with them.[36] The charters suggest that at Saint-Antoine early donors and recruits were often widows seeking a sisterlike status with the abbey, but who continued to live in their own homes until death. They made postmortem gifts of their domiciles in return for lifetime annuities and promises of anniversary masses.[37]

It is important to emphasize these urban widows who were early and continuing donors to the community of Saint-Antoine; the urban cartulary is replete with them.[38] In 1210 Basilia, widow of William Fovet, with their son granted a house in the Clos Brunel.[39] In 1217, Emelina, widow of Robert Torti of Saint-Séverin, gave a postmortem gift of two *cameras*, or chambers, which she had acquired by her own purchase on the left bank of Paris at Saint-Séverin near the Grande Rue Saint-Jacques; she gave this dwelling along with a courtyard (*platea*) and stable, all of which she would continue to use for her lifetime.[40] Likewise in 1218 a certain widow Agnes, for herself and her late husband Robert le Ber, gave the nuns a house in Paris; in 1225, the king's baker, Peter le Ber (a brother or son of the first?), and his wife, again an Agnes, gave rights over what appears to be the same house, located in territory owned by the canons of Saint-Médard.[41] In 1235, Petronilla, widow of Thibaut Forre, gave a house to the nuns and made arrangements to live as a sister in secular garb.[42]

Maria, widow of Richard Arconis, gave income from a house in the *censiva* of the lord King in 1258.[43] The widow Girendis in 1261 made a gift of a Parisian house with income that would fund a distribution of food to the poor along with an anniversary mass and pittance; that distribution of food to the poor was to be overseen by the abbess of Saint-Antoine and Richard Anglicus.[44] In 1263 another widow, probably also a bourgeois, Genovefa, the widow of the late Reguier the Fleming, also gave rents over a house in Paris.[45] Jeanne, widow of the late Nicholas of Tria, gave an increased rent of eleven livres in 1269.[46]

In 1284 Agatha of Lyons, widow of the late William Marshall, made a gift of income.[47]

Some of the gifts to the nuns of Saint-Antoine can show considerable generosity in the face of personal tragedy, when donors mentioned what had motivated a gift. Particularly poignant was the 1289 postmortem conveyance in which Philip Fauvel and Aveline, his wife, granted Saint-Antoine land in the countryside at Bourgeol near its grange at Aulnay: "Having no heirs of their bodies . . . and because of the great devotion they have for the nuns of Saint-Antoine and for the benefits of the Divine Office, prayers, almsgiving and other charitable activities done at that abbey each day."[48] In this case Saint-Antoine was the recipient of their wealth because the nuns' grange of Savigny/Aulnay was nearby.

There were also such cases from within the city. In 1208 William of Bonne Nouvelle, following the death of his son, promised the nuns a fourth of a Parisian house after his own death (granted ten years later). Those gifts made for a dying child brought Saint-Antoine portions of a house on the Île-de-la-Cité on a major thoroughfare, the Street of the Marmozets.[49] In 1242, another couple, presumably without heirs, gave all their property to the nuns after their deaths, but retained usufruct for their lifetimes.[50] These examples remind us of a tendency among late medieval urban populations to not reproduce themselves and for cities to require continual recruits from the country-side.[51] In only a few cases were donors to Saint-Antoine seen guaranteeing their heavenly repose by making gifts for anniversary masses to more than one religious community. Indeed it is exceptional when in 1275 a certain Agnes and her husband John Sarracen, a royal official, made postmortem gifts for anniversary masses at several religious foundations: three livres to Saint-Antoine, three livres to Maubuisson, and the same to the Benedictine nuns at Chelles, where two of Agnes's sisters were nuns.[52]

Recruits to Saint-Antoine gradually came to include younger women as well, often the daughters of bourgeois families. Among them was Blanche of Paciac, who had a charter made in 1277 in recognition of the cash donations she had made to Saint-Antoine when she entered the abbey circa 1259/60.[53] Blanche was the daughter of Raoul of Paciac, citizen and possibly notary of Paris, and his wife Sedilia; her parents made a donation to Saint-Antoine at the time of Blanche's entrance.[54] In 1259 just before she became a nun, Blanche had given 400 livres *parisis* to Saint-Antoine; she gave an additional 1,500 livres *tournois* in 1260.

Table 19. Saint-Antoine: Purchases Using Blanche of Paciac's Cash Donations

---

- One manor with all its appurtenances at Champagnes (for 280 livres)
- Three arpents of arable land there from Lord John of Champagnes, knight
- A quarter part of the *champart* at Savigny adjoining grange of the Aulnay
- Four arpents of arable land adjoining the Sauveté-Saint-Antoine
- Four arpents of land in the territory of Praelles/Pradelles near Aulnay
- Two arpents of land above the fishpond of Praelles/Pradelles near Aulnay
- The *Pressoir Majeur* at Montreuil-sur-Vincennes
- Fifteen arpents of land and rents at the grange of Bordes
- Eight livres annual rent from the *péage* (toll) at Franqueville, north of Paris
- Five livres annual rent on a house in Paris in the *censive* of Saint-Magloire

---

Source: Paris, AN, S*4386, fols. 24v–26r (1264) and 75r–76r (1277).

The funds Blanche brought allowed Saint-Antoine's nuns to consolidate major holdings, particularly at three centers that would become the nuns' major granges: Aulnay and Savigny, Champagnes, and Montreuil-sur-Vincennes. In 1277, those properties were recorded in a charter issued by the abbess of Saint-Antoine and the abbot of Cîteaux: "in order that Blanche may be remembered perpetually and especially after her death she be included in the prayers of the nuns serving the Lord at this house."[55] See the list in Table 19, but the purchases described in that charter are seen throughout this chapter.

Saint-Antoine's Early Abbesses and the Grange at Savigny/Aulnay

Noblewomen, also usually widows, from the countryside around Paris were Saint-Antoine's first leaders. One of them, Amicia de Savigny, in 1205 came before the dowager queen, Adele of Champagne, to register a conveyance to those nuns.[56] The charter records that Amicia, widow of the late Renaud de Savigny, had taken the religious habit at Saint-Antoine and had granted the nuns rights over tolls at Lieu-Saint-Sauve. She became an early abbess of Saint-Antoine.[57]

Another early charter is from Lady Agnes of Cressonessart dated 1206; it mentions the "brothers and sisters living at an infirmary" there.[58] Agnes was the widow of Dreux II of Cressonessart who had died on the road returning from Zara in 1203. Her brother, Robert of Mauvoisin, was a crusader as well, departing against the Albigensians in 1209. Just before his departure on that campaign, Robert of Mauvoisin had granted land at Aulnay with the consent of his wife, Cecilia of Chevreuse, and of his feudal overlord, Walter of Aulnay. The latter promised a gift of twenty-five livres in rents for Robert's soul "if he died on that campaign."[59] Upon his safe return in 1211 Robert confirmed his own earlier gift: "Forty arpents of arable land between Savigny and Aulnay and five arpents in the meadows of Aulnay at Pont David, with the tithe over those meadows and an arpent of land just outside the village of Aulnay where Robert had lordship and where the nuns were allowed to make a very large house for their shepherds."[60] Also in 1211 Robert confirmed an exchange of two arpents of land at Savigny between the nuns of Saint-Antoine and Ida, the wife of Bertrand, and their son Herman; a transaction also approved in 1212 by Adam of Beaumont and his wife Isabelle.[61]

An early chapel at Saint-Antoine was founded for Robert of Mauvoisin's soul. Conveyances for it were made by a number of crusading nobles with familiar names like Simon of Montfort.[62] Already in 1215 Robert's sister Agnes had made a gift for that chapel.[63] In 1223 the executors for Robert, including the crusader Simon of Montfort, funded this chapel at Saint-Antoine for his soul "and in honor of Saint Peter," making additional conveyances at Aulnay.[64] Already in 1216, the crusade leader Simon of Montfort had given Saint-Antoine five livres annual rent "for his own soul and for that of Robert of Mauvoisin"; gifts to Saint-Antoine from Matthew of Montmorency (whose sister was married to Simon of Montfort) may also have been for Robert of Mauvoisin's soul. In 1223 Robert of Longpoirier and his wife Isabelle confirmed to the nuns what was given in alms by Robert of Mauvoisin; they also gave to the nuns for their own souls an additional gift: "Whatever they had in the fief and *censives* at Aulnay and Savigny, whether in arable lands, meadows, vineyards or whatever other things, saving only their own and their heirs' rights in cens and *champart*."[65] Robert of Mauvoisin and his wife Cecilia of Chevreuse had also made gifts to Port-Royal, and in 1221, probably after Cecilia's death, Amicia, abbess of Saint-Antoine, retrieved that land at Aulnay that Robert had earlier given to Port-Royal.[66]

At the same time, following the successive deaths of her second husband and son, both named Dreux of Cressonessart, Agnes of Cressonessart, sister of Robert of Mauvoisin, became an important recruit and patron of Saint-Antoine. Already in 1208 Lady Agnes had purchased lands at Aulnay located near those of her brother Robert in order to convey them to the nuns of Saint-Antoine. She had paid 260 livres to Andrew of Ternel, his mother, Hersendis, and his wife, another Agnes, for land and a small dwelling at

Aulnay/Savigny.[67] As reported in a document from the bishop of Paris dated 1212, the funds for that purchase came from the earlier sale in 1208 by Agnes of Cressonessart to Lord Philip, bishop of Beauvais, of her marital property (*dotalicium*) at Gerberoy from her first marriage, that to William of Gerberoy.[68] (See Figure 10.) In 1212, that property at Aulnay was granted to Saint-Antoine as a postmortem gift by Lady Agnes for the salvation of her soul and those of her two late husbands, William of Gerberoy and Dreux II of Cressonessart, and for her deceased son, Dreux III of Cressonessart. Lady Agnes explained in her document from 1212 what she expected in the meantime: "The nuns were to cultivate that land at their own expense [*a propriis sumptibus*], giving half of what it produced each year to Agnes for the rest of her life;" in addition to their taking half of the produce, the nuns were to take an additional muid of winter wheat from Agnes's share of the produce to fund the anniversaries she had requested.[69] Agnes's confirmation of all this in 1213 also mentions another twenty arpents of woodland that she had conveyed to the nuns of Saint-Antoine.[70]

In 1214, a charter issued by her eldest surviving son, Thibaut, lord of Cressonessart, states that Agnes had made a gift to the sisters at Bruyères and that she had taken the religious habit as a sister of Saint-Antoine.[71] Since she had already made conveyances to Saint-Antoine that were to provide her an annuity for life, it is likely that what he referred to was her living in the status of a sister at the home she had retained. In 1216 Agnes made an additional gift to Saint-Antoine of whatever she held in fief at Aulnay from Lord Peter of Floriac; Lord Peter's confirmation of this conveyance definitely does not refer to Lady Agnes of Cressonessart as abbess there.[72]

With regard to Agnes's career as patron and sister associated with Saint-Antoine it is helpful to consider Saint-Antoine's acquisition of income from tolls at one of several ports on the Seine, downriver from Paris, at Mantes. In 1221 Agnes of Cressonessart and her sons from her second marriage granted the nuns of Saint-Antoine five livres from the tolls at the port at Mantes.[73] These original five livres were doubled in 1225, when the nuns purchased another five livres of that income from Agnes's son Thibaut of Cressonessart and his wife, Elizabeth, with the consent of Agnes's younger brother Guy, who had also confirmed the earlier gift for the chapel for Robert's soul.[74] By 1225/26 it appears that Agnes was no longer alive. Since the conveyances by Lady Agnes in 1221 show that she was not then abbess, the only possibility of her being so is during the brief window between 1221 and 1225. Although Agnes was buried in the church, it was probably as a "founder;" she probably did not become abbess.

Mauvoisin Family

Three siblings:
Guy of Mauvoisin, becomes Franciscan

Robert[1] of Mauvoisin (d. 1223) m. Cecilia of Chevreuse (d. ca. 1221?)

Agnes of Mauvoisin (d. 1225) m. William of Gerberey (no issue)
She became Lady Agnes of Cressonessart when she m. 1185

Cressonessart Family

Lady Hersendis of Cressonessart (mentioned 1145), her son
Dreux I (mentioned 1165) m. Emelina (mentioned 1177)

Dreux II of Cressonessart (d. 1203) son of Dreux I[2]
They have five children:

Dreux III of Cressonessart (d. ca. 1212)
Thibaut, lord of Cressonessart (1212–?), m. Elizabeth.
Robert? Adeline/Emeline? Beatrix?

Documents that support the argument that Agnes did not become abbess at Saint-Antoine:

1212 Agnes arranges endowment from Saint-Antoine in her own house for life; she was at least a quasi-nun[3]
1214 Her son Thibaut mentions her taking the religious habit; she may be a sister, but not abbess[4]
1214 Thibaut and Elizabeth confirm gift of tolls at Mantes to Saint-Antoine with Agnes
1221 Thibaut, Elizabeth, Agnes, and Guy of Mauvoisin confirm these tolls to Amicia, abbess of Saint-Antoine[5]
1225 Thibaut and Elizabeth confirm tolls at Mantes with Guy, but without Agnes. Did she die ca. 1225?[6]

Sources: *Cartulaire de Port-Royal*, Paris, AN, S*4386, *Cartulaire de Saint-Antoine*; Eugène de L'Épinois, *Recherches historiques et critiques sur l'ancien comtés et les comtes de Clermont en Beauvoisis du XIe au XIIIe siècle* (Beauvais, 1877). p. 204 n. 4; *Cartulaire de l'abbaye de Notre-Dame d'Ourscamp de l'ordre de Cîteaux, fondée en 1129, au diocèse de Noyon*, ed. Achille Piegné-Delacourt (Amiens: Lemens, 1865); Sean L. Field, *The Beguine, the Angel, and the Inquisitor: The Trials of Marguerite Porete and Guiard of Cressonessart* (Notre Dame, IN: Notre Dame University Press, 2012), pp. 270–72, nn. 70–76.

1. *Cartulaire de Port-Royal*, no. 26 (1216); 56 (1221/22); 15, 68 cf. Paris, AN, S*4386, fols. 62r–63r (1221).
2. On Drew II, see Épinois, p. 204 n. 4; *Cartulaire de Ourscamp* pp. 4, 384–87, where Agnes and Dreux II appear together in 1197 and 1202 at Ourscamp; by 1203 Dreux II had died, probably during return from Zara with Simon of Montfort.
3. Paris, AN, S*4386, fol. 61v (1212): bishop of Paris reported that property at Aulnay was granted to Saint-Antoine as a postmortem gift by Lady Agnes for her soul and those of her two late husbands, William of Gerberey and Dreux II of Cressonessart; by fol. 61v (1214), her son, Drew III, is dead; she expected the nuns to cultivate the land at their own expense, giving her half its produce for life, and to live in her house.
4. Paris, AN, S4373 (1213/14), Saint-Antoine loose parchments: Lady Agnes gives land at Courdemanche to the sisters of Bruyères; her son Thibaut mentioned that Agnes had taken religious dress; in AN L1014, liasse 1, she is described as Sister Agnes in 1215.
5. Paris, AN, S*4386, fol. 6r–6v (1221): Guy of Mauvoisin, a Franciscan, confirmed Agnes's gift of income from tolls at Mantes, having gotten the assent of her brother Robert and her son Thibault I. Abbess Amicia appears in 1221, but is this the same Amicia in 1230 and 1242/43? (See Sean Field, *The Beguine*, pp. 270–72 nn. 70–76.)
6. Paris, AN, S*4386, fol. 6r–6v (1225): Guy's confirmation without mention of Agnes of one hundred livres of income at Mantes sold by Thibault I and his wife Elizabeth.

FIGURE 10. Genealogy: Agnes of Cressonessart (Mauvoisin) and family.

Soon after the conveyance of tolls at Mantes, income from tolls on the Seine River at Conflans-Sainte-Honorine was also being acquired by Saint-Antoine from members of the Montfort and Montmorency families, friends of the Mauvoisin and Cressonessart families. By 1250 Saint-Antoine had annual rents of thirteen livres there. By 1340 those rents at Conflans-Sainte-Honorine had increased to thirty-six livres per year.[75]

While conveyances to the nuns of Saint-Antoine from the Mauvoisin and Cressonessart families were vital to its early existence, the nuns also acquired rights at Aulnay by purchase. In 1211 they paid the knight Peter of Beaumarchais and his wife Margaret thirty-six livres for twelve arpents of land located between Aulnay and Blanc-Mésnil; they also paid six livres to the knight John of Belfont for six sous in annual rents over those lands, receiving the seller's promise that his son, Little John, would confirm this; by 1220 it was probably the younger John of Belfont who granted land between Savigny and the village of Gonesse to the nuns of Saint-Antoine; they were in return to release two of his tenants from rents owed on that land.[76] In 1226 the nuns paid seven livres for two arpents of arable land at Aulnay, which Jeanne of Aulnay had inherited from her mother, Erembours. By 1236, when these holdings had come to be described as "in the lordship of Saint-Antoine," the nuns had acquired quarries from John of Chelles, as well as three arpents of land at Luat for construction of the grange at Savigny.[77] (See Map 6.)

In the 1230s Saint-Antoine began to acquire rights north of Aulnay and Savigny. At Louvres in 1233, the nuns acquired a mortgage over the tithes on thirty-three arpents of land at Fosse-Ibout for thirty livres; in 1238 they paid seventy-five livres to acquire *la main morte* over twenty-four sous of annual minute cens to be collected on seventy arpents of land there; in 1255 additional land at Fosse-Ibout was acquired in an exchange with Saint-Martin-des-Champs in Paris.[78] There were also acquisitions at Épiais and Mauregard in the 1240s and 1250s, including an *amortissement* for the nuns' acquisitions granted by Eudes, son of the Duke of Burgundy.[79] Saint-Antoine paid ten livres in 1247 for a single arpent of land at Mauregard that had been held by a priest called Lord Renaud of Montigny Neuve and by another Brother Renaud, the rectors of a *domus Dei* at Montigny Neuve, but there is no indication that this property at Montigny was incorporated into the holdings of Saint-Antoine.[80] Some of these acquisitions at Savigny and Aulnay from the 1260s had been purchases made with Blanche of Paciac's cash entrance gifts: the charter of 1277 lists ten arpents of arable land at Aulnay, of which

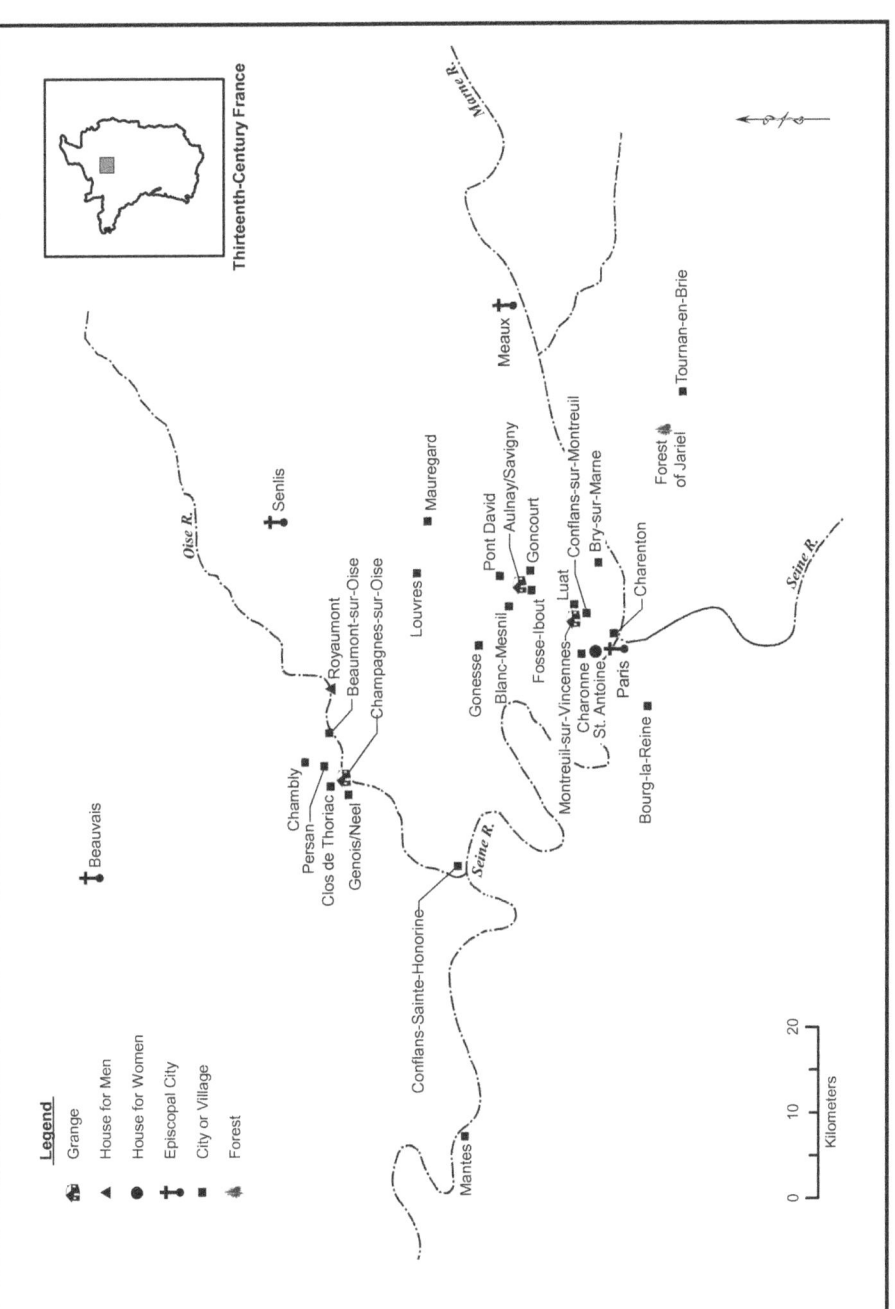

MAP 6. Saint-Antoine's granges and properties in the Parisian countryside. Map created by Gordon Thompson.

four adjoined the Sauveté-Saint-Antoine, four were at Praelles or Pradelles, and two were above the fishpond there.[81] (See Table 19 again.)

In 1261 the nuns of Saint-Antoine also began attempting to collect income they were owed at Aulnay by making written claims against Master Geoffrey of Beaumont, lord of Aulnay and canon of Beauvais. The nuns asserted that Master Geoffrey's late brother John of Beaumont had granted them a rent of forty sous (two livres) per annum for the celebration of his own anniversary. They stated that the abbey had not been paid this for the last fifteen years, and they were by then owed thirty livres. Additional sums were due, moreover, because Manasses, late dean of Orléans, another of Master Geoffrey's relatives, had left Saint-Antoine thirty livres for his soul, none of which had been paid. Master Geoffrey responded by paying the nuns an annual rent of one hundred sous (five livres) drawn from twelve arpents of arable lands in his *coutures* at Goncourt in Aulnay, but seemingly did not repay any of the arrears.[82] Still the nuns expanded their revenues from those twelve new arpents of land, paying eighteen livres in 1262 to purchase from John *dictus Vignor* of Aulnay and his wife Poncia their rights over the four arpents of arable land at Savigny that had been ceded earlier by Master Geoffrey.[83] New rents were granted to the nuns a decade later, when in March 1274/75 executors for the late nobleman Peter, once lord of Beaumont, Count of Montauban and Albi, *camerarius* of the king of Sicily (Charles of Anjou) paid seven livres in annual income for an anniversary mass for Peter's soul.[84]

Beginning in the 1260s the nuns' acquisitions at Aulnay and Savigny were smaller ones: often consolidating existing holdings and often sold to them by bourgeois investors. In 1265 the nuns paid Andreas of Aulnay, bourgeois of Saint-Denis, and his wife Eva twenty-four sous for half an arpent of land at Savigny; in 1267 the nuns paid two livres to Walter Pastillarius, a dealer in dyestuffs, for a piece of arable land at Aulnay; in 1268/69 they paid eight livres to Andreas, *dictus* Ensin, of Aulnay, and his wife Ysetia for the *champart* over three arpents of arable land; in 1272 they paid forty-five sous for an arpent of arable land at Aulnay to Peter Osanna and Emelina his wife; then in 1275 they paid three livres for an arpent and a half in the *champart* there to Beatrice Flament of Aulnay.[85] In 1279 again in a mixed gift and sale, the nuns paid forty sous for their rights in the *champart communal* to Anglicus and his wife Petronilla; the couple in turn gave the nuns additional rights over an area abutting one held already by the abbey.[86]

Another wave of such cash purchases at Aulnay occurred in the late 1290s, probably using the 320 livres that had come to the nuns in the conveyance in 1296 from Jean Popin following the entrance of his daughter Petronilla into the abbey.[87] In 1298 they paid ninety-five livres to Thibaut Creuse of Aulnay and Eremburgis, his wife, for twelve arpents of land in the territory of Aulnay; the majority of that land was adjoining that of the nuns on at least one side; they also paid thirty livres to William of Noisy and his wife Jeanne, residents of Gonesse, for four arpents of land between Gonesse and Savigny; in 1299 they paid seventeen livres to Jeanne Paridous of Gonesse for an arpent and a half of cultivable land, which she had inherited, in the *champart communal* of Aulnay adjoining that of the nuns.[88] Such purchases were enhanced in 1299 by a gift in alms made by Guibert of Fontenoy of three arpents of land at Aulnay in the *champart communal* of Savigny, also adjoining the land of the nuns.[89] Such acquisitions provided Saint-Antoine with a substantial estate of grain-producing properties at Aulnay, located less than twenty kilometers northeast of the abbey.

Suburban Properties: Charonne, Charenton, Bry, and the Grange of Montreuil

From an early date Saint-Antoine's nuns also began to acquire properties not far from the abbey site in the village of Charonne (near today's Père Lachaise cemetery), in the *censive*, or lordship, of the canons of Saint-Magloire. In 1218 Gautier of Senlis and his wife Halois granted Saint-Antoine a postmortem gift of seven quarts of wine paid annually during the octave of the feast of Saint-Rémy (October 1) from vines at Charonne near the *clos* of Saint-Martin-des-Champs.[90] Genovefa, widow of Eudes Coci of Saint-Magloire, in her last will granted ten sous directly to Saint-Antoine and an additional five to fund a pittance for the soul of her daughter, Annette.[91]

Such property at Charonne located in the *censive* of Saint-Magloire and conveyed to Saint-Antoine in wills that are found in Saint-Magloire's archives was often that which would be returned to Saint-Magloire by Saint-Antoine's nuns by way of property exchanges. Thus in 1230 Amicia, abbess of Saint-Antoine, ceded to Saint-Magloire income of three sous annually over a house in Saint-Magloire's lordship that the late Thibaut de la Chaîne had once granted to Saint-Antoine.[92] The late Terrence Ruf had given three arpents less one *quartier* of vineyards with a rent of five and a half sous annually paid in the octave of Saint-Denis to Saint-Antoine, as well as justice, tithes, and fees for pressing grapes into wine near the *roue* at Charonne.[93] The nuns conceded this income back to Saint-Magloire in return for other benefits that Saint-Magloire had given them, but the nuns retained the right to use the winepress at that *roue*.[94] In 1268, Saint-Magloire confirmed to Saint-Antoine's nuns their rights at Charonne: "In our *fundus* and lordship: half an arpent of vineyard sited at the *roue*, and a *quartier* of vineyards in *la main morte* on Plasterer's Street, which paid a rent of three sous."[95] The nuns were not to sell those rights to anyone else, and Saint-Magloire reserved its tithes and the fees for pressing grapes.

Such acquisitions close to the city also included income from a mill at Charenton, southeast of Paris. The same knight William of Galande who had given rights to tolls earlier, together with his wife Alice circa 1210 made the first gift of rights at Charenton to the nuns: a muid of grain to be paid to Saint-Antoine on Christmas from their mill there.[96] In 1227 Eustachia of Villespede gave those nuns another livre in cash to be paid annually from her rents at Charenton on the feast of Saint-Denis.[97] Then in 1244 a priest named John and another named Simon of Vincennes asserted that Simon's mother, the late Basilia of Vincennes, had left Saint-Antoine three sestiers of wheat from the mill at Charenton to be paid annually during the octave of the feast of Saint-Rémy.[98]

Sometimes early donors in the suburbs were clerics interested in gaining burial or anniversaries for female relatives, as in the case of Fontenay near Sarcelles, north of the city. Peter, the priest at Fontenay, and his brother Gazus in 1213 conveyed vineyards to the nuns for the soul of their mother who had elected to be buried at Saint-Antoine. They specified that if the nuns sold the three plots of vines and a garden next to the church of Fontenay, the abbey should replace those rights with other vineyards.[99]

Another early postmortem gift from a cleric allowed the nuns to acquire a fishing weir on the Marne River east of Paris and meadows, which may have included sheep grazing after hay was cut, at the port of Bry-sur-Marne. The details show how pieces of meadow were consolidated. In 1217 executors for Roger, a canon of Notre-Dame, gave Saint-Antoine two arpents of meadow at Bry. The nuns of Saint-Antoine may have been anticipating this gift, for they had paid eighty-five livres in 1214 for a single arpent of meadow on the Marne River along with the fishing weir there; the sellers, the knight Simon of Bry and his wife Margaret, along with Geoffrey of Toulon and his wife Heloise, promised that the third owner, the knight Peter of Bobez,

Table 20. Saint-Antoine: Acquisition of Meadows at Bry-sur-Marne

Years	Property Acquired	Cost
Before 1214	2 arpents of meadow	Bequest fulfilled in 1217
1214	1 arpent of meadow and 1 fishing weir	85 livres
1219	1 1/2 arpents of meadow and lordship	14 livres
1225–34	2 arpents of meadow and vineyards	29 livres in various acts
1247	2 arpents of meadow along the Marne	20 livres
1257	1 arpent of meadow	10 livres
Totals	9 1/2 arpents of meadow, etc., and 1 weir	158 livres

Source: Paris, AN, S*4386, fols. 18v–21v, early modern cartulary/inventory.

would confirm this conveyance once he had returned from fighting the Albigensian heretics; he did so.

The nuns' possession of this holding was secured in 1219 when the knight Bouchard of Bry and his relatives granted their rights of lordship. The nuns also purchased another arpent and a half from Adam Carpentarius of Bry and his son for fourteen livres in that year. Acquisitions in the next decade (1225–34) cost a total of twenty-nine livres for additional pieces of meadow and already-planted vineyards of about two more arpents. In 1247 another two arpents of meadow along the river were acquired for twenty livres. Overall, the nuns had acquired a weir, fishing rights and about eight and a half arpents of what was primarily meadowland and had spent 148 livres. In one last purchase made in 1257, presumably to round out their holdings in those meadows, the nuns of Saint-Antoine probably expended ten livres for a single additional arpent of meadow, described as "located between the meadow of the lord king and that of the lords of Bry," from the butcher John of Gournay, suggesting that the latter had been using the area for holding and fattening stock before slaughter.[100] This makes the total 158 livres. (See Table 20.)

The meadows and fishing at Bry, like properties at Charonne and Charenton, were relatively minor acquisitions just outside Paris. The grange at Montreuil-sur-Vincennes would be considerably more extensive and more costly. Acquisitions there also began early. In 1212 Peter of Nemours, bishop of Paris, confirmed to the nuns of Saint-Antoine a gift of three and a half arpents of vines at Montreuil-sur-Vincennes made by the late Hervé Marshal, probably a canon of the cathedral. These vineyards at Montreuil, located just outside the eastern walls of Paris, had been purchased by Hervé from the abbot of Saint-Victoire of Paris. Following the initial gift, over the next several decades the nuns developed an important grange for wine production at Montreuil and what had been described in 1212 as located "in the *censive* of Saint-Victoire" had been developed by 1232 into a holding that had begun to be described as "in the *censive* of Saint-Antoine."[101]

The process of development was relatively slow. In 1216 two local residents, Frederick and William of the Petit Montreuil, conveyed to Saint-Antoine's nuns two arpents of vineyards at Soucy or Saulsaie (literally, willow grove).[102] Two years later, in 1218, Hersendis, wife of Garnier of Saint-Lazare, confirmed their gift.[103] In 1220, John, Count of Beaumont-sur-Oise, confirmed the conveyance made by his late wife, the countess Jeanne, of thirty sous in annual rents over their lordship at Montreuil.[104] In 1237 Stephanie, widow of Stephen Ruf, gave the nuns another three arpents of arable land at Soucy.[105] In 1232 the nuns paid seven livres to Roger of Montreuil-sur-Vincennes, son of the late Galardus and his wife Ermensendis for three *quartiers* of vines in the *censive* of those nuns; in 1235 the nuns purchased three and a half arpents of land from Saint-Victoire, described as at Montreuil in the *censive* of Saint-Victoire. Some of these holdings adjoined the canons' land at Luat; the rest were located behind Saint-Victoire's house in the villa of Montreuil-sur-Vincennes. The nuns also acquired another arpent of land at Bourg-la-Reine from Saint-Victoire. In 1242 the nuns paid four livres to Aimeric Jules and Emelina his wife for a *quartier* of vines from her dowry lands at Montreuil. These adjoined the winepress of Luat, described as in the *censive* of Saint-Antoine. In 1252 the nuns paid twenty livres to Squire Peter of the Petit Montreuil for a rent of six muids of red wine to be paid annually by the residents of three houses in the nearby town of Villejuif.[106] In 1287 Marie, Countess of Grandpré and Lady of Montreuil, gave the nuns an annual rent of one muid of wheat for the relief of her soul and those of her ancestors and for services on the feast of the Purification of the Blessed Mary and at Easter; this muid of wheat was to be paid to the nuns at the time of the fair that the nuns held at Montreuil-sur-Vincennes.[107] The importance of the grange, where a fair would presumably be held annually, is underlined in this conveyance.

These conveyances are all found in the early modern cartulary Paris, AN, S*4386. On folio 45r of that cartulary, the copyist commented, "These next three conveyances from 1255 are of central importance for Montreuil." The first of these concerns the same Peter, squire of the Petit Montreuil, to whom the nuns had paid twenty livres in 1252. In 1255 Saint-Antoine's nuns paid more: fifty livres for what was ostensibly only a rent of fifteen deniers annually over two arpents of vineyards at Montreuil, but the next charter suggests there was more there, and it raises the possibility that the first document had been truncated when copied. That second charter from 1255 concerned "two *mansi* and nineteen arpents of woodland, sixty-eight arpents of arable land, two and a half arpents of vineyards, and sixty-two sous of minute cens at Montreuil." This was a conveyance by a different Peter, the knight Peter Cambellarius, granting all his rights in pure alms to Saint-Antoine in a larger fief earlier held from him by Squire Peter.[108] In 1255, the king granted to the nuns of Saint-Antoine an *amortissement* over this property at the time when the knight Peter Cambellarius's four sons confirmed their father's conveyance: they are described as knights and brothers, Peter and Adam Cambellarii, Matthew and Adam of Villebayonne.[109] These items are among those designated by the copyist as among the most important, probably because they constitute the grange center, but they constitute only the first of three groups of important items impacted by Blanche of Paciac's gift.

The second group would be those charters that concern a property at nearby Conflans-sur-Montreuil for which the nuns acquired rights from a group of urban purchasers, who may in fact have been land-speculators. In 1259 the nuns paid 46 livres to John of Bobigny, described as a draper and citizen of Paris, and his wife Margaret for their rights at Conflans. In the same year the nuns also paid 56 livres to Raoul Fourre for his rights there and then they paid 198 livres to Peter of Buciac, seen elsewhere among the urban charters, and his wife and heirs.[110] The amounts paid by the nuns in 1259 totaled 400 livres. The property at Conflans is described as consisting of "a winepress called the Pressoir Majeur, tithes over that winepress and its vines, twenty sous in minute cens over vineyards there, another two and a half arpents of vineyards, oats, twelve hens, and twenty-six deniers in minute cens at Parenciac," and so on. That third contract (for 198 livres) makes it clear that Peter of Buciac and his associates had earlier purchased those rights at Conflans from the knight Lord Thomas of Clamartis and his wife Lady Sedilia, who had been fief holders there.[111]

Thomas of Clamartis, in turn, held that fief from a group of three siblings, the knight Lord William of Montreuil-sur-Vincennes, his brother, Master Eustachius, and their sister, Lady Isabelle of Parenciac, some of whom still had claims. In 1265 the nuns of Saint-Antoine paid another one hundred livres to Squire Philip of Villecrane and his wife Domicella Isabelle (she is probably the Isabelle of Parenciac mentioned).[112] Claims at the intermediary level, those of Thomas of Clamartis and his wife Sedilia, were resolved only in 1277 when the nuns paid another one hundred livres to a different knight named Lord Peter of Cengle and his wife Lady Sedilia, probably the widow with dowry claims of Thomas of Clamartis, who had disappeared from the documents, presumably dead. Again the description of these vineyards was that they adjoined the nuns' holdings on two sides and included rights over an adjoining winepress, all in the nuns' *censive*.[113] The property was described as being at Parenciac and there were other members of a family from Parenciac involved, but how they fit in is not clear. What is clear is that some of it was associated with entrances into the abbey.

A third item among the "important conveyances" is the charter for January 1264/65, in which the fourteen-year-old Margaret, daughter of the late Andrew of Parenciac and his wife Euphemia, announced that she was of age. She entered the community of nuns at Saint-Antoine and gave her entire inheritance, probably that from her late father. In addition to rights over properties in Paris that produced two livres annually, Margaret conveyed holdings at Montreuil-sur-Vincennes: "Eighteen arpents of arable land in the *censive* of the Count of Grandpré and another two and a half arpents of land in the *censive* of Saint-Antoine, both holdings being burdened with minute cens of eight deniers per arpent."[114] It is likely that her mother, Euphemia, had already entered Saint-Antoine as a nun, for there is an abbess E. of Parenciac seen in a document from 1298.[115]

Other charters for Montreuil-sur-Vincennes suggest the intertwining of rights to vineyards that was the consequence of using contracts *ad medium* to establish new vineyards.[116] In a contract from 1269, the nuns paid sixty livres to Heloise, widow of Nicholas Carnifex, for her rights over seven *quartiers* of vines at Montreuil-sur-Vincennes, on which the nuns already had some rights, for it is stated that those vineyards owed fourteen deniers in cens to the nuns. The property was described as: "All one piece, in the *censive* and lordship of Saint-Antoine at Luat, adjoining Saint-Antoine's winepress on one side and Heloise's nephew's on the other."[117] Further light on this may be shed by a charter from 1272 in which the nuns paid thirty-two livres to John Bernier Carnifex, citizen of Paris, and his son Little John for four-fifths of their rights over the vineyards at Soucy in the nuns' *censive* at Montreuil. The sellers issued a separate charter of donation in 1272 for their souls and those of their predecessors, granting the fifth part of that holding to Saint-Antoine.[118] Overall, it was in such vineyards at Montreuil that the nuns made the most acquisitions, but also the largest investments (with the exception of purchases in the woods at Jariel discussed in Chapter 9). Seemingly the market for wine in Paris was becoming an attractive one.

The Grange of Champagnes near Beaumont-sur-Oise

The grange of Champagnes was located north and west of Paris, upstream from Pontoise and on the opposite side of the Oise from the castle of Beaumont-sur-Oise. The grange properties, like those at Aulnay/Savigny, were used for cereal production but also for viticulture. Most of the holdings there came into the nuns' hands in the 1260s, but they began to acquire scattered rights and properties there in the 1220s. The heirs of the late Matilda, wife of Philip of Tournasel, later disputed an annual rent of thirty-five sous and six deniers at Beaumont given to the nuns in 1224.[119] Between 1238 and 1244 rights in the fief and farm of Champagnes were granted by Raoul, nephew and executor of the late Dame Aye, and by Peter, manager, who forgave the nine deniers per annum that the nuns had owed to Dame Aye.[120] The nuns purchased four-fifths of a vineyard for fifty livres in 1249, when Dreux of Chartres and his wife Eve granted the other fifth of that vineyard (about an arpent) from her inheritance at Neel.[121]

As for clergy, the gift in 1248 of vineyards that Eudes, chaplain of the King's Chapel, purchased with his own funds has already been mentioned.[122] Then in 1254 Master Walter of Neuilly, priest of the nearby church of Saint Mary of Chambly, gave the nuns everything he had purchased over his lifetime: "A house in the villa [or manor] of Champagnes, half an arpent of vineyard next to the *mansus* of Adam of Pyril, vines in the territory of Neel, four arpents of arable land at Champ-Rémy next to what had been planted there as vineyard, an arpent of meadow at Mardella, another next to Prés-Girard owing five sous, three tenanted holdings, the *champart* over three arpents of arable land and whatever other rights he may have had in the fief of that villa of Champagnes once held from the king."[123] Another royal confirmation in April 1260 included three holdings sold to the nuns by the Squire Peter of Cengle of Mésnil-Saint-Denis and his wife Sedilia, who had ceded rights at Montreuil as well. At Beaumont these included rights in a vineyard called "Clos de Thoriac" and two arpents of meadow located next to the Beaumont bridge in the lordship of the Parisian canons of Saint-Germain-d'Auxerrois, and a field held from the lord king.[124] In 1261 the king also confirmed property granted by the knight Renaud of Champagnes.[125]

Such acquisitions were preliminary to Saint-Antoine's major purchase of the entire estate of Champagnes in 1264, using cash that had come from Blanche of Paciac (again, see Table 19). Thus, after the death of the knight Thibaut of Champagnes, the nuns paid 280 livres to his sons and heirs, the knight John of Champagnes and his brothers Henry and Robert and their widowed mother, Lady Jeanne, for a working estate: "A certain manor . . . which included a great hall or tower, a smaller hall, a winepress, a barn and smaller stables for cows, all surrounding a courtyard and three additional arpents of cultivated land and a *quartier* of vines, five and a half arpents of cultivated land, one and a half arpents of meadows, three arpents of planted vineyards and the cens owed there."[126] For the rents owed the nuns, see Table 21. The larger property, which would come to be called the Petit Saint-Antoine, had more than thirty tenants paying a share of the harvest as well as minute cens totaling thirty-eight sous annually. The nuns paid the executors for the late Thibaut an additional thirty livres to fulfill the gifts in alms listed in the deceased's will.

The nuns' acquisition of the manor at Champagnes in 1264 was accompanied by other acquisitions there, many of them involving vineyards granted *ad medium* for planting, but later reacquired by the nuns. In 1264 the nuns received back an arpent of meadow between the villa of Champagnes and the Oise River from Lawrence and his wife Maria, residents of Champagnes, who had earlier held that property *ad medium* for sixteen sous annual rent paid to the nuns. In 1269 Robert of Montigny, who described himself as a bourgeois of the villa of Champagnes, "gave and conceded to Saint-Antoine in pure, perpetual and irrevocable alms *inter vivos,* four arpents in the meadows of Champagnes and two arpents of vineyards in the *censive* of the abbey of Saint-Antoine at Genois and Neel." He and his wife Ermengardis retained usufruct for life. Colardus of Champagnes sold other vineyards there to the nuns in 1269. In 1269 as well, the nuns paid Nicholas of Champagnes, son of the village provost, thirty livres for four-fifths of his vineyards in the valley of Chambly; he granted the other fifth in alms.[127]

The original sellers of the manor, or villa, of Champagnes retained some property at Champagnes. In 1269 the nuns purchased an additional six arpents of arable land in two pieces (one in the common fields of Champagnes and the other near the vines planted by Colardus) for seventy-four livres from the eldest of the three sons, the knight John and his wife, a younger Lady Jeanne.[128] In 1269 at the time when his daughter entered the abbey of Saint-Antoine, this same John sold to Saint-Antoine's nuns for fifty livres, "an additional three arpents of arable land in *la main morte* between Champagnes and Persan with the crops still on them" and granted the nuns *amortissement* for another one hundred livres of acquisitions there.[129] Nearly a decade later, in 1278, John's wife, the younger Lady Jeanne, sold the nuns

Table 21. Saint-Antoine: Cens Owed to Nuns at Champagnes Manor, 1264

Tenant	Owed Annually	Property Tenanted
Guiard Bedin and his brothers	300 deniers	$^1/_3$ arpent of vines
Girard Forestarius	68.5 deniers	$^1/_2$ arpent of vines
Simon Major's widow	24 deniers	1 house (of John of Boules)
Robert of Montigny	12 deniers	$^1/_2$ arpent of vines at Genais
William of Paris	9 deniers	1 house and garden
Peter Mensuarius	8 deniers	$^3/_4$ arpent of vines at Rue Latronum
Guerin of Croy	6.5 deniers	$1^1/_4$ arpents of vines
Maria Cucufaria and G. Boulanger	6 deniers	1 arpent of vines
Thibaut of Montigny	4 deniers	1 arpent of vines at Clos
John of Boules	3.5 deniers	$^1/_4$ arpent of vines in Genais
John of Boules	2.5 deniers	$^1/_6$ produce for his garden
Martin Tonnelarius	2 deniers	1 arpent of vines at Longevigne
Margaret of Platea	2 deniers	1 arpent in John Souffle's vines
William Niger's widow	1.5 deniers	$^3/_4$ arpent of vines on Ruella Prepositi
Thibaut with Adenotus of Neuville	1.5 deniers	$^1/_2$ arpent of vines
John of Saint-Genovessa	1.5 deniers	$^1/_2$ arpent of vines at Logia
John of Montigny and a widow	1.5 deniers	1 arpent of vines at Teubert
Guerinus Vicariis and 2 widows	1.5 deniers	$^1/_2$ arpent of vines
Raoul of Prairie	1 denier	$^1/_4$ arpent vines at Fouques
John Golant	1 denier	$^1/_4$ arpent of vines at Fouques
Guerinus Vicariis	1 denier	$^1/_2$ arpent of vines at the Clos
Adelice of Poumiaus	1 denier	$^1/_2$ arpent of land *super aquam*
William of Paris	0.5 denier	$^1/_4$ arpent of vines at Roussein
William Niger's widow	0.5 denier	$^1/_4$ arpent of vines at Roussein
John of Montigny	Half return	For land at Genais
John of Montigny	Half return	For garden of Aquam
Nelinus Carnifex, familia	Cens	$^1/_4$ arpent of vines at Genais and tenants should use the nuns' press
Hugo of Zozon	Cens	$^3/_4$ arpent of vines at Rue Latronum
Godefrey Moran	Cens	1 arpent of vines at Via Leirier
Total annual income	460.5 deniers, which equals 38 sous, 4.5 deniers	

Source: Paris, AN, S*4386, fols. 24v–26r (1264).

half an arpent of vineyards at Genois for thirteen livres, declaring that another fifth of the property had been conveyed to the nuns as a gift in alms.[130]

John, the eldest of the three brothers, appeared again in 1284 along with his younger brothers, Henry and Robert, when they granted another *amortissement* to Saint-Antoine at the time of the death of their mother, the elder Lady Jeanne.[131] This John appeared at a Parisian court among executors for this Lady Jeanne's last testament, along with Master Walter of the church of Champagnes and Raoul, priest of the chapel of Champagnes. Lady Jeanne had instructed them to sell her properties and pay her debts, asserting that at the time of her writing she owned what she had acquired by her own purchase: two pieces of vineyard in the *censive* of Saint-Antoine at Genois in the territory of Champagnes, which owed six deniers of cens to those nuns. The three executors sold those rights to Saint-Antoine for twenty-four livres, describing themselves as executors for "the late Jeanne of Faisiac, once wife of Lord Thibaut of Champagnes, knight."[132]

This is not quite the end of the story. Lady Jeanne in a 1267 charter registered in Paris asserted that at the moment in 1264 when she and her sons had made the sale of Champagnes to Saint-Antoine, she had transferred all her rights to the nuns, except the fief, *champart*, and one obol of cens over a single house. In that 1267 document she used this last property at Champagnes to establish a life rent for herself with the nuns of Saint-Antoine, transferring all those rights in return for twenty livres annually to be paid out in quarterly amounts of five livres. After her death, however, the usufruct over three arpents of land between Champagnes and Chambly would go to the priory of Laye, where she had elected to be buried.[133]

In that document from 1267 Lady Jeanne, mother of John and Henry and Robert, described herself as "Lady Jeanne, widow of the late lord and knight Thibaut of Champagnes, and now wife of the knight Lord William Eschalez of Montreuil-sur-Vincennes."[134] Thus in 1267 Lady Jeanne established an annuity with Saint-Antoine for herself, just as Lady Agnes of Cressonessart had done in 1212. Agnes soon became some sort of lay sister at Saint-Antoine, but Jeanne chose to remarry and be provided income by those nuns, although she did eventually have a granddaughter who was a nun at Saint-Antoine.

Ceremonial and Other Income from Sources Outside Paris

The Saint-Antoine cartulary, Paris, AN, S*4386, has references scattered throughout, documenting gifts to Saint-Antoine of income from various sources. These were conveyances of income very like those found in the hold-ings of other abbeys of nuns: tolls on rivers and roads, tithes from beyond its own landholdings, or income from revenue-producing mills or *prévôtés*.[135] Often these were conveyances granted to the nuns on quasi-ceremonial occa-sions and often by wealthy, titled individuals who otherwise had little to do with the abbey and its nuns. They were drawn from outside Paris, like the income over fulling mills at Chartres confirmed by Countess Isabelle of Char-tres in 1236, or they might mark a specific event, such as Louis IX's departure on his 1248 crusade when property in Arras was granted by Robert of Artois, Louis IX's younger brother, or the twelve and a half livres annually from the gates of Troyes given in 1249 by Lady Margaret of Lisigniac, widow of the late marshal of Champagne, William of Guillac.[136]

The nuns also acquired woodlands and usage in them from various donors, but there were no recognizable conveyances of royal forest. Saint-Antoine had woodland or forest rights, probably including firewood, at Aul-nay and at Montjoie-en-Cressonessart near Beauvais—in both cases given by Agnes of Cressonessart and her family.[137] The abbey also got firewood and lumber by purchases and leases of rights to expanses in the forest of Jariel east of Paris between Tournan-en-Brie and Ozoir-la-Ferrière, as discussed in Chapter 9; it may be that it was Blanche of Paciac who suggested leasing there rather than additional purchases.

In 1351 the expected income from all Saint-Antoine's extra-urban sources, including from its grange properties, was listed in a *censier* found in Paris, AN, LL1595. The nuns appear to have summed up expected income from such rural sources in that year: 1,070 livres and 7 sous annu-ally. The list, however, is about failing expectations. The record of 1351 looked back at rents already beginning to disappear as a result of the pan-demic of 1348. In 1358 the nuns added annotations that suggest a precipitous drop in income as a result of that plague. While the information in that *censier* deserves a full study on its own, several examples suggest the consid-erable losses. See Table 22, which suggests losses of about 40 percent. There is no equivalent revision of the urban property list that had been made somewhat earlier.

Saint-Antoine's Properties in Paris

Paris was the center of a region in northern France of diverse agricultural, pastoral, and viticultural production, where demographic growth and

Table 22. Saint-Antoine: Examples from Rural *Censier* with Income Reductions After
1351

Reduced minute cens paid at the feast of Saint Rémy from fol. 78v				
	Sous Paid			
Location*	In 1351	In 1358	(Loss 1351–58)	(Reduction)
Our *hôtel* at Montreuil	120	72	(48)	(40%)
Châtillon-les-Baigneux	22	13	(9)	(41%)
Noisy-le-Sec	140	86	(54)	(39%)

Internal summary of reduced income in livres from fol. 79v				
	Livres Paid			
	In 1351	In 1358	(Loss 1351–58)	(Reduction)
Sum of rents/tolls	44	23	(21)	(48%)

Source: Paris, AN, LL1595, *Cartulaire de Saint-Antoine.*
*These are the first three items in a larger entry in the accounts.

increased rural production fueled an expansion of Capetian royal power. As
Paris became the royal capital its markets also expanded. The development
of merchant ports and artisanal areas on the right bank of the Seine in Paris
was matched by the bishop's growing cathedral school on the Île-de-la-Cité
and housing for students on the left bank. Moored on the bridges linking
both right and left banks to the Île-de-la-Cité were water-powered mills,
providing flour for bread to feed Paris's growing population and power for
industries like textile, leather, and parchment production.[138]

An increase in population density and an expansion in the total overall
area of early thirteenth-century Paris is apparent in improved roads, bridges,
castles, parish churches, water-powered mills, and the construction of the
Gothic cathedral and other churches. Before the year 1200 King Philip
Augustus had already recognized that growth, by beginning new city walls
and gates, giving greater access to the city for the many new churches and
monasteries like Saint-Antoine that were appearing in its vicinity as well as
to migrants from the countryside. As it grew, Paris came to be viewed by its
residents as consisting of various lordships, or *censives*, belonging to the king,
the bishop and his chapter, and to great religious communities like Saint-
Magloire, Saint-Médard, and Saint-Victoire. In those *censives*, new houses,
shops and workshops were being built. Tenants paid rents to landlords who

had put up buildings for which theoretically at least a ground rent (or cens) was paid to the *censive* holder, but ownership of *censives* was shifting, particularly in the suburbs, as new groups acquired properties.

On the edge of the growing city, on the right bank and north of the river, the abbey of Saint-Antoine was located just east of the new city walls. Its nuns soon received the patronage not only of rural elites from the Parisian countryside but of Parisian merchants and artisans, including those associated with services for the royal court. Most of its Parisian properties came from bourgeois families. Such artisans and guild members included Petronilla, wife of a Smith, Agnes the Butcheress, and Peter the Cook.[139] Many were citizens of Paris like "Petrus Coquillarius, civis parisiensis," mentioned in 1261, and "Stephanus dictus Carnifex [Butcher], civis parisiensis" cited in 1283.[140]

Names of donors suggest the diversity of Saint-Antoine's urban patronage and provide some measure of the donors' origins and distances from which their families had come.[141] They included Roger Anglicus and his wife Gille, who made a gift for an anniversary for their souls in 1227.[142] Tostennis of Chartres and Cecilia, his wife, who gave Saint-Antoine's nuns a house on the Grand Pont for their souls and those of their ancestors.[143] Robert of Nogent and his wife Christina who gave four houses in the city and two vineyards near the abbey.[144] Richard the Scot and his wife Theophania gave property in the Marais retaining usufruct for life and so on.[145] In 1296 the citizens of Paris making gifts to the nuns of Saint-Antoine included a family of merchant/bankers from Padua: "The children of the late Philip of Padua and his late wife Juliana, citizens of Paris, [those children named] Stephen, Little John, and Little Philip of Padua, and their sister Agnes, wife of Guiard of Latigny, citizen of Paris, confirmed to Saint-Antoine, where their parents had elected to be buried, their parents' conveyance of seventeen and a half livres over three bankers' benches on the Grand Pont of Paris and fifty sous annual rent over a house in the Truanderie (once the realm of vagabonds)."[146] Such gifts suggest the diversity of occupations encompassed by the term *civis*, or citizen, which included wives, as in 1291 when the plural *cives* is used to describe donors as "Johannes dictus le Chaus [Shoemaker?] et Petronilla eius uxor, cives parisiensis."[147] Such donors included Jacob Sarracen and Aalesia de Bosco who gave themselves and all their goods to the monastery in a postmortem gift in 1242, which allowed them to stay in their own house until their deaths; in this case, Sarracen may refer to hair color, rather than exotic origins.[148]

New Types of Investments in Paris

Given the city's varied industries and endeavors, and a growing demand for housing and workshop space, Parisians developed new means of investing in a very sophisticated real-estate market that allowed its housing and building stock to increase in value alongside the city's growth in both population and wealth. By at least the early thirteenth century, a new level of ownership was developing as landlords (old and new) built additional houses and workshops throughout the city of Paris by issuing new contracts that covered their investments called "augmentations of rent." This was a case not of speculation or of a "bubble" but of an addition in perpetuity to principal, often granted by owners, which allowed them to increase income over the long term from improved urban properties. Sometimes an augmentation in rent was promised to investors in an artisanal business, to those who had put up the capital for that endeavor.[149]

Saint-Antoine's nuns' investments in the city soon included using these new "augmented rents." The nuns' contracts for them took a variety of forms, as seen in Table 23. A donor could, out of piety, make a gift for additional spiritual benefits by establishing an augmentation of rent to be paid to those who would pray for his soul, in this case the nuns of Saint-Antoine. Most often, an additional layer of rental payment was agreed to by tenants in return for cash to be used to improve a property in some way. Loans for what we would call home improvements were granted in return for augmented rents to be paid in addition to existing rents in perpetuity. Indeed such contracts often made such reinvestment in the property explicit, indicating the amount "invested" or the time period in which improvements were to be made. Such contracts allowed owners in the city like the nuns of Saint-Antoine to keep properties from deteriorating and to increase income from them. Saint-Antoine's nuns embraced the use of such contracts for investments in the city and their "augmentations" over urban properties increased overall from about 60 livres per decade in the 1210s to between 90 and 120 livres per decade from the 1260s onward.

This brings us back to Blanche of Paciac, the nun who may have been advising the abbess to lease rather than buy forest at Jariel (as seen in Chapter 9), and it may have been Blanche as well who urged the nuns to make written claims against Master Geoffrey of Beaumont, lord of Aulnay and canon of Beauvais, who was in considerable arrears on what he owed them (as seen

Table 23. Saint-Antoine: Augmented Rents, Examples from Paris, AN, LL1595

Year (citation)	Type of Creation	Details
1211 (fol. 16v)	Existing augmented rent	Saint-Antoine received a house opposite that of Adam of Moulin *cum augmento census*
1216 (fols. 19r–20v)	Creation of augmented rent	Adam Herman and wife Sancia agreed to an augmented rent in return for "home improvement" loan)
1219 (fol. 32r)	Creation of augmented rent	Ada, widow of Stephen Berondi, gave Saint-Antoine an augmented rent or cens of forty sous annually over a house in Paris facing Saint-Mathurin in return for prayers
1228 (fol. 41v)	Creation of a postmortem one	Master William of La Tiniac, a canon of Châlons, gave Saint-Antoine ten livres' worth of annual "increased rent" over a house in Paris, for after his death
1218 (fol. 28r–v)	Sale of augmented rent	Maria, widow of Geoffrey the Goldsmith, sold an augmented rent or cens over half a house on the Quai des Orfèvres in return for thirteen livres from Saint-Antoine's nuns

Source: Paris, AN, LL1595. *Cartulaire de Saint-Antoine.*

above for Aulnay/Savigny). She had funded acquisition of rights in an important house in Paris across from that of the king over which five livres were acquired (see Table 19). Indeed, Blanche's urban expertise may have been equal to that of any abbess of Saint-Antoine, particularly in Parisian areas where her family had considerable property holdings, for instance, in the vicinity of a gate in the earlier city wall called the Porte Baudéer (today's Place Baudoyer). This had been a gateway through which the ancient Roman road to Melun and Sens had passed; part of it became the rue Saint-Antoine. Documents tell us that in 1234 executors for Marie, late wife of Richard li

Charronz, had granted to Saint-Antoine half a house and property behind it at the Porte Baudéer.[150] In 1262, probably on the advice of Blanche, the nuns had invested twelve livres in a house there in return for an augmented rent of twenty sous agreed to by Thomas Heres and his wife, Marie.[151] The nuns also invested thirty livres in the house of Thomas Juvenis Talementarius (baker/*patisseur*) and his wife Odeline, who agreed to an increased rent of sixty sous.[152] By the 1340s the urban *censier* lists payments owed to the nuns at Porte Baudéer, which amounted to sixty-two livres annually from five houses.[153] Saint-Antoine created in this way an increasingly large portfolio of urban properties using such contractual devices.

Expansion into city properties was a good investment and acquisitions of urban property are found for a variety of places in the city. Saint-Antoine's nuns often chose to invest in neighborhoods where they already had some property rights. In 1219 Adam Baldwin on his deathbed gave a rent of four sous and three deniers annually over a house near Saint-Gervais on the right bank near the Châtelet.[154] Another acquisition on the left bank began with a contract in 1218 of forty-six sous of cens over a house located between the old Roman baths and the church of Saint-Germain-des-Prés, given by Roger of Camera and his wife Jeanne. In this case the nuns then repurchased rights from Roger and Jeanne's lord for ten livres, but they also allowed the tenants to improve the holding—promising that the new rent of eleven livres per annum would be reduced for anything invested in improvements.[155] Another conveyance to Saint-Antoine in 1219 was of an augmented cens of slightly over one hundred sous: forty sous over a house at Saint-Mathurin and sixty sous over one in the terre d'Aletz outside the eastern walls; the donor of this rent, Ada, widow of Stephen Berondi, also gave ten arpents of arable land at La Chapelle-Saint-Genovese, north of Montmartre.[156]

Saint-Antoine's investments in the city by the time of its 1340s Old French *censier* of urban rentals amounted to about 150 properties, producing annual income of more than six hundred livres.[157] This rent roll provides something more than a list of rents owed, for it also provides evidence of a mental map of Paris, as understood by the nuns of Saint-Antoine. (See Map 7.) It included places where their families lived, and those to which the nuns went on their daily rounds: visiting the sick, hearing mass, attending funerals, sermons, and possibly even university lectures in other churches. The nuns would have come to know those areas of the city in which they had properties and collected quarterly rents; they knew the tenants from whom rents were collected, or who had proposals about improvements. They must have known

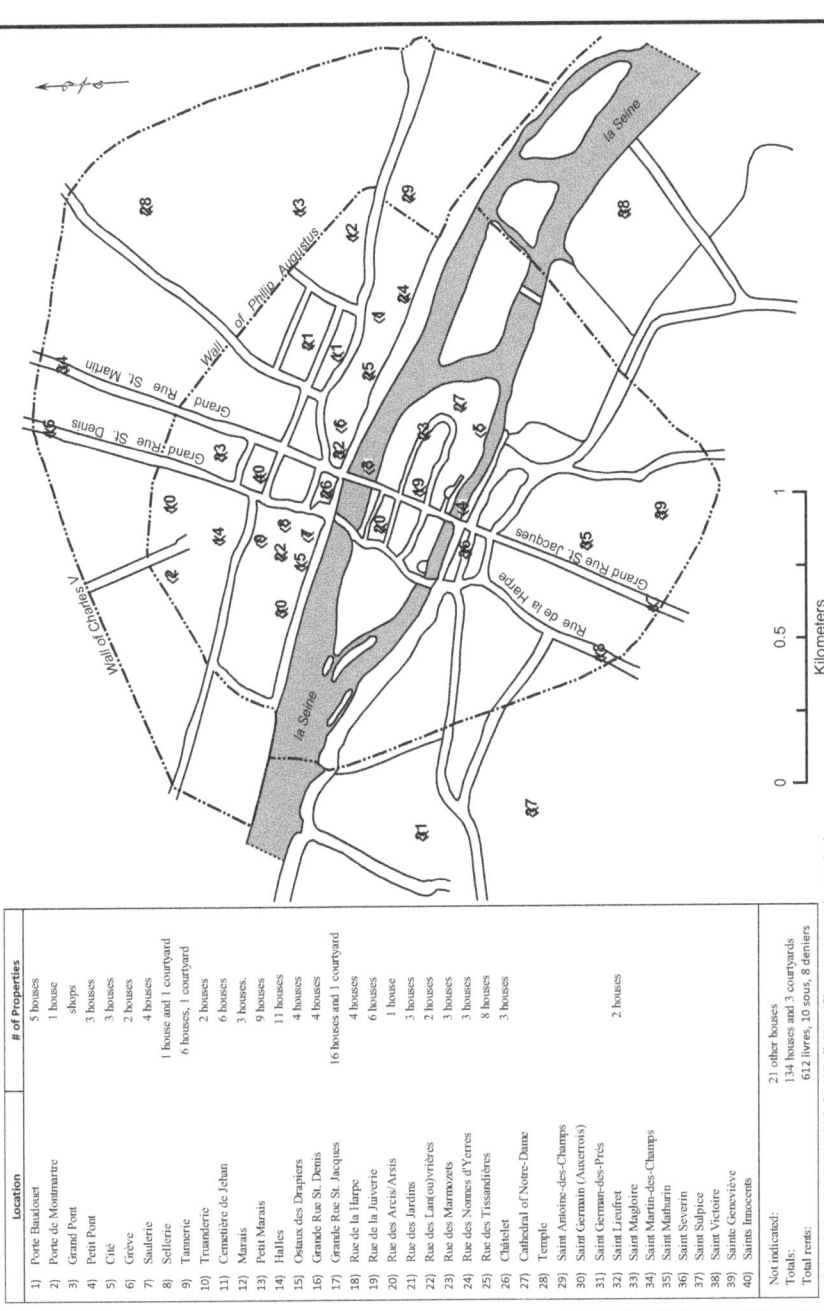

Location	# of Properties
1) Porte Baudoïet	5 houses
2) Porte de Montmartre	1 house
3) Grand Pont	shops
4) Petit Pont	3 houses
5) Cité	3 houses
6) Grève	2 houses
7) Saulerie	4 houses
8) Sellerie	1 house and 1 courtyard
9) Tannerie	6 houses, 1 courtyard
10) Truanderie	2 houses
11) Cemetière de Jehan	6 houses
12) Marais	3 houses.
13) Petit Marais	9 houses
14) Halles	11 houses
15) Ostaux des Drapiers	4 houses
16) Grande Rue St. Denis	4 houses
17) Grande Rue St. Jacques	16 houses and 1 courtyard
18) Rue de la Harpe	4 houses
19) Rue de la Juverie	6 houses
20) Rue des Arcis/Arsis	1 house
21) Rue des Jardins	3 houses
22) Rue des Lant(ou)vrières	2 houses
23) Rue des Marmozets	3 houses
24) Rue des Nonnes d'Yerres	3 houses
25) Rue des Tissandières	8 houses
26) Châtelet	3 houses
27) Cathedral of Notre-Dame	
28) Temple	
29) Saint Antoine–des–Champs	2 houses
30) Saint Germain (Auxerrois)	
31) Saint Germain-des-Prés	
32) Saint Lieufret	
33) Saint Magloire	
34) Saint Martin-des-Champs	
35) Saint Mathurin	
36) Saint Severin	
37) Saint Sulpice	
38) Saint Victoire	
39) Sainte Geneviève	
40) Saints Innocents	
Not indicated:	21 other houses
Totals:	134 houses and 3 courtyards
Total rents:	612 livres, 10 sous, 8 deniers

(Source: Paris, A.N. LL1595, fol. 87r ff. [1344?], annual rents in *censier*.)

MAP 7. Saint-Antoine's properties in Paris. Map created by Gordon Thompson. Source: Paris, AN, LL1595, fol. 87r ff. (1344?), *censier* of annual urban rents.

who were the boisterous occupants at one house, the struggling poverty in another, the need for repairs at a third that would necessitate some sort of augmentation of rents.

The *censier* for urban properties was organized into thirty-two districts or streets, with holdings and rents on each broken down further and identified by current or recent tenants. Many of the urban properties belonging to Saint-Antoine were on the right bank, not far from the abbey itself. At some locations there might be only one substantial house that owed sixty or eighty livres per year. In other cases, identical rents on an entire street suggest that the nuns may have built rows of domiciles of identical size.[158] Rental amounts usually described as quarterly payments were listed following each holding; most often it was on houses that rent was paid, although a few had stables or gardens. Although rents varied widely, many houses paid about sixty sous (three livres) per quarter, that is, twelve livres annually. Very few paid less than a livre per year. There were exceptions. On the street of the weavers (*tisserands*) the nuns had seven houses; one of these paid fourteen livres annually, another paid four livres and two other houses each paid eight livres, but the rest of the tenants paid three to five sous a year.

In terms of income produced in the 1340s as revealed by this *censier*, the most important areas were in the center of Paris. The highest rents were from houses opposite the royal palace at the Châtelet or nearby: one paid 156 livres per year and another 136 livres. On the left bank, where the nuns had rents over at least twenty-five houses, many were properties along the Grande Rue Saint-Jacques, or on the Île-de-la-Cité, where the nuns had acquired at least one house on its Rue des Marmozets and owned twelve in all, including properties on the bridges. On the right bank at the Halles of Paris, where the nuns had "notre grande maison des Halles," which owed eighty livres annually, they also had rents on another ten houses, including that of the late Nicholas Burgat, which owed thirty-six livres a year; that of the Welshman, nearly fifty livres; that of Robert of Latève, forty livres a year; that of the late John Thomas, thirty livres. On the Rue de la Harpe on the left bank, every house paid either ten or twenty livres. In contrast among the six houses on the Rue de la Juiverie, the house of Master Jean Pastourel owed thirty-six livres annually, two others each paid twelve livres, and three others paid four livres or less.

Just as communities of Cistercian nuns were investing in improvements to land in the countryside in agreements *ad medium* with tenants for planting vineyards, in the city of Paris the augmented rent provided a way to invest in amelioration of urban property. Such investments in city properties by Saint-Antoine's nuns created new wealth in which everyone in the city shared—refurbishing of the city with new or renovated houses, gardens, vineyards, and other facilities. This was not exclusively for the nuns' or their tenants' benefit, but for that of entire neighborhoods, providing housing, access to foodstuffs, and other amenities for the population of the city, including the elderly. Moreover, there appears to have been very little disadvantage to anyone else when the nuns introduced augmented urban rents. The augmented rent along with increased investment in urban properties appears to have been a win-win situation, particularly as compared to changes in the countryside where the nuns' land purchases may have been seen as contributing at least indirectly to a crisis among feudal families, as discussed in Chapter 4.

Bourgeois Recruits and Private Income

By the end of the thirteenth century such bourgeois patronage of Saint-Antoine and entrances of bourgeois daughters had stretched right to the top of merchant society and the issue of private income among nuns arose. In 1296 Jean Popin, that year's head or provost of the prestigious Parisian Marchands d'Eau, gave Saint-Antoine two livres' worth of annual rents and 320 livres in cash to purchase additional rents. The income was to provide pittances for Saint-Antoine's community on Easter, Pentecost, and Christmas, but it was also to be used to build a chapel for the family's souls. In addition it would provide a life income of six livres per year for his daughter Petronilla, a nun there.[159] In the view of a wealthy merchant like Jean Popin, his daughter, even as a nun, would need pocket money in the city of Paris for her own alms and other needs. Such "needs" for private income had developed in the second half of the thirteenth century at Saint-Antoine, but had developed gradually.

In 1243 such personal income was seemingly not yet needed for nuns at Saint-Antoine when John Sisonardi, canon of Saint-Honoré in Paris, made a gift of urban property for his niece Sibilia, admitted there as a nun "by the liberality and grace" of Saint-Antoine's nuns.[160] Similarly, in 1250 Master Jean of Gagniac gave for the soul of his late sister Gille and for her daughter Juliana, a nun at Saint-Antoine, eight livres of annual rent over a house in the square opposite the Petit Pont in Paris. Juliana's brothers joined their uncle in this gift, which was made to the nuns, not for Juliana's personal needs.[161] Such a need for pocket money for nuns may have been becoming the case in 1261 when Peter Coquillarius, citizen of Paris, assigned to Saint-Antoine six livres per year in the name of his sister, Margaret, a nun at that house, but this is not clear.[162] This is also the moment when a Parisian mother of three nuns at Maubuisson granted them private income as discussed in Chapter 6.

For other nuns access to such personal cash was increasing. In 1281 it was Jeanne, daughter of the late Lord Henry of Triânel, a member of the feudal elites, who took her vows at Saint-Antoine, bringing gifts that provided her clothing upon taking her vows and a life income of five livres per annum, while another rent of five livres went immediately to the abbey.[163] In her last testament dated 1282, Marie the Blanchière, widow of John Blancher, granted use of twenty-seven and a half sous annually to Agnes of Compiègne, a nun at Saint-Antoine.[164] In 1282 as well, Jeanne, widow of the late William Pidoe citizen of Paris, granted to their daughter Agnes, a nun at Saint-Antoine, a life rent of sixty sous over a house in Paris facing the cemetery of the Holy Innocents.[165] In 1287 the nuns Regina and Acelina Goutière received from their uncle, a cleric, an annual seven and a half livres of income over a house near Saint-Benedict that would fund anniversaries for the donor after those nuns' deaths.[166]

A sudden increase in the 1290s of the number of nuns with personal income is seen in Table 24. It was in this context that Jean Popin, head of the merchants' guild, had left income for his daughter Petronilla's personal use in the 1290s.[167] Whether or not it was done with the advice or endorsement of the abbot of Cîteaux is unclear, but the nuns appear to have decided to provide all nuns with such pocket money. This is suggested in Saint-Antoine's urban cartulary section entitled: "Here begin letters for rents that this church holds over houses in Paris, which are held by the lady nuns for life and will return to the church after their deaths."[168] The charters that follow reveal that in 1296 John of Forrenis, who called himself "Imperator and citizen of Paris," gave forty livres in cash and three arpents of vines at Montreuil when his daughter Jeanne entered Saint-Antoine, possibly partly held by her for life.[169] In 1296 Alice la Poissonière made a testamentary grant of income for her niece, a nun at Saint-Antoine.[170] In 1299 Simon of Saint-Benoît, draper, and his wife Agnes, both citizens of Paris, gave rental income over a Parisian house for their daughters, Agnesota and Mariota, nuns at Saint-Antoine.[171] In 1300 Peter the Draper and his wife Michaela granted their daughter, the nun Colette, income for life at Gentilly, that would

Table 24. Saint-Antoine Nuns with Income, 1280s into 1300s

Year	Number of Nuns with Income
1281	1
1282	2
1287	2
Total for decade	5 nuns
1293	2
1295	1
1296	1
1298	12
1299	3
Total for decade	19 nuns
1300	1
1301	4
1302	2
Total for decade	7 nuns

Source: Paris, AN, LL1595, fol. 63r ff.
Note: These are approximate numbers, because not all these nuns would have lived long.

devolve onto the abbey after her death, but was to be paid into her hands "for necessities" during her lifetime.[172] In 1302 William Brice, valet and furrier for the lord king, and his wife Katharine, the king's seamstress, gave four livres in annual rents "in pure and perpetual alms for their souls" to Saint-Antoine and for their daughter, Petronilla, a nun there; again seemingly it provided the daughter her pocket money for life.[173]

The practice is seen most clearly circa 1301 when the abbess Gile herself was granted income of ten livres per year by her cousin, Lady Marguerite of Beaumont-sur-Oise, widow of John of Montfort.[174] Having her own funds settled on her by a relative, Abbess Gile would no longer hesitate to set aside income from several Parisian properties in the abbey's endowment to provide "pocket money" for those nuns lacking it. What seems a prudent act under the circumstances is mentioned in another cartulary rubric:

Concerning the six livres parisis over a certain house located in the Halles of Paris, adjoining on one side the house of Henry Marshal and on the other the house of Peter called Cleric, located in the *censive* of the Lord King. Of these six livres, Sister Agnes of Compans, Sister Melania Bordone, and Sister Juliana of Roe [together]

hold 40 sous, which will continue to go to whichever of them out-
lives the others. Similarly Sister Agnes La Pidoe, Sister Jeanne of
Giroles, and Sister Genovefa will hold another 40 sous. The last 40
sous will be held for life by Sister Margaret Little, Sister Agnes of
Saint-Victoire, and Sister Agnes Little.[175]

Such life income settled on groups of nuns at Saint-Antoine may have prevented conflict that otherwise might have occurred between the more wealthy
noble and bourgeois nuns and their poorer sisters.[176] All could be equally pious
and happy to have become nuns, but still feel an inequality in their abilities to
give alms and otherwise pay for their needs in the city. It may be that the
increase in private income is what is at issue in the 1293 Cistercian General
Chapter statute: "That the disbursement [of funds?] to the nuns of Saint-
Antoine should be placed under the judgment of the abbot of Cîteaux."[177]

Saint-Antoine's Management

The management of its rural properties by Saint-Antoine's nuns at Saint-
Antoine's three major granges and smaller properties resembled very much
that by Maubuisson or Port-Royal. The evidence is limited but, as in those
cases, suggests a mixture of methods. Certainly there is no evidence that the
nuns of Saint-Antoine did not cultivate their landholdings in ways very similar to those of Cistercian abbeys of monks. Some land was taken under direct
cultivation but worked by hired laborers. At Savigny and Aulnay, *champart*,
the income from shares in the common fields, enters the discussion. In contrast there is little evidence for animal husbandry, but acquisition of meadows
at Bry-sur-Marne, as discussed above, underlines the importance of holding
places for animals near the city. With the exception of that case, however,
meadows and hay and animal production are little noted among Saint-
Antoine's acquisitions, except possibly for a reference to a house for shepherds at Aulnay.

   Certainly early conveyances like those from Agnes of Cressonessart and
her brother Robert of Mauvoisin carried the expectation that the nuns would
cultivate at their own expense.[178] Whether or not they used lay brothers or
hired laborers in the thirteenth century, Saint-Antoine's large uninterrupted
rural holdings had long been under cultivation and were probably being
improved using the rationalized "Cistercian grange agriculture" once thought

to be the exclusive preserve of the foundations of Cistercian monks.[179] In the village of Gonesse, Saint-Antoine's nuns, like those of Maubuisson seen in Chapter 6, acquired claims to income in an established agricultural regime in the great open fields north of Paris—*champart* income from land probably worked by traditional cultivators. Conveyances of land in the countryside such as these had often already moved from the hands of local lords into those of bourgeois individuals, sometimes land speculators, who then sold them to new abbeys of nuns, as was seen for Conflans-sur-Montreuil above.

While local lords were strapped for cash, Saint-Antoine's nuns, in common with other important communities of Cistercian nuns, had the wherewithal to take land out of grain cultivation and devote it to viticulture. As is implicit in the lists of income paid at the time of transfer of properties at Champagnes to the nuns (see again Table 21), such viticultural activities had begun even before acquisition by Saint-Antoine's nuns and may have been more profitable than cereal cultivation. Such arrangements probably continued beyond the terms of the formal *ad medium* contracts. That charters report secular owners' properties interspersed among those of the nuns at Montreuil suggests *ad medium* contracts in use at an earlier date. There at Montreuil and elsewhere east of Paris, Saint-Antoine's nuns must have been producing wine for internal consumption or for sale in the nearby markets of Paris.[180]

Like other similar houses of Cistercian nuns in the area, Saint-Antoine's nuns could frequently invest in making more profitable their cultivation in fields, meadows, and vineyards and in exploiting the possibilities of streams for establishing water-powered mills. The surviving evidence shows fragmented holdings consolidated into larger ones but also suggests introduction of more appropriate crops, allowing land to remain fallow longer, employing better tools and animals, getting crops under cover in adequate barns, and protecting flocks and herds from bad weather. As at Blanche of Castile's foundations, small expenditures in tools and better management may be inferred from more visible ones in new barns, or grange centers, in mills and weirs, and viticulture. All this produced agricultural efficiencies similar to those experienced by the order's monks.

Much of what has been said about Maubuisson and Lys and Port-Royal could be repeated here for Saint-Antoine, whose nuns soon became self-sufficient in food and wine production, but also able to sell surpluses. Noticeable is the fact that except at Gonesse, where both Maubuisson and Saint-Antoine acquired properties, each of these abbeys appears to have

maintained an exclusive zone of interest—not encroaching on the properties of other Cistercian nuns.

Saint-Antoine Conclusions

The abbesses of Saint-Antoine created a women's religious community that
was strong, powerful, well-managed, and devout, whose prayers were valued
by male and female, lay and clerical patrons. Those patrons built chapels,
financed pittances and anniversaries, and sent daughters or nieces to be educated or to become nuns. The abbesses of Saint-Antoine petitioned the General Chapter (as in 1213). They issued and probably drafted important
documents—a few had their own seals to be affixed alongside that of the
abbot of Cîteaux. They made decisions about which documents to copy into
the abbey's medieval cartulary. Indeed, there is considerable evidence that
Saint-Antoine's nuns were educated and literate, inspired by the sermons
preached by young clerics in their abbey church to pray but also to provide
social services, to take on the education of young orphan girls and care for
elderly boarders. The abbey may have been somewhat unusual in welcoming
both noble and bourgeois women.

Saint-Antoine's nuns and abbesses were particularly sagacious in their
management of property. Part of this came from judicious attention to
matching the expertise of abbesses, able managers of rural properties coming
from a feudal elite near Paris, with the perspicacious managerial skills brought
to the community by bourgeois women like Blanche of Paciac. Much more
could be said about Saint-Antoine from the surviving archives, but the story
told here of Saint-Antoine's development of rural properties balanced with
its acquisitions in Paris confirms the nuns' abilities. Indeed the evidence is
that Saint-Antoine's abbesses and nuns were often on the cutting edge of
thirteenth-century economic development in the city and its environs.

It is clear that Saint-Antoine, like Maubuisson and Lys, became a substantial community of Cistercian nuns, well able to support 120 nuns.[181] The
nuns provided for nearly all their own internal needs from granges, lordships,
mills, vineyards, rents, and tithes in cash and grain acquired in the surround-
ings of Paris as well as with the cash coming from their urban properties.
Such assets allowed them to survive war, plague, crop failure, and commendatory abbesses right up to the abolition of religion in the late eighteenth century, although with considerably reduced numbers.[182] Over the centuries the

abbey of Saint-Antoine became a site for local pilgrimage; the privileges granting indulgence for visits to Saint-Antoine's church on important religious festivals and in the surrounding days earned pilgrims some religious benefit on close to a third of all the days of the year.[183]

Although men acting as provosts or procurators for the nuns are found in the documents, they are rare. Women administrators appear more often, rarely resorting to male proxies.[184] Although the community had one or two lay brothers and priests, such men serving the nuns are not found frequently in the documents. Instead, when men are found in the records for Saint-Antoine, it is as patrons interested in obtaining the prayers of its nuns. They are knights like Robert of Mauvoisin and Simon of Montfort making gifts for their souls before they departed on the Albigensian Crusade or founding chapels for their companions who had died. They are wealthy bourgeois fathers making gifts for their daughters' reception by the abbey. They are sons funding anniversary masses for their parents' souls. They are young clerics learning to sermonize before a knowledgeable audience of nuns. They are priests and canons making bequests for prayers for their own souls or to assure the care of a loved one in old age. All this suggests the esteem in which Saint-Antoine's nuns were held in the Middle Ages and the lack of any skepticism about the value of their prayers.

Saint-Antoine: Postscript

Much of the history of the abbey of Saint-Antoine for later centuries remains to be written, but one mysterious reference for 1432 from a Parisian diarist suggests the importance of the community. In that year toward the end of the Hundred Years' War, Paris was held by the Burgundians supporting Charles VII and had been virtually surrounded by the English. The diarist, possibly a canon of the cathedral, reported: "At the end of August the abbess of Saint-Antoine and some of her nuns were put in prison. They were accused of having agreed with a nephew of this abbess, who made himself out to be a true friend of Paris, to betray the town by the Porte St. Antoine. The gatekeepers were to be killed first and then everyone in the town without exception; this was generally known after their arrest."[185] Whether or not true, such accusations that Saint-Antoine's abbesses could act on behalf of the enemy underlines the power and authority that they maintained then and right up to the French Revolution. But Saint-Antoine, like Maubuisson, Lys,

Port-Royal, and a number of other great abbeys, was more successful than some of the smaller houses of Cistercian nuns, especially those located in the eastern parts of the province of Sens, where their lack of strong patrons and the value of their viticultural assets aroused the envy of neighboring abbots. As seen in Chapter 8, by the end of the Middle Ages some of those houses of Cistercian nuns were suppressed.

CHAPTER 8

Nuns and Viticulture in Champagne

Houses of Cistercian nuns in this chapter, founded in those parts of Champagne that were part of the province of Sens, tended to be established by rivals of the counts of Champagne or by bourgeois associated with the growing industry and commerce of the Champagne fair towns.[1] At the outset, Cistercian nuns had considerable support from the rulers of Champagne. Countess Blanche of Navarre had founded the abbey of Cistercian nuns at Argensolles between 1222 and 1229.

Support for those nuns is seen in the will drafted in 1257 by her grandson Thibaut V (1253–70), who gave cash to seven abbeys of Cistercian nuns. He granted five hundred livres to the nuns of Argensolles, four hundred to those of Jardin, three hundred to Grâce-Notre-Dame, and one hundred livres each to Piété, Notre-Dame-des-Prés, Mont-Notre-Dame, and Pont-aux-Dames.[2] All these abbeys were established in the first half of the thirteenth century. Their foundations reflect the same interests in supporting prayers by Cistercian nuns as those found elsewhere but also suggest that Champagne was experiencing considerable demographic and economic growth at the time.[3]

Only circa 1300 did Champagne begin to lose its primacy in international trade. In 1284 it began to become part of France after the marriage of the last countess, Jeanne of Navarre, to the future King Philip IV (1285–1314). Cistercian nuns in this region became more vulnerable to suppression in this region, probably in part because they had less protection from secular patrons. During the last stages of the Hundred Years' War (1337–1453) some of those nuns' granges and vineyards were ravaged, particularly in the vicinity of Sens, and nuns fled temporarily to such nearby towns.[4]

Those events may have lent some verisimilitude to the claims by Cistercian abbots of economic problems for the nuns, but abbots made no effort to help those nuns rebuild damaged buildings or replant vineyards or to ensure any continued viability of those Cistercian women's houses. Instead abbots cast envious eyes on the valuable viticultural assets that those nuns had developed. As a consequence, land suitable for viticulture, vineyards, winepresses, and wine cellars came into the hands of leading abbots of the order, while communities of nuns were suppressed.

When Henry II, count of Champagne, departed on crusade in 1190, he left his mother, Marie of Champagne, in control, and designated his younger brother, Thibaut III, as his heir. Upon Henry II's death in 1197, Marie immediately recognized her second son, Thibaut III, as count of Champagne (1197–1201). Marie died in 1198, but the marriage she had arranged for the new count Thibaut III with Blanche of Navarre was celebrated in 1199. They produced two children, Marie and Thibaut, the latter born after his father's death. Thibaut III's wife, Blanche of Navarre, would act as regent for Thibaut IV until 1222 when he came of age. She then retired to found Argensolles, dying in 1229. Thibaut ruled on his own from 1222 until his death in 1253, becoming king of Navarre in 1234. He is recognized as an important French poet, Thibaut le Chansonnier.[5] (See Figure 11.)

Although Blanche of Navarre had acted quickly upon her husband's death to secure the inheritance of her son who was about to be born, she faced considerable challenges in a regency for him of nearly twenty years. Claims to the county came from the daughters of Count Henry II, who had departed for Jerusalem only to marry Isabelle, queen of Jerusalem, and take over the throne there. Henry and Isabelle had two daughters, Philippa and Alice.[6] In 1215, the elder daughter, Philippa, having married Érard, lord of Ramerupt (d. 1243), claimed Champagne. Although eventually thwarted, her claims led to the War of the Champagne Succession (1216–22). Soon after the foundation of Argensolles circa 1222 by the retired regent Blanche of Navarre, other houses of Cistercian nuns began to be fostered by such claimants from Jerusalem. Both Philippa and her sister Alice's daughter Marie founded an abbey of Cistercian nuns in the diocese of Troyes.

Foundations by Claimants to Champagne: Jardin and Piété

The abbey of Jardin-lez-Pleurs was founded near the town of Pleurs before 1229 by Alice of Cyprus's daughter Marie and Marie's husband Walter IV,

Marie of Champagne (1146–98) m. Henry I, Count of Champagne (r. 1152–81)

They had four children:

The elder son: Henry II (b. 1166–d. 1197), ruled as Count of Champagne (1181–97)
(twice under his mother's regency, in 1181–87 and 1190–97, and then continuing to rule until he died in 1197)

In 1190 he left for Jerusalem, making his brother Thibaut III his heir to the countship;
once Henry II arrived in Jerusalem he married Queen Isabelle of Jerusalem.

They had two daughters: Alice of Cyprus, Philippa of Brienne

The elder daughter, Marie (1173–1204), m. 1186 Baldwin of Flanders (d. 1205)

They had two daughters: Jeanne (d. 1244) and Marguerite (d. 1275), successive countesses of Flanders

The younger daughter, Scholastica (b. 1175), m. William IV of Mâcon (d. 1224), count of Mâcon

Their son Géraud II, count of Mâcon (d. 1224), m. Alix Guigonne

Their daughter was Alice of Mâcon (d. 1260), countess of Mâcon, m. John of Dreux (d. 1239)

In 1239 they sold the Mâcon to Louis IX. She became a nun in 1240 and abbess of Lys (1248–59/60).

The younger son: Thibaut III (b. 1179–d. 1201, Count of Champagne (1197/98–1201)
as Count of Champagne (1197/98–1201), m. 1199 Blanche of Navarre (d. 1229)

They had two children: Marie and Thibaut IV, born several weeks after his father's death

Thibaut IV (1201–53) ruled from birth as Count of Champagne, under his mother's regency until 1222

Source: Theodore Evergates, "Aristocratic Women in the County of Champagne," in *Aristocratic Women in Medieval France*, edited by Theodore Evergates, pp. 76–95 (Philadelphia: University of Pennsylvania Press, 1999).

FIGURE 11. Genealogy: Marie of Champagne, daughter of Eleanor of Aquitaine and Louis VII of France.

Table 25. Jardin: Acquisitions Before Blanche of Navarre's Death in 1229

Placename	Description
Estraellis	One *cortil* (small courtyard?), adjoining pond, of late Renaud Staboni
	One *cortil* from Robert the Raguerat
	One *hospicia* (little dwelling) (for a water mill) from Terri Poin
	One *cortil* located behind said mill
	One grange, house, and their property held by William of Courcel
Prés Bordini	One and a half *falcatae* (measure of hay production in a meadow?)
Bernetello	Minute cens and head taxes in various places
Calceya	House of late Lord Garnier of Lyée, the priest
Châtelet	One *cortil* next to Laurencia's
	One *cortil*, which had belonged to the late Thibaut Lescorchie
	Two parts of another *cortil*
	Four deniers over a *cortil* that belonged to Coletus Chevalier
	Half a *cortil* next to the nuns' mill at Pont d'Aube
Conanntre	A sixth of the tithe; a quarter of the straw; taxes over Morselly women, the wife of Leston, and the men and women of Lord John Corberant
Corroy	*Terrage* and eleven sous from Squire Walter of Sousgaye
	Six and a half livres in rents from John of Courgançon
Droueti	One piece of land planted with vines (*edificata ad vineam*)
At Sousgaye?	Land that was Peter la Boule's
Froidcult grange	Land that was Renaud of Pont's
Marigny	*Terrage* from Adam Fray le Margue and Thibaut Lambert
Val Refroy	*Terrage* from Thibaut le Solier
	Eight sestiers of wheat from Squire Raoul of Fera
	Four sous rent and half the *terrage* at Ouchiae

Source: "Chartes du Jardin," edited by Lex, nos. 22 and 23 (1295).

Count of Brienne (1205–46). Although there are a few surviving charters, a medieval obituary for Jardin provides much of the evidence.[7] That obituary describes Marie of Cyprus, Countess of Brienne, as its founder and supporter: "Obiit nobilis domina Maria comitissa de Brianna mater et sublevatrix ecclesie istius de Jardino."[8] The foundation of Jardin had to have occurred before Countess Blanche of Navarre's death in 1229, as is attested by a document from 1295 that lists the earliest properties. (See Table 25.) By 1231 a charter issued by Marie and her husband Walter IV of Brienne, confirmed the gift to Jardin of eighty sestiers of grain payable on All Saints' Day made by the knight John of Toreto, Walter of Brienne's "feudatory." In 1235 support came from Thibaut IV, Count of Champagne, who replaced the ten livres in annual rent at his grange at Sézanne that had been given earlier by that his mother Blanche of Navarre, because the monks of Chézy would not give up their claims there.[9]

The nuns' subsequent acquisitions included that of October 1237 (the first document to mention they were Cistercian nuns at Jardin), in which they bought a mill located between Jardin and Marigny, granting a lifetime annuity to the seller.[10] Later, in a charter from 1260/61 Guy de Louan conveyed half the rights at Marigny-lez-Pleurs (the nuns already owned the other half), including eighteen sestiers of mixed grain (including some rye or oats along with the wheat?), six sestiers of oats, eight sous in cens, sixteen hens, sixteen *fougaces* (hearth cakes eaten at the New Year), and sixteen deniers. In exchange Guy received five arpents of arable land and sixteen arpents of meadow elsewhere. Marigny (near Pleurs) became one of Jardin's granges. There were others at Connantre, Allemant, Saint-Loup-de-Broyes, and Longueville.[11] In December 1253, Isabelle, sister of the late Guy of Charny, confirmed the gift of Longueville made by her own late husband, the knight Jacob, lord of Plancy. This was a working estate "including land, meadows, men and women, rents, customs, rights to graze animals and any other rights Isabelle had there." The grange appears to have continued to be cultivated just as it had been earlier, but parts of it would be leased out in 1281.[12]

Other granges appeared. In 1275 the nuns paid 130 livres to the knight, John of Courberans, his wife Isabelle, and nephew Adam, for a sixth of the tithes at what became the grange of Connantre, as well as a fourth of the hay and straw and twenty-eight deniers of cens paid by the men of Connantre.[13] In 1276 the knight Thibaut of Broyes granted an *amortissement* to Jardin over a vineyard at Allemant that the late priest of Saint-Loup-de-Broyes had given to the nuns.[14] In 1290, Jardin paid eighty livres to John of Gougançon and his wife Margaret for rights "in cens, rents, *terrages*, arable land, meadows, vines, and other things" at Quoirat, Allemant, and Saint-Loup-de-Broyes; these too became granges.[15] Gifts to Jardin could be exemptions from tolls, usage rights in forest, or rights to expand cultivation into wasteland. Thus John, lord of Broyes, in 1239 granted pasture "in all his lands" for Jardin's animals and a cartload of firewood in the forest of Chapton. All this was confirmed by the next lord of Broyes who also granted "rights to make assarts, to reduce land to cultivation, and to construct granges or other buildings in that forest."[16]

Gifts came from a variety of patrons. In February 1254, the knight Hugh of Conflans made one for the anniversary of his late wife, Marie of

Nanteuil—an annual rent of fifty sous to be drawn on the Champagne fairs; it was soon converted into freedom from passage and market tolls at Pleurs.[17] In 1279 Raoul of Thourette left ten livres in annual rents to Jardin's nuns for the soul of the late Raoul, lord of Châtelliers.[18] In 1284 the chaplain of Saint-Rémy of Pleurs agreed to pay three sestiers of grain (half rye and half oats) to the nuns each year for land at Fosse-Martin.[19] By 1270 the nuns were leasing out rights to some of their lands. In June they granted a *hospicia* (little dwelling) in the street called "Voute de Broyes" and two vineyards at Bois d'Essart to Simonetus and Maria, his wife, for two sous of annual rent.[20] Such leasing out of parts of estates, but particularly of vineyards, along with grants to tenants of land *ad medium* to be planted in vines, suggests the importance of viticulture at Jardin.

Among the most long-lived patrons of these nuns was Lord John of Châteauvillain. In 1258 he confirmed a gift to the nuns of twelve sestiers annually of grain and allowed the castellan of Nanteuil to give Jardin a grange and its dependencies. Twenty-three years later, in 1281, it was this same John of Châteauvillain and his wife Jeanne who confirmed all of Jardin's acquisitions in their holdings. Another decade later, in 1292, he adjudicated a dispute over water rights between Jardin and the residents of Pleurs: the nuns wanted to close off their millpond, but the community of Pleurs feared that the proposed mill dam would prevent the stream from carrying off waste from Pleurs's sick house and would alter access to fishing and milling.[21] There is no evidence of any association between Jardin's nuns and that sick house—only proximity in properties.

While Jardin had been founded by Marie, the granddaughter of Henry II, the abbey of Cistercian nuns at Piété-Notre-Dame-lez-Ramerupt was founded by Henry's elder daughter, Philippa, circa 1231.[22] In 1232 Philippa and Érard's son, Érard II of Ramerupt, with his wife Felicity confirmed to Piété the gifts at Méry and Saint-Médard made earlier by Helissande of Marigny and Gerald of Triânel. Felicity in 1234 also confirmed rents of six muids of oats at Val-Cherbite and a single muid of wheat from her rights at Brual. She had earlier given this last muid of wheat at Brual to the lepers of Ramerupt and in her conveyance Felicity noted that unless Piété's nuns took over the leprosarium and ministered to its residents, that muid of wheat would not go to Piété. A 1235 record for the bishop's court confirmed the nuns' control of the leprosarium, but the documents make clear that the nuns and the community of lepers had originated separately.[23]

Philippa and Érard, founders of Piété, had daughters who also supported the nuns. Sibilia became abbess there. Their daughter Isabelle married Henry,

Count of Grandpré (eventually lord of Ramerupt), and confirmed to the nuns rights over woods and brush along the Aube River and over mills at Somme given earlier by her mother, all to be held by Piété in *la main morte*. Another daughter, Marie, had a son named Érard who was lord of Nanteuil, the latter in 1259 confirmed land producing twenty livres per annum, which had been given earlier by his grandmother, Philippa. Érard transformed that twenty livres into an annual payment of nine muids of wheat and two muids of oats; in 1277 his widow, Matilda of Nanteuil, confirmed this into the hands of his aunt Sibilia, abbess of Piété.

There were other early patrons at Piété, including the lord and lady of Marigny, whose gift was confirmed by Érard II in 1232; this conveyance of thirty sous annually at Méry and Saint-Médard is the first document referencing Piété's nuns as Cistercians. Piété also attracted the attention of Blanche of Castile, who in 1250 encouraged Thibaut IV of Champagne to grant *amortissement* to the nuns of Piété over all their earlier acquisitions in his holdings.[24] The abbey also benefited from the last testament of Marie of Esternay dictated in 1279 to another Marie, the prioress of the Paraclete; Marie of Esternay elected to be buried at Piété, giving that abbey and the Paraclete alike bequests of thirty livres *tournois*, but also making gifts to four sisters of Chappes, all nuns at Piété.[25]

Abbess Sibilia also received a bequest from the other branch of the Brienne family, from Walter IV, Count of Brienne (who with his wife, Marie of Cyprus, had founded Jardin). They gave a daily cartload of "long wood" in the East Woods. Their grandson, Walter V, Count of Brienne (1297–1311), later granted Piété the right to acquire land worth twenty livres annually within his holdings. This was donated into the hands of his own sister, Marie of Broyes, who had become abbess of Piété.[26] Such intertwined patronage between the two branches of the family probably eventually weakened both abbeys, since Piété and Jardin eventually may have had to vie for family patronage. Both Piété and Jardin were suppressed. Piété was closed by the Cistercian monks of Clairvaux in the 1440s and Jardin by the monks of Jouy in 1403.

Suburban Locations: Notre-Dame-des-Prés Outside Troyes

More substantial than Piété and Jardin were foundations made by bourgeois and knights from towns in this region where the international fairs were thriving: at Notre-Dame-des-Prés just outside Troyes and at Val-des-Vignes near Bar-sur-Aube. Notre-Dame-des-Prés had its origins circa 1230 at a farm at Chichéry outside the city walls of Troyes.[27] Stephen of Champguyon, citizen of Troyes, had allowed a group of religious women to establish themselves there with the encouragement of the Cistercian abbot of Fontenay. In 1235, the Cistercian abbots of Boulancourt, Arrivour, and Mores and the abbot of Cîteaux recognized that these nuns were part of the Cistercian Order, although the abbey of nuns was to be visited by the bishop of Troyes.[28] The nuns at Chichéry had already begun to acquire endowment: in 1233, Marie of Saint-Médard gave them rents in grain from several mills and in 1234 Hugh of Saint-Maurice and his wife Margaret, lady of Savières, granted a fourth of all their earthly goods to those nuns.[29]

Conflict about these nuns arose almost from the moment of their arrival at Chichéry. In July 1230 Gregory IX received a letter about them from the Benedictine monks of nearby Montier-la-Celle. The enregistered extracts from that account suggest that the monks were deliberately stirring up trouble; perhaps they knew that Gregory IX wanted to enclose religious women and place them under male authority. Information from the complaint was selected by chancery clerks, curial officials, or archivists to include in papal registers: "We have received from the monks of Celle the account of a quarrel over the chapel built by Stephen of Champguyon in the parish of Saint-André where certain women have settled by their own authority."[30] In this extract those women were referred to as "Filia Dei vulgariter appellantur," that is, "called daughters of God in the vernacular."[31] Elsewhere in the papal registers is a lengthier extract from the complaints of Celle's monks:

> Certain women, wearing nuns' dress by their own authority, have
> settled themselves in that chapel, which is near the monk's monas-
> tery [Celle], whence it is possible to hear their voices singing psalms.
> Saying that they are part of the Cistercian Order, they do not
> observe its practices, for they have neither been incorporated, nor
> do they maintain continuous residence in an enclosure or cloister,
> but instead frequently wander around through diverse places in the
> neighborhood of the monks' monastery, and have thus caused great
> scandal, and it [Celle] has been very much defamed, and the monks
> are fearful lest they themselves be destroyed because of any presump-
> tion of evil inferred from the presence of those women in the
> vicinity.[32]

This cannot be taken as an unprejudiced description of the nuns, their behavior, or their participation in any larger women's movement. Instead it amounts to a frantic rhetorical flourishing of misogynous clichés to attack the nuns.[33] Indeed, the entry needs to be treated with caution precisely because the later judgment on the nuns overturned the erroneous claims made by the monks. So the interesting point is that someone somewhere saw the errors in this complaint, for the churchmen sent to investigate absolved the women of all complaints and granted them "sanctioned status in the parish" as *moniales*.

In spite of such distractions the new abbey for Cistercian nuns was soon established.[34] In 1236 and in 1239 Stephen of Champguyon, citizen of Troyes, and his wife Andrea formally ceded rights over the property at Chichéry where the abbey had been founded, including rights in the parishes of Sainte-Savine and Saint-André and in the woods called Betton. Their son, John Magnus, citizen, and his wife Felicia, also a citizen, made a gift to Notre-Dame-des-Prés in 1236, granting the nuns rights over half an oven, land near the city wall and near one of its bridges; the other half of that oven was probably acquired in 1246 when Stephen and Andrea's daughter Isabelle, with her own daughters, confirmed a donation of rights within her dowry share there.[35] It was a good site because the abbey's suburban location allowed the nuns a certain amount of solitude, while they benefited from the abbey's proximity to Troyes's major international fairs and industrial production (particularly of woolen cloth).

Pope Innocent IV's confirmation from early 1247 recognized that the nuns of Notre-Dame-des-Prés followed the Rule of Saint Benedict and the institutes of the Cistercians, the usual designation for a house of Cistercians, whether of monks or nuns. The confirmation listed the abbey site and its granges at Chapelle-Saint-Luc, Méry, and Neuville, as well as houses and an oven in Troyes, and houses and woodlands in the parishes of Sainte-Savine and Saint-André. It granted to the nuns the typical thirteenth-century Cistercian tithe exemption—an exemption from tithes on the cultivation of their noval fields and on their animals and fishponds. Notre-Dame-des-Prés's documents contain a number of references to leprosariums and hospitals on lands adjoining those that came into their hands. Only one of these was ever attached to the nuns and that only after a decade and a half, that at Saint-Julian-de-Méry, which does not appear to be a leprosarium or hospital, but perhaps a hermitage.[36]

The *domus Dei* at Saint-Julian-de-Méry came into the nuns' hands by 1247, and they would manage it as a separate hospice; it was clearly independent of the abbey.[37] It had been granted as a postmortem gift to the nuns of Notre-Dame-des-Prés in 1239 by Jacob, priest of Saint-Benedict, who seems to have been a local man who had established himself there, probably as a hermit. He also confirmed his parents' gift of one hundred sous annually to be paid to the nuns at the fair of Saint-Rémy in Troyes. That rent derived from a house in the *draperie* of Troyes, adjoining the house of the Templars on one side and that of Master Robert the Goldsmith on the other. The priest, Jacob, was still living at Saint-Julian as a pensioner of Notre-Dame-des-Prés in 1245, but the property was described as part of the nuns' properties by the time of the 1247 papal confirmation.

What the priest Jacob had given was not the only source of urban rents for Notre-Dame-des-Prés's nuns. In 1245 the nuns acquired rents over two other houses in the Rue des Drapiers in Troyes and another two properties in the Boucherie of Troyes; others were acquired in 1251 with rents payable at the time of the fair of Saint-Rémy.[38] In 1263 Notre-Dame-des-Prés also acquired rents on the market stalls of the Poivrerie.[39] It was probably a result of the international status of those fairs at Troyes that in 1280 a citizen of Paris named Adam Boudin, having acquired rights over property in Troyes at some time in the past, granted that property in Troyes to Notre-Dame-des-Prés in return for an anniversary for his soul.[40]

Many of the principals in the charters for Notre-Dame-des-Prés, like the family of Stephen of Champguyon, but probably also that of Jacob, the priest, were citizens of Troyes. They often requested religious benefits from Notre-Dame-des-Prés: founding anniversaries for their souls, making gifts when their daughters entered the abbey, or setting themselves up with annuities for old age.[41] The nuns received several conveyances from a family of knights, the Jaucourts, who were dependents of the counts of Champagne and supporters of the nuns at Val-des-Vignes near Bar-sur-Aube as well.[42] One came to Notre-Dame-des-Prés in 1264 from Walter of Jaucourt, canon of the cathedral of Saint Stephen of Troyes.[43] Then in 1269 Érard of Jaucourt and his wife Agnes granted rights in Fontvannes, Prugny, and Vauchassis, a grant confirmed by their lord, Thibaut V, Count of Champagne (1256–69).[44] Thibaut V in 1269 also made concessions to Notre-Dame-des-Prés of income from tolls and taxes at the fair of Saint-Rémy in Troyes, to fund a pittance on the anniversary of his death. He also granted them an *amortissement* allowing them to acquire another thirty livres' worth of income in his fiefs.[45] In

Table 26. Notre-Dame-des-Prés: Rivière des Corps, Acquisitions, 1260s

Date	Donor/Seller	Property Transferred	Amount Paid by Nuns
1262	John of Fontaine and Matilda	gave 10 arpents of vineyards plus 3 arpents of arable land and 1 muid of wheat annually	
1263	William of Saint-Ouen and wife Felicia	sold various rents	85 livres
1266	Walter of Fontaine and John, his son	sold one-fourth arpent of land above Fontvannes and other rents	300 livres
1267	Peter Dores of Moussey	sold rights at Rivière	120 livres
1268	William of Rosières, knight	sold land there	100 livres
	Total for property at Rivière-des-Corps		605 livres

Source: Troyes, AD Aube, 23H178, 23H244, 23H269 Notre-Dame-des-Prés.

April 1270 the new count, Henry III (1270–74), granted rights for Notre-Dame-des-Prés's nuns to collect two hundred cartloads of firewood annually in Martin's Woods at Insula.[46]

The acquisitions by Notre-Dame-des-Prés's nuns within the city of Troyes were extensive, but they were matched or even exceeded by the nuns' acquisitions of vineyards outside the city. Some vineyards were located close to the abbey site, not far to the west, at Rivière-des-Corps, where the nuns expended over six hundred livres in the 1260s. (See Table 26.) They probably also had rights to vineyards farther west of Rivière-des-Corps, in the properties granted by the Jaucourts at Fontvannes, Prugny, and Vauchassis. What is most striking in these purchases is how often the charters describe land and vineyards adjoining those already held by the nuns, for instance in the common vineyards associated with the Babelini family where the abbess spent sixty-two livres in 1282 alone for such vineyards near Chaumont, Moussey, and Rivière.[47] The abbess Isabelle is described as acting directly in these charters and sealing them with her seal, only occasionally replaced by a lay brother named John, who acted as her assistant. (See Table 27.) Such acquisition of vineyards described as being interspersed among the nuns' holdings as well as leases of those vineyards to tenants suggest the giving back and forth of holdings that is characteristic of areas where contracts *ad medium* were used to bring vineyards under cultivation.[48]

Table 27. Notre-Dame-des-Prés: Abbess Isabelle's Purchases in 1282

Seller	Property Conveyed	Amount Paid
Peter of Vierna and wife Ysabelle	sold 1¼ arpents of land/vines at Chaumont, adjoining those belonging to the nuns and 1 arpent at Champ Thibert	14.6 livres
Herbert of Vierna and wife Babelet	sold ½ arpent in *finage* (adjacenies) of Sanoya and ½ arpent at Chaumont	9 livres
Herbert of Vierna and wife Babelet	sold land in *finage* of Arrivour and at Chaumont	9 livres
Sanche Margite of Vierna and wife Pastoris	sold meadow in *finage* of Moussey adjoining Notre-Dame-des-Prés's lands	5.75 livres
Magnus, son of Matthew of Sanoya and wife Babelet	sold ½ arpent in *finage* of Moussey	4 livres
Jacquinus, son of Matthew of Sanoya and wife Babelet	sold land at Champ-de-Rivière	4 livres
Henry of Nazat, goldsmith, and Peter Mollets, citizens	sold 1½ arpents in communal vineyards adjoining those of Babelini	3 livres
Total spent by Abbess Isabelle in 1282		49.35 livres

Source: Troyes, AD Aube, 23H245, Notre-Dame-des-Prés.

The abbey of Cistercian nuns at Notre-Dame-des-Prés, founded with the assistance of the abbots of nearby houses of Cistercian monks also bene-fited from their protection.[49] This may have been the case in 1289, when the nuns were investigated by papal commissioners seeking to collect a "crusader tithe." Those investigating officials reported that the nuns' income was "a total of 80 livres per annum and no more" and that "its population amounted to 41 in all: nuns, *conversae* (lay sisters), students and seculars." The threat of excommunication was soon lifted in an apologetic document making clear that there was no question of default by Notre-Dame-des-Prés's nuns.[50] Such cooperation between monks and nuns was not always the case, but it may help to explain why Notre-Dame-des-Prés was one of the few abbeys of nuns from this region not suppressed by the order's monks.

Suburban Locations: Val-des-Vignes near Bar-sur-Aube

The abbey of Cistercian nuns at Val-des-Vignes was at a second suburban location, just outside the walls of Bar-sur-Aube, where international fairs were held once a year. Unlike Troyes, Bar-sur-Aube was not the bishop's seat, but was subject to the bishop of Langres, although the nuns' primary properties were in the province of Sens. Bar's townspeople as a result were called burghers or bourgeois rather than citizens. Documents for the abbey of Val-des-Vignes usually date its foundation to 1232, but it may have appeared slightly earlier. The major founder was Lord Peter of Jaucourt, a knight whose lands were held directly from Count Thibaut IV; other knightly patrons included the lords of Chacenay. Peter of Jaucourt appears to have begun the foundation of Val-des-Vignes in a methodical way, first by requesting in 1236 an inspection of the site by Cistercian abbots.[51] Also in 1236, Peter of Jaucourt and his wife Alice gave a sixth of the entire fief they held from the Count of Champagne and an eighth of all the major tithes at Chaumont also held from the count.[52] The gift of tithes was confirmed in 1240 by the bishop of Langres and again by Peter of Jaucourt in 1242 when his wife Alice was on her deathbed.[53]

Documents dating from 1231 to 1237 refer to this community as "the abbey of Our Lady, Mother of the Savior [*Notre-Dame-Mater-Salvatoris*]." Indeed Gregory IX, in the fifth year of his pontificate (1231), addressed its nuns as "his dear daughters, the abbess and convent of the Blessed Mary, Mother of the Savior, of the Cistercian Order in the diocese of Langres."[54] In October 1232 the lord of Chacenay, Érard, and his wife, Ameline, gave those nuns rights to gather a daily two-horse cartload of dry wood for heating and cooking from the woods of Boccicaut.[55] Also in 1232, Maria, widow of Anseric or Aimeric, son of Machaut, gave land to the nuns between Ailleville and the monastery of Isles.[56] In 1232 Gerard of Vigne, squire, gave one journal of land to the nuns, selling them another two journaux for three livres *provinois*.[57] Without any site change the nuns soon came to be known as the Cistercian nuns of Val-des-Vignes.[58] Some of their properties were in the vicinity of a possible leprosarium at Bretonval near Bar, and there was also a *domus Dei* dedicated to Saint Nicholas nearby. The documents, early and late, however, distinguish between the three different institutions: an abbey of Cistercian nuns, the lepers of Bar, and the sisters of Saint Nicholas.[59] There was some oversight of the abbey's size by the end of the thirteenth century, when a document dated 1298 shows their abbot visitor, the abbot of Clair-vaux, attempting to limit the size of the community to twenty nuns, three *conversi*, one chaplain, and one confessor.[60]

The nuns of Val-des-Vignes acquired significant vineyards in the vicini-ties of Bar-sur-Aube and Chaumont, including those near the abbey at Aille-ville and Bretonville. (See Table 28.) In 1235 the nuns were given land near their own cemetery by Walter, son of the late Agnes, "mayoress" of Bar; the nuns of Val-des-Vignes then purchased additional vineyards at Ailleville from Walter for one hundred livres.[61] Conveyances nearby came from John and his wife Perrona in 1253, and in 1255 from Barnus of Pringey and his wife Osanneta.[62] Sometimes vineyards were exchanged, as in 1264 when Lawrence Berger and his wife Christina gave vineyards near the abbey in exchange for others elsewhere.[63]

In 1264 two townsmen of Bar, William of Monceaux and Lambert, son of Martin Panini, settled a dispute with the nuns over vineyards at Bretonval, which was very close to Ailleville.[64] (See Table 29.) In 1268, vineyards at Valle Tauron were given by Renard Panifex of Bar, who designated a gift worth ten livres for his niece's entrance as a nun at Val-des-Vignes; the rest of his gift was made so that he could enter religious life at Val-des-Vignes as a *conversus*, or lay brother.[65] Popularity among the bakers is striking: Lambelius of Chaumont, Boulanger, in 1268, and Bernard Panifex, in 1272, also made conveyances to the nuns.[66]

Only one formal grange is recorded for Val-des-Vignes, that at Chau-mont, a comital castle, near which there were a number of vineyards owned by the nuns. (See Table 30.) As seen above, in 1236 the Jaucourts had given an eighth of all their major tithes at Chaumont, which they held from the count, and in 1259 the nuns paid other owners forty-three livres for one twenty-fourth of those tithes.[67] Count Thibaut V in 1261 and again in 1267 confirmed to Val-des-Vignes their acquisitions of tithes at Chaumont, and he may have provided them with income and *amortissement* for additional acquisitions there.[68] The actual grange at Chaumont, with its winepress and wine cellar was purchased in 1268 from Simon Ventarius and his wife Felicia, burghers of that town, for 120 livres, and an additional 100 livres were spent on tithes and more land, presumably for vineyards.[69]

Table 28. Val-des-Vignes: Vineyards Acquired at Ailleville, 1257–77

Date	Seller	Conveyance	Amount Paid by Nuns
1257	Henry Cardesel of Bar	sold vineyards at Ailleville	5 livres
1257	Peter, son of late Aremburgis	sold vineyards	8 livres
1265?	Walter, son of Agnes, mayoress	sold rights at Ailleville	100 livres
1271	John of Monastery and Isabelle	sold land at Ailleville	28 livres
1271	Peter of Bar	sold land at Ailleville	7 livres
1271	Peter of Ailleville	sold various rights	4 livres
1271	Peter of Ailleville	sold land at Ailleville	1 livre
1271	Lawrence and Christina	sold vines at Ailleville	12 livres
1271	Peter Papelarz, cleric, and sister	sold 12 sous rents	9 livres
1272	Stephen T.	renounced rent of 4 sous	2 livres
1272	Agnes of Jaucourt	sold various rights	60 livres
1272	Bernard Panifex	sold vines free of rents	12.25 livres
1272	Érard Cacelie	sold vines at Ailleville	4 livres
1273	Peter Blanchard and Adeline, wife	sold various rights	20 livres
1273	Nicholas C.	sold vines at Tauron	40 livres
1273	Peter Blanchard	sold land at Ailleville	8 livres
1273	Guy of Champignon, Baker?	various	80 livres
1274	Agnes of Jaucourt	sold various land	53 livres
1274	John of Fontaine, knight,	sold rent in mill	60 livres
1274	Martin and Érard of Ailleville, clerics	sold land at Ailleville	9 livres
1275	Martin and Érard of Ailleville, clerics	sold land at Ailleville	21 livres
1275	Christian of Burville	exchanged land at Ailleville	
Total expenditures at Ailleville			543.25 livres
Life leases granted in those lands:			
1268	Jacob of Arras	over vineyard at Ailleville	
1273	Durand Pasque	over vineyard owing 2 sous/year	
1275	Girard le Mareschal	over vineyard owing 5 sous/year	
1277	Paginus, son of Perrin	over vineyard at Ailleville	

Source: Troyes, AD Aube, 3H4036, 3H4039, 3H4042, 3H4044, 3H4063 Val-des-Vignes.

There is evidence that the nuns of Val-des-Vignes, like those of Notre-Dame-des-Prés, rented out parts of their viticultural holdings. Charters show the nuns renting vineyards adjoining those that he already owned to Evrard, butcher, of Bar; also to Jacob of Arras and his wife, who would pay five sous annually to rent a vineyard near Ailleville; also to the widow Poncia for life;

Table 29. Val-des-Vignes: Vineyards at Bretonval, 1243–78

Date	Donors/Sellers/ Other Principles	Property in Question	Price in Livres (If any)
		Gifts	
1243	Jaucourt family	newly planted vineyard	
1256	Richerus of Porte	vines near Bretonval	
1256	Raoul, canon of Saint-Maclou (Bar) and Milo, provost of Chacenay and his wife, Maria	land and vines at Bretonval	
1261	Evrard of Porte and his wife	vineyards beyond Bretonval	
1266	O. Beaubourg and wife Margaret	vines at Bretonval	
1267	Ermengardis, widow	gave 9 livres annual rent from vines	
		Exchanges, Disputes, Planting Contracts and Leases	
1264	Lawrence Berger and wife Christina	exchanged vineyards near Bretonval	
1265	William of Monceaux and Lambert	dispute over vines at Bretonval	
1266	Ulric of Thierry	contract *ad medium vestum* for vines at Bretonval	
1266	Milo of Vire	got life lease	
1269	Lawrence and Cristiana	exchange of vineyards at Bretonval	
1278	John of Bar, priest	exchange of vines at Bretonval and Ailleville	
		Sales	
1242	Peter, son of Evrard of Porte	land at Bretonval	13
1242	Walter Coichet	land at Bretonval above Ailleville	5
1250	Peter of Porte	various rights	3
1255	Varnus of Porte	land near vines	7.5
1266	Guibelin and Johanna of Bar	land at Bretonval	11
1266	Stephen Bonsoeur	vines at Bretonval	18
1266	O. Beaubourg and wife Margaret	land and vines at Bretonval	120
1273	Guibelin and Johanna of Bar	land at Bretonval	11
Total livres paid at Bretonval by nuns			188.5

Source: Troyes, AD Aube, 3H4077, 3H4078, 3H4079, Val-des-Vignes.

Table 30. Val-des-Vignes: Chaumont Grange, Tithes, Land Acquisitions

Date	Donor/Seller	Transaction	Amount Paid by Nuns
1236	Jaucourt family	Gift of tithes at Chaumont	
1259	Thierry of Bourdon	Sale of tithes at Chamont	43 livres
1261	Count of Champagne	Confirmation of tithes at Chaumont	
1267	Deacon of Chaumont	Dispute over tithes of Chaumont	
1268	Simon *Ventarius* of Chaumont	Sale of grange at Chaumont	120 livres
1268	Peter, son of Warner of Chaumont	Sale of land at Chaumont	15 livres
1268	Walter of Chaumont	Sale of land at Chaumont	10 livres
1268	Drouz of Chaumont, *pelletier*	Sale of land at Chaumont	12 livres
1268	Lanbelins of Chaumont	Sale of land at Chaumont	20 livres
1274	Alice, daughter of Margaret of Chaumont	Gift of land at Chaumont when she entered the abbey	
Total expenditures at Chaumont (mostly in 1268)			220 livres

Expenditures for Acquisitions at Three Major Vineyard Sites by Val-des-Vignes
Total expended at Ailleville (Table 28):   543.25 livres   (1257–75)
Total expended at Bretonval (Table 29):   188.5 livres   (1242–73)
Total expended at Chaumont (Table 30):   220 livres   (1259–68)

Combined total for the three sites: 954.75 livres   (1242–75)

Source: Troyes, AD Aube, 3H4071, 3H4083, 3H4085, 3H4086, Val-des-Vignes.

also to a certain Jacob Udalric; and also to Durand Pasque and his wife Marie Bernarde; and also to Milo of Bar and his wife Marie.[70] Other economic activities undertaken by the nuns of Val-des-Vignes included animal husbandry and wool production, as is suggested by a confirmation of pasture rights for fifty animals by Count Thibaut V in 1263; markets for their fleece would be found in the growing fairs, but also in the local textile industries of Bar and elsewhere.[71]

Overall, the nuns of Val-des-Vignes concentrated their expenditures on acquiring vineyards, sometimes establishing tenants on them with life leases, in other cases in grants *ad medium*. Their substantial viticultural assets, which they appeared to be consolidating and improving with replanting campaigns, probably made the nuns' properties a good target for "takeover" by nearby abbeys of Cistercian monks. There was an attempted suppression in 1399, but it succeeded in 1445 when the monks of Clairvaux took over the vineyards and other properties of Val-des-Vignes.[72] Those monks appear to have recognized an important asset, as evidenced by their removal of the nuns' archives to be preserved among their own.[73]

Cour-Notre-Dame

Slightly farther away from a major city, Sens, the seat of the archbishop of
Sens, was Cour-Notre-Dame. The suppression of Cour-Notre-Dame by the
abbot of Cîteaux has been discussed elsewhere, but is discussed here within
the context of other such suppressions in this region.[74] The account begins
with the statutes of the Cistercian General Chapter for 1226, which record an
inspection of the abbey site by neighboring abbots before the women
arrived.[75] The archbishop of Sens had granted the prospective nuns what was
probably a partially constructed church near Michery as well as oversight of
a community of lepers at Viluis. The abbey of Cour became a medium-sized
house of nuns attached directly to the abbot of Cîteaux. Among local patrons
of Cour's nuns were supporters of the Cistercian monks of Vauluisant and of
Heloise and the Paraclete, like Dreux, lord of Triânel.[76]

The charters for Cour show its abbesses acquiring land at a variety of places
and carefully consolidating those acquisitions into larger holdings. The nuns
received the support and encouragement of Blanche of Castile, her sons Louis
IX and Alphonse of Poitiers, and local counts and bishops.[77] Pasture rights were
granted to its nuns by the bishops of Troyes, and Count Thibaut IV confirmed
pasture and other rights to the nuns in 1239 and 1250. The latter conveyance to
Cour records that it was done "as requested by the most excellent lady and my
cousin Blanche of Castile, Queen of France, for our souls and those of our
ancestors."[78] Louis IX confirmed a gift made to the nuns by John of Cour
consisting of two arpents of vines at Villeneuve-le-Roi.[79] A document issued by
Innocent IV at Lyons in 1245 confirms that they were Cistercian nuns and
lists Cour's acquisitions to that date: the monastic site, three granges, and two
dozen other places, including woods, mills, tithes, meadows, and vineyards at
Michery, Sesbonnes, Gissy, Sergines, Fossay, and houses in the city of Sens.[80]

Cour's early abbesses had charters made to record their acquisitions—
more than 280 were eventually copied into a cartulary, which provides considerable evidence for the early nuns' good management. Those charters show
the nuns acquiring nearly a third of their property before 1250. The third
quarter of the century saw another 24 percent of all acquisitions and the
fourth quarter saw 18 percent. Thus, slightly more than 75 percent of the
nuns' acquisitions were made in the thirteenth century, but they stretched
right up to the end of that century. There was no precipitous decline of
acquisitions after 1268 (a date at issue below). A quarter of all acquisitions,
however, still remained to be done in 1300. (See Table 31.)

Table 31. Cour-Notre Dame: Nuns' Acquisitions

Date Ranges	Aquisition Charters	Percent of Total	Cumulative Totals	%
1226–49	95	33%	95	33
1250–74	69	24%	164	57
1275–99	52	18%	216	76*
1300 and later	70	24%	286	100

Source: Auxerre, AD Yonne, H787.
*Just over three-quarters of the 286 acquisitions made by the nuns were made in the thirteenth century, from foundation in 1226 to 1299.

Overall the charters in the Cour-Notre-Dame cartulary confirm that the nuns had managed acquisition and its documentation with skill. Yet this is not the initial impression to be had from the cartulary, which was compiled only in the 1490s. Those charters, carefully stored by the nuns in geographical categories, would be copied into a cartulary for the abbot of Cîteaux, who was in the process of taking over the assets of Cour's nuns and replacing those women with a priory of monks.

The events of the late Middle Ages had been disruptive. During the last campaigns of the Hundred Years' War, the nuns of Cour, located not far north of the archbishop's seat at Sens, were forced to flee to safety at their properties inside the walls of Sens. Afterward they were discouraged from returning to their abbey, although they attempted to do so. Soon the nuns' rights to recover their granges and vineyards were challenged by their father visitors, the abbots of Cîteaux. The latter argued that the buildings were damaged, the vineyards needed to be replanted (and had never been very productive), and the lepers at Viluis were gone.

Jean de Cîrey, abbot of Cîteaux (1476–1501) at that time, commissioned a notary from Sens named Moret to copy the records for Cour into the cartulary, today Auxerre, AD Yonne, H787, *Cartulaire de la Cour*. But rather than celebrating the nuns' good management, the cartulary was organized so that the contracts of land acquisition by the nuns were hidden in its middle quires and pages, and given little prominence. The placement of so many contracts of acquisition deep within the folios of the 1490s cartulary allowed the abbot of Cîteaux and his associates to orchestrate a fictional account about the nuns' failure and inability to recuperate the productivity of their lands. Codicological examination of the volume, whose earliest part may have circulated separately as a dossier for the suppression, makes it clear that the

Table 32. Cour-Notre-Dame: Cartulary Organization

Cartulaire de la Cour-Notre-Dame, Auxerre, AD Yonne, catalog mark F, now MS H787
Physical description: Parchment volume from 1490s. It was bound in leather-covered wood with hasps. The volume contains 222 folios, consisting of a single bifolium followed by 17 quires identified alphabetically and a closing sheet that completes the index. Boards measure 36 × 27 cm and pages 33 × 26.5 cm. The main volume was produced by a single scribe, a notary of Sens named Moret, whose remark "Copie par moy, Moret" is at the bottom of each page ending a charter. A second, clearer hand (called rubricator's, although not in red) inserts commentary. The index and numbering are in the second hand. The quality of the parchment is poor and wavy, defying good reproduction. The interior guard page calls it "Censivement des propriétés . . . de la Court Nostre Dame."

Contents:

Part 1: Single folio numbered zero, in second hand (rubricator) text includes the comment "Not even the labours of Hercules . . ."

Part 2: Fols. 1r–37v. This section begins with the other half of the bifolium followed by three quires, A , B, and C in the hand of Moret. Commentary is added in the second hand, for instance, fol. 1v indicates that the abbot of Cîteaux had commissioned the copying; the opening of fols. 21r–23v comments on the testimony included by Abbess Constance in 1285.

Part 3: Fols. 38r–162v. Charters or title deeds organized by location, opening with those for the abbey's site at Michery and then chronologically. The twelve quires are identified as *D, E, F, G, H, I, K, L, M, N, O, P* (no quire *J*), each in the hand of Moret.

Part 4: Fols. 163r–221v. Charters or title deeds organized geographically and then chronologically including those for Viluis, the leprosarium. This part consists of five quires identified as *a, b, c, d,* and *e,* in Moret's hand. Fol. 163r contains a marginal note in the second hand reporting "These properties were transferred to pay off debts to Saint-Germain-des-Prés in Paris."

Part 5: fol. 222r completes an index begun at the end of quire e in the rubricator's hand.

cartulary presented the nuns of Cour in the worst possible light, making a strong case for their suppression. (See Table 32.)

On the first single page, in a manuscript hand different from that of the notary Moret, are arguments for the nuns' suppression. Composed in an ostentatious humanist rhetoric the opening statement, the diatribe or harangue in a legal argument, maintained "not even the labors of Hercules could restore these properties to productivity."[81] Arguments elsewhere, often in this same darker ink and tighter hand of the original rubricator took the side of the abbot of Cîteaux in denouncing the nuns. The first three full quires (part 2 in the description of Table 32) consist of selected items taken out of context. Among them is a papal act from Clement IV (1265–68) sent to the archbishop of Sens, William of Brosse, in 1267. The archbishop was told that size limitations should be imposed on all abbeys of nuns in his province. This act was accompanied by a letter also issued in 1267 from the abbot of Cîteaux, who limited the community at Cour-Notre-Dame "to forty nuns and other persons, plus their servants . . . unless their endowment should increase."[82] Clement IV during his brief pontificate appears to have circulated such requests widely, for a number of documents limiting the size of houses of nuns have survived for those years, including an act in which Clement himself imposed a limit of sixty nuns on the Franciscan nuns at Longchamp.[83]

Once one inspects the entire contents of the cartulary, it is clear that such a size limit established for Cour in 1267 "unless their endowment increased" would soon have been considered a dead letter, because the nuns were still acquiring new properties. Still, to demonstrate that the nuns had by 1285 wrongfully ignored and exceeded that limit, the cartulary makers introduced evidence about the testimony by Cour's Abbess Constance made before papal commissioners charged with collecting a crusader tithe. It was a tithe that the nuns did not owe, for Cistercian abbots had paid a lump sum in lieu of that tithe for the entire order. While there was no question of the nuns defaulting on an obligation (for they were not subject to that tithe), Abbess Constance was asked to list the number of her dependents (as was seen as well for Notre-Dame-des-Prés above). The abbess Constance asserted that she was responsible for "nearly fifty nuns, lay sisters, and dependents, including eighteen orphans, plus servants, and horses and oxen all needing to be fed." She stressed that some of the rents coming in were very small, pointing out that certain vineyards were producing "only five sous per year and no more."[84] Monastic servants, like Thibaut *carpentarius* of Viluis, who had accompanied her to Sens, added that the nuns' poverty had forced them "to beg in public."[85] By the late fifteenth century, some of the nuns' actions mentioned in this testimony may have been damning, but they were not so in 1285; yet the abbess's spirited testimony of 1285 had been turned into an indictment against her by ambitious, scheming monastic men.

This "proof" of mismanagement was presented early in the cartulary, where the opening comment accompanying the report of Constance's testimony was made very noticeable: "Sufficient evidence on the endowment and value of Cour-Notre-Dame, done in the year 1285 at which time the state of the endowment was in the best condition that it had ever been, and nonetheless it was concluded that the nuns need not pay."[86] Her testimony had become "proof" of the usual clichés about nuns' incompetence, profligacy, and failure to manage population size—part of a late fifteenth-century attempt to malign Cour-Notre-Dame's nuns.[87]

The peculiarities of this example should give historians pause. Indeed it is disconcerting, even before one considers the fact that the abbot of Cîteaux at the time, Jean de Cîrey, had inherited considerable debt, amounting to 25,448 gold florins in 1476.[88] As shown in Table 32 the cartulary of Cour-Notre-Dame, unlike most medieval cartularies, relegated evidence of Cour's extensive and well-managed property acquisitions in the thirteenth and fourteenth centuries to part 3. Moreover, buried deep within part 3, on folio 163r, at the beginning of a section on properties at Viluis that once housed lepers, is a marginal note revealing that assets from Viluis had been used to pay off Cîteaux's debts: "These properties were transferred to pay off debts to Saint-Germain-des-Prés in Paris."[89] So, whose failure was this?

More recently arguments that the nuns invested excessively in "a worthy church" have derived from assumptions about Cour's architecture. This was not elaborate or frivolous architecture, but the remains of what was no more than a simple chapel for a medium-sized community of nuns. The state of construction when the archbishop of Sens granted those nuns an existing church is unknown, but the site evidence suggests that the outlines of a cruciform church were already in place, but that a larger church, once planned, was never completed; possibly its very poorly articulated east end with a rose above lancets had already been started, but this was not extravagant. Indeed, its style and its name, cour or curtis, suggest that the earlier attempt at that place may have been for a Premonstratensian foundation.[90] (See Figure 12.) Whatever the impracticality or excessiveness of that early church undertaken or completed by its nuns, the medieval church was austere in comparison to la Cour's ostentatious doorway on the west wall in the Renaissance style, with its elaborate carvings with the inscription "Probatio dilectionis exhibitio ejus operis 1532." It was constructed by the monks who replaced the nuns.

There is no evidence, except in denunciations by Cistercian monks eager to take over the women's properties, that the nuns of Cour-Notre-Dame

Figure 12. Cour-Notre-Dame, east end.
Photograph by the author.

Figure 13. Cour-Notre-Dame, west end.
Photograph by the author.

Table 33. Abbeys of Cistercian Nuns Suppressed in Northern France Before 1500

Suppression Date	Abbey	Diocese	Reference No.	To Whose Benefit?
1312/1389	Rosiers	Reims	90	Clairvaux?
1393	Belfays	Langres	9	Morimond
1394/1436	Vauxbons	Langres	146	Auberive
1397	Benoîtevaux	Toul/Langres	13	Clairvaux
1399	Isles	Auxerre	85	Pontigny
1399	Mazures	Reims	86	Élan?
1399/1445	Val-des-Vignes	Troyes/Langres	143	Clairvaux
1399/1465	Mont-Notre-Dame	Sens	111	Preuilly
1402/1451	Joie-Notre-Dame	Soissons	64	Cîteaux
1403	Jardin	Troyes	49	Jouy
1432	Lézinnes	Langres/Sens	92	Clairvaux
1433	Droiteval	Toul	35	Morimond
1440s	Piété	Troyes	65	Clairvaux?
1460	Clairmarais	Reims	28	Igny/Clairvaux
1460	Marcilly	Autun/Sens	97	Cîteaux
1460	Monchy	Beauvais	110	Ourscamp
1464	Félipré	Liège/Reims,	38	Saint-Rémy
1466	Belleau	Troyes	10	Clairvaux
1477	Douais	Cambrai	34	Vaucelles
1490s	Cour-Notre-Dame	Sens	61	Cîteaux
1490s	Grâce-Notre-Dame	Troyes	62	Cîteaux

Source: Anne Bondéelle-Souchier, "Les moniales cisterciennes et leurs livres manuscrits dans la France d'Ancien Régime," *Cîteaux* 45 (1994): 193–337, for reference numbers.

were "failures." Indeed, if there were any failures in the late fifteenth century with regard to this suppression, they were the failures of the great Cistercian abbots whose excessive debts had encouraged their taking over of the properties at Cour that had once been given to support Cistercian nuns. These were misappropriations of women's property that were justified only by a blatant misrepresentation of the facts. That those monks were the interested parties and that it was their testimony that was biased becomes particularly clear in the larger context of this chapter about suppressions of houses of nuns wealthy in vineyards. (See Table 33.)

Cîteaux would suppress not only Cour-Notre-Dame, but also Grâce-Notre-Dame in the 1490s. It had earlier attempted to suppress Joie-Notre-Dame in the diocese of Soissons in 1402, but was only successful in 1451.[91] The abbot of Cîteaux was not alone in such suppressions, other abbots in Champagne followed suit and gave similar arguments for such suppressions.

In 1460, they were made by the abbots of Igny and Clairvaux about the nuns of Clairmarais near Reims (whose documents are found today among the Clairvaux documents). As remarked by Pamela Stucky Skinner, who edited the Clairmarais cartulary, letters authorizing investigation of conditions at this house imply that such suppression was a foregone conclusion.[92] There were also suppressions of Piété in the 1440s by Clairvaux and at Jardin by the monks of Jouy in 1403, and that of Val-des-Vignes, attempted in 1399 and accomplished in 1445 by Clairvaux.

Other Abbeys of Cistercian Nuns in the Region

More complicated are the interwoven histories of houses of Cistercian nuns near Provins and Nemours. Mont-Notre-Dame and Joie-lez-Nemours appear to have merged and separated several times. Mont-Notre-Dame-lez-Provins had been founded outside that important cloth and fair town in 1236 by a cleric of Provins, John Bouvier, who gave his entire inheritance to found this abbey of Cistercian nuns. Joie-lez-Nemours, in contrast, was founded in 1231 by a knight, Philip of Nemours, who had ties to the archbishop of Sens. Eventually he had given enough property to have it accepted by the order's abbots as an abbey of nuns.[93] It was this latter abbey that had ties to the properties at Mâlay eventually acquired by the nuns of Lys.[94] Had such houses of nuns for which there is so little surviving documentation once held attractive viticultural land?

There is almost no medieval evidence for the abbey of Cistercian nuns at Belleau, established in 1242, although there were remains of a church in the twentieth century.[95] The name is familiar because of a battle involving U.S. Marines at nearby Belleau Wood in World War I. By 1466 Belleau had become a priory of monks replacing the suppressed nuns. They were told by the Cistercian General Chapter to return to Grâce-Notre-Dame the third volume of a Bible that had been placed there for safekeeping; monks were attempting to convert Grâce too into a priory for men.[96]

Conclusions: Cistercian Nuns, Leprosariums, and Suppression in Champagne

There have been some attempts to explain the suppression of houses of Cistercian nuns in Champagne as the result of the disappearance of lepers.

Although a few abbeys of Cistercian nuns, like Cour-Notre-Dame and Piété, were associated with the care of lepers, this evaluation rejects the notion that suppressions were the result of a late medieval disappearance of leprosy. Indeed assumptions that most Cistercian nuns in this region had their origins in a wave of foundations of leprosariums or *domus Dei* are probably untrue. Certainly such ties were less prominent than once thought.[97] Thirteenth-century abbeys of Cistercian nuns, like the leprosariums that suddenly begin to appear in the twelfth century, tended to be founded outside the walls of the Champagne fair towns because these were the sites available for such foundations. Such sites provided both solitude and isolation, but references to leper houses adjoining the properties of Cistercian nuns most often refer only to their proximity.

A rise and fall in the numbers of lepers in the Middle Ages may have had more to do with dietary changes than anything else, but it turns out to be irrelevant as to why houses of Cistercian nuns were suppressed.[98] What once appeared to be strong evidence for medieval Cistercian nuns' association with the care of lepers has turned out to be unreliable. For instance, the *Life of Yvette of Huy*, the saintly woman engaged in the care of lepers in Belgium, was not tied to the Cistercians until after a Counter-Reformation preface was added to the opening of the *Vita*; the *Vita* itself had been written by a Premonstratensian confessor.[99] When examined closely, the suggestion of such an association based on the account of a conflict over property in 1234 between the lepers at Berneuil and the Cistercian nuns at Joie-Notre-Dame in the diocese of Soissons is also less convincing—at least as evidence of any concern among Cistercian women for lepers, although the case is an interesting one about rivalry for appropriate sites.[100] Jacob of Bazoches, bishop of Soissons, may have tried to impose the care of lepers at Berneuil on women who sought to found a religious community there, but the women's aim, eventually successful, was to have the lepers removed to make way for their own community of Cistercian nuns. There is no evidence that those nuns had any concerns about the care of lepers. Indeed, the bishop's 1234 letter seems to support their aims rather than any concern for the lepers, for it opens with praise of the women and then moves on to formulaic maligning of the lepers:

> Let everyone know that after certain women of our diocese, imbued with ecclesiastical discipline, wished to convert to the religious life [literally *transire:* cross over into], they humbly supplicated us that

we provide for them a tiny place [*habitaculum*] in our diocese, where
they might serve God by taking the garb and rules of monastic life.
Refusing to allow such a pious and praiseworthy proposal to be
impeded by any lack of concern or negligence on our part, and with
the counsel of good men, we have placed [*collocavimus*] those
women at the house of the lepers at Berneuil, moving the habitation
of those lepers into another adjoining house. [We are] placing those
women [there] because those lepers had dilapidated their goods by
evil living.[101]

Yet Cistercian nuns in Champagne and elsewhere were suppressed. The
nuns of the Cistercian Order, once valued for their prayers, began to be
ignored by father abbot visitors once so intent on their prerogatives of visitation of those nuns, except when those abbots could acquire the property that
those nuns had amassed by their earlier careful management. At Clairmarais,
near Reims, the abbot of Clairvaux and his associates abrogated their responsibilities to the nuns when they sent a monk so elderly and deaf that he
could not hear the nuns' confessions; in this case a father visitor was clearly
transferring the burden of "elder care" to the nuns.[102] Bondéelle-Souchier
reports that 20 percent of houses of Cistercian nuns in her study of Francophone areas had been suppressed by 1500. This means, however, that 80
percent of those abbeys for nuns survived, often until the French Revolution.[103] In both cases, whether they were suppressed by abbots seeking to
acquire their valuable property, or they managed to remain viable, such
abbeys of Cistercian nuns were a tribute to the good management by the
women who became Cistercian nuns and abbesses in Champagne (see
Map 8).

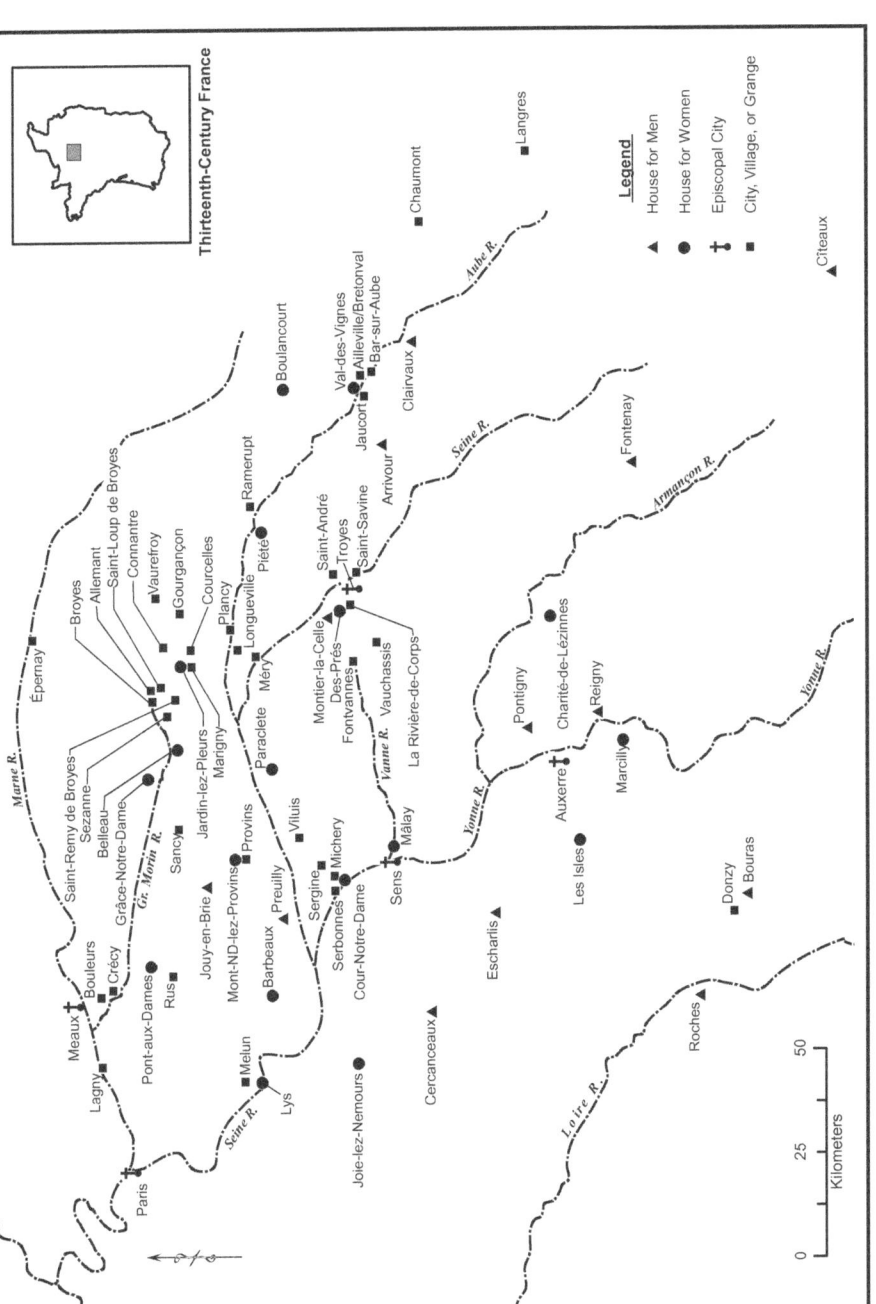

MAP 8. Cistercian abbeys for monks and nuns, Champagne fair towns, and viticulture in western Champagne. Map created by Gordon Thompson.

PART III

Comparisons and Conclusions

CHAPTER 9

Cistercian Nuns and Their Predecessors

This investigation of Cistercian nuns in the province of Sens began by con-firming the presence of abbeys of nuns within the Cistercian Order there. That these were Cistercian nuns, that they had been founded in a variety of circumstances, that they managed their properties well, and that their prayers for patrons were considered effective, are all established here. An unexpected bonus in this study of religious women is that it has uncovered considerable evidence about the activities of the great feudal *dominae*, or lady/lords of the thirteenth century, who were founders, patrons, and even occasionally abbesses of those communities of nuns. Powerful women founders and patrons, including queens and countesses, endowed masses for the souls of their loved ones or created chapels at such abbeys because they believed in the prayers of those nuns. Often they were women who ruled and could not give up their rule to become nuns, but would wait until death to enter the communities they had founded. Surviving documentation is strong—amounting to nearly three thousand charters—and shows a great expansion of those communities in this region in the half century up to 1250.

Comparison to Fontevraud and the Paraclete

Yet in the province of Sens, which included the Capetian heartland but was also close to Champagne and Burgundy where the Cistercian reform had begun, there were relatively few twelfth-century foundations for Cistercian nuns. This was perhaps because of the competition of other groups of reli-gious reformers in this region, including those associated with the western

French reformer Robert of Arbrissel at Fontevraud and those foundations made by the abbess Heloise at the Paraclete.[1] A glance at those earlier foundations at Fontevraud and the Paraclete highlights similarities and suggests that the most important of the differences was that twelfth-century foundations for nuns tended to be organized more hierarchically, with dependent priories. Abbeys of Cistercian nuns followed the organizational principals of the Cistercian Order, insofar as almost all monasteries of monks or nuns would be abbeys, equal to one another.

Although Cistercian abbesses and nuns were not included in the order's General Chapter of abbots and eventually tended to be visited by abbots of neighboring houses, the election of an abbess, among the Cistercians, like that of an abbot, was conducted internally and canonically by those who would be subject to the new head of a house; there was no imposition of an abbot or abbess from outside. Similarly, within the Cistercian organization there was no internal taxation of either monks' or nuns' houses. The Cistercian houses of nuns were full-scale abbeys that hired priests to celebrate mass for their founders and patrons. Each was separate, independent, and equal. In contrast, at the Paraclete and Fontevraud internal organization was monarchical, following the model of Cluny, with a single abbot or abbess as head. We know that prioresses assembled once a year in a chapter at Fontevraud, the abbey founded by Robert of Arbrissel in 1099–1101, and that all houses were priories subject to the abbess of the motherhouse, Fontevraud.[2] We also know that assets granted casually to Robert had to be carefully consolidated by those who followed.[3]

Fontevraud held a favored position under the patronage of counts of Anjou and of Anglo-Norman and Angevin kings and queens, and those patrons often offered them water rights and mills. In 1135 Fontevraud's first abbess, Petronilla of Chemillé, resolved a dispute over a mill the nuns had built at Asnières, giving recompense of forty sous for damage to another mill and fishing.[4] An earlier donor had granted the nuns various rights to fish and rivers, including delivery of five thousand eels per year in 1123.[5] Also in 1123, Amaury of Montfort, Count of Évreux, gave the nuns a mill at Beynes, one at Bardelle with a pond, lands at Mère and at Essarts, *minage* (for measuring salt?) at Épernon and one hundred livres annually at Bavent when his daughter entered Fontevraud as a nun.[6] Included in such support were gifts from Fulk V the Younger, who ruled Anjou from 1109 to 1129, then became king of Jerusalem (1131–43). He had provided Fontevraud with two mills at Chinon long before he departed for Jerusalem in 1229. Other types of rights were gained as well. At his departure Fulk the Younger gave other rights when his daughter Matilda entered Fontevraud as a nun; she served as abbess from 1149 until her death in 1154.[7] In 1135 Henry I of England (1100–1135) made a gift to Fontevraud of money rents at Rouen, London, and Winchester.[8] In that same year (1135) Geoffrey, Count of Anjou, invested the abbey with the *viguerie* (rights to high justice) over its mills on the Loire and other waterways.[9] The nuns also acquired rights over saltworks at Noirmoutier at the mouth of the Loire River.[10]

The centralized structure of the order of Fontevraud, with only priories as daughter houses, was partially paralleled by the leadership of Heloise at the Paraclete, for there too priories were usually the rule. The one exception was the foundation of a second abbey made in the 1140s by Countess Matilda, wife of Thibaut II of Blois, who assisted Heloise in founding a daughter abbey at Pommeraye where Matilda herself would be buried. The latter granted three muids of grain annually from her mill of Crevecoeur for the support of that second abbey.[11] Just as it shared liturgical practices with the Cistercians, the Paraclete had its own, quasi-Cistercian personality, with its organizational structure more mixed than that of Fontevraud.[12]

Priories Versus Abbeys: The Case of Eleanor of Vermandois

The Fontevraud practice had strong ties to the twelfth-century patrons who had supported its widely distributed priories, but that was beginning to change by circa 1200. A good example of this may be seen in the career of Eleanor of Vermandois (ca. 1145–1213/14), Countess of Saint-Quentin and Lady of Valois, the daughter of Eleanor of Aquitaine's younger sister, Petronilla. Among other religious patronage projects, Eleanor of Vermandois founded both a priory of Fontevrist nuns at Longpré circa 1180 and an abbey for Cistercian ones at Parc-aux-Dames in 1205.[13] Bruce Venarde describes Longpré's creation: "In the 1180s Countess Eleanor of Saint-Quentin restored an old house of regular canons . . . replacing it with a community of Fontevrist nuns."[14] The building campaign was to be supported by income from Eleanor's grange of Feigneux along with what she had already granted for it by 1190: "A mill and fishpond at Haramont, 3 muids of grain annually at the mill at Pontrond, the grange of Feigneux and its tithes, annual money rents amounting to 40 livres, a yearly 10 measures of salt from the passage tolls at Crépy-en-Valois, a daily load of dead or fallen wood from her forest at Retz, and pasture in her lands for the nuns' larger animals, excluding sheep and goats."[15] Some of this analysis derives from Louis Duval-Arnould's study of Eleanor's almsgiving; noticeable is that in 1201 when Eleanor established an anniversary for her own soul, she made a gift to the abbey of Fontevraud itself rather than to Longpré.[16] This suggests that Fontevraud's abbey, with its impressive church, was the designated locus for the celebration of anniversary masses for all donors to the order.[17]

So if there was a major difference between twelfth- and thirteenth-century foundations for nuns in northern France, it is that earlier groups had founded priories while Cistercian houses of nuns were abbeys. Such a difference may have had consequences having to do with anniversary masses. Were such abbeys (as opposed to priories) more likely to celebrate masses for souls, even if they had to hire priests for such duties? Were bequests for the celebration of anniversary masses for souls more often made to abbeys than to the dependent priories? Did the advantages of an abbey being more likely to celebrate anniversary masses encourage the elevation of priories to abbeys among the Cistercian houses of nuns in the mid-thirteenth century as was discussed in Chapter 2? Was this an issue of canon law or possibly of Cistercian privilege? On this issue more work needs to be done.

Recruiting Nuns and Acquiring Lands

Much of this expansion of abbeys for nuns in both the twelfth and thirteenth centuries had been possible because of an economic and demographic expansion in the central Middle Ages that allowed many more women to avoid the obligations of childbearing and become nuns, often entering new reform communities of nuns not as young virgins but as adult women. Indeed Venarde argues persuasively that new communities of nuns from eleventh-century Ronceray and Marcigny to twelfth-century Fontevraud and its priories were attractive not just to virgins but to "mature women" and that the convents in his study "were diverse communities that included virgins, widows, and wives, young and old."[18] Similarly he described the social class of donors to the Paraclete, referring to a papal confirmation of 1147: "Eugenius named more than fifty donors, including Count Theobald of Champagne (twice) and his countess, a viscountess, the bishop of Troyes, and the archbishop of Sens."[19] Some were widows who granted their resources in postmortem gifts to houses of nuns as a way of securing annuities for life. Others, having become skilled administrators in the secular world, entered to become abbesses. Still others resigned themselves to taking on monastic garb only on their deathbeds, *ad succurrendum*, because they had assumed the responsibilities of rulership.

Mary Martin McLaughlin also remarked on those who entered the Paraclete as being capable and well-trained widows and married women: "In at least eighteen cases up to 1147, donations were made specifically in behalf of daughters, sisters, nieces, and in one instance, a mother, who became nuns of the Paraclete."[20] Underlining the continuing power of female patrons and abbesses after Heloise died in 1164, McLaughlin compared properties listed in the papal confirmation of 1147 with those confirmed by Bishop Garnier of Troyes in 1194; she also noted the resolution of a dispute with the nearby Cistercian monks at Vauluisant arbitrated by Lady Ermancia of Triânel in 1196.[21] Although neither McLaughlin nor Venarde mentions it, the Paraclete cartulary makes it clear that its abbesses recognized the need to limit population size in accord with endowment.[22]

At these earlier houses of nuns it was endowment that was most similar in type to what those of Cistercian nuns would acquire. According to Venarde, "Heloise gathered wealth quite deliberately, perhaps frequently exchanging or buying lands nearby," and the Longpré holdings were made extensive by the efforts of Eleanor of Vermandois.[23] Moreover, as Venarde continues with regard to Heloise's foundation, the Paraclete's holdings were concentrated close together, often within fifteen kilometers of one another.[24]

As for Fontevraud's priories, Venarde's consideration of the priory of Longpré above is accompanied by that of a second priory located south of Poitiers at Montazais, founded on land given in 1119 to Fontevraud. Its expansion was somewhat hampered in comparison to the purchases made by Fontevraud itself. "Fontevraud was able to use its wealth to obtain title to more lands, often paying out substantial sums for new real estate."[25] This appears to have been less so for Montazais, where few purchases appear to be found among the over two hundred twelfth-century charters for Montazais. Venarde's analysis lends itself to a comparison over two intervals of the nuns' acquisitions (before and after 1165) of tangible (or immovable) assets: land, buildings, and mills, as opposed to those of intangible (movable) ones like rents. (See Table 34.) The Paraclete's nuns, like those of Fontevraud, also acquired income from river rights and mills from an early date when it was still possible to gain privileged access to water resources. By the thirteenth

Table 34. Montazais, Priory of Fontevraud: Types of Donations

Dates	Land, Buildings, Mills, Water Rights	Rents in Cash/Kind*	Total
1135–65	53	13	66
% (three decades)	80%	20%	
1165–1205	41	56	97
% (four decades)	42%	58%	
Total 1135–1205	94	69	163
% (seven decades)	58%	42%	

Source: Bruce Venarde, *Women's Monasticism and Medieval Society: Nunneries in France and England, 890–1215* (Ithaca, NY: Cornell University Press, 1997), p. 44, table 5.
*These are what Venarde calls "tributes."

century, the landscape was coming to be saturated by other owners of such rights.

Forest Rights at Jariel

In the twelfth and thirteenth centuries the Paraclete, like Fontevraud, also sought forest holdings for the needs of its communities. The Paraclete had holdings in the forest of Jariel east of Paris between Tournan-en-Brie and Ozoir-la-Ferrière. The Jariel forest's location, upriver and east of Paris, must have been a prime one for abbeys without access to royal forest, and except for Blanche of Castile's foundations at Maubuisson and Lys, which had extensive royal rights, abbeys of Cistercian nuns also sought rights in places like Jariel. The Paraclete's forest holdings included thirty-five arpents of woodlands associated with its grange called Essarts (the Clearances), and for those nuns the Paraclete's exemption from tithes on recently reclaimed lands (that must thus be considered noval or with noval tithes) may have been critical to making such newly acquired endowment profitable. Certainly such tithes were a recurring theme in the Paraclete cartulary, and they appear to have been associated with their clearance efforts.[26] (See Table 35.)

Cistercian nuns also purchased forest rights at Jariel. For Pont-aux-Dames what was critical was lumber. Those nuns had received an outright gift in 1239 of three hundred arpents of woodland near Lubeton in the forest of Crécy, but they were forbidden from cutting down anything there. They

Table 35. Heloise's *Cartulaire du Paraclet*: Charters Referencing Tithes

Date	Description/Location	Charter Number
1136/45	Tithes of Lesignes	no. 47
1154	Tithes of Saint-Martin-des-Champs and "Boat"	no. 55
1155	Tithes of Saint-Aubin (Roman privilege mentioned)	no. 56
1155	Tithes of Mesnil and Saint-Morice	no. 57
1162	Tithes at Cuchermoy	no. 59
1176	Tithes over mills	no. 62
1180	Tithes and income with Hospitallers	no. 67
1182	Tithes of Lesignes and Saint-Martin-des-Champs	no. 69
1184	Tithes "propriis sumptibus excolunt" with Hospital of Nangis	no. 70
1185	Tithes of priory of Chapelle at Villegruis	no. 71
ca. 1190	Tithes "quorumdam novorum essartorum"	no. 74
1191	Tithes of Quincey	no. 79
1192	Tithes "de novalibus de *Aspreselve*"	no. 80
1196	"Decimas omnium novalium ejusdem decimationis et nemorum, que infra eandem decimationem extirpata reducentur ad plantum"	no. 92
1197	Tithes "a quocumque excolantur"	no. 94
1198	*Novales* of Triânel	no. 97
1199	Tithes at Marigny	no. 101
1199	Tithes of "all assarts"	nos. 104, 105

Source: *Cartulaire du Paraclet*, ed. Lalore.

purchased other forest rights at Jariel, which was closer to the site at Rus to which they moved circa 1140 and where they could get building materials.[27] The most substantial purchases by Cistercian nuns in Jariel appear to be those that were made by the nuns of Saint-Antoine-des-Champs. In January 1243/44, John of Parrochey and his wife Aalydis claimed 130 arpents of woodlands at Jariel, which she had inherited and which they held in the *mouvance* (the overlord's territorial rights) of the children of the late William of Gleseria. Aalydis had paid a yearly rent or cens there of 2.5 deniers per arpent to William of Gleseria. This John of Parrochey and Aalydis sold their rights over those 130 arpents of woodland at Jariel to the nuns Saint Antoine "in *la main morte* and in perpetuity" for five livres *parisis* per arpent. Then Peter of Champs and his wife Julianne sold the nuns an additional 70 arpents for the same price.[28] The first sale amounted to 650 livres *parisis*; the second one to 350; thus the nuns expended 1,000 livres in the 1240s for 200 arpents at

Table 36. Forest of Jariel: Nuns' Acquisitions

Abbey	Date	Acquisition
Paraclete	1222	Nuns received rights associated with the grange of Essarts
	1264	Nuns rented out rights to Guy de Revel for life
	1269	Nuns received holdings in la main morte
Pont-aux-Dames	1238/39	Nuns received 22 arpents of forest at Villeneuve-le-Comte
	1240/41	Nuns of Pont received 40 arpents of woods that the community of Hermières* held from the late Philip of Couvray
	1240/41	Hugh of Châtillon confirmed gift to nuns of 20 arpents of woods adjoining Villeneuve-Saint-Denis by John of Marle.
	1240/41	Hugh of Châtillon confirmed sale of 8 arpents of said forest to Hermières by the knight Renaud of Marle, forbidding clearing land and reserving to himself pears, apples, acorns, nuts, and medlars
	1301	The nuns purchased 90 arpents of woods for 120 livres
Port-Royal	1239/1240	Nuns got 4 arpents at Jariel for 3 livres per arpent paid to Hugh Pilet
Saint-Antoine	1243/44	Nuns purchased 200 arpents in Jariel for 1,000 livres
	1261	Nuns rented 25 arpents there for 6 livres/year; later this was reduced to reduced to 25 sous per arpent.

Sources: *Cartulaire du Paraclet*, nos. 171, 271, and 287; *Pont-aux-Dames*, nos. 63, 74, 128, and 129; *Cartulaire de Port-Royal*, nos. 196, 197, and 198; Paris, AN, S*4386, *Cartulaire de Saint-Antoine*, fols. 11r–16r.
*Hermières was a community of Premonstratensian brothers located in that forest.

Jariel. This was the largest expenditure that is found in the archives for Saint-Antoine. (See Table 36.)

Nearly two decades later, in 1261, the nuns of Saint-Antoine found themselves in need of additional forest rights. But as suggested in Chapter 7, it may have been on the advice of one of the bourgeois nuns, like Blanche of Paciac, that the abbess Jeanne of Saint-Antoine decided to lease rights at Jariel from the abbot of Hermières, rather than purchasing them. Nearly 25 arpents of woodlands there at another place called Essarts were acquired for a rent of six livres, four sous, and four and a half obols annually, and the nuns of Saint-Antoine claimed tithe exemption on the noval lands they were creating there. Eventually, however, the nuns found that they were paying too much and would argue that they were paying more than the "just price" (that is, "the going rate") for their lease there; it was reduced to twenty-five sous, a little over one livre per arpent.[29]

Conclusions

Overall, the comparison between thirteenth-century abbeys of nuns in the region with earlier foundations for nuns there suggests little difference between the thirteenth-century foundations for the white nuns described in this study and those earlier ones. Moreover, abbeys of Cistercian nuns (like the communities dependent on the Paraclete or Fontevraud) could vary considerably in size, wealth, and location. Cistercian nuns managed their properties in ways that were not so different from those of earlier communities of nuns.

The records reveal as well that the types of properties held by Cistercian houses of nuns in the ecclesiastical province of Sens were not much different from those held by the order's earlier foundations for monks and that Cistercian nuns had very similar management practices to those of Cistercian monks. Thus Cistercian nuns held granges with arable land, vineyards, mills, fisheries, and some urban rights and properties that gave them access to markets in Paris and elsewhere (This is with the exception of Saint-Antoine, which had many urban rights.) They held tithes, or at least they held tithes over the production of their granges, which made their agriculture exempt from tithes. They held exemptions from tolls and market taxes, and they held pasture rights and access to woodland for building and heating needs. Maubuisson and Lys also had access to royal forest and areas of forest that were managed in a cycle of pollarding or coppicing. While abbeys of Cistercian monks had probably acquired much more property than did many of those of Cistercian nuns, this study concludes that the ways in which Cistercian monks and nuns supported themselves were quite similar. Moreover, as has been suggested earlier, all abbesses, including Cistercian ones, could give more attention to administration of property, recruitment, and solicitation of endowment, precisely because unlike abbots they were forbidden from undertaking priestly roles.

Founders for nuns were often different. Whereas many of the order's houses of monks had been founded by knights in the twelfth century, thirteenth-century abbeys of Cistercian nuns often had patrons from even higher social levels, including countesses or queens. Abbeys for nuns were also often founded by ladys/lords, *dominae*, whose power and authority had risen in part from a failure of male heirs and deaths associated with various crusades. Many of these abbeys for Cistercian nuns founded in the thirteenth century had strong, viable endowments, important patrons, and high numbers of recruits. Such monastic houses were popular places to send daughters, and lay and ecclesiastical patrons valued their prayers. Thirteenth-century popes and bishops, moreover, seem to have encouraged women's affiliation with the Cistercian Order, seeing Cistercian abbeys for nuns as ideal places for women to exercise their religious vocations, and often recommending them to the General Chapter. Those nuns were also appropriate recipients of tithes, as is seen at Voisins when noble patrons were encouraged by the bishop to grant "his nuns" the ecclesiastical tithes that had come into lay hands.

Moreover, whether we look at Heloise's Paraclete, Fontevraud, or the great Cistercian abbeys of the thirteenth century, communities of nuns elected able administrators, rather than those most pious or most elite. Women who had managed property outside the monastic communities, as regents or heiresses, were perhaps those most likely to be promoted to leadership within the Cistercian women's houses, but such communities were successful as well because not only did they recruit from among capable elite women but they also did not hesitate to admit bourgeois women. They listened to their bourgeois sisters about land acquisitions, for instance, those in Paris, but also possibly with regard to forest acquisitions.

While it is true that thirteenth-century abbesses were soon excluded from the Cistercian Order's General Chapter, they continued to leave their enclosure when necessary to manage their properties.[30] These abbesses were successful in managing endowment in part because they undertook record keeping, making charters and copies of charters to record land acquisitions. Even if they hired scribes to do the writing, the abbesses and nuns could read and organize the documents to the benefit of their communities. Those nuns as administrators reflect the strong abilities of all medieval women to manage property. Moreover, it is those documents that they produced, to be used in property management, that are testament to their existence and their accomplishments.[31]

Still it appears that what was considered sufficient endowment for such abbeys of nuns was often smaller than what had been acquired earlier by Cistercian monks. After circa 1200 Cistercian men's houses seem to have had declining numbers, but they retained that endowment. So at the same time that Cistercian women's numbers were increasing, men's houses had fewer inhabitants but more resources than did women's. Perhaps this is unimportant. As Roberta Gilchrist has suggested, our evaluations of communities of nuns and monks alike should not be based on the number of granges, attractive buildings, or even the contents of their wine cellars, but on how well those monastic foundations fulfilled their Christian duties to minister to the poor and to pray for souls.[32] Abbesses' priorities were not always focused on the material situation in which they found themselves, and nuns seem to have devoted more resources to the poor.[33] Thus the record shows that nuns at Voisins were willing to forgive rents owed by impoverished peasants and those of Saint-Antoine to lower their expectations for income after the Black Death, and those at Coyroux lived under considerably less ostentatious circumstances than the nearby Cistercian monks of Obazine.

Of more concern is a tendency by modern accounts of monasticism to dismiss medieval women's religious houses as filled with women who did not want to be in them. Many studies have disparaged houses of nuns as communities of women who broke their vows or as "dumping grounds" for unwanted, disabled, or possibly even recalcitrant daughters.[34] In addition many monks of the Cistercian Order tended to treat them as interlopers, as imitation Cistercians, and as uncontrollable women who had pushed their way into an order where they were not wanted. Indeed, a misogynous discourse has long poisoned our understanding of all nuns, but including Cistercian ones. Such misogyny, drawn from medieval sources that were obviously self-serving and used by abbots to wrest property rights from nuns, must not be mistaken for truth. Some abbeys of Cistercian nuns in Francophone regions closed by 1500; but more than three-quarters of them survived, often up to the French Revolution. In either case, they had abbesses who managed property well and nuns who were almost never sources of scandal.

Standard treatments of nuns in modern accounts of medieval history have often been based on misogynous tropes found in the monastic histories of the time, clichés brought out for use by ecclesiastical rivals when wealth or property was in question. Modern historians still incorporate those clichés into their own accounts of medieval history, contending that communities of nuns and their abbesses were unsuccessful because women were incompetent, frivolous, profligate of their wealth, and unable to avoid causing scandal or to maintain their monastic vows. The ability of Cistercian nuns and abbesses to manage their own affairs as demonstrated in this study has been ignored by earlier studies of medieval monasticism, which insisted that nuns had to be constantly enclosed and downgraded the value placed on their prayers by medieval men and women, secular and religious alike. The assumption, not based on any discernable facts, that women's houses would not be supported in the Middle Ages because women could not celebrate mass can no longer be upheld.[35]

When modern historians incorporate such misogyny about medieval nuns without question, it can only be concluded that they still adhere to some of its notions. Not to mince matters, the marginalization of religious women in modern histories of the medieval period has been an egregious distortion, perpetrated by modern historians who have accepted earlier misogynies. It is inexcusable, even in face of the fact that it had been espoused by the medieval discourse. Misogynies are not evaluative tools and our job as historians is to weigh and evaluate sources for bias and assess their reliability. Too often medieval monastic documents are still just taken at face value, misogyny and all, because men remain powerful.

This book is about resisting such familiar misogynies, about resisting diatribes about women and religious women from the standard narratives that have formed a significant part of medieval history until recently. Medieval monks and clerics once controlled the discourse of medieval monastic history, and their words have been naively taken as truth. The establishment of a new and different history of nuns and their women supporters has required opposing those misogynies with reconstructions of "what really happened" that are based on evidence that is less biased, but more difficult to use. Only the thousands of administrative records, documents of practice, account books, obituaries, and the like, which are used in studies like this, can provide a firm basis for rejection of that misogynous narrative—a narrative that has long impugned religious women, complained of the burden on religious men of the *cura monialium*, and even congratulated monks on resisting the attempts of those women to live religious lives. Feminist medievalists have begun to challenge such assumptions, but to refute them is an arduous task, for too often the medieval world has been romanticized into something it never was.

Those women's resistance (like our own) to a maligning narrative that was "standard operating procedure" whenever valuable medieval real estate was at issue was wielded at the same time that other mundane things, like efforts to feed their communities, were even more urgent. It is those nuns' efforts, the economic ones, and their very existence (despite centuries of denial) that this study has revealed. It is hoped that its conclusions will allow new considerations of medieval religious and secular women that can start from this point, rather than, as too often has happened, beginning again from scratch, and that it will contribute to a many-faceted image of medieval society.

Ad Medium, Amortissement, Augmented Rents, Measures, Money, Names

Ad medium: literally this is a "half/half" contract, also called *ad medium vestum, ad medium plantum, complant,* and *méplant,* usually used for vineyards or other sharecropping arrangements. This kind of contract is most often used by a lord to develop holdings like vineyards (but also mills) by granting a strip of land to a peasant for planting and cultivating vines; usually after a period of years the vineyard would be divided in equal and full ownership between lord and peasant. Sometimes a holding is described as *ad medium*, as, for instance, in the conveyance of land for Royaumont cited above in Chapter 6. Often the practice is indicated by indirect evidence, for instance, when it is found that Saint-Antoine's nuns had received a number of vineyards at Montreuil-sur-Vincennes, described as adjoining others already owned by the abbey, sometimes on more than one side; this would be the normal result of a series of an *ad medium* contract.

An early example at length, but one in which the division is not actually half and half but something more complicated, is found among the Maubuisson documents, but predating the abbey's foundation. See *Cartulaire de Maubuisson,* nos. 335 (1219) and 336 (1221), p. 341. It reads in part "Terre mee in cultura apud l'Ospitel de Frepeillon colendos ad vineam faciendam, ad medietatem vinorum, fructuum, et arborum in ea provenientium." In this case Raoul of Frépillon, son of Lord Aimard of Frépillon, transferred to Robert de Curia of Sognolles, a plot of land containing two and a quarter arpents, on which the latter was to plant vineyards. One-third of the wine produced was to be paid to Raoul, the original owner, with various other provisions about who fertilized the land, where the grapes were pressed, and so on. It is unusual to find such contracts surviving among the land acquisition documents (like a lease or mortgage, it might be destroyed once the contract had been fulfilled).

Amortissement: A concession required for the transfer of feudal/royal lands that was introduced by great lords and the king circa 1240. It was the outcome of attempts to limit the permanent alienation of feudal holdings into the hands of religious communities, that is, into *la main morte*, or "the dead hand," of the church. The church was an institution that never died, and, unlike an individual, its lands never had to pay feudal relief. Not only was land permanently alienated, but also income from relief was permanently lost. While kings and counts might forbid family members from making excessive alienations to the church, the more effective alternative was to insist that the ecclesiastical recipient acquire a license to do so in the form of an *amortissement*, which could be purchased or otherwise acquired from the feudal lord. Such grants of *amortissement*, however, could also become a form of currency that did not immediately draw down the treasury, but only reduced potential future income from relief. Insistence on such grants of *amortissement* probably began among the great royal vassals like the Count of Champagne, but it soon extended to royal holdings as well. See Evergates, *Aristocracy*, pp. 75–80; and Berman, "Two Medieval Women's Control."

In the 1240s, before leaving on crusade, Louis IX made grants of *amortissement* to religious communities, which would allow them to acquire lands without fine for values up to 500, 600, or even 1,000 livres in annual income. That such requirements had "teeth" is clear in a charter from 1295, "Chartes du Jardin," no. 22 (May 10, 1295), an act in which royal agents charged the nuns of Jardin a fine of eighty-eight livres because they had not acquired an *amortissement* for a list of holdings given by Blanche of Navarre. This act contains a useful list of early properties (see Table 25, "Jardin: Acquisitions Before Blanche of Navarre's Death in 1229"), and the fine was paid, but in fact the claim was anachronistic, for such grants of *amortissement* would not have been made in the 1220s.

Augmented rents: Contracts by which increased rent was promised to owners or investors by an artisanal business or by tenants in a building. Most often, an additional layer of rental payment was agreed to by tenants in return for cash to improve a property. Such contracts often made such reinvestment explicit, indicating the amount "invested" or the time period in which improvements were to be made. The contracts allowed owners to keep property from deteriorating and to increase income from tenants of improved holdings that otherwise would have declined in face of inflation. This was not a case of "speculation," but a legitimate addition to rent in perpetuity over the long term. See Table 23, "Saint-Antoine: Augmented Rents, Examples from Paris, AN, LL1595."

Money: Medieval French money through the mid-thirteenth century was based on the Carolingian system of twelve deniers to the sou and twenty sous to the livre, but only the denier and obol (the half denier) were actually minted until the mid-thirteenth century, and obols were relatively rare. After the Carolingians lost power, there were two developments in wider Francia.

First, the fineness of the Carolingian penny gradually declined until it was only about one-quarter silver; it still functioned as a currency because the economy grew at about the same rate as the money supply expanded. Indeed, inflation over the twelfth century has often been described as about 1 percent for the entire century. Things got worse by the end of the thirteenth century, and the complaints by the nuns of Lys (discussed in Chapter 6) about being paid in cash rather than kind reflect that deteriorating situation.

Second, the medieval pennies, or denier coins, fell out of royal control. They came to be issued by many "feudal" authorities, including those pennies circulated with Matilda of Auxerre's name on them in the 1240s that are mentioned in Chapter 4. Louis IX attempted to bring this under control in the 1260s, attempting to call in other feudal coinages and to put coinage again under royal control. Beyond local areas, he allowed only two royal coins, the *denier parisis* and *denier tournois*, which had a fixed relationship between them with five deniers *parisis* equal to four deniers *tournois*. The difference between *parisis* and *tournois* only occasionally comes up in the documents used here, as when Alice of Mâcon, the first abbess of Lys, is seen expending livres *tournois*. The *tournois* in this case may indicate that she was expending her own resources, for she was paid a life annuity of 900 (originally 1,000) livres *tournois* from the Norman exchequer after the sale of the county of Mâcon. My text follows the example of Baldwin, *Philip Augustus*, p. xv: "All *livres, sous, deniers*, and *marks* designate the money of Paris except when otherwise qualified." Marks appear very rarely in the charters used here. In 1266 a larger silver coin, a twelve-denier coin, began to be issued as the *gros tournois*, but it is irrelevant here as it does not appear anywhere in the documents for this study.

Measures: For weights and measures, only a general idea may be provided, because they varied from one region to the next. Most often in the charters used here, the liquid measure is the *muid*, which might be described as a very large cask or barrel made up of 288 pints (each about 1 US quart). There is a dry measure also called a *muid*, made up of 144 *boisseaux*, or 12 *setiers* or *sestiers* (the latter is closer to the medieval term). One sestier equaled twelve boisseaux; one *mine* (or *émine*) equaled six boisseaux or half a sestier. The *sestier* for flour or grain might be thought of as an 80- to 100-pound sack; the *muid* as a cartload. From "Units of Measurement in France Before the French Revolution," Wikipedia, accessed January 25, 2017.

Land measures include *arpents*, a commonly used unit of land measurement, probably smaller than an acre according to locality; a *quartier* seems to be a quarter arpent, but generally is only a measure of vineyards. Many such descriptions of expanses of land are not absolute but are based on how long it would take to plow; for instance, a *journal* (plural, *journaux*) is the amount of land that could be plowed in a day. Some measures describe an area to be sown with a particular measure of grain—thus, the *sestierade* is the area in which one *sestier* was sown, and so on. Terms indicating development include *mansus/mansi*, which refers to a typical peasant farm, *villa* an estate or manor, but was coming to mean village, *domus*/pl. *domus* was a typical family dwelling; *aula*, or hall, was a more noble residence. *Grange* may be a barn, or an expanse of land, with particular implications as discussed in Chapter 3.

Placenames and personal names: For placenames I have tended to use those most common, for instance, Rome or London. Placenames in the countryside have been identified when possible with modern French names in common usage, but there is inconsistency: Pacy for a mill west of Paris, but Paciac for the Parisian family name. For personal names, I have used those most familiar to medievalists' ears: Eleanor of Aquitaine, for example. Generally, however, women's names have not been Anglicized, so Marie of Champagne, Jeanne of Constantinople, Blanche of Castile, Petronilla, Jeanne, and Guillelma, but men's names are more likely to be so. Sometimes, however, the alternation between John and Jean allows two individuals to be kept straight. Note too that sometimes Saint Mary or Saint-Marie is replaced in the charters for "the blessed Mary"; it was a period when her status as saint was being disputed.

The Evidence: Cistercian Nuns' Charters and Charter Books

The primary evidence for this study consists of charters that record real estate transactions, documenting the conveyance of land and land-related rights by secular men and women to communities of Cistercian nuns. Such charters often survive in local French archives where they were transferred at the time of the French Revolution, but the survival of documents for abbeys in this study varies tremendously. Some are found in departmental depositories, but a few were taken to Paris when the religious community in question was moved into the city.[1] Some of those were later dispersed to more local depositories in the metropolitan area, when archives in the Seine department were dispersed into the archives of new departments, but many are still found in Paris. Medieval volumes of such charters can become valuable on the antiquarian market and end up in places far beyond the religious foundation from which they originated.

Most often originally recorded on parchment, such early charters were almost invariably in Latin, although by the thirteenth century there were lapses into the vernacular, particularly for the names of people and places. The models for these charters were imperial and royal *diplomata*, which in an earlier age had recorded donations by such rulers of land, estates, or income to religious communities. The private charters found in Cistercian collections often copy the form of those earlier great documents, but were most often written in the voice of the secular donor by monastic scribes or local notaries. Such private charters are not official acts, but private ones and list witnesses who might be called back in a dispute. Such charters could be used for almost any type of transaction—even when it records what was clearly (or only slightly disguised as) a sale or lease or pledge of property for a loan.

Whereas in the early middle ages and up through much of the twelfth century, the monastic charters were almost always private acts listing witnesses who could be called back to attest to a transaction, the thirteenth century saw a shift in the use of charters associated with the rise of royal, comital, and ecclesiastical bureaucracies. Such charters made before such an authority became dispositive, that is, became themselves proof of the transaction.[2]

The record of the acquisition and creation of endowment for houses of Cistercian nuns in the province of Sens may sometimes still be read from such charter originals. Sometimes a charter, often a foundation charter, collapses the events of several years onto a single date; that does not necessarily make it a forgery.[3] Sometimes such charters survive as loose parchments, sometimes even with their wax seals intact. Sometimes they were made in multiple "original copies" including those called "chirographs," which consisted of two copies of an original charter made on a single sheet of parchment and then cut apart along a line of letters or with a jagged line so that they could be fit back together.[4]

Such charters also survive in very early copies in charter-books or cartularies often made at nearly the same date as the charters themselves. The production of such charter books, however, doubled the already very expensive process of charter production and many poorer houses of nuns are less well documented today because such copies were never made. Obviously such charters survive remarkably well because they were made of parchment. Nevertheless such charters had an even better chance of surviving if they had been copied into the parchment pages of a medieval charter book or cartulary—which could survive anything short of direct fire.

Moreover the medieval cartulary is itself evidence. Whereas it was once the fashion to assign a lesser value to the cartulary copy of a charter than to the original charter, historians have begun to recognize the value of medieval cartularies themselves for they reflect someone's thinking about organizing and prioritizing individual acts within what was usually a codex.

Still a hazard in the use of cartularies (or the so-called cartularies that are in fact modern compendiums) is the insertion of acts that have the appearance of being charters but are actually ex post facto summaries of a series of events attached to a single date—what the French call *actes-notices*. There are also *pancartes,* which often summarize or omit details, and were made at a slightly later date, often by a bishop confirming many earlier conveyances at once. Charters can also sometimes be presented with rubrication directing a reader toward a specific conclusion.[5]

The foundation and endowment of an abbey of Cistercian nuns might produce hundreds of such private charters. Individual charters used in this study easily number more than three thousand distinct acts; see Appendix 3. Overall such charters provide a very different picture of Cistercian nuns from what is occasionally reported about them in the chronicles for this period.

APPENDIX 3

Specific Charters and Other Materials for This Study, with Earliest Date for Foundation

Date	Abbey (acts/charters)	Sources
Unpublished or partially unpublished:		
1198	Saint-Antoine (550 acts)	Paris, AN, LL1595, *Cartulaire de Saint-Antoine*; S*4386 *Cartulaire de Saint Antoine* Paris: AN H⁵ 3859¹ and H⁵3859² L1014, L1015: S4357–S4373
1226	Cour-Notre-Dame (300 acts)	Auxerre, AD Yonne, H787 (cat. F), *Cartulaire de Cour-Notre-Dame*, 222 fols.
1229	Piété-Notre-Dame (30 acts)	Paris, BnF, Collection Duchesne, vol. 4
1230	Notre-Dame-des-Prés (100 acts)	Troyes, AD Aube, 23H3–335
1231	Val-des-Vignes (120 acts)	Troyes, AD Aube, 3H4001–3H4023
1234	Maubuisson (500 acts)	Pontoise, AD Val d'Oise, 72H10 (later cartulary, 72H12 (account book), 72H80–72H143.
1244	Lys (100 acts)	Auxerre, AD Yonne, H Lhuillier, "Inventaire des titres." Melun, AD Seine-et-Marne, H566, Melun, *Inventaire du Lys* commissed by abbess Claire-Cécile Colbert. Paris, BnF Latin MS 13892, *Cartulaire du Lys* (see Prieur diss.)
Published:		
1204	Clairets (100 acts)	*Abbaye royale de N.-D. des Clairets*, ed. Hector de Souancé, 1894
1205	Port Royal (300 acts)	*Cartulaire de l'abbaye de Porrois . . . Port-Royal*, ed. Adolphe de Dion, 1903

1215	Voisins (170 acts)	*Cartulaire de N.-D. de Voisins de l'Ordre de Cîteaux*, ed. Jules Doinel, 1887
1220	Villiers (100 acts)	"Histoire . . . de Notre-Dame de Villiers . . . ," ed. Paul Pinson, 1893
1222	Lieu-Notre-Dame (150)	*Cartulaire de l'abbaye royale du Lieu-N.-D.-lès-Romorantin*, ed. Ernest Plat,1892
1226	Pont-aux-Dames (250 acts)	*L'abbaye du Pont-aux-Dames*, ed. Berthault, 1878
1226	Eau-lez-Chartres (70 acts)	*Cartulaire de l'abbaye de Notre-Dame de l'Eau*, ed. Charles Métais, 1908
1229	Jardin-lez-Pleurs (50 acts)	"Martyrologe et chartes de N.-D. du Jardin lez Pleurs," ed. Léonce Lex, 1884

Total: Approximately three thousand charters, several *censiers* or rent lists, inventories, cartularies, and one account book

Size Limits of Abbeys for Cistercian and Other Nuns

Date	Abbey	Limit Imposed	Source
1181	Vauxbons (Cistercian)	abbess, 12 nuns, 1 priest, 4 *conversi*	Bondéelle-Souchier, p. 329
1196	Longpré (Fontvraud priory)	60 nuns	*Epistolae*, ed. Loewenfeld, pp. 257–58
1196	Paraclete (Benedictine)	60 nuns	*Cartulaire du Paraclet*, nos. 20 (1196)
1201	Avenay (Benedictine)	40 nuns	Evergates, "Aristocratic Women," p. 218 n. 157
1217	N.D.-aux-Nonnains (Benedictine)	60 nuns	Evergates, "Aristocratic Women," p. 218 n. 157
1222 +	Argensolles (Cistercian)	90 nuns, 10 *conversae*, 20 clerics, *conversi*	Evergates, "Aristocratic Women," p. 218 n. 157
1230	Nun Cotton (Cistercian)	30 nuns and sisters, 12 lay brothers, 3 priests	*Acta of Hugh of Wells*, no. 447
1230	Les Blanches (Cistercian)	50 nuns	Lexington, "Registrum," (1233?)
1230	Moncey (Cistercian)	30 nuns, 6 *conversae*, 4 priests, 2 *conversi*	Lexington, "Registrum," (1230)
1232	Moncey (Cistercian)	28 nuns, 6 *conversae*, 4 *fam*, 4 priests, 2 *conversi*	Lexington, "Registrum," (1233)
1233	Port-Royal (Cistercian)	60 nuns	Lexington, "Registrum," 1233
1244	Borenx (Benedictine)	20 nuns	*Cartulaire du Paraclet*, no. 238
1244	Triânel (Benedictine)	20 nuns	*Cartulaire du Paraclet*, no. 239

1262	Maubuisson (Cistercian)	140 persons	*Cartulaire de Maubuisson*, no. 29
1267	Maubuisson (Cistercian)	140 nuns	*Cartulaire de Maubuisson*, no. 34
1267	Cour-Notre-Dame (Cistercian)	40 nuns and *conversae* and dep.	Auxerre, AD Yonne, H787, *Cartulaire de la Cour*
1268	Maubuisson (Cistercian)	120 nuns	*Cartulaire de Maubuisson*, no. 35
1268	Longchamp (Franciscan)	60 nuns	*Actes pontificaux*, ed. Barbiche, II, no. 1447
1270	Flines (Cistercian)	100 nuns, 2 priests, 18 *conversi/ae*	*Cartulaire de Flines*, no. 173 (1270)
1289	N.-D.-des-Prés (Cistercian)	41 total: nuns, *conversae*, et al.	Troyes, AD Aube 23H14 (1289)
1291	Saint-Antoine, Paris (Cistercian)	140 nuns	Bondéelle-Souchier, pp. 312–13
1298	Val-des-Vignes (Cistercian)	20 nuns, 3 *conversae*, 1 chap, 1 confrère.	Troyes, AD Aube, 3H4003

Numbers of Cistercian Nuns' Houses
According to Selected Historians

1935 Grundmann, *Religious Movement* (1995 trans.), p. 242	Asserts few: "Since Premonstratensians closed their ranks to the reception of new women's houses before 1200, and Cistercians in 1220."	
1967 Fontette, *Les religieuses*, pp. 33/41	Those houses described "*incorporatio pleno jure*":	
	Germany	320
	France	160
	Spain	98
	England	100
	Italy	70
	Belgium	57
	Portugal	10
	Holland	19
	Cyprus	1
	Palestine	1
	Tripoli	1
	Total	837
1974 Schneider, *Die Cistercienser: Geschichte, Geist, Kunst* (Köln: Wienand, 1974)	Cistercian nuns' houses added over time:	
	France	134
	Belgium	47
	Netherlands/Luxembourg	232
	Mittel Europe	319
	Total	523

1977 Lekai, *The Cistercians*, p. 351	"Incorporated houses of nuns"	211
	All nuns' houses	752
1990 Southern, *Western Society*, p. 317, n. 19	Women's houses	654
	Men's houses	742
1994 Bondéelle-Souchier, *Les Moniales*, passim.	In Francophone areas	153
2001 Lawrence, C. H, *Medieval Monasticism*, p. 180:	Nuns	654
	Monks	738
2017 Williams, David. See Figure 2 above, "The growth of the early Cistercian nunneries in ten-yearly cycles"		

NOTES

ABBREVIATIONS

AD   Archives Départementales
AN   Archives Nationales
BnF Bibliothèque nationale de France
PL   *Patrologiae cursus completus . . . sive Latinorum, sive Graecorum*, ed. Jean-Paul Migne
     (Paris: Migne, 1857–66), Latin volumes

PREFACE

1. Louis J. Lekai, *The Cistercians: Ideals and Reality* (Kent, OH: Kent State University Press, 1977), devoted a single, separate chapter, pp. 347–63, to nuns; on p. 352 he concluded, "at their peak the total number of convents was probably greater than that of the monasteries."

2. There is no gazetteer of women's houses of the Cistercian Order like that compiled for houses of Cistercian monks by Leopold Janauschek, *Originum Cisterciensium* (Vienna, 1877; repr., Ridgewood, NJ: Gregg Press, 1964); the promised second volume on nuns never appeared. Among recent surveys that emphasize such diversity, see Bernadette Barrière et al., eds., *Cîteaux et les femmes: Actes des rencontres de Royaumont* (Paris: Créaphis, 2001).

3. Jean-Berthold Mahn, *L'ordre cistercien et son gouvernement des origines au milieu du XIIIe siècle (1098–1265)*, 2nd ed. (Paris: Boccard, 1951), on the 1180s for exemption from episcopal visitation; on tithes, see Chapter 1 below.

4. On this point, J.-M. Canivez, "Cadouin," in *Dictionnaire d'histoire et de géographie ecclésiastiques*, ed. Alfred Baudrillart et al., vol. 11 (Paris: Letouzey et Ané, 1949), pp. 118–22, is useful.

5. Constance H. Berman, *The Cistercian Evolution: The Invention of a Religious Order in Twelfth-Century Europe* (2000; repr., Philadelphia: University of Pennsylvania Press, 2010).

6. Thus, a document for Clairvaux from 1190 reports that its practices were those of the Benedictine Rule and the institutes of the brothers of Cîteaux: *Recueil des chartes de l'abbaye de Clairvaux au XIIe siècle*, ed. Jean Waquet, Jean-Marc Roger, and Laurent Veyssière (Paris: CTHS, 2004), no. 277 (1190).

7. That the movements were rarely gender specific is true not just for the Cistercians but for other groups; see Yvonne Seale, "Reading the Premonstratensian Landscape: Women, Space, and Patronage in Northern France, c. 1120–1400" (PhD diss., University of Iowa, 2016).

8. See Erin L. Jordan, "Roving Nuns and Cistercian Realities: The Cloistering of Religious Women in the Thirteenth Century," *Journal of Medieval and Early Modern Studies* 42 (2012): 597–614; and Elizabeth Makowski, *Canon Law and Cloistered Women: Periculoso and Its Commentators, 1298–1545* (Washington, DC: Catholic University of America Press, 1997).

9. Ljubljana State and University Library, MS 32, opens with the vows to be made to the abbess by lay brothers.

10. For the more spiritual side of those nuns' lives, see Simone Roisin, "L'efflorescence cistercienne et le courant féminin de piété au 13ème siècle," *Revue d'histoire ecclésiastique* 39 (1943): 342–78; Roger de Ganck, "The Cistercian Nuns of Belgium in the Thirteenth Century Seen Against the Background of the Second Wave of Cistercian Spirituality," *Cistercian Studies* 5 (1970): 169–87; Caroline Walker Bynum, *Jesus as Mother: Studies in the Spirituality of the High Middle Ages* (Berkeley: University of California Press, 1982); and Bynum, *Wonderful Blood: Theology and Practice in Late Medieval Northern Germany and Beyond* (Philadelphia: University of Pennsylvania Press, 2007); Alistair Minnis and Rosalyn Voaden, eds., *Medieval Holy Women in the Christian Tradition, c. 1100–c. 1500* (Turnhout: Brepols, 2010); Anne E. Lester, *Creating Cistercian Nuns: The Women's Religious Movement and Its Reform in Thirteenth-Century Champagne* (Ithaca, NY: Cornell University Press, 2011); and June L. Mecham, *Sacred Communities, Shared Devotions: Gender, Material Culture, and Monasticism in Late Medieval Germany*, ed. Alison Beach, Constance H. Berman, and Lisa Bitel (Turnhout: Brepols, 2014).

11. See Jacques de Vitry, *The Historia Occidentalis of Jacques de Vitry: A Critical Edition*, ed. John Frederick Hinnebusch (Fribourg: University Press, 1972), p. 117.

12. See Lisa M. Bitel, *Isle of the Saints: Monastic Settlement and Christian Community in Early Ireland* (Ithaca, NY: Cornell University Press, 1990), pp. 73–98.

13. On *ad succurrendum*, see Giles Constable, *The Reformation of the Twelfth Century* (Cambridge: Cambridge University Press, 1996), pp. 82–87.

14. Erin L. Jordan, "Gender Concerns: Monks, Nuns, and Patronage of the Cistercian Order in Thirteenth-Century Flanders and Hainaut," *Speculum* 87 (2012): 62–94.

15. Eileen Power, *Medieval English Nunneries, c. 1275–1535* (1922; repr., Cambridge: Cambridge University Press, 2010), p. 25; on p. 29 it refers to a nunnery as a "dumping ground."

16. Emilie Amt, "Making Their Mark: The Spectrum of Literacy Among Godstow's Nuns, 1400–1550," in *Nuns' Literacies in Medieval Europe: The Kansas City Dialogue*, ed. Virginia Blanton, Veronica O'Mara, and Patricia Stoop (Turnhout: Brepols, 2015), pp. 310–14.

17. Two American studies have also long since taken on Power's conclusions about nuns, which were based in part on a biased examination of bishops' registers, which only collected instances in which women were censured, but none for men; see Penelope D. Johnson, *Equal in Monastic Profession: Religious Women in Medieval France* (Chicago: University of Chicago Press, 1991); and Marilyn Oliva, *The Convent and the Community in Late Medieval England: Female Monasteries in the Diocese of Norwich, 1350–1540* (Woodbridge: Boydell, 1998).

18. It included nearly all of the modern departments of Aube, Eure-et-Loir, Haute-Marne, Loire, Loir-et-Cher, Nièvre, Seine-et-Marne, Seine-et-Oise, and Yonne, as well as parts of the Val-d'Oise and the Marne.

19. Blanche's record book is now in Pontoise, AD Val d'Oise, 72H12, back cover reads: *Achatz d'heritages pour Maubuisson*; hereafter it is cited as *Achatz d'héritages*; see summary of contents in Chapter 6, Table 11. The conveyances listed here come from fols. 38v–39r (1241–46). Parts of the book's opening section were published by Henri de L'Épinois, "Comptes relatifs à la fondation de l'abbaye de Maubuisson, d'après les originaux des archives de Versailles," *Bibliothèque de l'École des Chartes* 29 (1858): 550–69, but it contains inaccuracies.

20. See Constance H. Berman, "Two Medieval Women's Control of Property and Religious Benefactions in France: Eleanor of Vermandois and Blanche of Castile," *Viator* 41 (2010): 151–82, and Chapters 6 and 9 below.

CHAPTER I

1. This chapter incorporates parts of Constance H. Berman, "Were There Twelfth-Century Cistercian Nuns?" *Church History* 68 (1999): 824–64.

2. Berman, *The Cistercian Evolution*, 1–42; and Ellen F. Arnold, *Negotiating the Landscape: Environment and Monastic Identity in the Medieval Ardennes* (Philadelphia: University of Pennsylvania Press, 2013), pp. 41–61.

3. See Uta-Renate Blumenthal, *The Investiture Controversy: Church and Monarchy from the Ninth to the Twelfth Century* (Philadelphia: University of Pennsylvania Press, 1991).

4. H. E. J. Cowdrey, "Archbishop Aribert II of Milan," *History* 51, no. 171 (1966): 1–15; Dyan Elliott, *Fallen Bodies: Pollution, Sexuality, and Demonology in the Middle Ages* (Philadelphia: University of Pennsylvania Press, 1999). That there may have been some truth in the accusation of priests granting land to their children is seen in Jean-Pierre Poly, *La Provence et la société féodale, 879–1166: Contribution à l'étude des structures dites féodales dans le Midi* (Paris: Bordas, 1976).

5. Jo Ann McNamara, "Canossa and the Ungendering of the Public Man," in *Render unto Caesar: The Religious Sphere in World Politics*, ed. Sabrina Petra Ramet and Donald W. Treadgold (Washington, DC: American University Press, 1995), pp. 131–50; Constance H. Berman, "Gender at the Medieval Millennium," in *The Oxford Handbook of Women and Gender in Medieval Europe*, ed. Judith M. Bennett and Ruth Mazzo Karras (Oxford: Oxford University Press, 2013), pp. 545–60.

6. Giles Constable, *Monastic Tithes: From Their Origins to the Twelfth Century* (Cambridge: Cambridge University Press, 1964).

7. Tithes are discussed in James S. Donnelly, *The Decline of the Medieval Cistercian Laybrotherhood* (New York: Fordham University Press, 1949), pp. 50ff.; on complaints, see Coburn V. Graves, "The Economic Activities of the Cistercians in Medieval England (1128–1307)," *Analecta Sacri Ordinis Cisterciensis* 13 (1957): 3–62, esp. pp. 45–54.

8. Constance H. Berman, "Cistercian Development and the Order's Acquisition of Churches and Tithes in Southern France," *Revue bénédictine* 91 (1981): 193–203; see Chapter 3 on Rifreddo and Chapter 4 on Port-Royal's tithes.

9. Giles Constable, "Forgery and Plagiarism in the Middle Ages," *Archiv für Diplomatik, Schriftgeschichte, Siegel- und Wappenkunde* 29 (1983): 1–41.

10. David J. Herlihy, "Treasure Hoards in the Italian Economy, 960–1139," *Economic History Review*, 2nd ser., 10 (1957): 1–14. More recently the complaint by Eleanor of Vermandois that the canons of Saint-Quentin had melted down a golden chalice that she had given them to pay for construction emphasizes the issue; see Ellen Shortell, "Erasures and Recoveries of Women's Contributions to Gothic Architecture: The Case of Saint-Quentin, Local Nobility, and Eleanor of Vermandois," in *Reassessing the Role of Women as "Makers" of Medieval Art and Architecture*, ed. Therese Martin (Leiden: Brill, 2012), p. 167. Expansion into deserted parts of late imperial towns often uncovered treasure that had long been buried, and spolia began to be used for new church buildings; see Dale Kinney, "Roman Architectural Spolia," *Proceedings of the American Philosophical Society* 145 (2001): 138–61.

11. On buildings, see Conrad Rudolph, *The "Things of Greater Importance": Bernard of Clairvaux's "Apologia" and the Medieval Attitude Toward Art* (Philadelphia: University of Pennsylvania Press, 1990); on accounting, Robert F. Berkhofer III, *Day of Reckoning: Power and Accountability in Medieval France* (Philadelphia: University of Pennsylvania Press, 2004).

12. See Constance H. Berman, *Medieval Agriculture, the Southern French Countryside, and the Early Cistercians: A Study of Forty-Three Monasteries* (Philadelphia: American Philosophical Society, 1986), p. 33 nn. 16 and 17 on a transfer from Saint-Michael of Cuxa to the Cistercians.

13. Ludo J. R. Milis, "Ermites et chanoines réguliers au XIIe siècle," *Cahiers de civilisation médiévale* 22 (1979): 39–80.

14. *Cartulaire de l'abbaye de Berdoues près Mirande*, ed. abbé Cauzarin (The Hague: Nijhoff, 1905), nos. 173 (1152), 189 (n.d.), 190 (1212), 222 (n.d.), 229 (n.d.), 231 (n.d.), 232 (n.d.), 253 (n.d.), and 266 (1155); Berman, *Medieval Agriculture*, p. 34 n. 23. There seem to have been many such tiny houses of reformers founded along the Languedoc coast that were eventually absorbed by abbeys like Valmagne; see Berman, *The Cistercian Evolution*, pp. 205–20.

15. Bede K. Lackner, *The Eleventh-Century Background of Cîteaux* (Washington, DC: Cistercian Publications, 1972).

16. Henrietta Leyser, *Hermits and the New Monasticism: A Study of Religious Communities in Western Europe, 1000–1150* (London: Macmillan, 1984).

17. On the *Exordium Parvum*, see many online versions and Latin text cited in note 40 below.

18. *Cartulaires de l'abbaye de Molesme, ancien diocèse de Langres, 916–1250*, ed. Jacques Laurent (Paris: Picard, 1907–11), vol. 2, nos. 79, 126, 135.

19. *Histoire du prieuré de Jully-les-Nonnains*, ed. Abbé Jobin (Paris: Bray, 1881), p. 29, nos. 1–12 (hereafter cited as *Histoire de Jully*).

20. *Histoire de Jully*, nos. 6 (1133), 3 (March 1128), 7 (before 1137), and 9 (1142). See also Alexis Grélois, "Humbeline-Héloise: Variations autour de deux figures du monachisme féminin au XIIe siècle," in *Universitas scolarium: Mélanges offerts à Jacques Verger par ses anciens étudiants*, ed. Cédric Giraud and Martin Morard (Geneva: Librairie Droz, 2011), pp. 329–46; my thanks to M. Grélois for providing me a copy.

21. Jean Leclercq, "Cisterciennes et filles de S. Bernard à propos des structures variées des monastères de moniales au moyen âge," *Studia Monastica* 32 (1990): 139–56, citing *Histoire de Jully*, no. 1 (n.d.); unless otherwise noted, all translation are the author's own, in this case from Leclercq's French.

22. "Cartulaire de l'abbaye de Boulancourt de l'ancien diocèse de Troyes," ed. Charles Lalore, *Mémoires de la Société académique de l'Aube* 33 (1869): 101–92.

23. Anne Bondéelle-Souchier, "Les moniales cisterciennes et leurs livres manuscrits dans la France d'Ancien Régime," *Cîteaux* 45 (1994): 193–337, at p. 316.

24. See *The Letters of Heloise and Abelard: A Translation of Their Collected Correspondence and Related Writings*, ed. Mary Martin McLaughlin and Bonnie Wheeler (New York: Macmillan, 2014); Mary Martin McLaughlin, "Heloise the Abbess: The Expansion of the Paraclete," in *Listening to Heloise: The Voice of a Twelfth-Century Woman*, ed. Bonnie Wheeler (New York: St. Martin's Press, 2000), pp. 1–17.

25. Laurent Veyssière, "Cîteaux et Tart, fondations parallèles," in Barrière et al., *Cîteaux et les femmes*, pp. 179–91.

26. It would eventually share the order's tithe privilege *Desiderium quod* possibly issued to Tart in 1147; see *Patrologiae cursus completus . . . sive Latinorum, sive Graecorum*, ed. Jean-Paul Migne (Paris: Migne, 1857–66), vol. 180, cols. 1199–1200. The text of *Desiderium quod* is

cited in full in Berman, *The Cistercian Evolution*, p. 294 n. 105; the Migne volumes are hereafter cited as *PL*.

27. Bondéelle-Souchier, "Moniales," p. 269.

28. Bondéelle-Souchier, "Moniales," p. 329.

29. Bondéelle-Souchier, "Moniales," pp. 238–39, 252.

30. Bondéelle-Souchier, "Moniales," pp. 249, 308.

31. Bondéelle-Souchier, "Moniales," pp. 255 and 308 and see discussion of Montreuil below in chapter 3.

32. Bondéelle-Souchier, "Moniales," p. 255, 308. My thanks to archivists in Laon, AD Aisne, who provided me with copies of documents for Fervaques and to those grad students who have worked on them, including Russell L. Friedman, Christopher Schabel, and Heather Wacha.

33. *Liber instrumentorum memorialium: Cartulaire des Guillems de Montpellier*, ed. A. Germain (Montpellier: Société archéologique de Montpellier, 1884–86), no. 96 (1172).

34. *Histoire de Jully*, no. 10 (1145): Eugenius's grant of authority over Jully and its daughter houses to Molesme may have been part of a systematic removal of references to female followers in the revisions of Bernard's *Vita Prima*, as described by Adriaan H. Bredero, *Bernard of Clairvaux: Between Cult and History* (Grand Rapids, MI: William B. Eerdmans, 1997), p. 214. A distancing from religious women may have been associated with a fear of heresy that began in the 1140s; see Constant J. Mews, "The Council of Sens (1141): Abelard, Bernard, and the Fear of Social Upheaval," *Speculum* 77 (2002): 342–82.

35. Jean de la Croix Bouton, "L'établissement des moniales cisterciennes," *Mémoires de la Société pour l'histoire du droit et des institutions des anciens pays bourguignons, comtois, et romands* 15 (1953): 83–116; and Bouton, "Saint Bernard et les moniales," in *Mélanges Saint Bernard: XXIVe Congrès de l'Association bourguignonne des sociétés savantes (8e Centenaire de la mort de Saint Bernard), Dijon, 1953* (Dijon: Marlier, 1954), pp. 225–47.

36. Berman, *The Cistercian Evolution*, 143; Janet Burton, *The Foundation History of the Abbeys of Byland and Jervaulx*, Borthwick Texts and Studies 35 (York: University of York, 2006), xxi.

37. Beverly Mayne Kienzle, *Cistercians, Heresy and Crusade in Occitania, 1145–1229: Preaching in the Lord's Vineyard* (York: York Medieval Press, 2001); Christine Thouzellier, *Hérésie et hérétiques: Vaudois, Cathares, Patarins, Albigeois* (Rome: Edizioni di storia e letteratura, 1969), also noted the incompetence of Cistercian abbots in that preaching.

38. See *The History of the Albigensian Crusade: Peter of les Vaux-de-Cernay's "Historia Albigensis,"* trans. W. A. Sibly and M. D. Sibly (Woodbridge: Boydell, 1998), pp. 68 and 85; and *Cartulaire de Notre-Dame de Prouille*, ed. J. Giraud (Paris: Picard, 1907).

39. Conrad of Eberbach, *Exordium Magnum Cisterciense, sive Narratio de initio cisterciensis ordinis*, ed. Bruno Griesser, Series Scriptorium Sacri Ordinis Cisterciensis 2 (Rome: Editiones Cistercienses, 1961; repr., Turnhout: Brepols, 1994); see also Conrad d'Eberbach, *Le Grand Exorde de Cîteaux, ou Récit des débuts de l'Ordre cistercien*, trans. Anthelmette Piébourg, intro. Brian P. McGuire (Turnhout: Brepols, 1998); *The Great Beginning of Cîteaux: A Narrative of the Beginning of the Cistercian Order; The "Exordium Magnum" of Conrad of Eberbach*, trans. Benedicta Ward and Paul Savage; ed. E. Rozanne Elder (Kalamazoo, MI: Cistercian Publications, 2012.)

40. See *Les plus anciens textes de Cîteaux: Sources, textes, et notes historiques*, ed. Jean de la Croix Bouton et Jean-Baptiste Van Damme (Achel: Abbaye cistercienne, 1974); and many

recent English translations of the *Exordium Parvum* online. See "Exordium Parvum," accessed June 19, 2017, http://www.ocso.org/resources/foundational-text/exordium-parvum.

41. An apostate abbess and the sister of Saint Benedict are the only women mentioned.

42. John Van Engen, "The 'Crisis of Cenobitism' Reconsidered: Benedictine Monasticism in the Years 1050–1150," *Speculum* 61, no. 2 (April 1986): 269–304; on Cluny, see Barbara H. Rosenwein, *To Be the Neighbor of Saint Peter; The Social Meaning of Cluny's Property, 909–1049* (Ithaca, NY: Cornell University Press, 1989); Dominique Iogna-Prat, *Order and Exclusion: Cluny and Christendom Face Heresy, Judaism, and Islam (1000–1150),* trans. Graham Robert Edwards (Ithaca, NY: Cornell University Press, 2002); and Constable, *Reformation of the Twelfth Century.*

43. Often cited is R. W. Southern, *Western Society and the Church in the Middle Ages* (Harmondsworth: Penguin, 1990), pp. 315–17; but see numbers in Appendix 5.

44. *Statuta capitulorum generalium ordinis cisterciensis ab anno 1116 ad annum 1786,* 8 vols., ed. Joseph-Marie Canivez (Louvain: Bureaux de la Revue, 1933–41), vol. 1, introduction; I have avoided citing *Twelfth-Century Statutes from the Cistercian General Chapter: Latin Text with English Notes and Commentary,* ed. Chrysogonus Waddell (Brecht, Belgium: Cîteaux, Commentarii cistercienses, 2002), because I disagree with his dating of manuscripts; see Berman, *The Cistercian Evolution,* pp. 46–92.

45. See Lekai, *The Cistercians,* pp. 348–49, citing *Statuta,* ed. Canivez, vol. 1 (1191, no. 27), "Domino regi Castellae, scribatur, quia non possumus cogere abbatissas ire ad Capitulum de quo scripsit et si vellent ire, sicut eis iam consuluimus, multum nobis placeret"; the response "that they had no authority to compel nuns" to attend meetings at Alphonso's foundation but "that they would be pleased if those nuns did attend such a chapter" is not a denial that Huelgas had Cistercian nuns. Indeed the king's request that the abbots compel Iberian Cistercian nuns to attend such a chapter reveals that there were already a number of communities of Cistercian nuns south of the Pyrenees when Huelgas was founded. Many of these abbeys in Spain remain to be studied, but see Ghislain Baury, *Les religieuses de Castille: Patronage aristocratique et ordre cistercien, XIIe–XIIIe siècles,* with preface by Adeline Rucquoi (Rennes: Presses Universitaires de Rennes, 2012); my sincere thanks to Professors Rucquoi and Baury for providing me copies of both the book and the earlier dissertation and other materials.

46. *Documentación del Monasterio de Las Huelgas de Burgos (1116–1230),* ed. José Manuel Lizoain Garrido (Burgos: J. M. Garrido Garrido, 1985), no. 11 (1187), the foundation document. Hereafter the collection is cited as *Documentación de Las Huelgas.*

47. One such chapter at Fontevraud is clearly documented for 1189; see Berenice M. Kerr, *Religious Life for Women, c. 1100–c. 1350: Fontevraud in England* (Oxford: Oxford University Press, 1999), pp. 8, 134, and 135. On chapters of Cistercian abbesses, see Chapter 2.

48. Herbert Grundmann, *Religiöse Bewegungen im Mittelalter: Untersuchungen über die geschichtlichen Zusammenhänge zwischen der Ketzerei, den Bettelorden, und der religiösen Frauenbewegung im 12. und 13. Jahrhundert* (Berlin: Ebering, 1935); an edition with revisions made in additional chapters was published in 1961 with those revisions republished in 1970 (Darmstadt: Wissenschaftliche Buchgesellschaft, 1970). Grundmann's work saw a resurgence following translation in 1995 into English of the 1961 version: *Religious Movements in the Middle Ages: The Historical Links Between Heresy, the Mendicant Orders, and the Women's Religious Movement in the Twelfth and Thirteenth Century, with the Historical Foundations of German Mysticism,* trans. Steven Rowan (South Bend, IN: Notre Dame University Press, 1995). While the 1961 and 1970 versions deal more extensively with religious women in added chapters, citation to Grundmann's first edition and translation of that original text, rather than to the added chapters, is

more appropriate in such a chronological survey. Quotations from Grundmann are from Rowan's translation.

49. Grundmann, *Religious Movements*, pp. 69–88.

50. See discussion of Lester, *Creating Cistercian Nuns*, in Chapter 8.

51. See *"Historia Occidentalis" of Jacques de Vitry*, p. 6 for date circa 1220, text on p. 117. It is cited in Grundmann, *Religious Movements*, p. 307 n. 41 and p. 309 n. 5.

52. Grundmann, *Religious Movements*, pp. 91–92.

53. Grundmann, *Religious Movements*, pp. 99 and 318 n. 57.

54. Ernst Günther Krenig, "Mittelalterliche Frauenklöster nach den Konstitutionen von Cîteaux," a volume of *Analecta Sacri Ordinis Cisterciensis* 10 (1954): 1–105. Translations from Krenig are my own.

55. Krenig, "Mittelalterliche Frauenklöster," p. 17.

56. Krenig, "Mittelalterliche Frauenklöster," pp. 17–20.

57. On papal provision, Krenig, "Mittelalterliche Frauenklöster," p. 21 n. 4, cites Catherine E. Boyd, *A Cistercian Nunnery in Mediaeval Italy: The Story of Rifreddo in Saluzzo, 1220–1300* (Cambridge, MA: Harvard University Press, 1943), p. 92, where she says: "Thus the legislation of the general chapter was fruitless in the face of papal determination to reform decadent nunneries through the agency of the Cistercians and to please the powerful patrons of nunneries by granting them affiliation with the popular order of Cîteaux." Here, the English is from her text but cited by Krenig.

58. Krenig, "Mittelalterliche Frauenklöster," p. 20.

59. Krenig, "Mittelalterliche Frauenklöster," pp. 15–16, in the original reads "sondern mehr als persönlicher Vermittler. . . . Infolgedessen sei Tart Cîteaux eigene Tochter."

60. Bouton, "L'établissement des moniales" and "Saint Bernard et les moniales."

61. The imagery is found on YouTube videos of 1953 newsreels.

62. Lekai, *The Cistercians*, p. 349.

63. Édouard de Moreau, *L'abbaye de Villers-en-Brabant aux XIIe et XIIIe siècles: Étude d'histoire religieuse et économique* (Brussels: A. Dewit, 1909); but Martinus Cawley, "Four Abbots of the Golden Age of Villers," *Cistercian Studies Quarterly* 27 (1992): 299–328, discussing "Abbot Walter of Utrecht: 1214–1221" on p. 316, suggests that the "resignation" of eight houses of Cistercians in the diocese of Liège to the abbot of Cîteaux by Walter of Villers could not have concerned only those of nuns. Cawley suggests that Walter, "faced with a depletion of seniors in his own house to serve as models for newcomers," had attempted to transfer the problem back to Cîteaux. In my view this should not be construed as evidence of an order-wide problem about the care of nuns' souls.

64. Sharon K. Elkins, *Holy Women of Twelfth-Century England* (Chapel Hill: University of North Carolina Press, 1988); Fiona Griffiths, " 'Men's Duty to Provide for Women's Needs': Abelard, Heloise, and Their Negotiation of the *Cura Monialium*," *Journal of Medieval History* 30 (2004): 1–24.

65. See Bondéelle-Souchier, "Moniales," p. 315, for Poulagny: see discussion of Rifreddo and Nonenque in Chapter 3.

66. Micheline de Fontette, *Les religieuses à l'âge classique du droit canon: Recherches sur les structures juridiques des branches féminines des ordres* (Paris: Vrin, 1967), pp. 9–11, my translation.

67. Moreover, as she remarks with regard to the Cistercians, she has deliberately left out any reference to what she describes as the "many communities that only practiced the [Cistercian] customs without being affiliated." Fontette, *Les religieuses*, p. 153 n. 2: "Nous avons fréquemment évoqué le phénomène de communautés pratiquant les 'coutumes' d'un ordre ou même dirigées par certains de ses membres et qui ne lui étaient juridiquement affiliées."

68. Fontette, *Les religieuses*, p. 34.

69. Fontette, *Les religieuses*, p. 30.

70. Fontette, *Les religieuses*, p. 29; here echoing Krenig, Fontette then explains that, like Tart, other such private foundations made by abbots "at Coyroux or at Morimond's foundation in 1125 of Belfays, for the wives of those who had entered Morimond . . . existed outside of any intervention by the general chapter" (p. 30).

71. Fontette, *Les religieuses*, p. 53.

72. Fontette, *Les religieuses*, pp. 33 and 41; on p. 63 she concluded that "Cistercian nuns' efforts bore immense fruit and Cistercian nuns succeeded very well, while women among the Premonstratensians just gave up the struggle." Recent study of the Premonstratensians might contest that; see Seale, "Reading the Premonstratensian Landscape"; the discussion of Yvette Huy at the end of Chapter 8; and work by Shelley Amiste Wolbrink, most recently, "Necessary Priests and Brothers: Male-Female Cooperation in the Premonstratensian Women's Monasteries of Füssenich and Meer, 1140–1260," in *Partners in Spirit: Women, Men, and Religious Life in Germany, 1100–1500*, ed. Fiona J. Griffiths and Julie Hotchin (Turnhout: Brepols, 2014), pp. 172–212.

73. Elizabeth Hyde, "The Cistercian Priory of Nun Cotton," paper presented at the Eleventh Conference on Medieval Studies, sponsored by the Medieval Institute, Western Michigan University, Kalamazoo, May 2–5, 1976 (based on what would be a 1977 dissertation, "The Cartulary of the Priory of Nun Coton in Lincolnshire"); my thanks to E. Rozanne Elder for confirming the date and title of this paper; obviously conferences in Kalamazoo spurred some of this research. The modern name is Nun Cotham.

74. Janet Burton, *The Yorkshire Nunneries in the Twelfth and Thirteenth Centuries*, Borthwick Paper 56 (York: University of York, 1979).

75. Coburn V. Graves, "English Cistercian Nuns in Lincolnshire," *Speculum* 54 (1979): 492–99.

76. On the practice, see Daniel Buczek, "Medieval Taxation: The French Crown, the Papacy and the Cistercian Order," *Analecta Cisterciensia* 25 (1969): 42–106; and Constance H. Berman, "Cistercian Women and Tithes," *Cîteaux* 49 (1998): 95–128.

77. My translation of Graves, "English Cistercian Nuns," p. 496 n. 28 citing *Calendar of Close Rolls, 1268–1272*, p. 301 (54 Henry III, 1270): "Venerabili et in Christo dilecto domino W. decano majori Linc' ecclesie frater Johannus dictus abbas Cyster' salutem. . . . Discrecioni vestre per presentes litteras intimamus quod abbatisse monialium de Stikeswolde, de Grenefeld, de Cotun, de Legburn', de Goukewell, de Sancto Michaele extra Stamf', licet habitum ordinis nostri portare videantur, non tamen sunt de ordine nostro nec eidem ordine incorporate, propter quod nec gaudere debent privilegiis et libertatibus ordinis nec de nostro ordine reputari. Datum apud Cisters' tempore capituli generalis. Anno Domini m.cc. septuagesimo." The letter is accompanied by another item of business concerning the archdeacon, suggesting that it was he who had had these items enrolled; his intervention suggests that he was not only being officious but seeking to find vulnerable communities from which he could collect the tithe.

78. Sally Thompson, "The Problem of Cistercian Nuns in the Twelfth and Early Thirteenth Centuries," in *Medieval Women: Dedicated and Presented to Professor Rosalind M. T. Hill on the Occasion of Her Seventieth Birthday*, ed. Derek Baker (Oxford: Ecclesiastical History Society, 1978), pp. 227–52, the assessment based on Thompson's work for *Women Religious: The Founding of English Nunneries After the Norman Conquest* (Oxford: Clarendon Press, 1991).

79. Sally Thompson, "Why English Nunneries Had No History: A Study of the Problems of the English Nunneries After the Conquest," in *Distant Echoes*, vol. 1 of *Medieval Religious Women*, ed. John A. Nichols and Lillian Thomas Shank (Kalamazoo, MI: Cistercian

Publications, 1984–85), pp. 131–49. Thompson reproduced assumptions about medieval nuns found in Power's 1922 *Medieval English Nunneries*; see Preface above.

80. Brigitte Degler-Spengler, "The Incorporation of Cistercian Nuns into the Order in the Twelfth and Thirteenth Century," in *Hidden Springs: Cistercian Monastic Women*, vol. 3, bk. 1 of *Medieval Religious Women*, ed. John A. Nichols and Lillian Thomas Shank (Kalamazoo: MI: Cistercian Publications, 1995), pp. 85–134, from Degler-Spengler's "Einleitung: Die Zister-zienserinnen in der Schweiz," *Helvetia Sacra* (Bern) 3 (1982): 507–74; cf. Degler-Spengler, "Die Zisterzienserinnen in der Schweiz," *Cistercienser-Chronik* 94 (1987): 124–32.

81. Berman, "Were There Twelfth-Century Cistercian Nuns?" (This paper was originally submitted in 1997, appearing only two years later because it was apparently lost.) See also Roberta Gilchrist, *Gender and Material Culture: The Archaeology of Religious Women* (London: Routledge, 1994), esp. pp. 22–40.

82. As seen in William C. Jordan, "The Cistercian Nunnery of La-Cour-Notre-Dame-de-Michery; a Community That Failed," *Revue bénédictine* 95 (1985): 311–20, which is discussed in Chapter 8.

CHAPTER 2

1. This chapter expands on Constance H. Berman, "Beyond the Rule of Saint Benedict: The Imposition of Cistercian Customs and Enclosure on Nuns in the Twelfth and Thirteenth Centuries," *Magistra* 13 (2007): 3–40; see also Berman, *The Cistercian Evolution*, pp. 46–92 and Mahn, *L'ordre cistercien*, pp. 1 and 50ff., which describe how papal privileges of exemption from episcopal visitation for houses of monks came to be order-wide in the 1180s. For Cluny's immunities and exemptions, see Barbara Rosenwein, *Negotiating Space: Power, Restraint, and Privileges of Immunity in Early Medieval Europe* (Ithaca, NY: Cornell University Press, 1999); and for Spain, Francesco Renzi, "The Bone of the Contention: Cistercians Bishops and Papal Exemption; The Case of the Archdiocese of Santiago de Compostela (1150–1250)," *Journal of Medieval Iberian Studies* 5 (2013): 47–68.

2. Lekai, *The Cistercians*, p. 50.

3. Canivez, "Cadouin."

4. *Les codifications cisterciennes de 1237 et de 1257*, ed. Bernard Lucet (Paris: Centre National de la Recherche Scientifique, 1977).

5. Voisins was visited by its founder, Manasses, bishop of Orléans, and successive bishops of Orléans; see *Cartulaire de Notre-Dame de Voisins de l'ordre de Cîteaux*, ed. Jules Doinel (Orléans: Herluison, 1887), hereafter cited as *Cartulaire de Voisins*; and Chapter 4.

6. See discussion below of visitation in the 1240s.

7. Hippolyte Bonnardot, *L'abbaye royale de Saint-Antoine-des-Champs de l'ordre de Cîteaux: Étude topographique et historique* (Paris: Féchoz et Letouzey, 1882), no. 2 (1204).

8. *Statuta*, ed. Canivez, 1226, no. 33, for Cour and see Chapter 8; on Maubuisson and Lys, see Chapter 6; for Saint-Antoine, see Chapter 7.

9. *Cartulary of the Cathedral of Holy Wisdom of Nicosia*, ed. Nicholas Coureas and Christopher Schabel (Nicosia, 1997), no. 63 (1222). This was not the only house of nuns in Nicosia associated with the Cistercians. See William Duba and Christopher Schabel, "A Documentary History of St Theodore Abbey," in *A Cistercian Nunnery in the Latin East: The History and Archaeology of St Theodore Abbey, Nicosia, Cyprus*. Edited by M. Olympios and C. Schabel. Leiden: Brill [forthcoming].

10. *Codifications*, ed. Lucet, pp. 351–52, no. 4 in 1237 and no. 6 in 1257 have same text: "Abbatisse que filias habent non intersint visitationibus que fient ab abbatibus, sed ipsi abbates per se visitent, corrigenda que corrigant, et statuant que secundum formam ordinis viderint statuenda. Abbatisse vero matres si postea accesserint, possunt caritative corrigere: si qua invenerint corrigenda, dummodo caveant pro omnibus, ne de hiis que statuerit visitator, minuere vel mutare omnino non presumant, vel in contrarium statuere, vel que ipse [iusserint] redigere in scripturam."

11. *Codifications*, ed. Lucet, p. 350, 1257, no. 3, says: "Nec abbatisse seu moniales quacumque de causa personaliter accedant ad capitulum generale."

12. *Cartulaire et documents de l'abbaye de Nonenque*, ed. C. Couderc and J.-L. Rigal (Rodez: Carrère, 1955), hereafter cited as *Cartulaire de Nonenque*, no. 88 (1267).

13. Constance H. Berman, "The Life of Pons de Léras, Knights and Conversion to the Religious Life in the Twelfth Century," *Church History and Religious Culture* 88 (2008): 119–37.

14. Herman of Tournay, *De miraculis sanctae Mariae Laudunensis*, in *PL*, vol. 156, cols. 962–1018.

15. See Chapter 3 on Obazine/Coyroux, and Chapter 1 on Jully.

16. See *Statuta*, ed. Canivez, 1243, nos. 55–68, which evidence attempts to install abbot visitors, but such non-abbatial visitation appears to have taken place in some instances until at least 1249; see below.

17. *Statuta*, ed. Canivez, 1295, no. 3.

18. *Statuta*, ed. Canivez, 1267, no. 71; 1268, no. 66.

19. Bondéelle-Souchier, "Moniales," p. 316

20. See Chapter 3.

21. Alexis Grélois, "L'expansion cistercienne en France: La part des affiliations et des moniales," in *Norm und Realität: Kontinuität und Wandel der Zisterzienser im Mittelalter*, Vita regularis: Ordnungen und Deutungen religiosen Lebens im Mittelalter, ed. Franz J. Felten and Werner Rösener (Berlin: Lit Verlag, 2009), pp. 287–325, notes on pp. 311–12 that Cistercian practices were used by the nuns of Yerres in a mixed practice associated with Victorines as well; this was confirmed by Alexander III in 1165. My thanks to M. Grélois for forwarding other studies and to Professor Franz Felten who forwarded this volume and many other studies to me. The difficulties of this mixed practice with regard to liturgy are seen in Janet Sorrentino, "In Houses of Nuns, in Houses of Canons: A Liturgical Dimension to Double Monasteries," *Journal of Medieval History* 28 (2002): 361–72.

22. *The Acta of Hugh of Wells, Bishop of Lincoln, 1209–1235*, ed. David M. Smith, Publications of the Lincoln Record Society 88 (Woodbridge: Boydell, 2000), no. 447.

23. Lexington had converted to the Cistercian life at Quarr Abbey on the Isle of Wight, became abbot of Sawley in England (1223–29), then of Savigny in Normandy (1229–43), and finally of Clairvaux (1243–56). In 1228, he had been sent to conduct a visitation of the Cistercian monasteries in Ireland that resulted in a dossier of 107 surviving letters. Many of them concern the lack of education and disorder in the Cistercian monasteries there. See Stephen of Lexington, *Letters from Ireland, 1228–1229*, trans. Barry W. O'Dwyer (Kalamazoo, MI: Cistercian Publications, 1982), from "Registrum epistolarum Stephani de Lexinton abbatis de Stanlegia et de Savigniaco," ed. Bruno Griesser, *Analecta Sacri Ordinis Cisterciensis* 2 (1946): 1–118 and 8 (1952): 234–57.

24. "Registrum epistolarum" (1952), p. 235, no. 11 (1231), Blanches-Abbaye (Mortain).

25. "Registrum epistolarum" (1952), pp. 241–42, no. 13 (1232), Blanches-Abbaye (Mortain) and Villers-Canivet. Both active and passive enclosure are apparent here; not only should nuns

not depart from the enclosure, but others should not enter; on this see Jane T. Schulenburg, "Strict Active Enclosure and Its Effects on the Female Monastic Experience (500–1100)," in *Distant Echoes*, vol. 1 of *Medieval Religious Women*, ed. John A. Nichols and Lillian Thomas Shank (Kalamazoo: Cistercian Publications, 1984), pp. 51–86.

26. "Registrum epistolarum" (1952), pp. 238–39, 240–41, 243–45, nos. 10 (1231) and 12 (1232) and 14 (1233), Moncey priory. See *Statuta*, ed. Canivez, 1213, no. 4, which already prevented the nuns of Saint-Antoine from having to receive male visitors: "Prohibitur firmiter ut nullus monachus vel conversus Ordinis nostri in domo monialium Sancti Anthonii iuxta Parisios comedat vel pernoctet."

27. Such maxima established for nuns' houses, offer an opportunity to gauge relative size; see Appendix 4, "Size Limits for Abbeys for Nuns, Cistercian and Other Nuns"

28. "Registrum epistolarum" (1952), p. 250, no. 21 (1233?); Blanches (Mortain) is censured for accepting too many women.

29. "Registrum epistolarum" (1952), pp. 238–39, 240–41, 243–45, nos. 10 (1231), 12 (1232), and 14 (1233); Moncey priory was reduced to twenty-eight nuns, rather than thirty, with the same six lay sisters, but now four *familiares*, or household servants, and the same four clerics and two conversi, if necessary. Stephen noted that the nuns needed to repair the armoire in which their books (and accounts) were stored, suggesting that he had been inspecting those accounts.

30. "Registrum epistolarum" (1952), p. 251, no. 23 (1233).

31. "Registrum epistolarum" (1952), p. 252, no. 24 (1233?).

32. *Cartulaire de l'abbaye de Maubuisson (Notre-Dame-la-Royale)*, ed. Adolphe Dutilleux and Joseph Depoin (Pontoise: Société Historique du Vexin, 1890–1913), hereafter cited as *Cartulaire de Maubuisson*, nos. 29 (1262), 34 (1267), and 35 (1268). See further discussion of the sources in Chapter 6.

33. Southern, *Western Society*, pp. 250–59; Lekai, *The Cistercians*, pp. 11–20.

34. "The Tract on the Conversion of Pons de Léras, and the True Account of the Beginning of the Monastery at Silvanès," trans. Beverly Mayne Kienzle, in *Medieval Hagiography: An Anthology*, ed. Thomas Head (New York: Routledge, 2001), pp. 495–513.

35. Charta Caritatis, chap. 7, accessed July 3, 2017, http://www.osb.org/cist/charta .html#Chap.7.

36. *Statuta*, ed. Canivez, 1226, no. 33.

37. *Codifications*, ed. Lucet, 1237, no. 15: 1.

De monialibus ordini non sociandis. Nulla monasteria monialium sub nomine vel iurisdictione ordinis nostri de cetero construantur vel ordini socientur. Qui vero contra hoc petitionem ad capitulum portaverit vel aliquid scienter per quod possit institutio tam utilis enervari si monachus aut conversus fuerit, a domo propria emitattur, non nisi per generale capitulum reversurus. Si abbas fuerit, omnia sexta feria sit in pane et aqua et extra stallum abbatis usque ad sequens capitulum generale, in ipso capitulo super hoc veniam petiturus. Si quas vero ex precepto domini pape, aut alia necessitate suscipere oportuerit, non prius ordini socientur donec peractis competenter edificiis, ita possessionibus et rebus necessariis sufficienter dotate fuerint quod possint moniales includi penitus et incluse secundum ordinem vivere, ita quod eas non oporteat mendicare.

38. Reference to begging at this time may be associated with the specific concerns of Cardinal Hugolino, later Gregory IX (1227–41), about mendicancy by religious women like

Clare of Assisi; see Lezlie S. Knox, *Creating Clare of Assisi: Female Franciscan Identities in Later Medieval Italy* (Leiden: Brill, 2008); and Catherine M. Mooney, *Clare of Assisi and the Thirteenth-Century Church: Religious Women, Rules, and Resistance* (Philadelphia: University of Pennsylvania Press, 2016).

39. Cf. Berman, *The Cistercian Evolution*, p. 86, which discusses establishment of such zones of patronage in southern France.

40. *Statuta*, ed. Canivez, 1218, no. 4: "Abbatiae monialium de cetero non construantur infra VI leucas a nostris abbatiis et infra se habeant distantiam x leucarum."

41. See Roisin, "L'efflorescence cistercienne"; John Freed, "Urban Development and the 'Cura Monialium' in Thirteenth-Century Germany," *Viator* 3 (1972): 311–27; and Degler-Spengler, "Incorporation of Cistercian Nuns."

42. *Statuta*, ed. Canivez, 1213, no. 3: "Item constituitur auctoritate Capituli generalis ut moniales quae iam etiam incorporatae sunt Ordini, non habeant liberum egressum." Again, all translations are my own. Cistercian leaders' concerns about gender separation were apparent already in the 1140s in the systematic erasure of evidence of ties between Bernard of Clairvaux and the nuns at Jully. See Chapter 1.

43. Dijon, AD Côte-d'Or 78 H 1042, on enclosure for Tart from Lucius III, December 1184: "Prudentibus virginibus." All this would be background to the eventual issuance of *Periculoso*; see Makowski, *Canon Law and Cloistered Women*.

44. *Statuta*, ed. Canivez, 1218, no. 84. "Moniales quae de cetero incorporantur Ordini, sicut definitum est, penitus includantur, et nullum habeant proprium. Liceat tamen abbatissae cum duabus egredi propter inevitabiles causas, de licentia abbatis cui commissae sunt, si potest fieri, quod tamen rarissime fiat et honeste. Qui visitator taxet numerum personarum quem transgredi non liceat." Cf. *Codifications*, ed. Lucet , 1237 no. 15: Latin text cited above in n. 38; see remarks by Erin Jordan, "Roving Nuns."

45. *Statuta*, ed. Canivez, 1220, no. 4: "Inhibetur auctoritate Capituli generalis ne aliqua abbatia monialium de cetero Ordini incorporetur. Moniales Ordinis nostri includantur, et quae includiae noluerint a custodia Ordinis se noverint eliminatas. Licet tamen abbatisse cum duabus, vel cellerariae ad procurandum negotia domus exire."

46. *Statuta*, ed. Canivez, 1228, no. 16, in full: "Nulla monasteria monialium de cetero sub nomine aut sub iurisdictione Ordinis nostri construantur, vel Ordini socientur. Si quod vero monasterium monialium nondum Ordini sociatum vel etiam construendum, nostras institutiones voluerit aemulari, non prohibemus; sed curam animarum earum non recipiemus, nec visitationis officium eis impendemus." It goes on to describe what might happen: "Qui vero super hoc faciendo petitionem ad Capitulum deportaverit, vel aliquid scienter procuraverit, per quod possit institutio tam utilis enervari; si monachus fuerit, vel conversus, a domo propria emittatur, non reversurus, nisi per Capitulum generale; si abbas fuerit, sit in pane et aqua extra stallum abbatis usque ad sequens Capitulum generale, in ipso Capitulo veniam petituris." These last clauses, often not cited, suggest that penalties might be imposed on those who made attempts to incorporate such nuns. The traditional discourse has seized on the term "to imitate" *"aemulari,"* to describe abbeys of Cistercian nuns as only pseudo-Cistercian.

47. *Statuta*, ed. Canivez, 1231, no. 6, "Omnes moniales Ordinis quaecumque sint loquantur de confessione per fenestram ad hoc, prout statutum est, deputatam, praeter graviter infirmantes et exceptis visitatoribus cum quibus in capitulo loqui possunt." See *Statuta*, ed. Canivez, 1225, no. 7, on limiting the numbers of nuns, which makes new reference to the confession window, ending with a reference to the 1220 statute: "Illae autem quae a quatuor annis incorporatae sunt, sicut statutum est, includantur, aut ab Ordinis corpore abscindantur."

That is, "Those that have been incorporated in the last four years, as was established, shall be cloistered, or they shall be cut off from the body of the order." Here's a sign that enforcing claustration is a problem, and, at this point, the pre-1220 nuns are told to be cloistered, but are not compelled to become so. These are part of repeated attempts by the abbots to cloister the nuns, becoming more strident, but having to face the reality of limited successes (hence the 1229 relaxation of the 1228 statute).

48. See Caroline A. Bruzelius, "Hearing Is Believing: Clarissan Architecture, ca. 1213–1340," in "Monastic Architecture for Women," special issue, *Gesta* 31, no. 2 (1992): 83–91; and Gilchrist, *Gender and Material Culture*, pp. 128–49.

49. See Chapter 6; *Statuta*, ed. Canivez, 1244, no. 4; and Anselme Dimier, *Saint Louis et Cîteaux* (Paris: Letouzey & Ané, 1954), pp. 169–70.

50. *Cartulaire de Maubuisson*, no. 244 (1245); Pontoise, AD Val d'Oise, 72H141, done at Maubuisson: and see Chapter 6.

51. *Codifications*, ed. Lucet, 1257, no. 4: "De non intrando claustrum monialium. Nullus preter visitores claustrum monialium ingrediatur, nisi fuerit tam reveranda et honesta persona, quod ei sine gravi dampno et scandalo ingressu ei nequeat denegari. Nec pueri in claustris monialium erudiantur. Mulieres autem seculares in claustris ipsarum vel in infirmitoriis non pernoctent." If this were to have been strictly enforced, it would have had repercussions for the nuns' abilities to take in students or boarders or to care for the elderly.

52. See *Codifications*, ed. Lucet, 1257, no. 3 (regarding personal property), which also says: "Nec abbatisse seu moniales quacumque de causa personaliter accedant ad capitulum generale"; and 1237, no. 6, and 1257, no. 8 (regarding clothing). Some historians have assumed that there had been a general chapter of abbesses from the late twelfth century; see Lekai, *The Cistercians*, p. 348. But this is not true any more than that there was any such organization in Spain; on this see Baury, *Les religieuses*, pp. 135, 144–45. On private property, see Chapter 7.

53. On Alice, see Chapter 6.

54. Documents survive for 1268, 1269, 1272, 1290, and 1302; they were published in *Les monuments primitifs de la règle cistercienne*, ed. Philippe Guignard (Dijon, 1878), 643–49; see Anselme Dimier, "Chapitres généraux d'abbesses cisterciennes," *Cîteaux* 11 (1960): 268–73; cf. G. Müller, "Generalkapitel der Cistercienserinnen," *Cistercienser-Chronik* 24 (1912): 65–72, 114–19.

55. Lekai, *The Cistercians*, p. 349, is here citing *Documentación de Las Huelgas*, no. 49 (where it is misdated in the sequence of charters). The document was issued from the Lateran on the 13 kalends of June in the second year of the pontificate of Innocent—it should be Innocent IV (1243–54), not Innocent III (1198–1216); Lekai appears to have followed the dating of A. de Manrique, *Annales Cistersiensis*, 4 vols. (Lyon, 1642–49). The problem of shorter papal documents having no A.D. dates is well-known; see most recently Olivier Guyotjeannin, Jacques Pycke, and Benoît-Michel Tock, *Diplomatique médiévale*, L'atelier du médiéviste 2 (Turnhout: Brepols, 1993), pp. 172–75.

56. *Les registres d'Innocent IV*, ed. Élie Berger, 4 vols. (Paris: E. Thorin, 1884–1921), no. 589, given at the Lateran, March 14, 1244, addressed to the abbot of Cîteaux: "De insana temeritate arrogantissimae abbatissae monasterie sanctae Mariae Regalis cisterciensis ordinis in que Berengariae sanctimoniali earum, immo exercrandum consecratum velum praesumpserit imponere, contradicente Burgensis episcopo, abbas Cistercii poenum eiusdem abbatissae per modo culpae imponat et omnibus abbatissis sui ordinis in Hispania constitutis inhibeat ne id ulterius praesumant attentare."

57. *Documentación de Las Huelgas*, no. 355, mentions "la infante donna Berengula circa 1245." The royal family of Castile appointed an unmarried daughter to serve as procuratrix for those nuns; see Andrea Gayoso, "The Lady of Las Huelgas: A Royal Abbey and Its Patronage," *Cîteaux* 51 (2000): 91–115.

58. *Registres d'Innocent IV*, no. 4463, identified as from Lyons, April 27, 1249:

> Abbati Cisterciensi et coabbatibus ejus Cisterciensis ordinis. Petitio vestra nobis exhibita continebat, quod cum correctio excessuum tam monachorum quam monialium vestri ordinis ad patres abbates secundum statuta dicti ordinis confirmata per sedem apostolicam pertinere noscatur, et in generali capitulo cisterciensi deliberatione provida, sit statutum ut moniales incorporatae ipsi ordini nulli alii confiteantur nisi patri abbati solummodo vel cui dictus abbas in hoc commiserit vices suas nonnulli religiosi et etiam saeculares non absque praesumptione damnabili falcem in alienam messem mittentes predictarum monialium confessiones absolvere ac ipsas de facto absolvere non verentur. Propter quod correctio vestra contemnitur, ipsaque moniales regularem effugiunt disciplinam in salutis animarum suarum dispendium et praefati ordinis iniuriam et contemptum. Quare fuit ex parte vestra nobis humiliter supplicatum ut super hoc congruum adhibere remedium dignaremur. Nos igitur [217r] statuta vestri ordinis cupientes illibata servari et animarum profectui providere, ne id de caetero fiat absque speciali mandato dictae sedis faciente plenam de statutis confirmatione ac inhibitione huiusmodi mentionem auctoritate praesentium districtius inhibemus. Nulli ergo, etc., nostrae inhibitionis, etc. Datum Lugduni quinti Kal. Maii anno sexto.

Transcription from RVAT 21A, fols. 216v–217r; and in manuscript, register 6, no. 470, fol. 40r (Potthast, 13308). My thanks to William Duba for discussions about this chapter and about Cistercian nuns more generally.

59. Bondéelle-Souchier, "Moniales," pp. 207–9.

60. *Statuta*, ed. Canivez, 1251, no. 4: "Cum a Summo Pontifice nostro Ordine sit indultum, ne ad incorporationem abbatiarum monialium per litteras apostolicas teneamur, statuit et praecipit Capitulum generale ut nulla deinceps quacumque de causa nostro Ordini incorporetur." There does appear to be a lessening of incorporation and founding of houses of nuns, but what does stop is the series of papal letters to the Cistercians regarding female foundations that show up in the statutes. Even then, however, the 1251 statute does not say that the pope will no longer send such letters, just that the Cistercians are not bound to accept them. Yet many were added; see, for instance, the petition for the nuns of the abbey of la Virginité in the diocese of Mans confirmed in *Statuta,* ed. Canivez, 1251, no. 17.

61. Lekai, *The Cistercians,* p. 352.

62. See Appendix 5, "Numbers of Cistercian Nuns' Houses According to Selected Historians," and Figure 2 in Chapter 3 from David Williams, "The Early Cistercian Nuns: 1125–1350," *Analecta Cisterciensia* 66 (2016): 177ff.

63. Nuns used written records to exert power and authority as did other women at a time when men may still have resorted to force; see Berman, "Gender at the Medieval Millennium"; see also discussion in the Preface, above, of the new volumes on nuns' literacy edited by Blanton et al.

64. The idea comes from reading Gary Macy, *The Hidden History of Women's Ordination: Female Clergy in the Medieval West* (Oxford: Oxford University Press, 2008); he is in no way responsible for my conclusion.

CHAPTER 3

1. Boyd, *A Cistercian Nunnery in Mediaeval Italy*, which drew on studies by Francesco Gosso, *Vita economica della abbazie piemontesi (sec. X–XIV)*, Analecta Gregoriana 22 (Rome: Gregorian University, 1940), and David Knowles, *The Monastic Order in England* (Cambridge: Cambridge University Press, 1940), pp. 215–16, and on documents from *Cartario della abazia di Rifreddo: Fino all'anno 1300*, ed. Silvio Pivano (Pinerolo: Chiantore-Mascarelli, 1902); cf. *Cartario della abazia di Staffarda*, vol. 1, ed. F. Gabotto, G. Roberti, and D. Chiattone (Pinerolo: Chiantore-Mascarelli, 1901) (hereafter *Cartario di Rifreddo* and *Cartario di Staffarda*).

2. One can see adaptations by Benedictines at places like Sauve Majeure; see *Grand Cartulaire de la Sauve Majeure*, ed. Charles Higounet and Arlette Higounet-Nadal, with Nicole de Peña (Bordeaux: Fédération historique du Sud-Ouest, 1996); or in the consideration of Benedictines in Flanders in Erin L. Jordan, *Women, Power, and Religious Patronage in the Middle Ages* (New York: Palgrave Macmillan, 2006), pp. 79–81. It is also clear that Cistercians and "new" Benedictines alike were most often involved in a second stage of reclamation, for instance, in maintaining existing drainage projects by construction of expensive dikes after land had already been cleared, drained, and brought under cultivation by anonymous peasants; see William H. TeBrake, *Medieval Frontier: Culture and Ecology in Rijnland* (College Station: Texas A&M University Press, 1985). The same could be said for monastic communities in the English Fens, with thanks to Brian Golding for discussion in the summer of 2013.

3. See Leyser, *Hermits and the New Monasticism*.

4. Such descriptions of twelfth-century reformers as frontiersmen were once embraced not only by monastic historians but also by economic historians seeking explanations for a pan-European expansion of cultivation. Somehow the clearance and reclamation movement was seen as leading to unexpectedly high yields—"bumper crops" in new lands and hence to the economic "takeoff" in the central Middle Ages. Such a view drew on analogies from the historiography of westward expansion in North America no longer viewed as valid. Cf. Frederick Jackson Turner, "The Significance of the Frontier in American History," in *Frontier and Section: Selected Essays of Frederick Jackson Turner*, ed. Ray Allen Billington (Englewood Cliffs, NJ: Prentice-Hall, 1961), pp. 37–62. New interpretations put Turner and his theory in context, such as those found in the work of Patricia Nelson Limerick, *The Legacy of Conquest: The Unbroken Past of the American West* (New York: W. W. Norton, 1997); and Kerwin Lee Klein, *Frontiers of Historical Imagination: Narrating the European Conquest of Native America, 1890–1990* (Berkeley: University of California Press, 1997). My thanks to colleagues Omar Valerio-Jimenez and H. Glenn Penny for discussion on this point. On European takeoff, see Robert S. Lopez, *The Commercial Revolution of the Middle Ages, 950–1350* (Engelwood Cliffs, NJ: Prentice-Hall, 1971); among its flaws is scant attention to women's work.

5. Parts of the discussion here build on Berman, *Medieval Agriculture*, but with new thoughts about the order's relationship to village formation and their reorganization of land for viticulture.

6. As French medievalist Robert Fossier remarked long ago in "L'économie cistercienne dans les plaines du nord-ouest de l'Europe," in *L'économie cistercienne: Géographie—Mutations du Moyen Age aux temps modernes*, Flaran 3 (Auch: Comité départemental du tourisme du Gers, 1983), pp. 53–74, "Cistercians were so late in the reclamation movement that they almost missed the train as it was leaving the station."

7. *Prima Collectio* or *Instituta* include "Where our abbeys are founded" and so on, in *Statuta*, ed. Canivez, vol. 1, p. 13; see Berman, *The Cistercian Evolution*, on its dating.

8. See Berman, *Medieval Agriculture*, pp. 61–93.

9. See "The Tract on the Conversion of Pons de Léras," trans. Kienzle. Latin text is available in *Cartulaire de l'abbaye de Silvanès.*

10. Arnold, *Negotiating the Landscape*, pp. 33–56; and Berman, *Medieval Agriculture*, pp. 11–30.

11. See Conrad Rudolph, *Violence and Daily Life: Reading, Art, and Polemics in the Cîteaux "Moralia in Job"* (Princeton, NJ: Princeton University Press, 1997).

12. Oliver Rackham, *Ancient Woodland: Its History, Vegetation and Use in England*, new ed. (Dalbeattie: Castlepoint Press, 2003).

13. On these marginal spaces for Cistercians, see Christophe Wissenberg, *Entre Champagne et Bourgogne: Beaumont, ancienne grange de l'abbaye cistercienne de Clairvaux* (Paris: Picard, 2007).

14. See Pierre Toubert, *Les structures du Latium médiéval: Le Latium méridional et la Sabine du IXe siècle à la fin du XIIe siècle*, 2 vols. (Rome: École française de Rome, 1973); Monique Bourin-Derruau, *Villages médiévaux en Bas-Languedoc: Genèse d'une sociabilité (Xe–XIVe siècle)*, 2 vols. (Paris: L'Harmattan, 1987); Robert Fossier, *La terre et les hommes en Picardie jusqu'à la fin du XIIIe siècle.* 2 vols. (Paris: Nauwelaerts, 1968); see also Laure Verdon, *La terre et les hommes en Roussillon aux XIIe et XIIIe siècles* (Aix-en-Provence: Publications de l'Université de Provence, 2001).

15. Such tithe exemption, however, was rarely exercised except by repurchase; see Berman, "Cistercian Development."

16. Berman, *Medieval Agriculture*, p. 120.

17. Berman, *Medieval Agriculture*, pp. 47–48; on displaced villagers, see also R. A. Donkin, *The Cistercians: Studies in the Geography of Medieval England and Wales* (Toronto: Pontifical Institute of Mediaeval Studies, 1978), pp. 44–51.

18. Herman of Tournay, *De miraculis sanctae Mariae Laudunensis, PL* 156:1001–2.

19. See Fossier, *La terre et les hommes.*

20. Arnold, *Negotiating the Landscape*, e.g., pp. 117–18. As for the assigning of textile work to women, see Constance H. Berman, "Women's Work in Family, Village and Town After AD 1000: Contributions to Economic Growth?" *Journal of Women's History* 19 (2007): 10–32.

21. Constance H. Berman, "Distinguishing Between the Humble Peasant Lay Brother and Sister and the Converted Knight in Medieval Southern France," in *Religious and Laity in Western Europe, 1000–1400: Interaction, Negotiation, and Power*, ed. Emilia Jamroziak and Janet Burton (Turnhout: Brepols, 2006), pp. 263–83; and Berman, *Medieval Agriculture*, pp. 55–56.

22. Berman, *Medieval Agriculture*, p. 74.

23. On tithes, see Chapter 1. The earliest lay-brother treatise concerns pastoralism; see Berman, *The Cistercian Evolution*, p. 65. These new affiliated communities could quickly adopt rules about the behavior of shepherds and lay brothers moving from one location to another or about the developing liturgical calendar and practices of the Cistercian customary. Less easily changed or jettisoned were the diverse landholdings and endowments in mills, tithes, and churches with which they may have come.

24. Brian Stock, *The Implications of Literacy: Written Language and Models of Interpretation in the Eleventh and Twelfth Centuries* (Princeton, NJ: Princeton University Press, 1983).

25. Berman, *Medieval Agriculture*, chapter 5, esp. p. 95.

26. Baury, *Les religieuses*, pp. 230–31.

27. *Recueil des pancartes de l'abbaye de la Ferté-sur-Grosne, 1113–1178*, ed. Georges Duby (Gap: Éditions Ophrys, 1953), introduction.

28. Whether by monks and nuns or their tenants, as I argue with regard to village women's labor in Berman, "Women's Work."

29. *Chartes et documents concernant l'abbaye de Cîteaux, 1098–1182*, ed. J. Marilier (Rome: Editiones cistercienses, 1961), nos. 40 and 41 (1218).

30. Baury, *Les religieuses*, p. 229.

31. On *ad medium*, see Appendix 1.

32. Boyd, *Cistercian Nunnery*, pp. 30–37, 41–43, esp. n. 32; see *Cartario di Rifreddo*, no. 9 (1221).

33. *Cartario di Rifreddo*, nos. 27 (1224), 29 (1225), 45 (1231), and 38 (1230); Boyd, *Cistercian Nunnery*, pp. 46–49 for Alice's death.

34. Staffarda had pressed claims against Alice for damages they claimed had been done by her late husband; see *Cartario di Staffarda*, no. 207 (1230); and see Boyd, *Cistercian Nunnery*, pp. 37–40.

35. *Cartario di Rifreddo*, no. 103 (1249) is Innocent IV's interpretation; see Boyd, *Cistercian Nunnery*, pp. 41–43.

36. *Cartario di Rifreddo*, no. 104 (1249). This is the tithe privilege for noval lands: "*Sane novalium;*" such privileges, however, are ambiguous insofar as they may refer to newly cultivated lands, or simply to lands on which new tithes had been established.

37. Lady Ruffina of Moncalieri, wife of the late Gardellus, "because of her own religious conversion, gave herself and all her movable and immovable goods into the hands of Lady Otta of La Roche, prioress of Saint Mary of Rifreddo, who received Ruffina at the common table of the nuns of that monastery." Lady Alasia, founder of the church or hermitage of Santa Maria Maddalene of Moncalieri also gave herself and her church to be a nun and sister at Rifreddo; she too would be provided for at the nuns' table: *Cartario di Rifreddo*, nos. 105 (1249) and 107 and 108 (both 1250).

38. *Cartario di Rifreddo*, nos. 24 and 25 (1224).

39. *Cartario di Rifreddo*, nos. 113 and 114 (ca. 1250).

40. *Cartario di Rifreddo*, nos. 177 and 178 (ca. 1260) and no. 152 (1257); a journal is the land worked in a single day.

41. On such mountain economies, see Chris Wickham, *Early Medieval Italy: Central Power and Local Society, 400–1000* (London: Macmillan, 1981), pp. 92–113.

42. Coincidence between lands and tithes is seen in *Cartario di Rifreddo*, nos. 14, 15, and 21 (1222), 104 (1249), and 178 (1256); no. 17 (1222) is a concession of noval tithes in the upper Po Valley by the bishop of Turin.

43. Such tithes were the only available rights based on a percentage of income, and their ownership (hardly ever in the bishop's hands) was one of the few ways in which a religious community like Rifreddo, whose tenants paid long-established fixed rents, could receive any benefit from the increased agricultural output of the time.

44. Boyd, *Cistercian Nunnery*, pp. 157–69; its community became Dominican in 1292.

45. See *Vie de Saint Etienne d'Obazine*, ed. Michel Aubrun (Clermont-Ferrand: Institut d'Études du Massif Central, 1970). Although dates in the 1140s have been proposed for the division of the double community into two, most likely it occurred after Stephen's death in 1154 and after acquisition of the property at Coyroux in 1159; see *Le cartulaire de l'abbaye cistercienne d'Obazine (XIIe–XIIIe siècle)*, ed. Bernadette Barrière (Clermont-Ferrand: Université

de Clermont-Ferrand II, 1989), hereafter cited as *Cartulaire d'Obazine*, no. 195 (1159), and Berman, *The Cistercian Evolution*, pp. 143–46.

46. Much of what we know about the two abbeys derives from the publication of documents, excavations and other work undertaken by the late Bernadette Barrière and her team. See Barrière, *L'abbaye cistercienne d'Obazine en Bas-Limousin: Les origines, le patrimoine*, with preface by Charles Higounet (Tulle: Conseil Générale de la Corrèze, 1977).

47. Bernadette Barrière, "The Cistercian Convent of Coyroux in the Twelfth and Thirteenth Centuries," *Gesta* 31 (1992): 76–82, has shown that the nuns' supplies were delivered by the monks into a passageway in the wall of the nun's compound; that passage could be locked at either end, with one key held by the monks and one by the nuns, so they could avoid any contact with one another. See the parallel about support of nuns between Jully and Molesme discussed in Chapter 1.

48. I am grateful for private conversations and site visits with the late Bernadette Barrière, who insisted on this point.

49. On marriage and concubinage among priests, deacons, subdeacons, monks, and nuns in the Second Lateran Council (1139), canons 6, 7, 11, see Papal Encyclicals Online, accessed April 21, 2017, www.papalencyclicals.net/Councils/ecum10.htm.

50. *Cartulaire d'Obazine*, nos. 30 (ca. 1159), 34 (n.d.), 225 (1166), 227 (1166), 289 (1169), 291 (1169), and 301 (1169), the last, a quarter of the woods of Veyrières. On terms for land holdings, see discussion in Appendix 1

51. *Cartulaire d'Obazine*, nos. 103 (1143–53) and 339 (1161); on such "*dévotées*," see Charles de Miramon, *Les "donnés" au Moyen Âge: Une forme de vie religieuse laïque v. 1180–v. 1500* (Paris: Cerf, 1999).

52. *Cartulaire d'Obazine*, no. 61 (n.d.) lists rents in at least twenty places, plus another eight places in his wife's right; see also nos. 268 (1150–59), 336 (1177), 291 (1169), 638 (by 1177), and 495 (1178/79), which includes a large purchase circa 1178 when 800 sous (40 livres) were paid to Geoffrey Toucheboeuf and his three brothers for the meadow of Las Juncheiras at Saint-Palavy.

53. *Cartulaire d'Obazine*, nos. 60 (1143–53), 65 (1153–56?), 62 (1155), 75 and 77 (1153–59), and 78 (1158/59) confirm that this was developed land; it included a gift by Peter Priest of Chavanac; nos. 750 (1190), 456 (1176), and 495 (1178/9) reveal agricultural tenants and a smith, Gerald Faber of Saint-Palavy.

54. *Cartulaire d'Obazine*, no. 88 (ca. 1153 acte-notice).

55. *Cartulaire d'Obazine*, nos. 170 (1162), 267 (1162), 269 (1162?), 196 (1164), and 337 (1170). Clearly the theory among Gregorian reformers about gifts not being required for the admission of monks or nuns was not applied here, but see Joseph H. Lynch, *Simoniacal Entry into Religious Life from 1000 to 1260: A Social, Economic and Legal Study* (Columbus: Ohio State University, 1976), pp. 162–63.

56. *Cartulaire d'Obazine*, nos. 270 and 276 (1159), 267 and 269 (1162/63), and 266 (1169).

57. *Cartulaire d'Obazine*, nos. 56(ca. 1142–59) and 88 (ca. 1153).

58. *Cartulaire d'Obazine*, nos. 57 (n.d.), 82 (1152), 106 (1158), 136 (1169), 292 (1170), 310 (1174), 441 (1179), 696 (1179), and 705 (1188). The couple apparently entered that abbey together (perhaps shortly before his death): "giving themselves into the hands of Stephen its first abbot" and giving land and tithes at Ramière; they promised that if the wife died without producing a child, the abbey would have all their possessions.

59. *Cartulaire d'Obazine*, nos. 179 (1163), 241 (1167), 183 and 194 (1164).

60. When its monks returned to their mother abbey at Landais in the diocese of Bourges in 1160, Obazine and Coyroux took over properties at Sourdain, La Serre, and Chadabec, all of which became granges, as well as vineyards at Alaca and a mill at Sourdain; Archambald V of Comborn transferred woods at Sourdain below the street and water and mills of La Serre, along with the grange of Chadabec and the vineyards of Alaca; some prayers were assigned to the nuns. *Cartulaire d'Obazine*, nos. 26 (1159 or later), 88 (ca. 1153), 853 and 854 (1190s).

61. *Cartulaire d'Obazine*, nos. 145, 187, 256–58, and 278 (all 1168), receiving back in exchange certain properties that his sister, Domizella, had earlier given when she became a nun there.

62. Berman, *The Cistercian Evolution*, pp. 117–23.

63. *Cartulaire de Nonenque*, nos. 12 (1170) and 13 (1170); the latter says, "Relinquimus eidem Domino nostro et monasterio in honore ipsius et Sancte Marie de Elnonencha edificato et priorisse Petronille et ceteris dominabus ipsius monasterii, presentibus scilicet et futuris." Cf. pp. x–xiii, nos. 1 (1139), 3 (1152), and 26 (1177), which mention lay brothers and lay sisters. On the relationship to Silvanès, see Constance H. Berman, "Men's Houses, Women's Houses: The Relationship Between the Sexes in Twelfth-Century Monasticism," in *The Medieval Monastery*, ed. Andrew MacLeish (St. Cloud, MN: North Star Press, 1988), pp. 43–52; and Berman, "Life of Pons de Léras."

64. These names in full provide access to wonderful on-line pictures of these granges.

65. See Giselle Bourgeois, "Les granges et l'économie de l'abbaye de Nonenque au Moyen Âge," *Cîteaux* 24 (1973): 139–60.

66. *Cartulaire de Nonenque*, nos. 8 and 9 (1167/8), 17 (1170), 26 (1177), and 18 (1171); in 1170 the Dowager Countess of Rodez, Ermengarde of Creyssels, entered Nonenque, granted Nonenque (with the confirmation of her son Hugh, Count of Rodez), her entire villa of Lioujas, north of the city of Rodez; it became an important grange. Disputes over Nonenque's pasture rights would arise later with Templars and Hospitallers, as described by Bourgeois, "Nonenque"; and Berman, *The Cistercian Evolution*, pp. 194–95.

67. Coburn V. Graves, "Stixwould in the Market-Place," in *Distant Echoes*, vol. 1 of *Medieval Religious Women*, ed. John A. Nichols and Lillian Thomas Shank (Kalamazoo, MI: Cistercian Publications, 1984), pp. 213–36.

68. Graves, "Stixwould," p. 226.

69. Graves, "Stixwould," p. 227. On the wool trade, see Donkin, *The Cistercians*, pp. 135–54; see also Elizabeth Freeman, "Cistercian Nuns in Medieval England: The Gendering of Geographic Marginalization," *Medieval Feminist Forum* 43 (2008): 26–39.

70. Graves, "Stixwould," p. 226.

71. *Chartulary of the Cistercian Priory of Coldstream with Relative Documents*, ed. Charles Rogers (London: Grampian Club, 1879), no. 8 (n.d.). Cf. *Historic Memorials of Coldstream Abbey, Berwickshire* (London: printed for private circulation, 1850) an earlier anonymous edition of the cartulary and related information. Here the 1879 edition is cited, hereafter as *Chartulary of Coldstream*.

72. *Chartulary of Coldstream*, no. 1 (n.d.): "Infra villam quam extra: scilicet in moris et in marisiis, in pratis et pascuis, in aquis, in stagnis, in piscariis et molendinis, et omnibus aliis sine aliqua subtractione."

73. Patrick also gave rights in Whitchester and Otterburn; see *Chartulary of Coldstream*, nos. 27–29 (n.d.).

74. *Chartulary of Coldstream*, nos. 35–39, quote from no. 38 (n.d.).

75. See *Chartulary of Coldstream*, nos. 48–52 (n.d.), for gifts at Berwick.

76. Emilia Jamroziak, *Survival and Success on Medieval Borders: Cistercian Houses in Medieval Scotland and Pomerania from the Twelfth to the Late Fourteenth Century* (Turnhout: Brepols, 2011).

77. *Documentación de Las Huelgas*, no. 11 (1187).

78. Baury, *Les religieuses*, pp. 201–2, 235–36.

79. Baury, *Les religieuses*, pp. 231–32.

80. Williams, "Early Cistercian Nuns." My sincere thanks to David Williams who provided me with this table.

81. As once argued by Bennett D. Hill, *English Cistercian Monasteries and Their Patrons in the Twelfth Century* (Urbana: University of Illinois Press, 1968).

82. Again, see Stock, *The Implications of Literacy*.

CHAPTER 4

1. Parts of this and the next chapter expand considerably on Constance H. Berman, "Noble Women's Power as Reflected in the Foundations of Cistercian Houses for Nuns," in *Negotiating Community and Difference in Medieval Europe*, ed. Katherine Allen Smith and Scott Wells (Leiden: Brill, 2009), 137–49, a volume in honor of Penelope D. Johnson, drawing on a paper originally delivered at the Berkshire Conference on Women's History, Smith College, 1984. For Voisins, a paper was presented at the Medieval Academy of America annual conference in Madison, Wisconsin, in the spring of 1989.

2. On the sources Appendix 2: "The Evidence: Cistercian Charters and Charter Books," and Appendix 3, "Specific Charters and Other Materials for This Study."

3. *Abbaye royale de Notre-Dame des Clairets: Histoire et cartulaire*, ed. Vicomte Hector de Souancé (Nogent-le-Rotrou, 1894), nos. 3 (1203), and 4 (1204), hereafter cited as *Cartulaire des Clairets*. For Clairets the 1894 publication draws on an early modern charter book for the nuns. I have checked the original, Paris, BnF Latin 17140, for items omitted from the publication, but there are only a few leases from much later dates that were not included by the editor.

4. *Cartulaire des Clairets*, nos. 4 (1204), 8 (1215), and 38 (1234).

5. *Cartulaire des Clairets*, nos. 5 (1213) and 7 (1215).

6. *Cartulaire des Clairets*, no. 9 (1216): "Pro molendinis nostris de Nogento-Rotrodi in pratis juxta Burgum-Novum positis, quae ipse de novo fundavit quartam portionem in eisdem molendinis; scilicet: in fullagio draporum et in mottura bladorum, et in piscatione et molneragium"; see also no. 10 (1217): "Ita quod nec a nobis nec ab heredibus nostris alia molendina ibidem vel alibi in detrimentum eorum poterunt edificari." He promised that if those mills were destroyed, the nuns' lost revenue would be replaced by eighty livres of annual income from other sources. Cf. no. 31 (1232); and no. 42 (1236) in which the nuns' Cistercian father visitor, Brother Walter of Trappe, resolved a dispute over those same mills with the Cluniacs of the priory of Saint-Denis in Nogent; the nuns would henceforth pay nine livres per annum in lieu of old tithes on those mills.

7. On England being under papal protection, see Ralph V. Turner, *King John* (Harlow: Longman, 1994), pp. 249–65; and John W. Baldwin, *The Government of Philip Augustus: Foundations of French Royal Power in the Middle Ages* (Berkeley: University of California Press, 1986), pp. 332–36.

8. *Cartulaire des Clairets*, nos. 12 (1218) and 13 (1218).

9. *Cartulaire des Clairets*, pancarte, no. 14 (1218). On sestiers and mines/émines, see Appendix 1.

10. *Cartulaire des Clairets*, no. 15 (1220): "Molendina nostra tam bladum molentia quam fullatoria, quae vocantur molendina Comitis." See also nos. 16 and 17 (1221); in the latter William confirmed that he had given his sixty sous (three livres) annual rent "on the day when the venerable father and lord Walter, bishop of Chartres, had installed and blessed the abbess."

11. In general the Tironists attempted to support themselves by short- and long-distance trade, work as artisans and craftsmen, and income from mills, churches, and tithes; in contrast Cistercians generally emphasized creating granges with tithe-free agriculture and pastoralism. Generally, however, there was a range of practices within either order. On Tiron, see Geoffrey Grossus, *The Life of Blessed Bernard of Tiron*, ed. and trans. Ruth Harwood Cline (Washington, DC: Catholic University of America Press, 2009); Richard D. Oram, *Domination and Lordship: Scotland, 1170–1230* (Edinburgh: Edinburgh University Press, 2006); and Kathleen Thompson, *The Monks of Tiron: A Monastic Community and Religious Reform in the Twelfth Century* (Cambridge: Cambridge University Press, 2014).

12. *Cartulaire de l'abbaye de la Sainte-Trinité de Tiron*, ed. Lucien Merlet (Chartres: Garnier, 1883), no. 358 (1225); and François Menant et al., *Les Capétiens: Histoire et dictionnaire, 987–1328* (Paris: Laffont, 1999), for political information.

13. We know the value when it was conveyed to the knight Guy of Villegrinosa by the Count of Perche. *Cartulaire des Clairets*, nos. 34 (1233/34), 35 (1233), and 40 (1235); Guy's two daughters and their husbands had sold their claims to that *feodum* to the nuns for 407 livres *parisis*, of which 60 livres *tournois* were held back by Clairets for the support of Guy's widow, Lady Heloise, who had retired there; so 60 livres *tournois* here constituted an entrance gift.

14. *Cartulaire des Clairets*, nos. 65 (1280) and 66 (1281): Lady Heloise of nearby Céton informed the nuns that the bishop of Mans would assure enough funds to hire that priest.

15. *Cartulaire des Clairets*, nos. 21 (1222) and 23 (1224): "tres partes molendini de Ruissellis ad cultellos et molendinos ad eam jure hereditario pertinentes." This included rights to take millstones from a nearby quarry. These mills also appear to have been used for some sort of chopping or pounding process (*ad cultellos*). Such income from mills may have come from farther afield if Isabelle, Countess of Chartres, indeed gave Clairets one hundred sous (five livres) of annual rent on her fulling mills of Chartres at an unknown date. It is possible that the income mentioned by her successors had been given back to Isabelle by Bishop William of Châlons; see Chapter 5.

16. *Cartulaire des Clairets*, nos. 36 and 37 (1234) and 60 (1274): "Et pourront les devant dites noneyns les davant dits boes arracher et mettre à terre gaagnable si il i veyent leur profit."

17. *Cartulaire des Clairets*, nos. 62 (1276), 63 (1279), 69 (1282), and 79 (1295).

18. *Cartulaire des Clairets*, nos. 22 (1223) and 29 (1230).

19. Bondéelle-Souchier, "Moniales," pp. 330–31; mendicants appear to have transferred to the nuns of Villiers those tithes that had been given earlier by Amicia of Breteuil's husband. Those nuns at Villiers were identified as Cistercian by 1227. There is no evidence that I have seen that this was ever a mendicant house.

20. For Villiers, the evidence is found primarily in an obituary, although there are a few scattered charter copies elsewhere. See "Histoire de l'abbaye royale de Notre-Dame de Villiers, de l'Ordre de Cîteaux, au diocèse de Sens (1220–1669)," ed. Paul Pinson, *Annales de la Société historique et archéologique du Gâtinais* 11 (1893): 1–125, hereafter cited as *Histoire de Villiers*. It is the account by Dom Basile Fleureau, *Briefve histoire de l'abbaie Nostre Dame la Roiale de Villiers proche la ville de la Ferté-Aales*, written in 1669, published without change but with additional

documents. Villiers was not a foundation made by the crown, but its location in the Île-de-France inspired several royal interventions in disputes concerning its nuns.

21. *Histoire de Villiers*, p. 9: "Omnibus presentes litteras inspecturis, Petrus Dei gratia Senonensis archiepiscopus in Dominio salutem. Noverint universi quod nos ad petitionem Amiciae nobilis feminae dominae Britollii concedimus, ut fundetur abbatia monialium apud Villiers item quod conventus monialium ibidem Deo serventium tenebit in perpetuum decimas omnes quas ibi tenuerunt canonici de ordine Praedicatorum de domini bonae memoriae Johannis Briardi, salvo jure presbyteri parochialis, qui coram nobis concessit ut ibidem fundetur abbatia supradicta. Actum anno gratiae MCCXX, mense maio."

22. *Statuta*, ed. Canivez, 1220, no. 60, records the General Chapter's approval of a foundation for nuns (at Villiers) advocated by the lady of Breteuil. Jean of Ferté had earlier given two muids of rye and four of wine from those tithes to the Cistercian monks of Barbeaux; see *Histoire de Villiers*, no. 1 (1181); Barbeaux disputed Jean of Briard's claims in 1225. The archbishop ordained that William, the priest of Cernay, who had been there for a long time, should receive annually from the nuns one muid of winter wheat and one of oats, as well as ten muids of wine in the measure of Étampes for the rest of his life. His successors would get only half as much: five muids of wine and one of grain, with the rest reverting to the nuns; see *Histoire de Villiers*, no. 2 (1227).

23. *Histoire de Villiers*, no. 3 (August 1227)

24. *Histoire de Villiers*, no. 4 (1235), confirmation by Louis IX; see also Corbeil, A.D. Essonne, 71H8, March 1228/29: Andrew of Plessis gave them the eighth part of the tithes and one mine of grain—half mixed and half oats. Some document copies that were unavailable at the time of my visit to those archives were mailed to me by archivists at Corbeil, A.D. Essonne; my sincere thanks.

25. *Histoire de Villiers*, pp. 115–16; Pinson's summary of Fleureau's text on pp. 6–35; the latter is probably Philip of Montfort, lord of Castres and Ferté-Alais; in 1247 he was about to depart on Louis IX's first crusade, on which he died in 1249.

26. *Histoire de Villiers*, no. 6 (February 1237/38): "Totum vivarium, totum pratum, totum fossatum quod est [*sic*] a parte Sarniaci, et totam calciatam que sunt subtus ecclesiam dictarum monialium apud Vilers, contigua prato dictarum monialium, et aquam descendentem a rota molendini domini Johannis Briardi, militis, euntem in dictum vivarium et omnia alia que sunt in predicti."

27. *Histoire de Villiers*, pp. 117–20.

28. *Histoire de Villiers*, pp. 6–35.

29. Dimier, *Saint Louis et Cîteaux*, p. 159, no. 47 (1233), p. 161, no. 64 (1235), p. 162, no. 72 (1235), p. 171, no. 165 (1246), pp. 171–72, no. 166 (1246).

30. *Histoire de Villiers*, no. 5 (1235).

31. Dimier, *Saint Louis et Cîteaux*, p. 167, no. 122 (1241–42), p. 173, no. 179 (1247), p. 174, no. 193 (1248), p. 175, no. 206 (1248), p. 194, no. 409 (1270).

32. Dimier, *Saint Louis et Cîteaux*, p. 198, nos. 437 and 441; Marguerite gave thirty-eight arpents in the woods of the lordship of Bouville for a chapel for Louis IX.

33. *Histoire de Villiers*, nos. 13 (1251), 14 (1252), 15 (1255), and 16 (1257).

34. In this case and that of Jardin-lez-Pleurs (see Chapter 8), surviving evidence comes from an obituary, which may overreport the widows; but the appeal to widows of prayers from Cistercian nuns is clear, particularly as discussed in Chapter 7 on Saint-Antoine's prayers; see also Table 1 for Voisins.

35. *Cartulaire de Voisins*, nos. 18 (1212), 49 (1249), 51 (1232), 54 (1260), 58 (1268), 80 (1220), 94 (1248). Earlier lay owners of tithes could thus simultaneously rid themselves of forbidden revenues and receive prayers from those nuns. See Constable, *Monastic Tithes*. For Voisins, *Cartulaire de Voisins*, an edition of about 170 documents, organized under the categories of a later inventory, was the "cartulary" edited and published by Jules Doinel in 1887; the originals were destroyed in World War II. Several documents were published earlier from an account by A. du Faur, comte de Pibrac, "Histoire de l'abbaye de Voisins," *Mémoires de la Société d'agriculture, sciences, belles-lettres et arts d'Orléans* 22 (1881): 177–348; on p. 180, Pibrac justifies the study of Voisins, but not of its women: "C'est à ce triple point de vue [historical facts, life of monastics, and archaeology] que l'histoire d'une abbaye de femmes peut encore présenter quelque intérêt."

36. On earlier hermits there see *Cartulaire de Voisins*, nos. 1 (1207), 149 (1208), 2 (1217) 23 (1220), and 3 (1231). The charter from 1207 describes John, prior and brother of Bucy, promising to celebrate an anniversary mass for a donor and his father; so does that from 1208. In no. 2 (1217) Herveus Chesneaux and his wife Isabelle gave the new site, where there would be at least one priest and one cleric to celebrate masses for benefactors and founder. In 1220, Bucy is mentioned as a grange. In 1231 there was a confirmation of rights to nuns of Voisins and the brothers and sisters serving there.

37. *Cartulaire de Voisins*, nos. 135 (1219), 102 (1244), 146 (1248), 103 (1249), 104 (1251).

38. *Cartulaire de Voisins*, nos. 173–77 (1218) concern rights near Janville that came to Voisins after Margaret Buticularis gave those rights to the Cistercian nuns of Moncey near Tours (on which see Chapter 5); Ermengarde, prioress of Moncey immediately sold these rights for fifteen livres to the nuns of Voisins. There are several conveyances by the countesses and counts of Chartres and Blois. In 1256 Lady Matilda of Amboise, Countess of Chartres, for anniversary masses, left forty sous annual rents from the treasury of Chartres to the nuns of Voisins. Matilda's heir, Jean of Châtillon, Count of Blois and Chartres, with his wife Alice of Brittany, transformed that into a rent on the *festagium* (hearth tax) of Blois; *Cartulaire de Voisins*, no. 50 (1256) records Matilda's gift, and nos. 33 (1272) and 34 (1289) record those by Jean and by Jeanne, his daughter.

39. *Cartulaire de Voisins*, no. 9 (1219), cites Honorius III; but Pibrac, "Histoire," no. 9 (1234), cites Gregory IX; it could be that there were two such documents, one issued by each pope.

40. *Cartulaire de Voisins*, no. 129 (1245): "De libris vero suis dedit et concessit eisdem monialibus: mesale in duabus partibus, epistolarium, breviarium grossum, antiphonarium novum in duabus partibus, sequentialium grossum, psalterium majus, duos passionarios, omeliarium novum, et vitam Patrum." They were his own books.

41. *Cartulaire de Voisins*, no. 13 (1234).

42. *Cartulaire de Voisins*, nos. 6 and 39 (1246), 40 (1259), 34 (1289), and 7 (1300).

43. Vineyards at Saint-Jean de Bray and Saint-Jean de la Ruelle: *Cartulaire de Voisins*, nos. 86 (1217), 84 (1218), 79 and 80 (1220), 48 (1222), appendix no. 2 (1224), nos. 117 and 118 (1225), 90 (1226), 87 (1227), 90 and 91 (1226), 92 (1227), 126 (1227), 51 (1232), 30 and 127 (1235), 93 (1245/46), 85 (1259), 94 (1248), 88 (1274), 89 (1292), and 95 (1314).

44. *Cartulaire de Voisins*, nos. 27 (1233), 121 (1238), and 123 (1277).

45. *Cartulaire de Voisins*, nos. 18 (1212), 49 (1232), 51 (1232), 54 (1260), 58 (1268), 80 (1220), 94 (1248), and so on.

46. *Cartulaire de Voisins*, nos. 28 (1248) and 60 (1312).

47. Bondéelle-Souchier, "Moniales," pp. 332–33.

48. For Port-Royal a two-volume cartulary was produced circa 1270 and was published in 1903. *Cartulaire de l'abbaye de Porrois, au diocèse de Paris, plus connue sous son nom mystique Port-Royal,* ed. Adolphe de Dion (Paris: Picard, 1903), hereafter cited as *Cartulaire de Port-Royal.* Although citing the original charter numbers, the 1903 publication followed the vogue for esteeming charter "originals" and published them in chronological order.

49. *Cartulaire de Port-Royal,* nos. 1 (before 1204), 2 (1204), 4 (1206), 183 (in fact 1223/24), and 68 (1223/24), the last act by Matilda of Garlande, who died circa 1223/24.

50. *Cartulaire de Port-Royal,* no. 4 (1206), and Bonnardot, *Saint-Antoine,* no. 1 (1206).

51. The campaigns against those heretics would figure largely in Port-Royal's early history; see below. Its later history included a second settlement for the community of Port-Royal in Paris that was associated with Jansenism; see Ellen F. Weaver, *The Evolution of the Reform of Port Royal: From the Rule of Cîteaux to Jansenism* (Paris: Beauchesne, 1978).

52. *Cartulaire de Port-Royal,* nos. 10 and 11 (1208).

53. *Cartulaire de Port-Royal,* nos. 12, 13, and 14 (1209).

54. On the first campaign of the Albigensian Crusade when he was accompanied by his mother; see *Peter of les Vaux-de-Cernay's "Historia Albigensis,"* pp. 68 and 85. Bouchard is referred to as lord of Châteaufort as well as of Marly in *Cartulaire de Port-Royal,* no. 46 (1213).

55. *Cartulaire de Port-Royal,* nos. 17, 18, 19, 21, and 22 (1214/15). Only in 1214, and then for one hundred sous, did the priest of Magny give up his claims to tithes over the abbey site; *Cartulaire de Port-Royal,* no. 20 (1214); Robert of Ivry, a monk from Vaux-de-Cernay, received these tithes for Port-Royal in 1214. In mid century a rent was still owed by the nuns to a parish priest at Magny; see Table 3. Port-Royal: Samples from *Censier* (1262/63).

56. *Cartulaire de Port-Royal,* no. 22 (1214/15); an extract by the editor from the bishop's cartulary: "Quod apud Porrois fiat abbatia mulierum Cisterciensis ordinis, que abbatie Vallium Sarnaii sit subjecta." The nuns may have had some difficulty in recruiting priests. In 1220 Philip of Valmaurier and his wife Eremburgis made a postmortem gift for their souls of the fifth part of all their inheritances in vineyards, lands, and other property, from which the nuns were to pay the church of Saint-Lambert five sous annually for the celebration of an anniversary mass for the donors; Eremburgis herself entered Port-Royal to become its fourth abbess; see *Cartulaire de Port-Royal,* nos. 47 (1220), 82 (1227), and 219 (1242/43).

57. *Cartulaire de Port-Royal,* no. 21 (1214/15). Peter of Nemours, bishop of Paris, later left gifts to Port-Royal in his will; see *Cartulaire de Port-Royal,* no. 37 (1218). Eventually too it was clear that Port-Royal answered to the abbot of Cîteaux and no longer to the abbot of Vaux-de-Cernay; see *Cartulaire de Port-Royal,* no. 144 (November 1233). Stephen of Lexington's visit (see Chapter 2) established that it should have sixty nuns.

58. *Cartulaire de Port-Royal,* no. 39 (1218).

59. *Cartulaire de Port-Royal,* nos. 6 and 7 (1207) and 8 (1208).

60. *Cartulaire de Port-Royal,* nos. 49 (1220)

61. *Cartulaire de Port-Royal,* nos. 190 and 194 (1239).

62. *Cartulaire de Port-Royal,* no. 213 (1241/42).

63. *Cartulaire de Port-Royal,* nos. 26 (1216), 55 and 56 (1221/22), and 190 (1239) and Paris, AN, S*4386, *Cartulaire de Saint-Antoine,* fols. 62v–63r (1221); shortly after Cecilia's death, Amicia, abbess of Saint-Antoine, would acquire the Aulnay holding in exchange for giving rents at Gratelou to Port-Royal. On Robert of Mauvoisin, see Chapter 7.

64. *Cartulaire de Port-Royal,* nos. 216, 217, and 218 (1242); this rent is seen in the *censier*; see Table 3.

65. *Cartulaire de Port-Royal*, nos. 68 (1223/24), 69 (1224), and 183 (1238); Matilda of Garlande gave this property to Port-Royal in 1223, her son Bouchard confirmed this in 1224; Bouchard's wife, Matilda of Châteaufort, got property elsewhere in exchange.

66. *Cartulaire de Port-Royal*, nos. 71 and 73 (1224).

67. *Cartulaire de Port-Royal*, nos. 62 and 63 (1223) and 130 (1231/32) when her husband Aimery of Narbonne confirmed the vineyard at Marly and gave an additional one hundred sous in rents when Marguerite's *filiola* (granddaughter or goddaughter?) named Marguerite and the latter's sister Alice entered Port-Royal as nuns. Marguerite is referred to as lady of Narbonne in the Port-Royal *censier*; see Table 3.

68. *Cartulaire de Port-Royal*, nos. 85 and 86 (May 1226).

69. This was Saint Thibaut of Marly, abbot of Vaux-de-Cernay (1235–47), who promised Louis IX and Marguerite of Provence (who married in May 1234) eleven children, although she had yet to conceive when they visited Vaux-de-Cernay; they eventually did have eleven, the first born in 1240.

70. *Cartulaire de Port-Royal*, p. 153, for her death. The nuns placed Bouchard first as if the "founder" of Port-Royal, an action probably encouraged by Bouchard's widow.

71. *Cartulaire de Port-Royal*, nos. 23 (1215) and 28 (1217): when Peter gave "partem terre ad edificandam granchiam apud Sanctum Accobilium ad partem sue decime recondendam."

72. *Cartulaire de Port-Royal*, no. 50 (1220): "in decimas de Rupturis contenente duodecim modios seminis, sita in parrochia Sancti Scubiculi." Enormous, to judge from the amount of seed planted; that it was called "de Rupturis" suggests recent clearing. The terms of a medieval *mort-gage,* in which the fruits did not reduce the principle, were very onerous and the contracts were not often redeemed.

73. *Cartulaire de Port-Royal*, nos. 127 (1231) for fifty-five livres and 138 (1233) for sixty-five livres.

74. *Cartulaire de Port-Royal*, nos. 292 (1262), 24 and 25 (1216), 133 (1232), and 226, 227, and 228 (1244).

75. *Cartulaire de Port-Royal*, nos. 29 (1216) and 30 (1217).

76. *Cartulaire de Port-Royal*, nos. 79 and 80 (1224).

77. *Cartulaire de Port-Royal*, no. 150 (1234) says that the nuns paid ten livres per arpent to the knight William of Issy and his wife Sedilia for eleven arpents of land at Saclay.

78. *Cartulaire de Port-Royal*, nos. 205–9 (1241) and 212 (1241/42).

79. *Cartulaire de Port-Royal*, nos. 294 and 295 (1262/63). This fief was transferred with its inhabitants and had seven tenancies paying a total of twenty-seven sous of minute cens, etc., to be held perpetually by Port-Royal in *la main morte*. These two charters are particularly important in dating the *censier*, if as appears likely, they provide an earliest date for the censier's list of Villeray holdings that are listed in Table 2.

80. *Cartulaire de Port-Royal*, no. 69 (1224) and no. 76 (1224) are conveyances by Bouchard including the land over which he once paid rent of fifteen sous to Walter of Escrones, which the nuns should now pay; his mother's repayment to Matilda of Châteaufort for her holdings there at Chagny is found in no. 183 (but it should be dated to ca. 1223, not 1238/39; his mother died ca. 1223).

81. *Cartulaire de Port-Royal*, no. 121 (1230): "Et dicte moniales responderent quod cum sint Cistercienses privilegiatos sunt in hoc quod de hiis que propriis manibus vel sumptibus excolunt, decimas solvere non tenentur. Et ipse dictas terras propriis sumptibus ad culturam redigi faciunt; quare dicto presbytero dictas decimas reddere non tenebantur." The rent of fifteen sous was reduced to one sou in no. 145 (1233) and in nos. 223 and 224 (1243) the nuns

acquired further rights at Chagny from Adam and Philip of Galardon, first for thirty livres and then sixty livres.

82. *Cartulaire de Port-Royal*, no. 121 (1230).

83. On noval tithes, see Donnelly, *Medieval Cistercian Laybrotherhood*, pp. 50ff. At issue was whether the noval tithe exemption applied to newly instituted tithes or to noval lands; in either case such an exemption had to be purchased. This was already true in the twelfth century; see Berman, "Cistercian Development."

84. In comparison, rents for Lieu discussed in the next chapter do not mention oats, but only wheat and rye. See Table 5, "Lieu-Notre-Dame: Annual Payments in Kind," in Chapter 5.

85. Dimier, *Saint Louis et Cîteaux*, p. 175; *Cartulaire de Port-Royal*, no. 224 (1243), land "de feodo Domini Regis."

86. *Cartulaire de Port-Royal*, nos. 243 (1247) and 247 (1248).

87. *Cartulaire de Port-Royal*, nos. 251–52 (1248). He was the grandson of Simon of Montfort, the Albigensian crusader, and son of Amaury VI of Montfort who had received the French holdings when splitting up the inheritance with his brother Simon of Montfort who received the English ones.

88. *Cartulaire de Port-Royal*, no. 51 (1220).

89. *Cartulaire de Port-Royal*, nos. 42, 43, 44, and 48 (1220), a house on that little square in the *censive* (lordship) of the lord king that had been occupied by the late Hugh Petrarii and had been given by Emelina's late brother, Simon of Braye, along with twenty livres for the support of a chapel in their church for his son, as confirmed by King Philip Augustus and the abbot of Vaux.

90. *Cartulaire de Port-Royal*, nos. 286 and 287 (1262) and 291 (1263). On augmented rents, see Chapter 7.

91. Most nuns brought either land or rents with them, although according to canon law it was illegal for abbesses to demand an entrance gift or dowry; see Lynch, *Simoniacal Entry*, pp. 162–63. Some donors insisted on such charters, as in the case of Blanche of Paciac in Chapter 7.

92. *Cartulaire des Clairets*, no. 6 (1214); cf no. 18 (1220) when another entrant also named Agnes gave herself and all her property to Clairets to be a nun, believing that she was the sole legitimate heir of her father. The nuns later had to pay forty livres against claims made by a certain Margaret, who claimed to be Agnes's legitimate sister, but born elsewhere; possibly she was a stepsister.

93. *Cartulaire de Port-Royal*, no. 98 (1228); the donor Odeline retained a rent of two deniers per arpent at the feast of Saint-Rémy and required that the nuns use her winepress until they had their own.

94. *Cartulaire de Port-Royal*, nos. 130 (1231/32), 225 (1245), 303 (1264), and 307 (1267), the last is a confirmation in French by the lord of Marly for the four orphan girls.

95. *Cartulaire de Port-Royal*, no. 333 (1280).

96. *Cartulaire de Port-Royal*, no. 274 (1259): "super terram patris mei in conquestu Albigense." This Guy is found as well in the *censier*. The girls were granddaughters of Simon of Montfort, the Albigensian crusader.

97. Stephen D. White, *Custom, Kinship, and Gifts to Saints: The Laudatio Parentum in Western France, 1050–1150* (Chapel Hill: University of North Carolina Press, 1988).

98. For the earlier situation, see Lisa M. Bitel, *Land of Women: Tales of Men and Gender from Early Ireland* (Ithaca, NY: Cornell University Press, 1998), pp. 74–83, 103–30, and 175–77

and suggestive items in Georges Duby, *The Early Growth of the European Economy: Warriors and Peasants from the Seventh to the Twelfth Century*, trans. Howard B. Clarke (Ithaca, NY: Cornell University Press, 1974), pp. 11–26.

99. It was really only in the early Italian Renaissance that women began to enter religious communities because they lacked other options; this turning point seems to be captured in the study by Sharon T. Strocchia, *Nuns and Nunneries in Renaissance Florence* (Baltimore: Johns Hopkins University Press, 2009).

100. *Cartulaire de Port-Royal*, no. 173 (1238).

101. *Cartulaire de Voisins*, nos. 104 (1251), 103 (1249), and 102 (1244).

102. *Histoire de Villiers*, pp. 6–35.

103. *Cartulaire de l'abbaye royale du Lieu-N.-D.-lès-Romorantin*, ed. Ernest Plat (Romorantin, 1892), hereafter cited as *Cartulaire de Lieu*, nos. 116 (1237), 117 (1239), 118 (1243), and 119 (1245), but see more discussion in Chapter 5.

104. Paris, AN, S*4386, fol. 64r–v (1231 and 1234); the sisters were Aelidis and her husband the knight Guarin of Conches; Beatrice and her husband the knight Guarin of Gagniac; and the unmarried sisters were Margaret and Agnes.

105. *Cartulaire de Port-Royal*, no. 34 (1217/18)

106. *Cartulaire de Port-Royal*, no. 94 (1227).

107. *Cartulaire de Port-Royal*, no. 102 (1228).

108. *Cartulaire de Port-Royal*, no. 169 (1237).

109. *Cartulaire de Port-Royal*, nos. 319 and 320 (1269).

110. *Cartulaire de Voisins*, nos. 67 (1259) and 320 (1270). In 1270 the income was granted "for only as long as my sister lives."

111. *Cartulaire de Port-Royal*, nos. 305 (1266), 306 (1266), 311 (1267), and 315 (1269).

112. Guy Bois, *Crise du féodalisme: Économie rurale et démographie en Normandie orientale du début du 14e siècle au milieu du 16e siècle* (Paris: Presses de la Fondation nationale des sciences politiques; Éditions de l'école des hautes études en sciences sociales, 1976). On some of the effects on the highest nobles, see Gabrielle M. Spiegel, *Romancing the Past: The Rise of Vernacular Prose Historiography in Thirteenth-Century France* (Berkeley: University of California Press, 1993).

113. See Constance H. Berman, "Cistercian Agriculture in Female Houses of Northern France, 1200–1300," in *Crisis in the Later Middle Ages: Beyond the Postan-Duby Paradigm*, ed. John Drendel (Turnhout: Brepols, 2014), pp. 339–63.

114. See Jonathan Riley-Smith, *The First Crusaders, 1095–1131* (Cambridge: Cambridge University Press, 1998), and Michael Lower, *The Barons' Crusade: A Call to Arms and Its Consequences* (Philadelphia: University of Pennsylvania Press, 2005).

CHAPTER 5

1. My thinking on this has been influenced by that of my student Erin L. Jordan, who, in *Women, Power, and Religious Patronage*, pp. 64–66, argues for the use of religious patronage by the countesses of Flanders to support their rule. Those countesses endowed a number of religious foundations including those for Cistercian nuns, to which they retired only on their deathbeds. Jordan describes them founding houses of nuns on sites where the King of France had refused to allow them to build castles—those abbeys occupied the same spaces that castles would have.

2. Elisabeth van Houts, *Memory and Gender in Medieval Europe, 900–1200* (Toronto: University of Toronto Press, 1999).

3. On women's use of written documents, see *The Cartulary of Countess Blanche of Champagne*, ed. Theodore Evergates (Toronto: University of Toronto Press, 2009); and Bruce L. Venarde, "Making History at Fontevraud: Abbess Petronilla of Chemillé and Practical Literacy," in *Nuns' Literacies in Medieval Europe: The Hull Dialogue*, ed. Virginia Blanton, Veronica O'Mara, and Patricia Stoop (Turnhout: Brepols, 2013), pp. 19–31, but see volume in general. See also Blanton, O'Mara, and Stoop, *The Kansas City Dialogue*; and a forthcoming third volume, *The Antwerp Dialogue*.

4. As is evidenced in letters they wrote or received, these thirteenth-century women were more educated and had more access to wealth; see "Epistolae: Medieval Women's Letters," accessed July 24, 2015, https://epistolae.ccnmtl.columbia.edu.

5. See Michelle Armstrong-Partida, "Mothers and Daughters as Lords: The Countesses of Blois and Chartres," *Medieval Prosopography* 26 (2005): 77–107. There is confusion about Marguerite's husbands, but no question that the last, present already in 1218, was Gautier of Avesnes. A third sister, Alice, had entered Fontevraud where she was abbess between 1209 and 1218; it is unclear whether she was still alive when the division of the counties occurred.

6. Baldwin, *Philip Augustus*, p. 342; cf. A. Dupré, "Les Comtesses de Chartres et de Blois: Étude historique," *Mémoires de la Société archéologique d'Eure et Loir* 5 (1872): 224–27; Marguerite and Isabelle were ruling heiresses to those counties, rather than the wives of inheriting counts, and were thus relegated to a footnote.

7. See Baldwin, *Philip Augustus*, e.g., pp. 277–79, 341–42; that Philip was less aggressive with regard to the marriages of feudatories, particularly in Normandy, is also suggested by Daniel Power, *The Norman Frontier in the Twelfth and Early Thirteenth Centuries* (Cambridge: Cambridge University Press, 2004), pp. 239–41. Cf. Turner, *King John*, pp. 104–5; perhaps Philip was subtler or slightly less greedy than John.

8. See Chapter 6; but Blanche as a child had lived in the vicinity of the great new foundation of Cistercian nuns at Huelgas made by her parents; see Élie Berger, *Histoire de Blanche de Castille, reine de France* (Paris: Thorin, 1895), p. 3.

9. *Cartulaire de Lieu*, no. 1 (1247), Isabelle's will: "Et pro hiis omnibus supradictis dicte moniales tenentur in dicta abbacia tenere capellanum, qui pro anime mee et domine Blanche franchorum regine, maritorum, antecessorum et successorum meorum salute singulis diebus divina celebrabit." See also no. 33 (1222), the actual foundation charter.

10. Bondéelle-Souchier, "Moniales," pp. 306–7; Moncey was visited by Stephen of Lexington; see Chapter 2.

11. Only a handful of documents survive for Moncey. Among the scraps in Tours, AD Indres-et-Loire, H799 and H800 is the act from 1214 listing six children, which suggests that Isabelle must have been born by 1180.

12. *Cartulaire de Voisins*, nos. 173–77 (1218/19–1220); no. 50 (1256) refers to Matilda of Amboise's last testament, in which she gave 40 *sous* annually to Voisins' nuns; that has not been found.

13. *Cartulaire de Lieu*, nos. 25 and 32 (1239) and 56–60 (1225, 1237, 1239).

14. In *Cartulaire de Lieu*, no. 91 (1238), John appears just before his death.

15. *Cartulaire de l'abbaye de Notre-Dame de l'Eau*, ed. Charles Métais (Chartres: Ch. Métais, 1908), hereafter cited as *Cartulaire de l'Eau*; the editor reports that the archives for Eau burned during the Wars of Religion; this "cartulary" is his own collection of surviving charters from various sources.

16. *Cartulaire de Lieu,* p. 7, opens with "Incipiunt transcripta cartularum et litterarum reddtualium monialium loci beate Marie iuxta Remorentinum cysterciensis ordinis," before the first charter from Isabelle (that of 1247, which might be described as the most important); it describes Isabelle providing 120 livres per year. The editor kept the original order of charters in the cartulary (that from the late thirteenth century), so that the initial foundation charter is no. 33 (1222). On p. 24 of the published text is a reproduced rubric after charter 25: "Explicit cartule pecuniarie," explaining that the initial charters contained money rents amounting to nearly 229 livres per year.

17. André Chédeville, *Chartres et ses campagnes (XIe–XIIIe s.)* (Paris: Klincksieck, 1973), p. 97, describes hostility to those acquiring land there near Chartres.

18. *Cartulaire de l'Eau,* no. 3 (1226).

19. *Cartulaire de l'Eau,* nos. 4, 5, 6, and 7 (all 1226) and 29 (1240).

20. *Cartulaire de l'Eau,* no. 10 (1227); this had been held from the late Louis, Count of Blois (d. 1205), from whose son, Thibaut VI (d. 1218), Isabelle and her sister had inherited. See Figure 4.

21. *Cartulaire de l'Eau,* nos. 13 (1228), and 27 (1239): Eau was to receive three muids of wheat annually in the countess's mills at Coudray and three muids of wine from her winepress there. There were also five arpents of meadow at Vauféry. Donors later took back rights over the vineyard of Lucent, in return for another two muids of wine at Coudray.

22. *Cartulaire de l'Eau,* no. 15 (1229): they ceded a house, vineyards, land, gardens, meadows, and their appurtenances at the abbey site, and she was to remain in the house for life. Her son, Perry, in consideration of his poverty and the good things he had done for the nuns, was to receive an annual pension of one hundred sous for life, even after his mother's death.

23. *Cartulaire de l'Eau,* no. 16 (1229), barrels called *costerez,* of which six made a muid of Chartres—so a muid and a third of wine; cf. *Cartulaire de l'abbaye de Saint-Père de Chartres* ed. M. [Benjamin Edme Charles] Guérard (Paris: Crapelet, 1840), no. 104 (1229), the only one for Eau in that volume.

24. *Cartulaire de l'Eau,* no. 18 (1231). On usurpations by managers of Benedictine estates see Berkhofer, *Day of Reckoning.*

25. *Cartulaire de l'Eau,* nos. 11 and 12 (1228).

26. *Cartulaire de l'Eau,* nos. 11, 12, 14, 15, (1228–30), 19, 21 (1232), and 23 (1235).

27. *Cartulaire de l'Eau,* nos. 31 (1241) and 37 (1248).

28. *Cartulaire de l'Eau,* nos. 38 (1250) and 43 (1251).

29. *Cartulaire de l'Eau,* nos. 53–55 (1257).

30. *Cartulaire de l'Eau,* nos. 32–33 (1243) and 34 (1244).

31. *Cartulaire de l'Eau,* nos. 25 (1237) and 82 (1274).

32. *Cartulaire de l'Eau,* no. 35 (1247).

33. *Cartulaire de l'Eau,* nos. 29 (1240/41) and 31 (1242), both of which were clearly done after John's death; they say "quam [ego] tunc de novo fundaveram." In the second charter Isabelle added seven more muids of wine from the press of Valféry with any deficit made up at her winepress at Luisant. On William, see Chapter 4.

34. B. F. Harvey, "Monastic Pittances in the Middle Ages," in *Food in Medieval England: Diet and Nutrition,* ed. C. M. Woolgar, D. Serjeantson, and T. Waldron (Oxford: Oxford University Press, 2006), pp. 215–27, describes the poor of Westminster, who flocked to that abbey's gates on the dates of such extra distributions of food (pittances) to the monastic community.

35. The poverty of the nuns is mentioned in *Cartulaire de l'Eau*, no. 85 (1278), when two daughters entered as nuns, and their parents granted four muids of wheat annually from their manor of Chenais "because of the poverty of those nuns and the affection that said John Jourdain and his wife Jacqueline had for that abbey." As for conflating the monastic poor, the *pauperes Christi*, with the truly indigent, the tendency goes back at least to the Rule of Saint Benedict; see Michel Mollat, *The Poor in the Middle Ages: An Essay in Social History*, trans. Arthur Goldhammer (New Haven, CT: Yale University Press, 1986), esp. pp. 3–40; Constable, *Reformation*, pp. 146–50; something more is said about this by Peter Brown in *Through the Eye of a Needle: Wealth, the Fall of Rome, and the Making of Christianity in the West, 350–550 AD* (Princeton, NJ: Princeton University Press, 2012), pp. 232–36.

36. *Cartulaire de Lieu*, nos. 25 and 32 (1239); there is no naming of the recipients of those alms.

37. Matilda's conveyances as countess are listed in *Cartulaire de l'Eau*, no. 50 (1256).

38. *Cartulaire de Lieu*, no. 33 (1222).

39. *Cartulaire de Lieu*, no. 1 (1247).

40. *Cartulaire de Lieu*, no. 33 (1222).

41. *Cartulaire de Lieu*, no. 24 (1232); the daughter and son-in-law gave to Lieu, "de novo constitute et religosis monialibus Deo famulantibus," a *métarie* in the woods of Calmont (belonging to Richard of Beaumont if we are to believe a charter rubric for no. 25 that called him lord of Calmont). Isabelle did this "for the amelioration of those lands" (in melioribus terris incultis usque ad centum arpenta).

42. *Cartulaire de Lieu*, no. 34 (1224, not 1254, for John died around 1238).

43. *Cartulaire de Lieu*, nos. 93, 94 (1232), and 132 (1234).

44. These four women were discussed in Chapter 4.

45. *Cartulaire de Lieu*, nos. 116 (1237), 117 (1239), 118 (1243), and 119 (1245).

46. *Cartulaire de Lieu*, nos. 105 (1245), 106 and 107 (both 1254); one donor wanted an annuity in bread and wine.

47. *Cartulaire de Lieu*, nos. 120 (1246), 121 (1246), 122 (1247), and 123 (1254).

48. *Cartulaire de Lieu*, no. 55 (1254); *in bloveriis* is probably a mistranscription of *in ploveriis*, a variant of *in paluderiis*—in marshes.

49. *Cartulaire de Lieu*, nos. 124 (1260), 125 (1260), and 126 (1261). The nuns paid another twenty-two livres to Hervy in 1260 and in 1261 to protect their mills and fishing there and thirty-seven and a half livres to Matthew of Charnay.

50. *Cartulaire de Lieu*, no. 134 (1237).

51. *Cartulaire de Lieu*, nos. 112 (1244), 114 (1269), and 115 (1248).

52. *Cartulaire de Lieu*, nos. 133 (1245), 129 (1246), 139 (1251), 65 (1246), and 131 (1260).

53. *Cartulaire de Lieu*, no. 113 (1262).

54. *Cartulaire de Lieu*, no. 81 (1242).

55. *Cartulaire de Lieu*, p. 24.

56. *Cartulaire de Lieu*, p. 95.

57. *Cartulaire de Lieu*, no. 91 (1238), rubric p. 65: "De terris inter cheminum et magnum stagnum et de la Ploardiere, et xii arpentis nemorum iuxta stagnum, de terragio dou Pin, de Plein Bois et de Combreu, de viii arpentis vinearum iuxta terras nostras. Item de duobus stagnis abbacie contiguis."

58. *Cartulaire de Lieu*, no. 65 (1246): "Quicquid habeo vinearum magnam et parvam forestiam in territorio Lanthenaci et Remorentini prout via protenditur Blesensium apud locum qui vocatur Rangeroulx et ab alia meta per marescum et stagnum Guillermi de Furno militis

et forestiam sitam iuxta viam que ducit de Remorentino ad Mur, et ex inde usque ad aliam metam positam iuxta grangiam sancti Lazari, et ab alia via que vadit pelliceam plateam cum omni iure et dominio quod habeo in eadem." In *Cartulaire de Lieu*, no. 101 (1249), Reginald sold to the nuns whatever he had in the vineyards "in parva foresta in territorio Remorentini" for another forty livres *tournois*.

59. See *Cartulaire de Lieu*, pp. 107–20.

60. *Cartulaire de Lieu*, no. 90 (1270).

61. *Cartulaire de Lieu*, nos. 66 (1234), 68 (1234), 67 (1244), and 71 (1247); this was confirmed by Matilda as Countess of Chartres in no. 69 (January 1249/50).

62. *Cartulaire de Lieu*, nos. 70 and 71 (1249), 76 and 77 (1252), and 79 (1263); in 1252 William Ternerii, knight, had granted usage in the woods of Briode in a place called Telleau to the nuns, and they granted to him usage and free of all payments in the territory of Morais.

63. *Cartulaire de Lieu*, nos. 61 and 62 (1252), 95 and 96 (1249), and 97 (1252); in 1252 Petronilla's son, William Ternerii, then sold the nuns a meadow at Laçay for thirty livres. In 1260 the tithes at Lanthenay and Romorantin were granted away by the nuns as a lifetime annuity to some of their former servants, but the tithes were ceded back again to the nuns in 1264 by Maria, widow of Bernard Carnifex, butcher and bourgeois of Romorantin; for this see nos. 87 (1264), 88 and 89 (1265), 129 (1246), 130 (1251), 131 (1260), and 128 (1261).

64. *Cartulaire de Lieu*, no. 1 (1247): "Totum nemus meum quod vocatur le Druillay situm iuxto viam que ducit de Millenciaco apud Romorentinum, prout continet clausura fossati dictum nemus claudentis, cum omni videlicet iure et dominio que in dicto nemore habebam vel habere poteram. . . . Volui siquidem, et concessi, quod dicte moniales dictum nemus possint conservare, vendere, dare, extirpare, et ad agriculturam redigerem et voluntatem suam de terris et de nemoribus facere."

65. *Cartulaire de Lieu*, no. 1 (1247); and nos. 36 and 37 (1249/50), her daughter's confirmation.

66. *Cartulaire de Lieu*, nos. 4 (1227), 5 (1230), 6 (1249), and 7 (1249).

67. *Cartulaire de Lieu*, no. 37 (1249).

68. *Cartulaire de Lieu*, no. 36 (1249).

69. See *Cartulaire de Lieu*, nos. 40 (1201), 41 (1201), 42 (1194), and 43 (1203), which include a conveyance to Barzelles by Hervé of Donzy, lord of the nearby castle of Saint-Aignan, and his wife, Matilda of Auxerre, on whom see below. The charters involved suggest that the monks of Barzelles had directed such reclamation since early in the thirteenth century.

70. *Cartulaire de Lieu*, no. 44 (1248): "Noverint universi quod grangiam nostram de Podiis Sauverons sitam in castellania de Remorentino Aurelianensis dyocesis cum omnibus pertinenciis tam in domibus quam etiam, vineis, pratis, terris, boscis, aquis, decimis, terragiis, et aliis redditibus quos habemus in parrochia de Giacho [Gy], de Soemio [Soings] and Aubereia [Aubèrière] ad dictam domum pertinentibus abbatisse et conventui monialium de Loco Beate Maria . . . vendidimus." It was sold for five hundred livres *tournois*.

71. *Cartulaire de Lieu*, no. 64 (1239); the nuns could take either tithes of wine or of wheat.

72. See Berman, *Medieval Agriculture*.

73. See Joseph Avril, "Les fondations, l'organisation et l'évolution des établissements de moniales dans le diocèse d'Angers," *Religieuses en France au XIIIe siècle*, ed. Michel Parisse (Nancy: Presses Universitaires de Nancy, 1985), pp. 27–67; on pp. 35–37 he described Perray as a house of monks established circa 1190, dependent on the neighboring abbey of Bellefontaine. Bondéelle-Souchier, "Moniales," p. 281, mistakenly identified Matilda of Amboise, wife of

Richard of Beaumont, as Matilda of Blois; it is Matilda of Amboise, eventually Countess of Chartres, who was married to that Richard and associated with Perray.

74. See similar rivalries described for Denmark by Brian Patrick McGuire, "Cistercian Nuns in Twelfth- and Thirteenth-Century Denmark and Sweden: Far from the Madding Crowd," in *Women in the Medieval Monastic World*, ed. Janet Burton and Karen Stöber (Turnhout: Brepols, 2015), pp. 167–84.

75. *Cartulaire de l'Eau*, no. 50 (1256).

76. *Cartulaire de l'Eau*, no. 51 (1256).

77. *Cartulaire de l'Eau*, nos. 59 (1259) and 59 bis (1280), pp. 76–77, and p. 77 n. 1. The Cistercian nuns at Grâce-Notre-Dame near Montmirail are discussed in Chapter 8.

78. *Cartulaire de l'Eau*, no. 56 (1257).

79. *Cartulaire de l'Eau*, no. 60 (1260).

80. *Cartulaire de l'Eau*, nos. 64 (1263) and 65 (1261).

81. *Cartulaire de Lieu*, nos. 8 (1259) and 35 (1261); the latter is the last instance in which Alice appears in the charters.

82. *Cartulaire de Lieu*, no. 9 (1268).

83. *Cartulaire de Lieu*, nos. 49 and 50 (1261).

84. *Cartulaire de Lieu*, nos. 140 and 141 (1266).

85. *Cartulaire de Lieu*, no. 26 (1270).

86. *Cartulaire de l'Eau*, no. 87 (1279).

87. *Cartulaire de l'Eau*, nos. 82, 89, 90, and 91 (1282) are Peter's concessions, nos. 99 and 100 (1285) are Jeanne's.

88. The following section draws on an honors' thesis written at the University of Iowa by Susan Cray in 1991. She based her study primarily on René de Lespinasse, *Le Nivernais et les comtes de Nevers*, 3 vols. (Paris: H. Champion, 1909–14); Lespinasse, *Chronique ou histoire abrégée des évêques et des comtes de Nevers écrite en latin au seizième siècle et publiée pour la première fois* (Nevers: Fay, 1870); and Ernest Petit, *Histoire des ducs de Bourgogne de la race capétienne: Avec des documents inédits et des pièces justificatives*, 9 vols. (Paris: E. Thorin, 1885–1905). My thanks to Ms. Cray for her enthusiastic work on this project.

89. A source of confusion is that among claimants to Auxerre was Peter's younger brother Robert of Courtenay. His wife Matilda (of Courtenay) was lady of Mehun-sur-Yevre and she founded houses of Cistercian nuns at Beauvoir in 1223 and Bussières in 1234 in the archdiocese of Bourges; my thanks to William Jordan for providing a clarification about the two Matildas and to archivists in AD Cher in Bourges, who provided numerous photocopies for the charters for those two houses of nuns, which nonetheless eventually fell out of the boundaries of this study; that work remains to be done.

90. Hubert Verneret, *Mahaut de Courtenay, 1188–1257: Comtesse de Nevers, Auxerre et Tonnerre* (Précy-sous-Thil: Éditions de l'Armançon, 2002), provides some maps and family trees of interest, but it is more novel than biography. A slightly different version of the lives of Matilda of Auxerre and her husband Hervé of Donzy is found among legends concerning the Caulite foundation of Épeau; see Phillip C. Adamo, *New Monks in Old Habits: The Formation of the Caulite Monastic Order, 1193–1267* (Toronto, Ont.: Pontifical Institute of Mediaeval Studies, 2014), pp. 115–19.

91. One of their earliest surviving acts after their marriage was Matilda and Hervé's grant of land at Saugirard to the Cistercian monks of Barzelles, confirmed by Louis, Count of Blois, and later sold to Lieu; see *Cartulaire de Lieu*, nos. 40 and 41 (1201).

92. *Les Chartes des Comtes de Saint-Pol (XIe–XIIIe siècles)*, ed. Jean-François Nieus (Turnhout: Brepols, 2008), hereafter cited as *Chartes de Saint-Pol*, no. 189 (May 1221), in which Guy of Châtillon and his brother Hugh of Châtillon confirmed arrangements with Philip Augustus about Guy's marriage to Agnes, daughter of Hervé, Count of Nevers, and Matilda of Courtenay.

93. *L'abbaye du Pont-aux-Dames (ordre de Cîteaux), assise en la paroisse de Couilly . . . 1226–1790)*, ed. [Claude-Hyacinthe] Berthault (Meaux: Librairie le Blondel, 1887), no. 6 (1226), this edition hereafter cited as *Cartulaire de Pont-aux-Dames*.

94. *Chartes de Saint-Pol*, nos. 222 (1227), a gift made to Cercamp, and 238 (1231), a similar one to Cîteaux.

95. Constance H. Berman, "A Thirteenth-Century Coin Hoard Found in the Collection of the American Numismatic Society and a Penny from the Cluniac Priory of Souvigny," *Trésors monétaires* 8 (1986): 115–27 and plate 41.

96. *Gallia Christiana in provincias ecclesiasticas distributa: qua series et historia archiepiscoporum, episcoporum et abbatum Franciae vicinarumque ditionum . . . opera et studio Domni Dionysii Sammarthani, presbyteri et monachii ordinis Sancti Benedicti et congregatione Sancti Mauri nec non monachorum ejusdem congregationis*, ed. B. Hauréau (Paris: various imprints, 1812–96), vol. 12, col. 480, "*Insulae*": "Beatae Mariae dicatur parthenon fundatoremque agnoscit Guillelmum de Seignelay episcopum Autissiodorensis circa an. 1219 monasterium virginum, quas ex Parisiensis S. Antonii de Campis arcessivit, uno ab urbe milliari eo in loco condidit, cui nomen olim Cellae locum donante Gerardo Baleine B. Mariae canonico illudque monasterium abbati Cisterciensi subjecit." Bondéelle-Souchier, "Moniales," p. 236. Auxerre, AD Yonne, H 1749 "Isles" includes several copies of gifts for the soul of Hervé to Isles in 1229: Matilda gave three stalls in the market of Auxerre. See also René Courtet, "Histoire de l'abbaye des Iles, anciennement de Celles," *Bulletin de la société des sciences historiques et naturelles de l'Yonne* 120 (1988): 47–69.

97. Bondéelle-Souchier, "Moniales," pp. 282 and 294; Marcilly's community was later moved to Réconfort in the diocese of Autun.

98. Bondéelle-Souchier, "Moniales," pp. 291–92.

99. *Cartulaire de Pont-aux-Dames*, nos. 66, 67 (1239/40), 68, 71, 73 (1240), and 83, 84, and 85 (1248), in the last of which he gave the nuns of Pont-aux-Dames twenty-three livres' worth of income for his own soul. Despite the contention to the contrary of H. de Flamare, who quotes Joinville on his glorious knighthood, in "La Charte de départ pour la Terre-Sainte de Gaucher de Châtillon, Baron de Donzy," *Bulletin de la Société nivernaise des lettres, sciences et arts* 13 (1886–89): 174–82, Gaucher had probably never married; although there was a proposal for his marriage, it probably never occurred; see *Chartes de Saint-Pol*, no. 254 (1236) an agreement for Gaucher made by his uncle Hugh of Châtillon that was a future promise of marriage.

100. *Cartulaire de Pont-aux-Dames*, no. 6 (1226).

101. *Cartulaire de Pont-aux-Dames*, nos. 2–4 and 6 (1226); to have Cistercian nuns answering to a bishop was not unusual at the time; see Chapter 2. Much later the abbey would occasionally be called Pont-aux-Dames-lez-Crécy-en-Brie; see no. 142 (1345).

102. *Cartulaire de Pont-aux-Dames*, no. 5 (1226); this must be six muids, not sixty—the error suggests the muddle in the published documents. Some information is also found in charters for the counts of Saint-Pol.

103. *Cartulaire de Pont-aux-Dames*, no. 39 (1231). See also *Chartes de Saint-Pol*, no. 242 (1233), which mentions Hugh's wife Marie; no. 263 (1239); it is about herrings and butter for Pont from Cercamp and appears to be the last charter in which she appears; she had died by 1241, but her husband would continue as Count of Blois until his death in 1248.

104. *Cartulaire de Pont-aux-Dames*, no. 38 (1230).

105. *Cartulaire de Pont-aux-Dames*, nos. 45 and 46 (1232).

106. *Cartulaire de Pont-aux-Dames*, no. 41 (1231).

107. *Cartulaire de Pont-aux-Dames*, no. 48 (1232).

108. *Cartulaire de Pont-aux-Dames*, no. 61 (1237).

109. *Cartulaire de Pont-aux-Dames*, no. 64 (1239).

110. *Cartulaire de Pont-aux-Dames*, no. 47 (1242), a postmortem gift.

111. *Cartulaire de Pont-aux-Dames*, nos. 42–44 (1231) and 48–50 (1232). Hugh supported the nuns' claims to half the tithe of wine at Bouleurs against the canons of La Chapelle (a dependency of Saint-Martin-des-Champs in Paris).

112. *Cartulaire de Pont-aux-Dames*, nos. 90 (1258) and 94 (1260), the rights to celebrate mass in their granges as long as they did not admit local laypeople.

113. *Cartulaire de Pont-aux-Dames*, nos. 54–56 (1233/34), except those sold earlier to the chapter of Meaux.

114. *Cartulaire de Pont-aux-Dames*, nos. 51–53 (1233/34).

115. *Cartulaire de Pont-aux-Dames*, nos. 66 and 67 (1239/40).

116. *Cartulaire de Pont-aux-Dames*, nos. 70 (1240), 19, and 20 (1227).

117. *Cartulaire de Pont-aux-Dames*, no. 66 (1239).

118. *Cartulaire de Pont-aux-Dames*, no. 106 (1263).

119. *Cartulaire de Pont-aux-Dames*, nos. 68, 69, 73, 75, 76 (1240), 77 (1248), and 78 (1264).

120. *Cartulaire de Pont-aux-Dames*, nos. 128 and 129 (1301): ninety arpents of woods were sold to the nuns for 120 livres; acquisitions at Jariel are treated further in Table 36 in Chapter 9.

121. *Cartulaire de Pont-aux-Dames*, nos. 23, 24, 25, 26, and 28 (1228); in no. 88 (1249) he gave the fief of Lubeton woods, but kept hunting rights there. In no. 91 (1259) a different Gaucher, Hugh of Châtillon's son (as opposed to his nephew), rented out 160 arpents of woods; no. 109 (1265) is the sale to Pont of twenty-seven arpents of woods in three places in Lubeton in the *bois de l'abbaye* for 180 livres, 112 sous, and two horses worth forty livres *tournois*. Much later the nuns acquired fifteen arpents of woods at Lubeton near those they already owned; see nos. 122 and 123 (1290).

122. My thanks to Jeroen Laemers for this insight.

123. *Cartulaire de Pont-aux-Dames*, nos. 62 (1238), 93, 97 (1260), 98 (1261), 113 (1269), 114 (1270), 134, 135 (1312), 136 (1328).

124. *Chartes de Saint-Pol*, no. 278 (1246). He had departed only slightly earlier, having confirmed his gifts to Pont-aux-Dames; see *Pont-aux-Dames*, no. 81 (1247).

125. Bondéelle-Souchier, "Moniales," establishes the large numbers of those houses of nuns in francophone areas.

126. Riley-Smith, *First Crusaders*; and Theodore Evergates, *The Aristocracy in the County of Champagne, 1100–1300* (Philadelphia: University of Pennsylvania Press, 2007).

127. It is possible that in the cases of Matilda of Auxerre and Isabelle of Chartres, like that of Eleanor of Vermandois, Philip Augustus had miscalculated the life expectancies of these women; and see Berman, "Two Medieval Women's Control."

CHAPTER 6

1. Some arguments here were initially presented in Berman, "Two Medieval Women's Control."

2. For Blanche's life, see Berger, *Histoire de Blanche de Castille*; Gérard Sivéry, *Blanche de Castille* (Paris: Fayard, 1990); Lindy Grant, "Blanche of Castile and Normandy," in *Normandy and Its Neighbours, 900–1250: Essays for David Bates*, ed. David Crouch and Kathleen Thompson (Turnhout: Brepols, 2011), pp. 117–31: and Grant, *Blanche of Castile, Queen of France* (New Haven, CT: Yale University Press, 2016).

3. Dimier, *Saint Louis et Cîteaux*, pp. 158–61, nos. 26–64, notes her advocacy for others' abbeys of Cistercian nuns.

4. See Erin Jordan, *Women, Power*: and Jordan, "Female Founders: Exercising Authority in Thirteenth-Century Flanders and Hainaut," in "Secular Women in the Documents for Late Medieval Women," ed. Constance H. Berman and Michelle Herder, special issue, *Church History and Religious Culture* 88, no. 4 (2008): 535–61, where she reports that Jeanne founded Ath in 1216, Marquette in 1224, Osteeklo in 1228, and Doornzele in 1234. Marguerite founded Ter Hagen in 1230 and Flines in 1234. In their counties more than thirty houses of Cistercian nuns were founded by 1250; at least half had women founders.

5. *Recherches historiques et critiques sur les anciens comtes de Beaumont-sur-Oise, du XIe au XIIIe siècle*, ed. L. Douet d'Arcq (Amiens, 1855), nos. 54–55 (1206) and 56 (1207).

6. *Feudal Society in Medieval France: Documents from the County of Champagne*, ed. Theodore Evergates (Philadelphia: University of Pennsylvania Press, 1993), no. 40 (1199). On Eleanor, see further discussion in Chapter 9 below.

7. See Lester, *Creating Cistercian Nuns*, pp. 28–33 for Argensolles. Berenguela of Navarre, widow of Richard I, founded the abbey of Cistercian monks at L'Épau near Mans in 1229; she entered and was buried there on December 23, 1230; see Dimier, *Saint Louis et Cîteaux*, p. 157.

8. Grant, *Blanche of Castile*, pp. 54–58.

9. See *Cartulaire de Lieu*, no. 1 (1247).

10. Matilda was Blanche's cousin; their mothers were sisters; see Figure 3 in Chapter 4.

11. See Menant et al., *Les Capétiens*; and Sean L. Field and M. Cecilia Gaposchkin, "Questioning the Capetians, 1180–1328," *History Compass* 12 (2014): 567–85.

12. There is considerable dispute on their financial state. Sivéry, *Blanche de Castille*, argued that they were short of funds because Blanche had to beg Philip for support for the Lincoln expedition; Baldwin, *Philip Augustus*, pp. 332–36, argues that there was plenty of money in the royal treasury, but that Philip refused to fund his son's invasion of England. Grant, *Blanche of Castile*, p. 45, argues that the young couple had adequate funds because they were set up in a separate court and, on p. 207, that a gift to a hospital in Issoudun, founded in 1234, points to Blanche's use of some of the original dowry lands.

13. Anselme Dimier collected all the references he could find to almsgiving to the Cistercians by Louis IX's parents, but he has very few entries for bequests even by Louis IX in those early years. See Dimier, *Saint Louis et Cîteaux*, pp. 155–56. His no. 1, p. 155 is not found in the archives today and is probably apocryphal, making the earliest Capetian grant to Saint-Antoine Dimier's no. 16; on this point I agree with Robert Branner, *St. Louis and the Court Style in Gothic Architecture* (London: A. Zwemmer, 1965), p. 31, note 1.

14. *Layettes*, vol. 2, 1710 (1225); see discussion below.

15. See Dimier, *Saint Louis et Cîteaux*, pp. 155–56.

16. On Adele's religious propensities, see Arnaud Timbert and Yves Gallet, "Une foundation royale du début du XIIIe siècle: L'abbaye Saint-Jean-Baptiste du Jard," in *Art et architecture à Melun au Moyen Age*, ed. Yves Gallet (Paris: Picard, 2000), pp. 201–21.

17. Dimier, *Saint Louis et Cîteaux*, pp. 155–56, nos. 6–14 and *Statuta*, ed. Canivez, 1227, no. 12.

18. Paris, BnF, Latin MSS 9166–69, *Cartulaire de Royaumont*, fol. 1157 (1228), hereafter *Cartulaire de Royaumont*; the foundation charter is published in H. Duclos, *Histoire de Royaumont: Sa fondation par Saint Louis et son influence sur la France*, 2 vols. (Paris: Ch. Douniol, 1867), 1:37–42.

19. Indeed, M. Cecilia Gaposchkin, *The Making of Saint Louis: Kingship, Sanctity, and Crusade in the Later Middle Ages* (Ithaca, NY: Cornell University Press, 2008), pp. 125–29, argues that Louis IX identified with Cistercian monks and particularly with Royaumont throughout his life.

20. See Caroline A. Bruzelius, "Cistercian High Gothic: The Abbey Church of Longpont and the Architecture of the Cistercians in the Early Thirteenth Century," *Analecta Cisterciensia* 35 (1979): 90–110. The term "court style" originates with Branner, *St. Louis and the Court Style*, but he discusses Royaumont only on pp. 30–34.

21. Bruzelius, "Cistercian High Gothic," beginning on p. 90.

22. Bruzelius, "Cistercian High Gothic," p. 97.

23. On difficulties in Blanche's early regency, see Berger, *Histoire de Blanche*. Studies like those of Ernst Kantorowicz, *The King's Two Bodies: A Study in Mediaeval Political Theology* (Princeton, NJ: Princeton University Press, 1957), and Andrew W. Lewis, *Royal Succession in Capetian France: Studies on Familial Order and the State* (Cambridge, MA: Harvard University Press, 1981), suggest some of the symbolic importance of such a gesture.

24. *Cartulaire de Royaumont*, fol. 1157 (June 1228); see Appendix 1 for *ad medium*.

25. *Cartulaire de Royaumont*, fols. 7–10 (August 1228).

26. See *Cartulaire de l'abbaye du Paraclet*, ed. Charles Lalore, Collection des principaux cartulaires du diocèse de Troyes, vol. 2 (Paris: E. Thorin, 1878) hereafter cited as *Cartulaire du Paraclet*, no. 193 (August 1228); the king gave the prioress of Borenc arable land at Baern (thirty-two arpents) and five muids of oats in annual rent in that villa, and at Pont-de-Beaumont seven livres and six sous in annual rent. He also gave eighty livres and fifteen sous for the cost of rebuilding a grange elsewhere for the nuns.

27. *Cartulaire de Royaumont*, fol. 1137 (September 1229).

28. See *Cartulaire de Royaumont*, fol. 646 (1230) and fols. 909–19 (1231–32); such references to tenants suggest that the existing manorial regime was continued.

29. Often such gifts represented 20 percent of the value of a property conveyed, with "donors" paying for the other 80 percent; see more examples of this for Cistercian nuns in Chapter 7.

30. *Cartulaire de Royaumont*, fol. 646 (1230); the purchase price for such a life rent might have been as much as four hundred livres.

31. *Cartulaire de Royaumont*, fols. 1642–45 (1239).

32. *Cartulaire de Royaumont*, fols. 1189ff. (1249). Such lavish royal support of animal husbandry and in particular of sheep raising by the Cistercian monks at Royaumont set its monks on an economic course of mixed agriculture and animal husbandry similar to that of earlier foundations of Cistercian monks in this region. See Charles Higounet, *La grange de Vaulerent: Structure et exploitation d'un terroir cistercien de la plaine de France, XIIe–XVe siècle* (Paris: SEVPEN, 1965); and François Blary, *Le Domaine de Châalis, XIIe–XIVe siècles: Approches archéologiques des établissements agricoles et industriels d'une abbaye cistercienne* (Paris: Éditions du CTHS, 1989).

33. There are no alms rolls for Blanche of Castile until 1240, and only fragments of several later ones. One is in *Layettes*, vol. 5, no. 448 (1242/43). The other, London, British Museum, Additional Charter 4129 (1241/42), is a running list of monies paid out. For instance, there were

"ten sous to the nuns of Val-des-Vignes at Bar-sur-Aube," "ten sous for the arms of Gerard," "five livres for a psalter," and so on; its dorsal indications have been papered over in an attempt to keep it from crumbling and are not legible. Evidence is also limited by dependence on Dimier's list, which collected only those bequests involving Cistercians, but see Dimier, *Saint Louis and Cîteaux*, p. 157, no. 22; and Leonie V. Hicks, *Religious Life in Normandy, 1050–1300* (Woodbridge: Boydell, 2007), pp. 27–28 and 201.

34. Branner, *St. Louis and the Court Style*, describes the Sainte-Chapelle, for which the king spent 40,000 livres and which was completed only in 1248; in addition the gold reliquary housed there reputedly cost another 100,000 livres.

35. *Layettes*, vol. 2, no. 2884 (1240).

36. On the will, see *Layettes*, vol. 2, no. 1710 (1225); cf. Charles Petit-Dutaillis, *Étude sur la vie et le règne de Louis VIII* (Paris: É. Bouillon, 1894), no. 219 (1224/25), p. 479.

37. *Layettes*, vol. 5, no. 514 (1248).

38. Contrary to Prieure, as discussed below.

39. See *Cartulaire de l'abbaye de Maubuisson (Notre-Dame-la-Royale)*, ed. Adolphe Dutilleux and Joseph Depoin (Pontoise: Société Historique du Vexin, 1890–1913), no. 302 (July 1253): "Ludovicus Dei gratia Francorum Rex. Notum facimus quod cum karissima domina mater nostra pie recordationis Blanche, quondam Francorum Regina, ad opus abbatie sue Beate Marie Regalis juxta Pontysaram," and no. 94 (August 1253), also from Sidon and addressed to his friend Master Garnier of Cergy (who would become chaplain at Maubuisson), which again treated his mother with great respect. Garnier was allowed to exchange properties that had been in her dower lands and he would later advise the nuns on their sale of part of the forest of Breteuil (see below).

This published edition of charters for Maubuisson is hereafter cited as *Cartulaire de Maubuisson*. The Dutilleux and Depoin edition was also published as *L'abbaye de Maubuisson, histoire et cartulaire: Publiés d'après les documents entièrement inédits*, 4 vols. (Pontoise: Amedée: Paris, 1882–85), but the document numbering is the same and here it is still identified as *Cartulaire de Maubuisson*. The published text, in fact, is not a real medieval cartulary but a recueil, or collection of medieval charters, many gleaned from separate bundles (*liasses*) in the archives, which were once in Versailles, but are today housed in Pontoise. Some but not all were published at least in summary by Dutilleux and Depoin in *Cartulaire de Maubuisson*; complete charters are found in Pontoise, AD Val d'Oise, 72H80–72H143, a very extensive collection. Pontoise, AD Val d'Oise, 72H10 is the manuscript *Cartulaire de Maubuisson* from 1688. On the other notable codex, see next note.

40. Pontoise, AD Val d'Oise, 72H12, *Achatz d'héritage pour Maubuisson*, (hereafter *Achatz d'héritages*) fol. 5r: "Anno Domini millesimo ducentesimo tricesimo sexto fundata fuit nova abbacia iuxta Ponthisarium ab illustria Blancha Dei gratia Regina Francorum. Et hec est recepta Magistri Richardi de Torni pro operibus dicte abbacie que fundata fuit prima ebdomada post Penthecosten." The week after Pentecost in 1236 was May 19 to 24. Excerpts from opening sections on construction expenses were published by Henri de l'Épinois, "Comptes relatifs à la fondation de l'abbaye de Maubuisson, d'après les originaux des archives de Versailles," *Bibliothèque de l'École des Chartes* 29 (1858): 550–69, but they are limited, sometimes rearranged, and give no attention to other sections; a new edition is being prepared.

41. *Achatz d'héritages*, fol. 6r.

42. *Achatz d'héritages*, fol. 15r.

43. *Achatz d'héritages*, fol. 15v, "Pro V^C III quarreaus, de quarreaus à fenestres et vitree: XII libr. II sol. III den.," may be referring here to cut stone for bar tracery.

44. *Achatz d'héritages*, fol. 18r, "Item summa summarum a principio operis usque Pascha anno XLII [1242] recepta de Templo: XXIIII^M IIII^C XXXI libr. XV sol. IIII den." Such lists and totals provide an index of building costs for this part of the thirteenth century.

45. *Achatz d'héritages*, fol. 13r, col. a, reports "Summa totalis a principio pagarum: XVII^M IX^CC IIII^XX XI £., XIIII s., X den. usque ad Paschum anno XL II," that is, 17,991 livres and 14.5 sous.

46. *Achatz d'héritages*, fol. 10r–v (1237).

47. *Achatz d'héritages*, fol. 20r.

48. *Achatz d'héritages*, fols. 20v and 21r (June 1238 to All Saints' Day 1239, seventeen months).

49. Again, this is rare documentation for such activities at this time. The only comparable things are found in Howard Colvin, *The History of the King's Works*, 4 vols. (London: HMSO, 1963).

50. On such inspections, see that for Cour-Notre-Dame: *Statuta*, ed. Canivez, 1226, no. 33.

51. *Statuta*, ed. Canivez, 1237, no. 27; *Cartulaire de Maubuisson*, no. 7 (September 1244), is a letter of affiliation from the order. Both of Blanche's abbeys would answer directly to the abbot of Cîteaux and be part of a mini-filiation of nuns' abbeys associated with Saint-Antoine in Paris; see Chapter 7; and Terryl Kinder, "Blanche of Castile and the Cistercians: An Architectural Re-evaluation of Maubuisson Abbey," *Cîteaux* 22 (1969): 161–88.

52. She became the first abbess of Lys. On Alice's sale of her county and her gift to Maubuisson, see discussion below.

53. *Cartulaire de Maubuisson*, no. 1 (1241/42), variants in Pontoise, AD Val d'Oise 72H115. The published cartulary, the original cartulary, and the account book often do not overlap; but it is worth noting that *Cartulaire de Maubuisson*, no. 87 should not be dated 1234, but 1237, as it is in the original manuscript cartulary; similarly *Cartulaire de Maubuisson*, no. 88, dated 1236, must be from 1239 or later, because it confirms *Cartulaire de Maubuisson*, no. 89 (1239).

54. *Cartulaire de Maubuisson*, nos. 300 (1239), 304 (December 1259), and 305 (1263); so these towns were already in the queen's hands by 1239.

55. *Cartulaire de Maubuisson*, nos. 465–70 (1239), and 487–90 (1247); and *Achatz d'héritages*, fols. 39v (1246) and 41v, totaling 971.5 livres; in 1246 Maubuisson paid one hundred livres to the Cistercian monks of Notre-Dame-du-Val for residual claims there. In March 1247/48 William of Avesnes and his family were paid 287 livres, 13 sous, and 8 deniers, for four muids of winter wheat and eight sestiers of oats from the tithes of Hérouville that had been part of the marriage portion of their mother, Garsendis.

56. *Cartulaire de Maubuisson*, no. 112 (1244).

57. *Cartulaire de Maubuisson*, nos. 10 (1248), 156–59 (1239/48), and 291–92 (May 1248); page 133 refers to a donation by Blanche (described as no. 634, but the printed cartulary ends with no. 633).

58. Robert, his wife Odeline, and their son Nicholas received 402 livres from the queen, of which forty were reserved for the couple's other son, Enjorrand, when he came of age.

59. *Cartulaire de Maubuisson*, nos. 91 (1241), the grant by Joyenval's abbot, and 92 (1243), the confirmation of Robert's grant by Hugh Rigoud and his wife Sebilia; see also *Achatz d'héritages*, fols. 40v–41r. Founded before 1227, the Premonstratensian house of Joyenval was located south of Poissy near Chambourcy in the diocese of Chartres. See A. Dutilleux, *Notice sur l'abbaye de Joyenval* (Versailles: Cerf, 1891); according to recent work by Yvonne Seale there

is no evidence that there had ever been Premonstratensian sisters at Maubuisson's site or at Joyenval.

60. *Achatz d'héritages*, fol. 38v (1242); *Cartulaire de Maubuisson*, no. 68 (1247); Armelle Bonis, *Abbaye cistercienne de Maubuisson (Saint-Ouen-l'Aumône, Val-d'Oise): La formation du temporel, 1236 à 1356* (Saint-Ouen-l'Aumône: Conseil général du Val-d'Oise, Service départemental d'archéologie du Val-d'Oise, 1990), p. 29, suggests that tithes at the site in the villa of Aulnay were conveyed by Saint-Martin of Pontoise; I have not found evidence of this, but the conclusion that either Saint Martin or Saint Peter of Pontoise had claims to the major tithes there makes sense. Bonis's valuable treatment, particularly in its maps, requires two minor corrections to its table 2 (as clarified by the account book): Blanche's gift at Meulan was confirmed (not supplemented) by Louis IX and his confirmation of one hundred livres from the exchequer of Normandy was given by Alice of Mâcon, not the king; see Pontoise, AD Val d'Oise, 72H10, the manuscript *Cartulaire de Maubuisson* from 1688 and further discussion of Alice below.

61. Acquisition of such tithes was through repurchase; see Berman "Cistercian Development."

62. *Cartulaire de Maubuisson*, no. 87 (1237); three years later he sold Maubuisson rights at the "Plasterium" of Bessancourt for seven livres as reported in *Achatz d'héritages*, fols. 26r and 30r (1240).

63. *Cartulaire de Maubuisson*, no. 167 (January 1238/39): "Abbacie quam Karissima domina nostra Blanca, Francium Regina illustris, juxta Pontisarum edificare incepit." Here she is literally the lady/lord.

64. *Achatz d'héritages*, fol. 29r.

65. *Cartulaire de Maubuisson*, no. 175 (1247).

66. *Cartulaire de Maubuisson*, no. 532 (1239).

67. *Achatz d'héritages*, fols. 38v–39r (1241–46).

68. Bonis, *Abbaye cistercienne de Maubuisson*, p. 26.

69. *Cartulaire de Maubuisson*, no. 5 (1244).

70. *Achatz d'héritages*, fol. 23r.

71. *Achatz d'héritages*, fols. 29v–30r (1239); she also purchased for sixty livres from Philip and his brother William of Hérouville, with the consent of their brother, Lord Adam of Hérouville (who held the fief in chief), annual rents at Sognolles: five *sestiers* and a mine (half sestier) of oats, eleven hens, and eleven cakes at Christmas. The purchase also included five *quartiers* in the vineyards at Bessancourt. See *Cartulaire de Maubuisson*, nos. 88, 89, 167, 169 (1239); and Pontoise, AD Val d'Oise, 72H132 (1239) for the ninety livres paid to Heluyus d'Atrio. Such a series of cash purchases made over several years from the same sellers suggests that the cash needs of local owners enhanced Blanche's ability to consolidate endowment for her new community of nuns.

72. *Achatz d'héritages*, fol. 30r (1240).

73. *Achatz d'héritages*, fol. 40r (1240, probably actually 1246) it reads:

Item per manu Domine Abbatisse Domino Theobaldo de Fic' [probably Frépillon] militi, pro nemore empta ab ipso sita retro Mahut, VII^{XX} £. Item Heluysi de Atrio et famulie ipsius pro laudem predicti nemoris XVI £. XIII s. IIII d.

74. *Cartulaire de Maubuisson*, no. 168 (1240); cf. *Achatz d'héritages*, fol. 30r.

75. *Cartulaire de Maubuisson*, no. 169 (1240).

76. *Cartulaire de Maubuisson*, no. 170 (1242).

77. *Cartulaire de Maubuisson*, no. 193 (1261); is he the same as Robert la Truie, knight and castellan of Évreux, who in no. 343 (1258) is giving for his own soul and that of his wife Agnes *la main morte* at Frépillon and Vaccaria? A puzzle remains about whether "de Atrio" is actually "de la Truie," and if these are all the same family.

78. *Cartulaire de Maubuisson*, nos. 168 (1244), 179 (1252), 180 (1254), 186 (1258), and 187 (1257); and *Achatz d'héritages*, fol. 38v (1244) and fol. 22v (1253).

79. *Cartulaire de Maubuisson*, no. 337 (1246).

80. *Cartulaire de Maubuisson*, nos. 340 (1254), 341, 341bis (1254/55), 342 (1255).

81. *Cartulaire de Maubuisson*, nos. 338 and 339 (1248), 344 (1258), 345 (1260), 347 (1269), and 348 (1271); *Achatz d'héritages*, fol. 39r (1245).

82. *Achatz d'héritages*, fol. 29v (1239): the queen paid two and a half livres to Richeudis (described as mayoress of the fief of Mateigne) and her daughters for half an arpent of land at Mateigne for which the sellers owed three sous at Easter to Michaela Messent; the latter held it from the daughter of John Salnerias; on fol. 38v it shows that in 1246 the abbess paid fourteen sous to Albert of Vaccaria for two arpents of land at Vaccaria and five livres to William of Vaccaria for five arpents there.

83. Pontoise, AD Val d'Oise, 72H141 (1253); and *Cartulaire de Maubuisson*, nos. 511–20 (1257–60): Maubuisson paid eight and a half livres for part of a vineyard at Mateigne adjoining that belonging to the nuns; ten livres for three small vineyards at Mateigne and rent on a fourth one; five livres for a vineyard at Mateigne called Mauquartier, and so on.

84. *Cartulaire de Maubuisson*, no. 305 (1263).

85. *Cartulaire de Maubuisson*, nos. 294 (1247), 295 and 296 (1256), and 297–99 (1258). She paid 140 livres to Squire William of Arsy and to Matilda, his wife, for her inheritance, 50 livres to Pernelle of Halatte with the consent of her brother, a knight, for fifteen arpents there, and 250 livres to Jacques of Moncy for rents over that villa.

86. *Cartulaire de Maubuisson*, nos. 539–45 (1262, 1265); Henry VI's survey (see *Cartulaire de Maubuisson*, pp. 273–78) reveals that Nonciennes was valuable still in 1421.

87. Bonis, *Maubuisson*, p. 56, describes the nuns of Maubuisson as "never having made a complete acquisition of the seigneurie." See also tables in Bonis, *Maubuisson*, pp. 30, 33, 49, 52, and 55, listing expenditures for each group of granges of about one thousand livres each.

88. *Cartulaire de Maubuisson*, nos. 319 (1255) and 320 (1256).

89. *Cartulaire de Maubuisson*, nos. 321 (1256), 323 (1257), 322 and 324 (1258) and 325 (1282); a copy of the 1269 confirmation is found in Pontoise, AD Val d'Oise, 17H124.

90. Dimier, *Saint Louis et Cîteaux*, p. 175; but to acquire lands producing that amount of income would have required spending about ten times the amount. Some of these sums had probably come from the sale of some of the nuns' rights to income in the forest of Breteuil in the 1250s discussed below.

91. *Cartulaire de Maubuisson*, no. 439 (1269), done at Maubuisson, nos. 244 (1245), 251 (1268), 439 (1269), done at Maubuisson, and 440 (1270); Pontoise, AD Val d'Oise, 72H141, done at Maubuisson; and see Dimier, *Saint Louis et Cîteaux*, p. 170.

92. *Cartulaire de Maubuisson*, no. 441 (1274).

93. *Cartulaire de Maubuisson*, no. 589 (1240).

94. *Cartulaire de Maubuisson*, nos. 590 (1252) and 591 (1254).

95. *Cartulaire de Maubuisson*, no. 600 (1289); this is an excellent return on that investment.

96. *Cartulaire de Maubuisson*, nos. 605 (1294), 607–19 (1302–5).

97. *Cartulaire de Maubuisson*, nos. 592–94 (1256, 1279) and 600 (1289)

98. This practice began to be found frequently after mid-thirteenth century at Saint-Antoine, Paris. Was the association with Paris the common factor? See further discussion in Chapter 7.

99. *Cartulaire de Maubuisson*, nos. 244 (1245), 251 (1268), 439 (1269), and 440 (1270); Pontoise, AD Val d'Oise, 72H141; Dimier, *Saint Louis et Cîteaux*, p. 170.

100. *Cartulaire de Maubuisson*, no. 69 (1262).

101. *Cartulaire de Maubuisson*, nos. 72 (1296) and 73 (1308); these provide a multiplier for the purchases of annuities of ten times the annual amount.

102. *Cartulaire de Maubuisson*, no. 104 (1310).

103. *Cartulaire de Maubuisson*, no. 454 (1326).

104. *Cartulaire de Maubuisson*, no. 604 (1292).

105. *Cartulaire de Maubuisson*, no. 101 (1294).

106. *Cartulaire de Maubuisson*, nos. 103 (1309) and 105 (1311).

107. *Cartulaire de Maubuisson*, no. 222 (1324).

108. *Cartulaire de Maubuisson*, no. 334 (1323).

109. On the General Chapter of 1244, see Dimier, *Saint Louis et Cîteaux*, pp. 169–70, nos. 138–48; *Statuta*, ed. Canivez, 1244, nos. 1, 4, 9, 10, 11, 12, 13, and 16.

110. William C. Jordan, *Louis IX and the Challenge of the Crusade: A Study in Rulership*. (Princeton, NJ: Princeton University Press, 1979), pp. 3–14; and Grant, *Blanche of Castile*, pp. 129–30. Whereas Louis IX doubled the size and endowment of Royaumont, his mother had begun founding a second abbey of Cistercian nuns. See *Statuta* ed. Canivez, 1244, no. 1; and Dimier, *Saint Louis et Cîteaux*, p. 87.

111. On the family ties, see Figure 11 in Chapter 8.

112. Michael Lower, *The Barons' Crusade; A Call to Arms and Its Consequences* (Philadelphia: University of Pennsylvania Press, 2005), mentions John of Mâcon a number of times and suggests that he died in the East, not in the presence of his wife. On the sale to the crown made with her husband John (a younger brother of Peter of Dreux) for ten thousand livres and a yearly life income of one thousand livres *tournois* from the exchequer of Normandy, see *Layettes*, vol. 2, no. 2776 (1238/39).

113. Pontoise, AD Val d'Oise, 72H10 *Cartulaire de Maubuisson* 1688, fol. 1a, "Ludovicus dei gratia francorum Rex. Notum facimus quod nos de centum libris Turonensis annui redditus quas delecte nostre Aaeli; quondam comitisse M" was allowed to be used.

114. Dimier, *Saint Louis et Cîteaux*, pp. 167–68. On the heart burial, see Alain Erlande-Brandenburg, "Le tombeau de coeur de Blanche de Castille à l'abbaye du Lys," in *Art et architecture à Melun au Moyen Age*, ed. Yves Gallet (Paris: Picard, 2000), pp. 255–57.

115. Melun, AD Seine-et-Marne H566, *Inventaire du Lys*, 1685.

116. Original parchments taken to Melun at the Revolution are said to have been used to stuff gunpowder into munitions. Only those taken to Auxerre survive; see Théophile Lhuillier, "Inventaire des titres concernant la seigneurie que les religieuses de l'abbaye royale de N.-D. du Lys, près Melun, possédaient à Mâlay-le-Roi," *Bulletin de la Société archéologique de Sens* 10 (1872): 347–57.

117. Paris, BnF, Latin MS 13892, *Cartulaire du Lys*, no. 10 (1252).

118. *Cartulaire du Lys*, no. 35 (1306), Philip IV gave 40 livres from the *ferme* of the woods of Mâlay, and in no. 36 (1311) gifts for an anniversary for Jeanne de Navarre and himself; nos. 39 and 40 (1311) were his confirmations of payments in kind. The cartulary ended up in the royal library in Paris, as did most similar volumes, whereas the abbey's documents were sent to Melun and Auxerre.

119. On the area, see Charles Higounet, *Défrichements et villeneuves du Bassin parisien, XIe–XIVe siècles* (Paris: CNRS, 1990); and Richard Keyser, "The Transformation of Traditional Woodland Management: Commercial Sylviculture in Medieval Champagne," *French Historical Studies* 32 (2009): 353–84.

120. Lys had a property in Melun called Voute with a winepress and cellars. Vineyards included those at Colléon once held by the queen: "en planter de la Reyne." See Melun, AD Seine-et-Marne H566, *Inventaire du Lys*, 1685, section 20.

121. Lhuillier, "Inventaire," p. 348, December 1252.

122. Lhuillier, "Inventaire," p. 348, December 1253, included a total of forty-five arpents of land at Mâlay along with five arpents of willow groves, ten of vineyards, a house and barn, and access to a large amount of pasture.

123. This was presumably part of what Louis IX confirmed to Lys in December 1260; see Lhuillier, "Inventaire," p. 350, December 1260.

124. Melun AD Seine-et-Marne H566, *Inventaire du Lys*, 1685, section 35, no. 1 (1253) lists a "foullerie," or cloth-fulling mill, there at Mâlay. Lhuillier, "Inventaire," p. 347 (1253), mentions Guy Legaigneur of Mâlay, but is in error about this being a house associated with the "Order of Clairvaux." Clairlieu must be the Caulite (Val-des-Choux) foundation near Nemours, rather than the abbey of Cistercian monks of that name near Nancy; see Adamo, *New Monks*, p. 95 n. 6. Lester, *Creating Cistercian Nuns*, p. 133, mentions a *domus Dei* granted to the Cistercian nuns at Notre-Dame-de-Nemours in 1247 and its founder Guy de Lucrator of Mâlay; he is probably identical with Guy Legaigneur. Guy had rented rights (to cut wood?) in the king's forest at Mâlay for forty livres a year. Louis IX transferred those rights to the nuns of Lys in June 1255, shortly after his return from his first crusade; see Lhuillier, "Inventaire," p. 350 (1255).

125. Lhuillier, "Inventaire," pp. 348–50.

126. Lhuillier, "Inventaire," p. 348 (1254).

127. Lhuillier, "Inventaire," p. 349 (1254).

128. Lhuillier, "Inventaire," pp. 349–50.

129. Lhuillier, "Inventaire," pp. 348–49. Louis IX would confirm some of these rights in March 1268/69, not long before his departure on his second crusade.

130. Lhuillier, "Inventaire," p. 351.

131. Melun, AD Seine-et-Marne H566, *Inventaire du Lys*, 1685, section 25, contains an acquisition from 1254 in which Alice paid six hundred livres to Hugh of Grange for rights at Orsonville where Villers was sited.

132. A bar tracery window used less stone than a punched out one and probably involved cutting the tracery parts before transport. So the weight of stone was less and so was its transport. The problem is that earlier churches were smaller, and Gothic ones larger; there must have been considerable differences in the amount of stone and its cost by the thirteenth century. Thus, rather than being a budget item for the houses of nuns (as some studies have asserted), construction costs in this case were borne by the founder, Queen Blanche. That the founder paid for construction in these cases at Maubuisson and Lys suggests the same elsewhere; see Constance H. Berman, "The 'Labours of Hercules,' the Cartulary, Church and Abbey for Nuns of La Cour-Notre-Dame-de-Michery," *Journal of Medieval History* 26 (2000): 33–70. My thanks for a Mellon grant at CASVA at the National Gallery of Art in Washington, DC, to study this question.

133. Bruzelius, "Cistercian High Gothic," p. 97, reports that the abbots complained about Royaumont in 1263.

134. Branner, *St. Louis and the Court Style*, p. 86 n. 1, suggests it was completed only circa 1252. On population sizes, see Appendix 4; there are also some references to population size in Bondéelle-Souchier, "Moniales."

135. See Chapter 4.

136. There is evidence in the account book suggesting a regular cycle of cutting; see *Achatz d'héritages*, fol. 43r (1273?): "Ce sont les coupes des bois de Rosières et des autres bois autour de Bertencuria ens arpentz du Roy."

137. *Achatz d'héritages*, fol. 39r (1241/46).

138. *Achatz d'héritages*, fol. 22v (1253). Here it is the priest Walter, who uses the Blessed Mary as opposed to Saint Mary, but he was not alone; there are other examples of replacing Saint Mary with the Blessed Mary, for there was considerable discussion at the time about which was correct.

139. *Achatz d'héritages*, fol. 36r (1241).

140. *Achatz d'héritages*, fol. 36v (1241).

141. *Cartulaire de Maubuisson*, no. 8 (May 1245).

142. *Cartulaire de Maubuisson*, no. 244 (October 1245), among others.

143. *Cartulaire de Maubuisson*, no. 245–48 (1250).

144. *Cartulaire de Maubuisson*, nos. 171–74, 189–91, 198, 204 (1247–71).

145. *Achatz d'héritages*, fol. 4r–v.

146. *Cartulaire de Maubuisson*, nos. 252 (1246), 256 (1248), and 257 (1248); see discussion of the Marly family, founders of Port-Royal in Chapter 5. The young Bouchard, at least twenty years old, was probably preparing to leave on crusade with Louis IX, and this payment may not have been charged against Maubuisson but against the queen's personal accounts. Perhaps this explains why it was not recorded in the abbey records.

147. *Cartulaire de Maubuisson*, nos. 252 (1246) and 256 (1248); no. 257 (1248) is Louis IX's confirmation. The purchase of the other half of this mill is found in *Cartulaire de Maubuisson*, nos. 506 (1251) and 588 (May 1260).

148. *Cartulaire de Maubuisson*, no. 329 (1246) is a concession of 400 livres per year, not 40; Bonis, *Maubuisson*, p. 57, repeats the error of the *Cartulaire de Maubuisson* rubric. This income from Normandy is mentioned in *Achatz d'héritages*, fol. 41v; see Table 13 and documents in the next note that show that it was 400 livres' worth of income.

149. *Cartulaire de Maubuisson*, nos. 287 (1253), 285 (1256), 94 (1253), and 330–33 (1293); a continued dispute over tithes at Breteuil, led Abbess Guillelma in 1256, with the king's permission, to sell a little more than half of those lands (those producing 250 livres' worth of income) to the nuns of Saint-Sauveur of Évreux for 5,000 livres. Dispute continued because Brother Garnier de Cergy, at this point chaplain of Maubuisson, received only 1,600 livres for the nuns of Maubuisson from the abbess Marie of Saint-Sauveur. On Brother Garnier, see note 39 above.

150. *Achatz d'héritages*, fol. 8v.

151. *Cartulaire de Maubuisson*, no. 68 (1247).

152. *Cartulaire de Maubuisson*, no. 251 (1268), and on Bonfosse, nos. 244–51.

153. *Cartulaire de Maubuisson*, nos. 529–30 (1272).

154. *Cartulaire de Maubuisson*, nos. 326 and 327 (1307).

155. Berman, *Medieval Agriculture*, pp. 89–93.

156. *Cartulaire de Maubuisson*, no. 196 (1263).

157. *Cartulaire de Maubuisson*, p. 241.

158. Armande Prieure, "Histoire de l'abbaye Notre-Dame du Lys-la-Royale au diocèse de Sens" (Thesis deposited in Melun, AD Seine-et-Marne, ref. 100J149). It is summarized in *École nationale des chartes: Positions des thèses de 1945* (Paris, 1945) (my translation).

159. See Frances A. Underhill, *For Her Good Estate: The Life of Elizabeth de Burgh* (New York: Palgrave, 2000), pp. 140–44.

160. Prayers for Blanche have been obscured by a narrative about the college in the history of the order that has focused almost entirely on Stephen of Lexington, abbot of Clairvaux, being at fault for its foundation, but see Daniel M. LaCorte, "Pope Innocent IV's Role in the Establishment and Early Success of the College of Saint Bernard in Paris," *Cîteaux* 46 (1995): 289–303, which shows that Stephen of Lexington's role was probably overemphasized. Innocent IV was, of course, Blanche's great friend and ally in many causes. Not long thereafter, Royaumont founded a college for its monks studying in Paris in the Faubourg-Saint-Marcel; see *Cartulaire de Royaumont*, fol. 152r (1259).

161. See Collège des Bernardins, Paris, website, accessed March 31, 2017, at https://www.collegedesbernardins.fr/a-propos/huit-sieclesdhistoire.

162. Robert of Artois granted Saint-Antoine's Cistercian nuns rents over a house in Arras in 1248; see Paris, AN, S*4386, *Cartulaire de Saint-Antoine*, fols. 5v–6r.

163. Caroline A. Bruzelius, *The Stones of Naples: Church Building in Angevin Italy* (New Haven, CT: Yale University Press, 2004), pp. 28–36.

164. In 1242 Isabelle and Louis IX had made a gift of two sestiers of salt annually to the Cistercian nuns of Lieu-Notre-Dame; see *Cartulaire de Lieu*, no. 81 (1242), but on Isabelle see Sean Field, *Isabelle of France: Capetian Sanctity and Franciscan Identity in the Thirteenth Century* (South Bend, IN: Notre Dame University Press, 2006), pp. 28, 42–63; and A. H. Allirot, "Longchamp et Lourcine, deux abbayes féminines dans la construction de la mémoire capétienne (fin XIIIe–première moitié du XIVe siècle)," *Revue d'histoire d'église de France* 94 (2008): 23–38. Louis VIII had granted 20,000 livres to Isabelle for her marriage. In 1253 Isabelle claimed them in support of a foundation of Franciscan nuns; in *The Writings of Agnes of Harcourt: The Life of Isabelle of France and the Letter on Louis IX and Longchamp*, ed. and trans. Sean L. Field (Notre Dame, IN: University of Notre Dame Press, 2003), that sum had become 30,000.

CHAPTER 7

1. Parts of this chapter were published earlier as Constance H. Berman, "Cistercian Nuns and the Development of the Order: The Abbey of Saint-Antoine-des-Champs Outside Paris," in *The Joy of Learning and the Love of God: Essays in Honor of Jean Leclercq, OSB*, ed. E. Rozanne Elder (Kalamazoo: Cistercian Publications, 1995), pp. 121–56. On walls and city expansion, see Simone Roux, *Paris in the Middle Ages*, trans. Jo Ann McNamara (Philadelphia: University of Pennsylvania Press, 2009); and John W. Baldwin, *Paris, 1200* (Stanford, CA: Stanford University Press, 2010).

2. I am very grateful to the personnel of the Archives Nationales (AN) in Paris, including those in the cartographic records department (Cartes et Plans) who provided me access to the oversized atlas, but also those in the reading room who provided me space to photograph entire series of documents for Saint-Antoine early in this project. Many of those Parisian properties were houses with tiny gardens as shown in an atlas created in the 1720s, which also shows their enclosure and buildings: See Paris, AN, Cartes et plans, N/III/Seine Atlas de Saint-Antoine. There is a smaller copy of this in the reading room of the AN, but the original, which is huge,

includes incredible detail about individual holdings; my sincere thanks to conservators who allowed me to look and photograph. See also the exhibition catalog *Du faubourg Saint-Antoine au bois de Vincennes: Promenade historique dans le 12e arrondissement; Exposition organisée par le Musée Carnavalet et la délégation à l'action artistique de la ville de Paris; Mairie annexe du 12e arrondissement, 26 janvier–20 février et 19 mars–20 avril 1983; Paris, Musée Carnavalet, 26 avril–5 juin 1983* (Paris: Musées de la Ville de Paris, 1983), esp. pp. 24–27. The abbey's location so near the city of Paris, but outside its thirteenth-century walls, allowed its neighborhood to escape the jurisdiction of the Parisian medieval guilds, making it an oasis of luxury furniture production in the early modern period. There is a novel about the abbey by Jean Diwo, *Les Dames du Faubourg* (Paris: Noël, 1984). My thanks to Professor Olivier Guyotjeannin, who referred me to Sandrine Delaforge-Marchand and her "Édition du chartrier de l'abbaye de Saint-Antoine-des-Champs (1191–1256)," *École nationale des chartes: Positions des thèses de la promotion, 1994* (Paris, 1994), pp. 43–51. I thank her for providing me with additional codicological evidence; the dissertation remains unpublished.

3. See *"Historia Occidentalis" of Jacques de Vitry*, pp. 99–100.

4. Bonnardot, *Saint-Antoine*, nos. 1 (1204), and 2 (1206). Cf. Maurice Garsonnin, *Histoire de l'Hôpital Saint-Antoine et de ses origines: Étude topographique, historique et statistique* (Paris: Henri Jouve, 1891). Port-Royal would become an independent abbey circa 1215; see Chapter 4.

5. Bonnardot, *Saint-Antoine*, no. 3 (1208).

6. *Statuta*, ed. Canivez, 1213, no. 5: "Prohibitur firmiter ut nullus monachus vel conversus Ordinis nostri in domo monialium Sancti Anthonii iuxta Parisios comedat vel pernoctet." The abbess had probably complained of the enormous burden placed on her community at a time when the order had no Parisian hospice for Cistercian monks and personnel—something not founded in Paris until mid-century; see Chapter 6.

7. Saint-Antoine was visited by the abbot of Cîteaux; see Paris, AN S*4386, fols. 75r–76r (1277). Its practices were introduced at abbeys of Cistercian nuns at Isles near Auxerre (see Chapter 5) and at Cour-Notre-Dame (see Chapter 8). No association with Tart is mentioned in Jean de la Croix Bouton, Benoît Chauvin, and Elisabeth Grosjean, "L'abbaye de Tart et ses filiales au moyen âge," *Mélanges Dimier* 1984, 2:3:19–61.

8. Stephen of Lexington, "Registrum Epistolarum" (1952), p. 252, no. 24 (1233?): "Moderatio institutionis domus S. Antonii auctoritate abbatis Cisterciensis facta per Stephanum abbatem Savigniac." Grant, *Blanche of Castile*, p. 174, cites this series of decrees by Stephen of Lexington as evidence that Stephen thought the ties between the queen and Saint-Antoine were undesirable; I read them as being more matter-of-fact.

9. Paris, AN, LL1595, fol. 35r–35v (1243).

10. A point emphasized by Grant, *Blanche of Castile*, pp. 72–73.

11. Paris, AN, S*4386, fols. 41r–v, 42r (1261/62).

12. Paris, AN, LL1595, fols. 36v–37v (1261, 1258); this is the same transaction as in the confirmation charter in the previous note, but without the royal confirmation; she had granted money for pittance meals earlier.

13. See Erin Jordan, "Gender Concerns."

14. This quote is from a sermon delivered to Saint-Antoine's nuns on May 6, 1273, by Nicolas du Mans, a Dominican who studied and preached in Paris, and later became the confessor for Philip III's eldest son; I wish to thank Professor Nicole Bériou, author of *L'avènement des maîtres de la parole: La prédication à Paris au XIIIe siècle* (Paris: Institute d'études augustiniennes, 1998), who provided this reference.

15. Paris, AN, LL1595, *Cartulaire de Saint-Antoine*, fol. 91r, lists rents held by the nuns personally; there is an urban *censier*, fols. 87r–91r; and then lists of non-urban rents on fols. 77v–84v (from 1351). The latter include about 1,070 livres in annual cash payments from sources outside the city: tolls, mills, and an oven. This cartulary was included in the *fichiers* compiled by Anne Terroine at the Institut de recherche et d'histoire des textes (IRHT) and her findings included in the study based on those *fichiers* by Boris Bove, *Dominer la ville: Prévôts des marchands et échevins parisiens de 1260 à 1350* (Paris: CTHS, 2004).

16. Paris, AN S*4386, *Cartulaire de Saint-Antoine*. The contents of this early modern volume were not included in Terroine's *fichiers* at the IRHT. It was not used by Bove, *Dominer la ville*. Some of these charters for both volumes also survive as individual charters in the archival collections of Paris, AN L1014, etc. See bibliography.

17. Robert's sister was the widow Lady Agnes of Cressonessart; see below.

18. Paris, AN, LL1595, fols. 47v–48v (1219).

19. Paris, AN, LL1595, fol. 43r–v (1243).

20. Paris, AN, LL1595, fol. 27r–v (1246).

21. Dimier, *Saint Louis et Cîteaux*, p. 194, no. 409. Louis IX made bequests to Saint-Antoine in his 1270 will, but also to Maubuisson, Lys, Cîteaux, Parc-aux-Dames, Trésors, Villers, Biaches Saint-Sauvoir at Laon. In 1272 Louis's widow, Marguerite of Provence, founded chapels for his soul at Maubuisson, at Saint-Antoine, and at Villiers; see Dimier, *Saint Louis et Cîteaux*, p. 198, no. 439 (1287), and Paris AN H⁵3859² (1286), the gift by Marguerite of income from Corbeil for that chapel.

22. Paris, AN, LL1595, fol. 34r (1260).

23. The church at Saint-Antoine, which was consecrated in the early 1230s, appears to have been built in the new Cistercian Gothic style; see Kinder, "Blanche of Castile," who reports that whatever remained of its medieval church was built over in the 1950s, so available evidence comes only from earlier plans and sketches. Saint-Antoine's church may be the link between Cistercian Gothic at places like Longpont, and Cistercian Gothic churches in Normandy, which may have been built at about the same time as Royaumont and Maubuisson; see Lindy Grant, *Architecture and Society in Normandy, 1120–1270* (New Haven, CT: Yale University Press, 2005).

24. Paris, AN, LL1595, fol. 42v (1210); located between the Mont-Sainte-Geneviève and the river.

25. Paris, AN, LL1595, fols. 38r–v (1213, 1218) and 40r (1210); the last confirmed by the abbot of Saint-Magloire.

26. Paris, AN, S*4386, fol. 23r–v (1244, 1248).

27. Paris, AN, S*4386, fol. 47r–v (1285/89).

28. Paris, AN, LL1595, fols. 28v–29r (1229); the normal rental rate from an investment of thirty livres should have been three livres per annum.

29. Paris, AN, S*4386, fol. 3r (1209), along with other bequests made with the permission of his brother Manasses.

30. Paris: AN H⁵ 3859¹: for 1226 for Marly gifts.

31. Paris: AN L1014, "Ad utilitate anime karissime Alienordis quondam uxoris mee que in dicta ecclesia tradita est ecclesiastice sepulture ut ibidem eius anniversarium annuatim in perpetuum celebretur."

32. Paris: AN S4359, S4360.

33. Paris, AN, L1014, Liasse 2, (1256).

34. Paris, AN, S*4386, fols. 65 r–v (1261), 66v–67r (1263).

35. Funding an increased rent at a house at the Baudéer gate; Paris, AN, LL1595, fols. 9v–10r (1285).

36. As Shortell comments in "Erasures," p. 151, "This action is typical of widows who placed their property in the hands of the church in order to free themselves from the burdens of property management, devote themselves to charitable works and spiritual lives, and/or to repay the clergy for protection and perpetual prayer."

37. See such bequests also in Tanya Stabler Miller, *The Beguines of Medieval Paris: Gender, Patronage, and Spiritual Authority* (Philadelphia: University of Pennsylvania Press, 2014).

38. Paris, AN, LL1595, fol. 20v (1248), describes a house given by Jean of Villeneuve, miller, and Roger Excoriator (probably he stripped bark from trees) that adjoined houses on one side occupied by Peter the White Cat and on the other side by the widow, Reynaudis la Dangereuse.

39. Paris, AN, LL1595, fols. 42v–43r (1210).

40. Paris, AN, LL1595, fol. 47r (1217).

41. Paris, AN, LL1595, fols. 12v–13r (1218) and (1225).

42. Paris, AN, LL1595, fol. 32v (1235).

43. Paris, AN, LL1595, fol. 31r–v (1258).

44. Paris, AN, LL1595, fol. 31v (1261), and see discussion in Harvey, "Monastic Pittances."

45. Paris, AN, LL1595, fol. 16r–v (1263).

46. Paris, AN, LL1595, fol. 18v–19r (1269).

47. Paris, AN, LL1595, fol. 55v–56r (1284).

48. Paris, AN, S*4386, fol. 76r–v (1289).

49. Paris, AN, LL1595, fol. 40r–v (1210 and 1218).

50. Paris, AN, LL1595, fol. 16v (1242).

51. Regarding Italian cities for which the same is known, see David Herlihy, *Pisa in the Early Renaissance: A Study of Urban Growth* (Port Washington, NY: Kennikat, 1973).

52. Paris, AN, LL1595, fols. 34v–35r (1275).

53. Paris, AN, S*4386, fols. 75r–76r (1277).

54. Paris, AN, LL1595, fol. 34r (1260); Bove, *Dominer la ville*, p. 156, cites them as recognizable citizens of Paris a century later.

55. Paris, AN, S*4386, fols. 75r–76r (1277).

56. Dimier, *Saint Louis et Cîteaux*, pp. 156, 175; but there were few Capetian bequests. I agree with Branner, *St. Louis and the Court Style*, p. 31 n. 1, that Dimier, *Saint Louis*, p. 155, no. 1, is not the earliest Capetian grant; rather the earliest is Dimier, *Saint Louis*, p. 156, no. 16; the first may not have ever existed, but it is certainly now missing from the archives.

57. Paris, AN, H⁵3859, no. 3 (1205); this Amicia probably became abbess and, acting in that role, in 1221 exchanged property with Port-Royal. See Paris, AN, S*4386, fols. 62v–63r (1221); *Cartulaire de Port-Royal*, no. 56 (April 1221/22). Abbess Amicia is also found in the charters of Saint-Magloire; see *Chartes et documents de l'abbaye de Saint-Magloire*, ed. A. Terroine and L. Fossier (Paris: CNRS, 1998), hereafter cited as *Chartes de Saint-Magloire*, no. 107 (1230).

58. The double community soon was a house of nuns only; see Paris, AN, H⁵3859, no. 1 (1206), which is the gift of one hundred sous (five livres) in rents by Agnes of Cressonessart to the "infirmarie Sancti Antonii Parisiensis," granting rents to "tam fratrem quam sororem."

59. Paris, AN, S*4386, fol. 60r–v (1209): "si decesserit in hac peregrinatione de Albigensio."

60. Paris, AN, S*4386, fols. 60v–61r (1211) and 62r (1213).

61. Paris, AN, S*4386, fol. 61r–v (1212).

62. On these individuals, see Monique Zerner-Chardavoine, "L'abbé Gui des Vaux-de-Cernay, prédicateur de croisade," in *Les Cisterciens de Languedoc (XIIIe–XIVe siècle)*, Cahiers de Fanjeaux 21 (Toulouse: Privat, 1986), pp. 185–204; and Zerner-Chardavoine, "L'épouse de Simon de Montfort et la croisade albigeoise," in *Femmes, Mariages, Lignages, XIIe—XIVe siècles: Mélanges offerts à Georges Duby* (Brussels: De Boeck Université, 1992), pp. 449–70; *Cartulaire de Notre-Dame de Prouille*, e.g., no. 278 (1212); and Daniel Power, "Who Went on the Albigensian Crusade?" *English Historical Review* 128, no. 534 (2013): 1047–85.

63. Paris, AN L1014, Liasse 1 (1215).

64. Paris, AN, S*4386, fol. 63r (1223), "in honor of Saint Peter," was approved by a number of relatives and associates. Thus Adam, lord of Beaumont, and Isabelle, his wife, approved "quandam capellam constituendam."

65. Paris, AN, S*4386, fol. 63r–v (1223).

66. See also Chapter 4. On giving rents at Gratelou to Port-Royal, see *Cartulaire de Port-Royal*, nos. 26 (1216), 56 (April 1221/22), and 15 and 68 (possibly 1233, but conflated); cf. Paris, AN, S*4386, fols. 62v–63r (1221); Robert's wife, Cecilia of Chevreuse, was from a family of Port-Royal's early benefactors. That the exchange was with an abbess Amicia in 1221, when Lady Agnes was still alive, precludes almost any possibility that Agnes was abbess.

67. Paris, AN, S*4386, fols. 60r–61v (1208, 1209, 1211, 1212).

68. Paris AN, S*4386, fol. 61v (1212).

69. Paris AN, S*4386, fol. 61v (1212).

70. Paris, AN, S*4386, fol. 62r (1213).

71. Paris AN, S4373 (1214); and see Figure 10; my thanks to Sean Field for discussions about this charter's implications.

72. Paris, AN, S*4386, fols. 61r–v (1211), 62r–62v (1214–21), among others; Bonnardot, *Saint-Antoine*, iii, 12, and 23 n. 4, reports that he saw a tombstone with Agnes of Cressonessart's name on it and attaches it to an abbess Agnes from 1233 to 1240; this was definitely not Agnes of Cressonessart, who died circa 1225.

73. Paris, AN, S*4386, fol. 6r–6v (1225/6), when the next son, Thibaut, is described as lord of Cressonessart.

74. Paris, AN, S*4386, fol. 6r–6v; Guy of Mauvoisin gave twenty sous in annual rents from the river tolls at Mantes.

75. See Paris, AN, S*4386, fols. 3v–5v.

76. Paris, AN, S*4386, fols. 60r–v (1211), 62v (1220), and 65r–v (1261), for Gonesse.

77. Paris, AN, S*4386, fol. 64v (1236); cf. fols. 68v (1267) and 71v–72r (1270).

78. Paris, AN, S*4386, fols. 81r–82v (1218, 1221, 1238, 1255).

79. Paris, AN, S*4386, fol. 82v (1256); he must be the great-grandson-in-law of Matilda countess of Auxerre—see Figure 5.

80. Paris, AN, S*4386, fol. 82r (1247).

81. Paris, AN, S*4386, fols. 71r–v (1267), 75r–v (1277).

82. Paris, AN, S*4386, fols. 65v–67r (1261, 1264).

83. Paris, AN, S*4386, fols. 65r–66v (1262).

84. Paris, AN, S*4386, fol. 73r–v (1274).

85. Paris, AN, S*4386, fols. 68v (1265), 68v–69r (1267), 70r (1269/70), 72v (1272), and 74v (1275).

86. Paris, AN, S*4386, fol. 71r–v (1279).

87. Paris, AN, LL1595, fols. 50v–51r (1291 and 1296) and Paris, AN, S*4386, fol. 77r–v (1297), a small conveyance of *gaignable* (developable?) land at Savigny, which was sold to the nuns for thirty sous by the widow of William of Delices. On Petronilla; see below.

88. Paris, AN, S*4386, fols. 77v–79r (1298), mentions Saint-Antoine's mill near Praelles.

89. Paris, AN, S*4386, fols. 79v–80r (1299).

90. For a good description of urban *censives*, see *Chartes de Saint-Magloire*, introduction and no. 86 (1218). A more general survey of building in the city is found in Meredith Cohen, "Metropolitan Architecture, Demographics, and the Urban Identity of Paris in the Thirteenth Century," in *Cities, Texts, and Social Networks, 400–1500: Experiences and Perceptions of Medieval Urban Space*, ed. Caroline Goodson, Anne E. Lester, and Carol Symes (Burlington, VT: Ashgate, 2010), pp. 65–100.

91. *Chartes de Saint-Magloire*, no. 106 (1229).

92. *Chartes de Saint-Magloire*, no. 107 (1230).

93. The *roue* might be a turnstyle leading to and from the village.

94. *Chartes de Saint-Magloire*, nos. 106 (1229/30) and 162 (1247).

95. *Chartes de Saint-Magloire*, no. 234 (1268).

96. Paris, AN, S*4386, fol. 1r (1210?)

97. Paris, AN, S*4386, fol. 1r (1227).

98. Paris, AN, S*4386, fol. 1r–v (1244).

99. Paris, AN, S*4386, fol. 9r–v (1213).

100. Paris, AN, S*4386, fols. 18v–21v (1214, 1217, 1219, 1225, 1229, 1234, 1234, 1247, 1257, 1258, 1261). The amount in 1257 is unclear; it could be 100 livres, or 100 sous (five livres), but most likely the copying error is reading C for X, which makes most sense under the circumstances.

101. Paris, AN, S*4386, fol. 44r–v (1212, 1220, 1235).

102. Paris, AN, S*4386, fol. 58r (1216).

103. Paris, AN, S*4386, fol. 58r (1218).

104. Paris, AN, S*4386, fol. 44r–v (1220).

105. Paris, AN, S*4386, fol. 17r (1237).

106. Paris, AN, S*4386, fols. 44v–45r (1235), 51r (1232), 51v (1242).

107. Paris, AN, S*4386, fol. 44v–45r (1287)

108. Paris, AN, S*4386, fols. 45r–v (1255) and 46v (1264).

109. Paris, AN, S*4386, fol. 45v (1255), lists four sons, two named Adam.

110. Peter of Buciac is also seen in Paris, AN, LL1595, fol. 14r (1260).

111. Paris, AN, S*4386, fols. 54r–56r (1259).

112. Paris, AN, S*4386, fol. 56r–v (1265).

113. Paris, AN, S*4386, fols. 56r–57r (1277); Peter of Cengle and Sedilia appear in the documents for Champagnes as well; see below.

114. Paris, AN, S*4386, fols. 45v–46r (1264).

115. This involves both cartularies. Paris, AN, S*4386, fols. 45v–46v (1264), is the gift from Margaret of Parenciac. Paris, AN, LL1595, fol. 26r (1298), identifies E. of Parenciac as abbess.

116. Paris, AN, S*4386, fols. 56v–57v (1277); this contract suggests that nuns and their tenants had divided up rights earlier to vineyards planted *ad medium*; see Appendix 1.

117. Paris, AN, S*4386, fols. 51r–52r (1269).

118. Paris, AN, S*4386, fols. 51r–52r (1269) and 58r–59r (1272).

119. Paris, AN, S*4386, fols. 21v–22r (1224).

120. Paris, AN, S*4386, fols. 22v–23r (1238, 1240, 1244).

121. Paris, AN, S*4386, fol. 23v (1249).

122. Paris, AN, S*4386, fol. 23r–v (1248).

123. Paris, AN, S*4386, fol. 24r (1254; the king confirmed this in 1255).

124. Paris, AN, S*4386, fol. 22r–v (1260, 1261); Lady Sedilia wife of Peter of Clamartis, must have been widowed soon thereafter; she appears to have then married Lord Peter of Cengle and they conveyed rights at Champagnes; later in 1277 she and Peter are paid for claims at Conflans. See note 113.

125. Paris, AN, S*4386, fols. 24r (1251) and 22v (1261).

126. Paris, AN, S*4386, fols. 24v–26r (1264): cf. fols. 42v–43r (1331).

127. Paris, AN, S*4386, fols. 26v (1264), 28v–29r (1265), 30v–31v (1269), 38r–39r (1269 and 1270).

128. Paris, AN, S*4386, fols. 31v–32r (1269).

129. Paris, AN, S*4386, fols. 32r–v and 37r–v (1269); three similar acts.

130. Paris, AN, S*4386, fol. 34r (1278).

131. Paris, AN, S*4386, fols. 38r–39r (1284).

132. Paris, AN, S*4386, fols. 33v–34r (1284); the price and rent do not compute.

133. Paris, AN, S*4386, fol. 36r–v (1267).

134. Paris, AN, S*4386, fol. 36r–v (1267); and see also fol. 87r (1305), which mentions a knight Lord Peter Escharaz, living near Montreuil-sur-Vincennes, who may have been related to her second husband.

135. Those rights are then referred to in a *censier* of non-Parisian rents found in Paris, AN, LL1595, fols. 78–84

136. Paris, AN, S*4386, fols. 5v–6r.

137. Paris, AN, S*4386, fol. 8r.

138. Jean Gimpel, *The Medieval Machine: The Industrial Revolution of the Middle Ages* (New York: Holt, Rinehart and Winston, 1976), pp. 16–17. There were eventually more than eighty water-powered mills; for illustrations of how such mills were tied to the bridges of Paris, see Virginia Wylie Egbert, *On the Bridges of Mediaeval Paris: A Record of Early Fourteenth-Century Life* (Princeton, NJ: Princeton University Press, 1974). There are also a few indications of wind-powered mills in the vicinity by the mid-thirteenth century.

139. Paris, AN, LL1595, fols. 32v (1227), 11r (1260), and 11v (1261).

140. Paris, AN, LL1595, fols. 11v–12r (1261) and 53r (1283).

141. On immigrants to Paris, see Bove, *Dominer la ville* and Sharon Farmer, *The Silk Industries of Medieval Paris: Artisanal Migration, Technological Innovation, and Gendered Experience* (Philadelphia: University of Pennsylvania Press, 2017).

142. Paris, AN, LL1595, fol. 32v (1227).

143. Paris, AN, LL1595, fol. 38r–v (1218).

144. Paris, AN, LL1595, fol. 19r (1242).

145. Paris, AN, LL1595, fol. 41r–v (1279).

146. Paris, AN, LL1595, fol. 33r–v (1295/96).

147. Paris, AN, LL1595, fol. 50r (1291)

148. Paris, AN, LL1595, fol. 16v (1242).

149. Bove, *Dominer la ville*, pp. 114–27, saw them as an investment bubble, but in my view such augmented rents reflected real value granted to tenants or invested in businesses. They are seen in other Parisian cartularies as well; for instance in *Recueil des chartes et documents de l'abbaye de Saint-Martin-des-Champs, monastère parisien*, ed. Joseph Depoin, 5 vols. (Ligugé, 1912–21).

150. Paris, AN, LL1595, fols. 7v–8r (1234), 6r–7v (1262) on Paciac family; see also Bove, *Dominer la ville*, p. 156.

151. Paris, AN, LL1595, fol. 6v (1262).

152. Paris, AN, LL1595, fol. 7r–7v (1262).

153. Paris, AN, LL1595, fols. 87ff., *censier*.

154. Paris, AN, LL1595, fol. 49r–v (1219).

155. Paris, AN, LL1595, fol. 47v (1218).

156. Paris, AN, LL1595, fol. 32r (1219).

157. Paris, AN, LL1595, fols. 87ff. Most helpful for locating such Parisian locations is an article by Wendy Pfeffer, "The *Dit des monstiers*," *Speculum* 73 (1998): 80–114.

158. Multiple identical rents on a single street suggest development by religious communities; for other later medieval cities, see Felicity Riddy, "'Burgeis' Domesticity in Late-Medieval England," in *Medieval Domesticity: Home, Housing and Household in Medieval England*, ed. Maryanne Kowaleski and P. J. P. Goldberg (Cambridge: Cambridge University Press, 2011), pp. 14–36; at p. 22 she writes, "In York the Vicars Choral built cottages in the 1330s for the lower end of the market; these were rented by 'tenants employed in the building industry, in various types of service (as porters and cleaners), as well as in various aspects of the leather and clothing industries,' while many of the cheapest houses were rented by women" (citing Sarah Rees Jones, "Women's Influence in the Design of Urban Homes," in *Gendering the Master Narrative: Women and Power in the Middle Ages*, ed. Mary C. Erler and Maryanne Kowaleski [Ithaca, NY: Cornell University Press, 2003], pp. 190–211, esp. pp. 204–9).

159. Paris, AN, LL1595, fols. 50r–51v (1291, 1296); the 1296 testament of Jean Popin was registered before Raoul of Paciac, notary; could this be Blanche's relative?

160. Paris, AN, LL1595, fols. 37v–38r (1243).

161. Paris, AN, LL1595, fol. 46r–v (ca. 1250).

162. Paris, AN, LL1595, fols. 11v–12r (1261).

163. Paris, AN, LL1595, fol. 68r–v (1281).

164. Paris, AN, LL1595, fol. 69r–v (1282/87).

165. Paris, AN, LL1595, fols. 69v–70r (1282).

166. Paris, AN, LL1595, fols. 68v–69r (1287).

167. Paris, AN, LL1595, fols. 50v–51v (1291, 1296).

168. Paris, AN, LL1595, fol. 63r.

169. Paris, AN, S*4386, fol. 52r–v (1296)—this was part of the estate of his late wife Marguerite and administered by him on behalf of his children.

170. Paris, AN, LL1595, fol. 64r–v (1296).

171. Paris, AN, LL1595 fols. 66v–67r ff. (1299).

172. Paris, AN, LL1595, fols. 64v–66v (1300).

173. Paris, AN, LL1595, fols. 24v–25r (1264), where he is described as tailor, furrier and valet de chambre and 67r–68r (1302), where there daughter is listed.

174. Paris, AN, LL1595, fols. 73r–75r (1301).

175. Paris, AN, LL1595, fol. 70r; the rubric reads: "De sex libris parisis super quadam domus sitam in alis (Halles) parisius contiguam ex una parte domui Henrici Marescalli et ex altera domui Petri dicti Clerici in censiva Domini Regis quarum sex librarum Soror Agnes de Compans, Soror Milina la Bordone et Soror Juliana de la Roe tenent xl solidos in solidos et quilibet pro se que supervixerit; item eodem modo tenent alios quadraginta solidos Soror Agnes la Pidoe, Soror Johanna de Giroles et Soror Genovespha la Pidoe, et alios xl solidos tenent eodam modo ad vitam Soror Marguerite la Petite, Soror Agnes de Sancto Victore et Soror

Agnes la Petite." The contract itself is the purchase in 1302 by Saint-Antoine of an augmented rent of six livres over a specific house; that was then assigned to the three groups of nuns. Other such assignment is found in Paris, AN, LL1595, fols. 71r–73r (1299 and 1301).

176. For other abbeys of Cistercian nuns, see Gabriel Lepointe, "Réflexions sur des textes concernant la propriété individuelle des religieuses cisterciennes dans la région Lilloise," *Revue d'histoire ecclésiastique* 49 (1954): 743–69; and Mecham, *Sacred Communities, Shared Devotions*.

177. *Statuta*, ed. Canivez: 1293:15: "Item, dispersio [more likely *dispertio*] monialium de Sancto Antonio prope Parisios domino Cisterciensi committitur, ut inde, per se vel per alium, faciat prout melius iudicaverit opportunum."

178. The nuns agreed to provide Agnes of Cressonessart an annuity from the produce of their cultivation of what had once been her lands; see above at discussion of Aulnay.

179. Berman, *Medieval Agriculture*.

180. In contrast, the wine produced from considerable vineyards northwest of Paris, in the vicinity of Beaumont-sur-Oise and the grange of Champagnes-sure-Oise, must have been intended for markets at places downstream on the Oise and Seine Rivers.

181. On size, see Bondéelle-Souchier, "Moniales," no. 122; and *Recueil de plans d'églises cisterciennes*, ed. Anselm Dimier, 4 vols. (Grignan: Abbaye Notre-Dame d'Aiguebelle; Paris: Librairie d'art ancien et moderne, 1949–67); both suggest that the church was similar in size to Maubuisson.

182. Bondéelle-Souchier, "Moniales," p. 300.

183. Paris, AN, S*4384 (eighteenth-century inventory), fols. 7–8, lists indulgences for about 120 days a year.

184. See Paris, AN, S*4386, fols. 63v–64r (1226), "Brother Bernard of Saint-Antoine" who may have been a lay brother; Paris, AN, S*4386, fol. 22r–v (1260, 1261), mentioned that Eudes, chaplain of Saint-Antoine, carried payments for them; Paris, AN, LL1595, fol. 69 (1282), has another cleric acting for the nuns.

185. *A Parisian Journal, 1405–1449*, trans. Janet Shirley (Oxford: Clarendon Press, 1968), p. 281. It is also available in French as *Journal d'un bourgeois de Paris: de 1405 à 1449*, ed. Colette Beaune. (Paris: Librairie générale française, 1990), where editions and several late medieval copies of this text are described.

CHAPTER 8

1. Parts of this chapter draw on Berman, "The 'Labours of Hercules.'" The chapter also draws on documents in Troyes, AD Aube, 3H series and 23H series, photographed in 1987 and other microfilms supplied at that time. The author thanks the archivists in Troyes for permitting me to take photographs of several whole series of documents, making them accessible to me at a time when the new archive building had just opened. This chapter concentrates on the economic aspects of those nuns' history and is thus complemented by the treatment by Lester, *Creating Cistercian Nuns*, which focuses more on spirituality and specific families.

2. *Feudal Society in Medieval France*, ed. Evergates, no. 53 (1257); those at Jardin, Grâce, Piété, Notre-Dame-des-Prés, and Mont-Notre-Dame are discussed in this chapter; on Pont, see Chapter 5.

3. On the fairs, see Elizabeth Chapin, *Les villes de foires de Champagne, des origines au début du XIVe siècle* (Geneva: Slatkine Reprints, 1976).

4. The classic account is Henri [Heinrich] Denifle, *La désolation des églises, monastères, et hôpitaux en France pendant la guerre de cent ans*, 2 vols. in 3 (Paris: Picard, 1897–99).

5. On the regency, see Baldwin, *Philip Augustus*, pp. 277–78.

6. Alice, the elder of Henry II's daughters born in Jerusalem, became queen of Cyprus in 1210; her daughter Marie's claims were pursued in 1233; again this was to no avail.

7. "Martyrologe et chartes de l'abbaye Notre-Dame du Jardin lez Pleurs (Marne), ancien diocèse de Troyes," ed. Léonce Lex, *Mémoires de la Société académique d'agriculture . . . du département de l'Aube* 48, 3rd ser., no. 21 (1884): 365–93 (hereafter cited as "Chartes du Jardin"), published materials from Paris, BnF Latin 5553, the obituary or martyrology dated between 1250 and 1350, from the Champagne collection and from a short cartulary, Paris, BnF. Latin MS nouv. acq. 2230; its doc. no. 5, dated 1231, is a confirmation by Walter of Brienne that is not in Lex. Like that for Villiers (see Chapter 4), the obituary's evidence tends to emphasize the activities of widows who may have entered the abbey *ad succurrendum*.

8. "Chartes du Jardin," p. 368, quote from fol. 52r of obituary.

9. "Chartes du Jardin," no. 1 (1235).

10. "Chartes du Jardin," no. 2 (1237).

11. "Chartes du Jardin," no. 8 (1260/61).

12. "Chartes du Jardin," nos. 5 (1253) and 16 (1281).

13. "Chartes du Jardin," no. 13 (1275).

14. "Chartes du Jardin," no. 14 (1276).

15. "Chartes du Jardin," no. 19 (1290).

16. "Chartes du Jardin," nos. 3 (1239) and 4 (1247).

17. "Chartes du Jardin," nos. 6 (February 1253/54) and 9 (1262).

18. "Chartes du Jardin," no. 15 (1279).

19. "Chartes du Jardin," no. 18 (1284).

20. "Chartes du Jardin," no. 11 (1270).

21. "Chartes du Jardin," nos. 7 (1258), 12 (1274), 17 (1281), 20 and 21 (1292); on him, see Evergates, *Aristocracy*, p. 220.

22. The proper medieval name was Piété-Notre-Dame; see Bondéelle-Souchier, "Moniales," no. 65. What we know about this abbey's foundation derives almost entirely from copies made by the Benedictine scholar André Duchesne; Paris, BnF, Collection Duchesne, vol. 4, fols. 35–41, contains the information cited below, including on folio 38v (1234), another gift to the lepers from Peter of Claverdez.

23. Lester, *Creating Cistercian Nuns*, p. 131, cites episcopal records AD Aube G3186 (1235), the resolution of a dispute over tithe exemption between the nuns, the lepers, and the cathedral canons. The abbess had to pay one hundred livres to the canons in order for the nuns' tithe exemption to apply to the lepers; this appear to be the nuns' repurchasing of that tithe.

24. Paris, BnF, Collection Duchesne, vol. 4, fols. 35–41.

25. *Feudal Society in Medieval France*, ed. Evergates, no. 54 (1279), found in *Cartulaire de l'abbaye du Paraclet*, no. 294.

26. Paris, BnF, Collection Duchesne, vol. 4, fols. 35–41.

27. See Troyes, AD Aube, 23H series. Many of these were edited by Noel Becquart, "Notre-Dame-des-Prés, abbaye cistercienne au diocèse de Troyes" (diss., École des chartes, Paris, 1945). Lester, *Creating Cistercian Nuns*, consulted as well Troyes, AD Aube, archival series G (secular clergy) and entries in the papal registers of Gregory IX, that expand on the *Gallia Christiana* reference in note 28.

28. *Gallia Christiana*, vol. 12, item LXI (1235), col. 291; such visitation by bishops was *not* unusual at the time, but see Chapter 2.

29. Troyes, AD Aube, 23H150 (1233) mentions Fontenay; so does 23H9, a later cartulary.

30. Entered into the published registers of Gregory IX. *Les registres de Grégoire IX*, ed. Lucien Auvray, 3 vols. (Paris: Bibliothèque des écoles francaises d'Athènes et de Rome, 1896–1907), vol. 1, cols. 1281–82, no. 2479 (Lateran, July 3, 1230) were extracts from the account of a quarrel: "Querelam dilectorum filiorum . . abbatis et conventus monasterii de Cella Trecensis recepimus, continentem quod St[ephanus] de Campo Guidonis, civis Trecensis, infra limites parrochie ipsorum ecclesie Sancti Andree quandam capellam, eorum et presbiteri parrochialis irrequisito consensu, construxit, contra suorum privilegiorum tenorem temere veniendo, in quod quedam mulieres que Filie Dei vulgariter appellantur, auctoritate propria se temere intruserunt, in eorum prejudicium et gravamen" (ellipses are in the publication); the two preceding entries, 2477 and 2478, date to 1235; so does no. 1900.

31. *Registres de Grégoire IX*, ed. Auvray, 1:1282, no. 2479.

32. My translation of the Latin with bracketed clarifications of *Registres de Grégoire IX*, ed. Auvray, 1:1038–39, no. 1900 (1234); the Latin text reads:

> Qua quedam mulieres, in monachali habitu auctoritate propria intruse ibidem . . .
> [cum in ea capella, que ipsorum monasterio adeo est vicina, quod hinc inde voces
> psallentium audiuntur] mulieres sint posite antedicte, que verbo Cisterciensem
> ordinem profitentur, sed facto non observant eundem, cum nec incorporate sint ei,
> nec in claustro continuam residentiam faciant, qui[n] potius frequenter per diversa
> loca vagentur, per quarum vicinitatem eorum monasterium, quod fuit hactenus
> magne fame, plurimum diffamatur, et timendum est ne, occasione vicinitatis
> hujusmodi, que presumptionem malam inducit, penitus destruatur.

Lester, *Creating Cistercian Nuns*, pp. 16 and 17 n. 7, dropped the parts of the text that are bracketed here, although they were included in her discussion.

33. Citing *Registres de Grégoire IX*, ed. Auvray, 1:1280–81, no. 2477 (1235), Lester, *Creating Cistercian Nuns*, pp. 17–18, warns against its rhetorical position: "The monks' *libellus* is a carefully crafted text, designed to present the women at Chichéry in a negative light"; but Lester treats its details as reliable, giving it credence as a picture of a larger movement: "In their comportment and demeanor and their disinterest in an organized religious affiliation, they were part of a movement of religious renewal taking hold in Champagne and throughout Europe that saw similar groups of women adopt a life of penance and religious conversion" (p. 15).

34. Troyes, AD Aube, 23H150 (1260), rights over mills granted to Notre-Dame-des-Prés in 1260, by Adam, son of the late Jacob, Viscount of Joigny; 23H287 (1271) records conflict about access to that river and a milling monopoly claimed by the monks.

35. Troyes, AD Aube 23H268 and 23H334 (1236, 1239, and 1246).

36. Troyes, AD Aube, 23H11 (1247).

37. Troyes, AD Aube, 23H232 (1239, 1243); 23H313 (1245).

38. Troyes, AD Aube, 23H313 and 23H316 (1245) and 23H327 (1251).

39. Troyes, AD Aube, 23H178 (1263/64).

40. Troyes, AD Aube, 23H313 (1280).

41. Troyes, AD Aube, 23H256, 23H268, 23H302, on entrances into the abbey.

42. Bar was much closer to the familial castle of Jaucourt; see Evergates, *Aristocracy*, p. 188.

43. Troyes, AD Aube, 23H5 (1264); his quarter of the rights there sold for thirty-eight livres.

44. Troyes, AD Aube, 23H244 (1267), 23H181 (1269), and 23H5 (1268).

45. Troyes, AD Aube, 23H181 (1269).

46. Troyes, AD Aube, 23H215 (1270).

47. Troyes, AD Aube, 23H245 (all 1282).

48. See Troyes, AD Aube, 23H301b (1258) and 23H257 (1263), the latter a postmortem gift involving a life lease; on *ad medium*, see Appendix 1.

49. Lester, *Creating Cistercian Nuns*, p. 175 n. 12, cites Troyes, AD Aube, G3101 (1251), on oversight by the abbot of Arrivour.

50. Troyes, AD Aube, 23H14 (1289 and 1290).

51. *Statuta*, ed. Canivez, 1236, no. 67.

52. Troyes, AD Aube, 3H4082 (1236).

53. Troyes, AD Aube, 3H4011 (1242) and 3H4082 (1240 and 1260).

54. Troyes, AD Aube, 3H4003 (1231).

55. Troyes, AD Aube, 3H4076 (1232) and copy in 3H4074 (1261).

56. Troyes, AD Aube, 3H4037 (1232).

57. Troyes, AD Aube, 3H4077 (1232).

58. Troyes, AD Aube, 3H4003, includes the papal documents.

59. Troyes, AD Aube, 3H4058 (1266), the conveyance of land and vines at Bretonval by Oliver Beaubourg and his wife Margaret clearly distinguishes between the nuns of Val-des-Vignes and the sisters of Saint Nicholas.

60. Troyes, AD Aube, 3H4003 (1298). Cf. Appendix 4, "Size Limits for Abbeys for Nuns, Cistercian and Other Nuns."

61. Troyes, AD Aube, 3H4037 (1235).

62. Troyes, AD Aube, 3H4037 (1253) and 3H4077 (1255).

63. Troyes, AD Aube, 3H4079 (1264).

64. Troyes, AD Aube, 3H4079 (1264).

65. Troyes, AD Aube, 3H4074 (1268/69).

66. Troyes, AD Aube, 3H4074 (1268 and 1272).

67. Troyes, AD Aube, 3H4082 (1259, 1261, 1269).

68. Troyes, AD Aube 3H4082, 3H4011 (vidimus of May 1270 for an earlier grant by Thibaut V, who died in 1269); it is presumably this gift of income for five years of twenty livres per year that constitutes the windfall mentioned by Lester, *Creating Cistercian Nuns*, p. 191.

69. Troyes, AD Aube, 3H4085 (1268); possibly *Ventarius* means he operated a windmill.

70. Troyes, AD Aube, 3H4062 (1257), 3H4043 (1268), and 3H4090 (1273).

71. Troyes, AD Aube, 3H4011 (vidimus 1282), 3H4011 (1263).

72. Bondéelle-Souchier, "Moniales," no. 143.

73. Troyes, AD Aube, 3H series includes the charters for Clairvaux, Val-des-Vignes, and a cartulary for Clairmarais.

74. Berman, "The 'Labours of Hercules,'" which responds to the earlier characterization by William Jordan, "The Cistercian Nunnery." Jordan had perhaps not adequately evaluated the reliability of an opening notice in the late fifteenth-century cartulary within the context in which a number of houses of Cistercian nuns were suppressed in the fifteenth century. The opening of that cartulary, created for the abbot of Cîteaux in the fifteenth century, contended that "not even the labors of Hercules could restore these properties to productivity." These findings were first presented at the College Art Association; see Constance H. Berman and

Caroline Bruzelius, "Introduction," in "Monastic Women's Architecture," special issue, *Gesta* 31, no. 1 (1992): 73–75, but this study suggests that such adherence to the narratives of clerical and monastic men can lead to erroneous conclusions.

75. *Statuta*, ed. Canivez, 1226, no. 33.

76. Auxerre, AD Yonne, H787, *Cartulaire de la Cour*, fols. 111r–112r, mentions the Albigensian heretics; on the family Triânel and the Paraclete, see Chapter 9.

77. Auxerre, AD Yonne, H787, *Cartulaire de la Cour*, fols. 38ff., 76r, 84r, 94r, 107r–108v, 165r, 172r–173v; houses in Sens (fol. 138r) provided a retreat for the nuns during the Hundred Years' War.

78. Auxerre, AD Yonne, H787, *Cartulaire de la Cour*, fols. 32r–v and 85r. The ties of the founder, Walter Cornut, archbishop of Sens, to Blanche of Castile have been noted by Grant, *Blanche of Castile*.

79. Auxerre, AD Yonne, H787, *Cartulaire de la Cour*, fol. 102r.

80. Auxerre, AD Yonne, H787, *Cartulaire de la Cour*, fol. 2, Bull of Innocent IV, 1245, printed in *Cartulaire générale de l'Yonne: Recueil des documents authentiques*, ed. Maximilien Quantin, 2 vols. with supplement, *Recueil de pièces pour faire* . . . (Auxerre: Perroquet, 1854, 1860, 1901), vol. 3 is hereafter cited as Quantin, *Recueil*. Under discussion here is no. 503.

81. Auxerre, AD Yonne, H787, *Cartulaire de la Cour*, fol. 0.

82. Auxerre, AD Yonne, H787, *Cartulaire de la Cour*, fol. 6v ff.; the papal letter and that of the abbot of Cîteaux have been conflated in Quantin, *Recueil*, no. 640.

83. *Les actes pontificaux originaux des Archives nationale de Paris*, ed. Bernard Barbiche (Vatican City: Biblioteca Apostolica Vaticana, 1975), vol. 2, no. 1447; and Appendix 4, "Size Limits of Abbeys for Cistercian and Other Nuns"; the 1270 limit for Flines, included in Appendix 4, was also directly in response to Clement IV's decree.

84. There is no apologetic letter like that found for Notre-Dame-des-Près, but in both cases there was no question of default. In comparison to Notre-Dame-des-Près, which had 80 livres for forty-one inhabitants in 1289. See Troyes, AD Aube, 23H14 (1289 and 1290). Auxerre, A.D. Yonne, H787, *Cartulaire de la Cour*, fols. 21r–23v, reports that Cour had 295 livres and 7.5 sous for fifty inhabitants. As for small cash returns at some of Cour's vineyards, the Abbess also reported more typical rents of twenty shillings per annum for vineyards; small rents probably reflected vineyards under contract for planting.

85. Even after Boniface VIII's *Periculoso* in 1296 nuns were enjoined to leave the abbey only to conduct business in groups of two or three. Makowski, *Canon Law and Cloistered Women*, provides a text of the medieval *Periculoso* as an appendix; it differs considerably from the Trent version; see also Erin Jordan, "Roving Nuns."

86. Auxerre, AD Yonne, H787, *Cartulaire de la Cour*, fols. 21r–23v, rubrication "Ample information sur l'estat et valeur de la Cour Nostre Dame faict dan mil cc oct v en quelle tempe ladicte est a estois en meilleur estate quelle fut jamais et neanmoins decedes ces ne doivent point payer." It goes on to state that they had "no more than 295 livres, 7 sous, and 10 deniers of income and no more," but there were obviously other types of income than cash that are not mentioned; in the end the commissioners agreed they should not pay and that they did not default.

87. This even extended to reports in the Cistercian General Chapter. See *Statuta*, ed. Canivez, 1463, nos. 67–68, which mentions "scandal" involving Sister Antonia de-la-Court, "former abbess" of the community in 1463; and 1469, no. 14, ordering Jacqueline Danoul, nun at Marcilliac, "to keep perpetual silence" about her "pretensions" to the dignity of abbess of Cour-Notre-Dame. See Andrée Mignardot, *Michery: Histoire d'un village du Nord-Sénonais*

(Michery: Mignardot, 1996), p. 152, who suggests that such claims by women to the abbacy of Cour-Notre-Dame continued long thereafter. My thanks to Mme Mignardot, who provided me a copy of this volume and also took me to visit the abbey.

88. Lekai, *The Cistercians*, p. 325.

89. Auxerre, AD Yonne, H787, *Cartulaire de la Cour*, fol. 161r.

90. The term *curtis* is found frequently for communities of Premonstratensians; see Seale, "Reading the Premonstratensian Landscape."

91. This abbey, Gaudium at Nemours, is not to be confused with Joie at Soissons discussed below.

92. "The Cartulary of Clairmarais, a Monastery of Cistercian Nuns at Reims, France, c. 1220–1460: Edition and Commentary," ed. Pamela Stucky Skinner (PhD diss., University of Iowa, 2005), based on Troyes, AD Aube, series H non coté, *Cartulaire de Clairmarais*.

93. Bondéelle-Souchier, "Moniales," no. 111, for Mont, and no. 114, for Joie.

94. Lester, *Creating Cistercian Nuns*, p. 133, mentions Nemours's *domus Dei* at Mâlay-le-Roi in 1247; it eventually came to Lys; see Chapter 6.

95. Marcel Aubert, *L'architecture cistercienne en France*, 2 vols. (Paris: Vanoest, 1947), vol. 2, plate 532, p. 190.

96. See *Statuta*, ed. Canivez, 1466, 5:184, "Mandat priori Beatae Mariae de Bella Aqua, quatinus citissime redimat iocalia sive vasa argentea reliquiis plena atque librum tertiam partem bibliae continentem per se impignorata, atque priori et prioratui de Gratia Beatae Mariae pertinentia ipsaque priori de Gratia restituat," as cited by Bondéelle-Souchier, "Moniales," p. 237. Here is the prior who has used the Bible as security for a loan. There was an early tie to the lords of Montmirail and especially with John of Oisy, whose major support of Cistercian nuns was in the county of Chartres; see *Cartulaire de l'Eau*, no. 59 (1257): it mentions ten livres of income given to Grâce, and see discussion in Chapter 5.

97. My own early linking of some of these abbeys with leprosariums was incorrect. Moreover, despite contentions by Grundmann and his followers (discussed in Chapter 1), those houses of nuns did not originate in a separate women's movement. Lester, *Creating Cistercian Nuns*, appendix, lists some ties that can no longer be justified; see my discussions of Pont, Jardin, Piété, Val-des-Vignes, Lys and Nemours, Notre-Dame-des-Prés; note that Saint-Loup did not become Cistercian until the early modern period.

98. Richard C. Hoffmann, *An Environmental History of Medieval Europe* (Cambridge: Medieval Textbooks, 2014), p. 287, suggests that leprosy may be a disease of the overfed, in which case it would have declined with late medieval famines. Indeed, the literature on leprosy in the Middle Ages does not suggest a general decline of its numbers in the fifteenth century. See the review article by Elma Brenner, "Recent Perspectives on Leprosy in Medieval Western Europe," *History Compass* 8, no. 5 (2010): 388–406. I thank Monica Green for this reference.

99. "*The Life of Yvette, Anchoress of Huy*, by Hugh of Floreffe," trans. Jo Ann McNamara, ed. Anneke B. Mulder-Bakker, in *Living Saints of the Thirteenth Century: The Lives of Yvette, Anchoress of Huy; Juliana of Cornillon, Author of the Corpus Christi Feast; and Margaret the Lame, Anchoress of Magdeburg*, ed. Anneke B. Mulder-Bakker (Turnhout: Brepols; 2011), p. 53 n. 9, p. 71 nn. 1 and 2; and cf. Anneke B. Mulder-Bakker, *Lives of the Anchoresses: The Rise of the Urban Recluse in Medieval Europe*, trans. Myra Heerspink Scholz (Philadelphia: University of Pennsylvania Press, 2013), pp. 66–68.

100. Louis Carolus-Barré, "L'abbaye de la Joie-Notre-Dame à Berneuil-sur-Aisne (1234–1430)," *Mélanges à la mémoire du père Anselme Dimier*, ed. Benoît Chauvin, part 2, vol. 4 (Arbois: B. Chauvin, 1984), pp. 487–504.

101. Carolus-Barré, "La Joie," pp. 499–500, a document from July 1, 1234. Although the earliest surviving copy of this text is from the seventeenth century, Carolus-Barré, p. 489, argues persuasively for its authenticity. The bishop wrote that, after a short period of co-residence, the nuns and lepers soon went their separate ways; Gregory IX in mid-August 1234 recognized the women as Cistercians.

102. "The Cartulary of Clairmarais," ed. Skinner.

103. Bondéelle-Souchier, "Moniales," pp. 207–11. The evidence of such suppressions moves far beyond Cistercian nuns and far beyond France, as in just two examples: Gilchrist, *Gender and Material Culture*, p. 23ff., reports that stories of scandal and too few occupants allowed the late medieval suppression of the nuns at Saint Radegund's in Cambridge, England, so that a college for young men could replace the nuns. The offense was subtler in the case of Abbot Sugerius of Saint-Denis, whose forgeries allowed his "takeover" of rich viticultural lands belonging to the nuns of Argenteuil; see Thomas A. Waldman, "Abbot Suger and the Nuns of Argenteuil," *Traditio* 41 (1985): 239–72.

CHAPTER 9

1. Too little is yet known about the women's communities among the Premonstratensians, but see the forthcoming work of Yvonne Seale and Heather Wacha.

2. See Kerr, *Religious Life*, p. 132.

3. Karen Ann Christianson, "Female Leadership and Male Submission: The Order of Fontevraud in Twelfth-Century France" (PhD diss., University of Iowa, 2009).

4. *Grand Cartulaire de Fontevraud*, ed. Jean-Marc Bienvenu, Robert Favreau and Georges Pon, 2 vols. (Poitiers: Société des Antiquaires de l'ouest, 2000, 2005), no. 885 (1135); the charter asserts that the nuns' mill had totally destroyed all fishing: "ut piscaturam omnino eis auferrat."

5. *Grand Cartulaire de Fontevraud*, no. 649 (1123).

6. *Grand Cartulaire de Fontevraud*, no. 652 (1123); note that the term *assarts* or *essarts* reflects already accomplished cutting and uprooting.

7. *Grand Cartulaire de Fontevraud*, nos. 854 (1109–12/13), 864 (1109–16), and 867 (1129).

8. *Grand Cartulaire de Fontevraud*, no. 874 (1135).

9. *Grand Cartulaire de Fontevraud*, no. 868 (1135).

10. *Grand Cartulaire de Fontevraud*, no. 678 (1118–49).

11. *Cartulaire du Paraclet*, no. 48 (1142 or later).

12. As Mary Martin McLaughlin argued, in "Heloise the Abbess," pp. 1–17.

13. On Eleanor of Vermandois, see Shortell, "Erasures" and studies cited below.

14. Bruce L. Venarde, *Women's Monasticism and Medieval Society: Nunneries in France and England, 890–1215* (Ithaca, NY: Cornell University Press, 1997), p. 150, opines: "Despite generous gifts . . . Longpré was already under economic stress only a decade or so after its foundation." An agreement between the abbess of Fontevraud and Pope Celestine III limited Longpré to sixty nuns; *Epistolae pontificum Romanorum ineditae*, ed. Samuel Loewenfeld (Leipzig: Veit, 1885), pp. 257–58, as cited by Venarde. But as seen in this study's Appendix 4, "Size Limits for Abbeys for Nuns, Cistercian and Other Nuns," a community of sixty nuns was not small.

15. Louis Duval-Arnould, "Les aumônes d'Aliénor, dernière comtesse de Vermandois et dame de Valois," *Revue Mabillon* 60 (1984): 395–463, at pp. 431–32, no. 1 (1192), no. 2 (1194);

and Petit-Dutaillis, *Étude sur la vie et le règne de Louis VIII*, p. 493, no. 329. Eleanor lived until 1213/14. See Berman, "Two Medieval Women's Control." I am grateful to Caroline Bruzelius, who brought the Duval-Arnould study to my attention.

16. *Recueil des actes de Philippe Auguste, roi de France*, ed. Élie Berger and H.-François Delaborde (Paris: Impr. nationale 1916–), vol. 2, no. 705 (1201).

17. Kerr, *Religious Life*, pp. 117–22, suggests that English houses followed the same calendar of commemoration, but nothing is said of anniversary masses. On the organization of priories at Fontevraud for Foissy, founded circa 1160, see Anne Elisabeth Lester, "Gender and Social Networks in Medieval France: The Convents of the Country of Champagne" (PhD diss., Princeton University, 2003), p 307, where she reports, "It should be noted that there are no papal confirmations in Foissy's document. This is perhaps explained in part because Foissy is a priory [and] therefore any papal confirmations would have gone to Fontevrault. The role of the Abbess of Fontevrault in resolving disputes is prominent."

18. Venarde, *Women's Monasticism*, pp. 96–97.

19. Bruce L. Venarde, "*Praesidentes Negotiis*: Abbesses as Managers in Twelfth-Century France," in *Portraits in Medieval and Renaissance Living: Essays in Memory of David Herlihy*, ed. Samuel K. Cohn Jr. and Steven A. Epstein (Ann Arbor: University of Michigan Press, 1996), p. 200, citing *Cartulaire du Paraclet*; that volume, and in particular no. 6 (1147), has been used widely as a description of the nuns' holdings; notable are references to *ad medium* for vines.

20. McLaughlin, "Heloise the Abbess," pp. 7 and 12 n. 18.

21. McLaughlin, "Heloise the Abbess," note 34. McLaughlin found that many of the women who entered the Paraclete made benefactions of property that they held in their own right.

22. *Cartulaire du Paraclet*, no. 238 (1244), E., abbess of the Paraclete:

Ad universorum igitur noticiam volumus pervenire, quod, cum moniales prioratus nostri de Bosranco, quarum numerus superfluus facultatem excedit in pluribus quantitatem, a parte optima Marie quam elegerant, cogantur penitus recedere ut Marte operibus perseverent, ita quod unguenti suavitas a muscis mordentibus paupertatis auferatur, ordinare voluimus, de consensu conventus nostri, quod dictarum monialium numerus minuatur, et ad certam reducatur, statuentes et observandum in virtute obedientie districte percipientes, ne amodo aliqua in predicto prioratu in monialem vel sororem recipiatur quousque, procedente tempore, ad XX deveniant predicti prioratus moniales.

23. Venarde, *Women's Monasticism*, p. 123.

24. Venarde, *Women's Monasticism*, pp. 121–22.

25. Comparison is possible because separate charters for Montazais survive. See Venarde, *Women's Monasticism*, pp. 144–45; the measure, probably a muid, would be about a cartload. In my table I have called these categories annual income rather than annual "tributes."

26. *Cartulaire du Paraclet*, no. 21 (1198), p. 37; the word *Sane* (typical in tithe exemption clauses) has been mistranscribed as *sive*, but the rest is the standard text introduced by Alexander III; see Constable, *Monastic Tithes*.

27. *Pont-aux-Dames*, nos. 91, 109, 122, 123,128, 129, and 130.

28. Paris, AN, S*4386, fols. 11r–14r (1243–47).

29. Paris, AN, S*4386, fols. 14v–15v (1261, 1272, 1278), included participation by the abbot Guy of Cîteaux.

30. Erin Jordan, "Roving Nuns."

31. See documents written as if by nuns ("our holdings") in *Chartrier de l'Abbaye-aux-Bois*, ed. Pipon; and discussion in Venarde, "Making History at Fontevraud," pp. 19–31; and Appendix 3, "Specific Charters and Other Materials for This Study."

32. See Gilchrist, *Gender and Material Culture.*

33. Barrière, "The Cistercian Convent of Coyroux."

34. See discussion of Eileen Power, *Medieval English Nunneries*, above in preface at note 15.

35. C. H. Lawrence, *Medieval Monasticism: Forms of Religious Life in the Middle Ages*, 3rd ed. (London: Longman, 2001), p. 220, makes that assertion but provides no evidence for it.

APPENDIX 2

1. On transfer of archives to Paris, see *Le chartrier de l'Abbaye-aux-Bois (1202–1341)*, ed. Brigitte Pipon, Mémoires et documents de l'École des chartes 46 (Paris: École des chartes, 1996), p. 13, but see also her discussion of the cartulary for this abbey, which ended up in Chicago.

2. This change appeared at different times in different places. Thirteenth-century charters for northern France gradually came to be registered before a public authority who attested to the legal validity of the transaction by affixing a seal to the charter. See Brigitte Miriam Bedos-Rezak, *When Ego Was Imago: Signs of Identity in the Middle Ages* (Leiden: Brill, 2010), chaps. 1 and 2; and remarks by Michel Parisse in *Les cartulaires: Actes de la table ronde organisée par l'École nationale des chartes et le G.D.R. 121 du C.N.R.S.*, ed. Olivier Guyotjeannin, Laurent Morelle, and Michel Parisse (Paris: École des Chartes, 1993).

3. Vivian H. Galbraith, "Monastic Foundation Charters of the Eleventh and Twelfth Centuries," *Cambridge Historical Journal* 4 (1934): 205–25, on pp. 221–22, describes how a monastic foundation might be accomplished over several years, but its events attached to a single date. This could mean that not all participants in the process were necessarily still alive or were identified with the correct titles. This does not mean that such a foundation charter should be rejected as a forgery.

4. On French charters and their copies in general, see Guyotjeannin, Pycke, and Tock, *Diplomatique médiévale*, which in many ways is the counterpart to *Les cartulaires*, cited in note 2 above.

5. Some of these problems are discussed with regard to the Cour-Notre-Dame cartulary, above in Chapter 8. See also discussion in Heather Wacha, "La Puissance du Choix: Women's Economic Activity in Twelfth- and Thirteenth-Century Picardy" (PhD diss., University of Iowa, 2016) and in William O. Duba, "The Cartulary of Vauluisant: A Critical Edition," ed. William Owen Duba (Master's thesis, University of Iowa, 1994); and in the discussion of Paris AN LL1595, *Cartulaire de Saint-Antoine*, in Chapter 7.

BIBLIOGRAPHY

UNPUBLISHED DOCUMENTS

Angers, AD Maine-et-Loire, 253H10, 253H11, Perray.
Auxerre, AD Yonne, H787, *Cartulaire de la Cour-Notre-Dame*, 222 fols. earlier mark F.
Auxerre, AD Yonne, H8–57; H511–12; H2063–64.
Bourges, AD Cher, H34–37; H38–54; 8H58, Beauvoir and les Bussières
Cambridge University Library, MS Mm.5.31.
Chicago, Newberry Library, MS, *Cartulaire de l'abbaye aux Bois*.
Corbeil, AD Essonne, 1H1–40; 71H8.
Dijon, AD Côte-d'Or, 11H 4,11; 78 H 1042.
Laon, AD Aisne, Fervaques, H series.
Ljubljana State and University Library, MS 32.
London, British Museum, Additional Charter 4129 (1241/42).
Melun, AD Seine-et-Marne, H550, H556–65; H648–64.
Melun, AD Seine-et-Marne, H566, *Inventaire du Lys*.
Paris, AN, Cartes et plans, N/III/Seine Atlas de Saint-Antoine.
LL154, *Notre Dame du Val*.
Paris, AN, Port-Royal L1034, H⁵4039, S4517, S4519, boxes of loose charters.
Paris, AN, Saint-Antoine registers:
   LL1595, *Cartulaire de Saint-Antoine*, medieval
   S*4384 (eighteenth-century inventory) listing days on which indulgences were granted
   S*4385, *Inventaire de Saint-Antoine* duplicates S*4386
   S*4386, *Cartulaire de Saint-Antoine*, early modern
Paris: AN Saint-Antoine, loose charters in boxes or bundles (liasses), containing from a single
   charter to dozens from the twelfth and thirteenth centuries:
   Paris: AN H⁵ 3859¹ and H⁵3859²
   Paris: AN L1014, Liasse 1, Liasse 2, Liasse 5, Liasse 7, Liasse 8, Liasse 9, Liasse 10, Liasse
      11, Liasse 12, Liasse 13, Liasse 14, Liasse 15, Liasse 16, Liasse 17, Liasse 21, Liasse 22,
      Liasse 24, Liasse 25
   Paris: AN L1015
   Paris: AN S4357
   Paris: AN S4359, Liasse 1, Liasse 2, Liasse 3, Liasse 4
   Paris: AN S4360, Liasse 1, Liasse 3, Liasse 4, Liasse 5
   Paris: AN S4364
   Paris: AN S4365, Liasse 1, Liasse 2, Liasse 3

Paris: AN S4366A, Liasse 1, Liasse 4, Liasse 5, Liasse 6, Liasse 7, Liasse 8

Paris: AN S4369

Paris, AN S4370

Paris, AN S4371

Paris: AN S4372

Paris: AN S4373

Paris: AN S4374

Paris: AN S4375

Paris, BnF, Collection Duchesne, vol. 4, Piété-Notre-Dame.

Paris, BnF, Latin MSS 1099 and 1098, *Cartulaire de Porrois.*

Paris, BnF, Latin MSS 9166–9169, *Cartulaire de Royaumont.*

Paris, BnF, Latin 10944, *Cartulaire de Pont-aux-Dames.*

Paris, BnF, Latin MS 11071, *Cartulaire de Fervaques.*

Paris, BnF, Latin MS 13892, *Cartulaire du Lys.*

Paris, BnF, Latin MSS 9220, 12665 and 17140, *Cartulaires des Clairets.*

Paris, BnF, Latin MS, nouv. acq. 2230, Jardin-lez-Pleurs documents.

Pontoise, AD Val d'Oise

    72H10, *Cartulaire de Maubuisson* (1688)

    72H12, *Achatz d'héritages pour Maubuisson*

    Maubuisson liasses (numbered bundles, multiple bundles or boxes, most with ten to thirty
    pre-1350 documents): 72H80, 72H81, 72H82, 72H83, 72H84, 72H86, 72H87, 72H88,
        72H90, 72H91, 72H92, 72H94, 72H97, 72H99, 72H100, 72H101, 72H103, 72H106,
        72H107, 72H109, 72H110, 72H112, 72H114, 72H115, 72H122, 72H124, 72H127,
        72H130, 72H131, 72H132, 72H133, 72H134, 72H135, 72H138, 72H141, 72H143

Tours, AD Indres-et-Loire, H799 and H800 (Moncey).

Troyes, AD Aube, 3H4001, Cartulaire de Val-des-Vignes.

Troyes, AD Aube, liasses: 3H4002, 3H4003, 3H4009, 3H4010, 3H4011, 3H3032, 3H4036,
    3H4037, 3H4038, 3H4039, 3H4040, 3H4042, 3H4043, 3H4044, 3H4058, 3H4060,
    3H4062, 3H4063, 3H4064, 3H4069, 3H4071, 3H4073, 3H4074, 3H4076, 3H4077,
    3H4078, 3H4079, 3H4080, 3H4082, 3H4083, 3H4085, 3H4086, 3H4086, 3H4087,
    3H4089, 3H4090, 3H4095, 3H4096, 3H4099, 3H4100, 3H4105, 3H4110, 3H4111, 3H4112,
    3H4113, 3H4114, 3H4117, 3H4118; 3H4118bis, 3H4119, 3H4120, 3H4021, 3H4023 (all the
    Val-des-Vignes documents are found in the 3H Clairvaux collection)

Troyes, AD Aube, series 23H3–335 Notre-Dame-des-Prés.

23H5, *Cartulaire de Notre-Dame-des-Prés* (early modern) 95 fols. 172 acts from 1236–1546.

23H9, 1234 report by Hugh of Saint Maur.

23H11, 1245 papal bull.

23H12, 23H13, 23H14, 23H16.

Troyes, AD Aube, Liasses: 23H142, 23H150, 23H151, 23H153, 23H160, 23H169, 23H171, 23H178,
    23H179, 23H180, 23H181, 23H182, 23H184, 23H203, 23H205, 23H210, 23H211, 23H215,
    23H232, 23H233, 23H236, 23H240, 23H244, 23H245, 23H247,23H256, 23H257, 23H266,
    23H268, 23H269, 23H270, 23H273, 23H275, 23H287, 23H293, 23H295, 23H300, 23H301,
    23H302, 23H305, 23H308, 23H312, 23H313, 23H314, 23H316, 23H327, 23H330, 23H333,
    23H334, 23H335, 23H338, 23H339.

Troyes, AD Aube, series H non coté, *Cartulaire de Clairmarais.*

PUBLISHED TEXTS, DOCUMENTS

L'abbaye du Pont-aux-Dames (ordre de Cîteaux), assise en la paroisse de Couilly . . . 1226–1790. Edited by [Claude-Hyacinthe] Berthault. Meaux: Librairie le Blondel, 1878.

Abbaye royale de Notre-Dame des Clairets: Histoire et cartulaire. Edited by Vicomte [Hector] de Souancé. Nogent-le-Rotrou, 1894.

The Acta of Hugh of Wells, Bishop of Lincoln, 1209–1235. Edited by David M. Smith. Publications of the Lincoln Record Society 88. Woodbridge: Boydell, 2000.

Les actes pontificaux originaux des Archives nationale de Paris. Edited by Bernard Barbiche. 2 vols. Vatican City: Biblioteca Apostolica Vaticana, 1975.

Agnes of Harcourt. *The Writings of Agnes of Harcourt: The Life of Isabelle of France and the Letter on Louis IX and Longchamp.* Edited and translated by Sean L. Field. Notre Dame, IN: University of Notre Dame Press, 2003.

Cartario dell'a abazia di Rifreddo: Fino all'anno 1300. Edited by Silvio Pivano. Pinerolo: Chiantore-Mascarelli, 1902.

Cartario dell'a abazia di Staffarda. Vol. 1. Edited by F. Gabotto, G. Roberti, and D. Chiattone. Pinerolo: Chiantore-Mascarelli, 1901.

Le cartulaire de l'abbaye cistercienne d'Obazine (XIIe–XIIIe siècle). Edited by Bernadette Barrière. Clermont-Ferrand: Université de Clermont-Ferrand II, 1989.

Cartulaire de l'abbaye de Berdoues près Mirande. Edited by the abbé Cauzarin. The Hague: Nijhoff, 1905.

"Cartulaire de l'abbaye de Boulancourt de l'ancien diocèse de Troyes." Edited by Charles Lalore. *Mémoires de la Société académique d'agriculture de l'Aube* 33 (1869): 101–92.

Cartulaire de l'abbaye de Flines. Edited by Edouard Hautcoeur. 2 vols. Lille, 1873.

Cartulaire de l'abbaye de la Sainte-Trinité de Tiron. Edited by Lucien Merlet. Chartres: Garnier, 1883.

Cartulaire de l'abbaye de Maubuisson (Notre-Dame-la-Royale). Edited by Adolphe Dutilleux and Joseph Depoin. 2 vols. Pontoise: Société Historique du Vexin, 1890–1913. Also published as *L'abbaye de Maubuisson, histoire et cartulaire: Publiés d'après les documents entièrement inédits.* 4 vols. Pontoise: Amédée Paris, 1882–85.

Cartulaire de l'abbaye de Notre-Dame de l'Eau. Edited by Charles Métais. Chartres: Ch. Métais, 1908.

Cartulaire de l'abbaye de Notre-Dame d'Ourscamp de l'ordre de Cîteaux, fondée en 1129 au diocèse de Noyon. Edited by Achille Piegné-Delacourt. Amiens: Lemens, 1865.

Cartulaire de l'abbaye de Porrois, au diocèse de Paris, plus connue sous son nom mystique Port-Royal. Edited by Adolphe de Dion. Paris: Picard, 1903.

Cartulaire de l'abbaye de Saint-Père de Chartres. Edited by M. [Benjamin Edme Charles] Guérard. 2 vols. Paris: Crapelet, 1840.

Cartulaire de l'abbaye de Silvanès. Edited by P.-A. Verlaguet. Rodez: Carrère, 1910.

Cartulaire de l'abbaye du Paraclet. Edited by Charles Lalore. Collection des principaux cartulaires du diocèse de Troyes, vol. 2. Paris: E. Thorin, 1878.

Cartulaire de l'abbaye royale du Lieu-N.-.D.-lès-Romorantin. Edited by Ernest Plat. Romorantin, 1892.

Cartulaire de Notre-Dame de Prouille. Edited by J. Giraud. Paris: Picard, 1907.

Cartulaire de Notre-Dame de Voisins de l'ordre de Cîteaux. Edited by Jules Doinel. Orléans: Herluison, 1887.

Cartulaire et documents de l'abbaye de Nonenque. Edited by C. Couderc and J.-L. Rigal. Rodez: Carrère, 1955.

Cartulaire générale de l'Yonne: Recueil des documents authentiques. Edited by Maximilien Quantin. 2 vols., with supplement *Recueil de pièces à faire suite au Cartulaire générale de l'Yonne.* Auxerre: Perroquet, 1854, 1860, and 1901.

Cartulaires de l'abbaye de Molesme, ancien diocèse de Langres, 916–1250. Edited by Jacques Laurent. 2 vols. Paris: Picard, 1907–11.

"The Cartulary of Clairmarais, a Monastery of Cistercian Nuns at Reims, France, c. 1220–1460: Edition and Commentary." Edited by Pamela Stucky Skinner. PhD diss., University of Iowa, 2005.

Cartulary of Countess Blanche of Champagne. Edited by Theodore Evergates. Toronto: University of Toronto Press, 2009.

Cartulary of the Cathedral of Holy Wisdom of Nicosia. Edited by Nicholas Coureas and Christopher Schabel. Nicosia: Cyprus Research Centre, 1997.

"The Cartulary of Vauluisant: A Critical Edition." Edited by William Owen Duba. Master's thesis, University of Iowa, 1994.

Chartes de l'abbaye cistercienne de Vaucelles au XIIe siècle. Edited by Benoit-Michael Tock. Turnhout: Brepols, 2010.

Les chartes des comtes de Saint-Pol (XIe–XIIIe siècles). Edited by Jean-François Nieus. Turnhout: Brepols, 2008.

Chartes et documents concernant l'abbaye de Cîteaux, 1098–1182. Edited by J. Marilier. Rome: Editiones cistercienses, 1961.

Chartes et documents de l'abbaye de Saint-Magloire. Edited by A. Terroine and L. Fossier. Paris: CNRS, 1998.

Le chartrier de l'Abbaye-aux-Bois (1202–1341). Edited by Brigitte Pipon. Mémoires et documents de l'École des chartes 46. Paris: École des chartes, 1996.

Chartulary of the Cistercian Priory of Coldstream with Relative Documents. Edited by Charles Rogers. London: Grampian Club, 1879. Cf. *Historic Memorials of Coldstream Abbey, Berwickshire* (London: printed for private circulation, 1850), an earlier anonymous edition of the cartulary and related information.

Christina of Markyate. *The Life of Christina of Markyate.* Edited by Samuel Fanous and Henrietta Leyser, based on original translation by C. H. Talbot. Oxford: World's Classics, 2010.

Cistercian Lay Brothers: Twelfth-Century Usages with Related Texts. Latin text with concordance of Latin terms, English translations and notes. Edited by Chrysogonus Waddell. Brecht, Belgium: Cîteaux, Commentarii cistercienses, 2000.

Les codifications cisterciennes de 1237 et de 1257. Edited by Bernard Lucet. Paris: Centre National de la Recherche Scientifique, 1977.

Conrad of Eberbach. *Exordium Magnum Cisterciense, sive Narratio de initio ciserciensis ordinis.* Edited by Bruno Griesser. Series Scriptorium Sacri Ordinis Cisterciensis 2. Rome: Editiones Cistercienses, 1961. Reprinted, Turnhout: Brepols, 1994. Also published as *Le Grand Exorde de Cîteaux ou Récit des débuts de l'Ordre cistercien,* translated by Anthelmette Piébourg, introduction by Brian P. McGuire (Turnhout: Brepols, 1998); and as *The Great Beginning of Cîteaux: A Narrative of the Beginning of the Cistercian Order; The "Exordium Magnum" of Conrad of Eberbach,* translated by Benedicta Ward and Paul Savage, edited by E. Rozannne Elder (Kalamazoo, MI: Cistercian Publications, 2012).

Decrees of the Ecumenical Councils. Edited by N. P. Tanner. 2 vols. London: Sheed & Ward; and Washington, DC: Georgetown University Press, 1990.

Documentación del Monasterio de las Huelgas de Burgos (1116–1230). Edited by José Manuel Lizoain Garrido. Burgos: J. M. Garrido Garrido, 1985.

L'édition romaine des consiles généraux et les actes du premier concile de Lyon. Edited by Stephan Kuttner. Rome: SALER, 1940.

"Epistolae: Medieval Women's Letters." Accessed July 24, 2015. https://epistolae.ccnmtl .columbia.edu.

Épinois, Henri de l'. "Comptes relatifs à la fondation de l'abbaye de Maubuisson, d'après les originaux des archives de Versailles." *Bibliothèque de l'École des Chartes* 29 (1858): 550–69.

Epistolae pontificum Romanorum ineditae. Edited by Samuel Loewenfeld. Leipzig: Veit, 1885.

Exordium Parvum. See *Les plus anciens textes de Cîteaux: Sources, textes, et notes historiques,* edited by Jean de la Croix Bouton and Jean-Baptiste Van Damme (Achel: Abbaye cistercienne, 1974) and on-line translations like "Exordium Parvum," accessed June 19, 2017, http://www.ocso.org/resources/foundational-text/exordium-parvum.

Feudal Society in Medieval France: Documents from the County of Champagne. Edited by Theodore Evergates. Philadelphia: University of Pennsylvania Press, 1993.

Gallia christiana, in provincias ecclesiasticas distributa: qua series & historia archiepiscoporum, episcoporum & abbatum Franciae vicinarumque ditionum . . . opera et studio Domni Dionysii Sammarthani, presbyteri et monachii ordinis Sancti Benedicti e congregatione Sancti Mauri nec non monachorum ejusdem congregationis. Edited by B. Hauréau and D. de Sainte-Marthe. Paris: various imprints, 1812–96.

Geoffrey Grossus. *The Life of Blessed Bernard of Tiron.* Edited and translated by Ruth Harwood Cline. Washington, DC: Catholic University of America Press, 2009.

Grand Cartulaire de Fontevraud. Edited by Jean-Marc Bienvenu, Robert Favreau, and Georges Pon. 2 vols. Poitiers: Société des Antiquaires de l'Ouest, 2000, 2005.

Grand Cartulaire de la Sauve Majeure. Edited by Charles Higounet and Arlette Higounet-Nadal, with Nicole de Peña. Bordeaux: Fédération historique du Sud-Ouest, 1996.

Herman of Tournay. *De miraculis sanctae Mariae Laudunensis.* PL, vol. 156, cols. 962–1018.

"Histoire de l'abbaye royale de Notre-Dame de Villiers, de l'Ordre de Cîteaux, au diocèse de Sens (1220–1669)." Edited by Paul Pinson. *Annales de la Société historique et archéologique du Gâtinais* 11 (1893): 1–125.

Histoire du prieuré de Jully-les-Nonnains, avec pièces justificatives. Edited by the abbé Jobin. Paris: Bray, 1881.

Histoire générale de Languedoc. Edited by Claude Devic and J. Vaissete. 18 vols. Toulouse: Privat, 1873–1983.

Hugh of Floreffe. "*The Life of Yvette, Anchoress of Huy,* by Hugh of Floreffe." Translated by Jo Ann McNamara. Edited by Anneke B. Mulder-Bakker. In *Living Saints of the Thirteenth Century: The Lives of Yvette, Anchoress of Huy; Juliana of Cornillon, Author of the Corpus Christi Feast; and Margaret the Lame, Anchoress of Magdeburg,* edited by Anneke B. Mulder-Bakker, 47–141. Turnhout: Brepols, 2011.

———. *The Life of Yvette of Huy.* Translated by Jo Ann McNamara. Toronto: Peregrina Publications, 1986.

Jacques de Vitry. *The Historia Occidentalis of Jacques de Vitry: A Critical Edition.* Edited by John Frederick Hinnebusch. Fribourg: University Press, 1972.

———. *The Life of Marie d'Oignies.* Translated by Margot H. King. Toronto: Peregrina, 1993.

Layettes du trésor des chartes. Edited by Alexandre M. Teulet, Joseph M. de Laborde, Élie M. Berger, and Henri-François Delaborde. 5 vols. Paris: Plon, 1863–1909.

The Letters of Heloise and Abelard: A Translation of Their Collected Correspondence and Related Writings. Edited by Mary Martin McLaughlin and Bonnie Wheeler. New York: Macmillan, 2014.

Lhuillier, Théophile. "Inventaire des titres concernant la seigneurie que les religieuses de l'abbaye royale de N.-D. du Lys, près Melun, possédaient à Mâlay-le-Roi." *Bulletin de la Société archéologique de Sens* 10 (1872): 347–57.

Liber instrumentorum memorialium; Cartulaire des Guillems de Montpellier. Edited by A. Germain. Montpellier: Société archéologique de Montpellier, 1884–86.

"Martyrologe et chartes de l'abbaye Notre-Dame du Jardin lez Pleurs (Marne), ancien diocèse de Troyes." Edited by Léonce Lex. *Mémoires de la Société académique d'agriculture . . . du département de l'Aube* 48, 3rd series, no. 21 (1884): 365–93.

Monastic Matrix, online. Currently at http://monasticmatrix.osu.edu. Accessed September 1, 2017.

Monasticon Anglicanum: A History of the Abbeys and Other Monasteries, Hospitals, Friaries, and Cathedral and Collegiate Churches, with Their Dependencies, in England and Wales. Edited by Roger Dodsworth and William Dugdale. London: Longman, Hurst, Rees, Orme & Brown, 1817–30.

Les monuments primitifs de la règle cistercienne. Edited by Philippe Guignard. Dijon, 1878.

A Parisian Journal, 1405–1449. Translated by Janet Shirley. Oxford: Clarendon Press, 1968. Also available in French as *Journal d'un bourgeois de Paris: De 1405 à 1449,* ed. Colette Beaune. Paris: Librairie générale française, 1990.

Patrologiae cursus completus . . . sive Latinorum, sive Graecorum. Edited by Jean-Paul Migne. Paris: Migne, 1857–66,

Peter of Les Vaux-de-Cernay. *The History of the Albigensian Crusade: Peter of les Vaux-de-Cernay's "Historia Albigensis."* Translated by W. A. Sibly and M. D. Sibly. Woodbridge: Boydell, 1998.

Les plus anciens textes de Cîteaux: Sources, textes, et notes historiques. Edited by Jean de la Croix Bouton and Jean-Baptiste Van Damme. Achel: Abbaye cistercienne, 1974.

Recherches historiques et critiques sur l'ancien comtés et es comtes de Clermont en Beauvoisis du XIe au XIIIe siècle. Edited by Eugène de l'Épinois. Beauvais, 1877.

Recherches historiques et critiques sur les anciens comtes de Beaumont-sur-Oise, du XIe au XIIIe siècle. Edited by L. Douet d'Arcq. Amiens, 1855.

Recueil de plans des églises cisterciennes. Edited by Anselm Dimier. 4 vols. Grignan: Abbaye Notre-Dame d'Aiguebelle; Paris: Librairie d'art ancien et moderne, 1949–67.

Recueil des actes de Philippe Auguste, roi de France. Edited by Élie Berger and H.-François Delaborde. Paris: Impr. nationale 1916–.

Recueil des chartes de l'abbaye de Clairvaux au XIIe siècle. Edited by Jean Waquet, Jean-Marc Roger, and Laurent Veyssière. Paris: CTHS, 2004.

Recueil des chartes et documents de l'abbaye de Saint-Martin-des-Champs, monastère parisien. Edited by Joseph Depoin. 5 vols. Ligugé, 1912–21.

Recueil des pancartes de l'abbaye de la Ferté-sur-Grosne, 1113–1178. Edited by Georges Duby. Gap: Éditions Ophrys, 1953.

Les registres d'Innocent IV. Edited by Élie M. Berger. 4 vols. Paris: E. Thorin, 1884–1921.

Les registres de Grégoire IX. Edited by Lucien Auvray. 2 vols. Paris: Bibliothèque des écoles francaises d'Athènes et de Rome, 1907.

Statuta capitulorum generalium ordinis cisterciensis ab anno 1116 ad annum 1786. 8 vols. Edited by Joseph-Marie Canivez. Louvain: Bureaux de la Revue, 1933–41.

Stephen of Lexington. *Letters from Ireland, 1228–1229.* Translated by Barry W. O. Dwyer. Kalamazoo, MI: Cistercian Publications, 1982.

———. "Registrum epistolarum Stephani de Lexinton abbatis de Stanlegia et de Savigniaco." Edited by Bruno Griesser. *Analecta Sacri Ordinis Cisterciensis* 2 (1946): 1–118; 8 (1952): 181–378.

Stephen of Obazine. *Vie de Saint Etienne d'Obazine.* Edited by Michel Aubrun. Clermont-Ferrand: Institut d'Études du Massif Central, 1970. Recent English edition in *Lives of Monastic Reformers, 1: Robert of La Chaise-Dieu and Stephen of Obazine.* Introduced and translated by Hugh Feiss, Maureen M. O'Brien, and Ronald Pepin. Trappist, KY: Cistercian Publications; Collegeville, MN: Liturgical Press, 2010.

"The Tract on the Conversion of Pons de Léras and the True Account of the Beginning of the Monastery at Silvanès." Translated by Beverly Mayne Kienzle in *Medieval Hagiography: An Anthology,* edited by Thomas Head, pp. 495–513. New York: Routledge, 2001. Latin text is available in *Cartulaire de l'abbaye de Silvanès.*

Twelfth-Century Statutes from the Cistercian General Chapter: Latin Text with English Notes and Commentary. Edited by Chrysogonus Waddell. Brecht, Belgium: Cîteaux, Commentarii cistercienses, 2002.

SECONDARY SOURCES

Abbayes et prieurés de l'ancienne France. Edited by Dom Beaunier and Jean-Martial Besse. 4 vols. Paris, 1910. Additional entries follow in *Archives de la France monastique* and *Revue Mabillon.*

Adaine, Jean-Luc. "Le domaine de l'abbaye royale et cistercienne de Maubuisson: Essai d'Inventaire Archéologique." Master's thesis, University of Paris, 1992.

Adamo, Phillip C. *New Monks in Old Habits: The Formation of the Caulite Monastic Order, 1193–1267.* Toronto: Pontifical Institute of Mediaeval Studies, 2014.

Ahlers, Gerd. *Weibliches Zisterziensertum im Mittelalter und seine Klöster in Niedersachsen.* Berlin: Lukas-Verlag, 2002.

Allirot, A. H. "Longchamp et Lourcine, deux abbayes féminines dans la construction de la mémoire capétienne (fin XIIIe–première moitié du XIVe siècle)." *Revue d'histoire d'église de France* 94 (2008): 23–38.

Amt, Emilie. "Making Their Mark: The Spectrum of Literacy Among Godstow's Nuns, 1400–1550." In *Nuns' Literacies in Medieval Europe: The Kansas City Dialogue,* edited by Virginia Blanton, Veronica O'Mara, and Patricia Stoop, pp. 307–25. Turnhout: Brepols, 2015.

Armstrong-Partida, Michelle. *Defiant Priests: Domestic Unions, Violence, and Clerical Masculinity in Fourteenth-Century Catalunya.* Ithaca, NY: Cornell University Press, 2017.

———. "Mothers and Daughters as Lords: The Countesses of Blois and Chartres." *Medieval Prosopography* 26 (2005): 77–107.

———. "Priestly Wives: The Role and Acceptance of Clerics' Concubines in the Parishes of Late Medieval Catalunya." *Speculum* 88 (2013): 166–214.

Arnold, Ellen F. *Negotiating the Landscape: Environment and Monastic Identity in the Medieval Ardennes.* Philadelphia: University of Pennsylvania Press, 2013.

Aubert, Marcel. *L'architecture cistercienne en France.* 2 vols. Paris: Vanoest, 1947.

Aurell, Martin. "Les Cisterciennes et leurs protecteurs en Provence rhodanniene." In *Les Cisterciens de Languedoc (XIIIe–XIVe s.),* pp. 235–67. Cahiers de Fanjeaux 21. Toulouse: Privat, 1986.

————. *Une famille de la noblesse provençale au Moyen Age: Les Porcelet.* Avignon: Aubanel, 1986.

Avril, Joseph. "Les fondations, l'organisation et l'évolution des établissements de moniales dans le diocèse d'Angers." In *Les religieuses en France au XIIIe siècle*, edited by Michel Parisse, pp. 27–67. Nancy: Presses Universitaires de Nancy, 1985.

————. "Le IIIe Concile du Latran et les communautés de lépreux." *Revue Mabillon* 60 (1981): 21–76.

Baldwin, John W. *The Government of Philip Augustus: Foundations of French Royal Power in the Middle Ages.* Berkeley: University of California Press, 1986.

————. *Paris, 1200.* Stanford, CA: Stanford University Press, 2010.

Barrière, Bernadette. *L'abbaye cistercienne d'Obazine en Bas-Limousin: Les origines, le Patrimoine.* With preface by Charles Higounet. Tulle: Conseil Générale de la Corrèze, 1977.

————. "The Cistercian Convent of Coyroux in the Twelfth and Thirteenth Centuries." In "Monastic Architecture for Women," special issue, *Gesta* 31, no. 2 (1992): 76–82.

————. "Les Cisterciens d'Obazine en Bas-Limousin (Corrèze, France): Les transformations du milieu naturel." In *L'hydraulique monastique: Milieux, réseaux, usages*, edited by Léon Pressouyre, Paul Benoît, Armelle Bonis, and Monique Wabont, pp. 13–33. Paris: Créaphis, 1996.

Barrière, Bernadette, Marie-Élizabeth Henneau, Armelle Bonis, Sylvie Dechavanne, and Monique Wabont, eds. *Cîteaux et les femmes: Actes des rencontres de Royaumont.* Paris: Créaphis, 2001.

Baury, Ghislain. *Les religieuses de Castille: Patronage aristocratique et ordre cistercien, XIIe–XIIIe siècles.* With preface by Adeline Rucquoi. Rennes: Presses Universitaires de Rennes, 2012.

Becquart, Noel. "Notre-Dame-des-Prés, abbaye cistercienne au diocèse de Troyes." Diss., École des chartes, Paris, 1945.

Bedos-Rezak, Brigitte Miriam. *La Châtellenie de Montmorency des origines à 1368: Aspects féodaux, sociaux et économiques.* Pontoise: Société historique et archéologique de Pontoise, du Val-d'Oise et du Vexin, 1980.

————. *When Ego Was Imago: Signs of Identity in the Middle Ages.* Leiden: Brill, 2010.

Bell, David N. "La Charité-lès-Lézinnes." In *Les Cisterciens dans l'Yonne*, edited by Terryl N. Kinder, pp. 159–62. Pontigny: Amis de Pontigny, 1999.

————. "Vins et vignobles cisterciens de l'Yonne." In *Les Cisterciens dans l'Yonne*, edited by Terryl N. Kinder, pp. 73–82. Pontigny: Amis de Pontigny, 1999.

Benoît, Paul, and Monique Wabont. "Mittelalterliche Wasserversorgung in Frankreich; Eine Fallstudie: Die Zisterziener." In *Die Wasserversorgung im Mittelalter*, edited by Klaus Grewe, pp. 185–226. Vol. 4 of the *Geschichte der Wasserversorgung*. Mainz, 1991.

Berger, Élie. *Histoire de Blanche de Castille, reine de France.* Paris: Thorin, 1895.

Bériou, Nicole. *L'avènement des maîtres de la parole: La prédication à Paris au XIIIe siècle.* 2 vols. Paris: Institut d'études augustiniennes, 1998.

————. "Les lépreux sous le regard des prédicateurs d'après les collections de sermons ad status du XIIIème siècle." In *Voluntate dei leprosus: Les lépreux entre conversion et exclusion aux XIIème et XIIIème siècles*, edited by Nicole Bériou and François-Olivier Touati, pp. 33–80. Spoleto: Centro italiano di studi sull'alto Medioevo, 1991.

Berkhofer, Robert F., III. "The Canterbury Forgeries Revisited." *Haskins Society Journal* 18 (2006): 36–50.

————. *Day of Reckoning: Power and Accountability in Medieval France.* Philadelphia: University of Pennsylvania Press, 2004.

Berlow, Rosalind Kent. "The Development of Business Techniques Used at the Fairs of Champagne from the End of the Twelfth Century to the Middle of the Thirteenth Century." *Studies in Medieval and Renaissance History* 8 (1971): 3–31.

Berman, Constance H. "Abbeys for Cistercian Nuns in the Ecclesiastical Province of Sens: Foundation, Endowment and Economic Activities of the Earlier Foundations." *Revue Mabillon* 73 (1997): 83–113.

———. "Les acquisitions rurales des abbayes cisterciennes féminines en l'Ile-de-France." *Paris et Île-de-France: Mémoires* 48 (1997): 113–20.

———. "Beyond the Rule of Saint Benedict: The Imposition of Cistercian Customs and Enclosure on Nuns in the Twelfth and Thirteenth Centuries." *Magistra: A Journal of Feminine Spirituality in History* 13 (2007): 3–40.

———. "Cistercian Agriculture in Female Houses of Northern France, 1200–1300." In *Crisis in the Later Middle Ages: Beyond the Postan-Duby Paradigm*, edited by John Drendel, pp. 339–63. Turnhout: Brepols, 2014.

———. "Cistercian Development and the Order's Acquisition of Churches and Tithes in Southern France." *Revue bénédictine* 91 (1981): 193–203.

———. *The Cistercian Evolution: The Invention of a Religious Order in Twelfth-Century Europe.* 2000. Reprint, Philadelphia: University of Pennsylvania Press, 2010.

———. "Cistercian Nuns and the Development of the Order: The Abbey of Saint-Antoine-des-Champs Outside Paris." In *The Joy of Learning and the Love of God: Essays in Honor of Jean Leclercq, OSB*, edited by E. Rozanne Elder, pp. 121–56. Kalamazoo: Cistercian Publications, 1995.

———. "Cistercian Women and Tithes." *Cîteaux* 49 (1998): 95–128.

———. "Distinguishing Between the Humble Peasant Lay Brother and Sister and the Converted Knight in Medieval Southern France." In *Religious and Laity in Western Europe, 1000–1400: Interaction, Negotiation, and Power*, edited by Emilia Jamroziak and Janet Burton, pp. 263–83. Turnhout: Brepols, 2006.

———. "Dowries, Private Income, and Anniversary Masses: The Nuns of Saint-Antoine-des-Champs (Paris)." *Proceedings of the Western Society for French History* 20 (1993): 3–20.

———. "Fashions in Monastic Patronage: The Popularity of Supporting Cistercian Abbeys for Women." *Proceedings of the Western Society for French History* 17 (1990): 36–45.

———. "Gender at the Medieval Millennium." In *The Oxford Handbook of Gender in Medieval Europe*, edited by Judith M. Bennett and Ruth Mazzo Karras, pp. 545–60. Oxford: Oxford University Press, 2013.

———. "Les granges cisterciennes fortifiées du Rouergue." *Les Cahiers de la Ligue Urbaine et Rurale; Patrimoine et Cadre de Vie* 109 (1990): 54–65. Originally published in *The Medieval Castle. Romance and Reality*, edited by Kathryn Reyerson. Dubuque, IA: Kendall and Hunt, 1984.

———. "How Much Space Did Medieval Nuns Have or Need?" In *Shaping Community: The Art and Archaeology of Monasticism; Papers from a Symposium Held at the Frederick R. Weisman Museum at the University of Minnesota, March 10–12, 2000*, edited by Sheila McNally, pp. 100–116. BAR International Series 941. Oxford: Archaeopress, 2001.

———. "The 'Labours of Hercules,' the Cartulary, Church and Abbey for Nuns of La Cour-Notre-Dame-de-Michery." *Journal of Medieval History* 26 (2000): 33–70.

———. "The Life of Pons de Léras: Knights and Conversion to the Religious Life in the Twelfth Century." *Church History and Religious Culture* 88 (2008): 119–37.

———. *Medieval Agriculture, the Southern French Countryside, and the Early Cistercians: A Study of Forty-Three Monasteries*. Philadelphia: American Philosophical Society, 1986.

———. "Men's Houses, Women's Houses: The Relationship Between the Sexes in Twelfth-Century Monasticism." In *The Medieval Monastery*, edited by Andrew MacLeish, pp. 43–52. St. Cloud, MN: North Star Press, 1988.

———. "Monastic Hospices in Southern France: The Cistercian Urban Presence." *Revue d'histoire ecclésiastique* 101 (2007): 747–74.

———. "Noble Women's Power as Reflected in the Foundations of Cistercian Houses for Nuns." In *Negotiating Community and Difference in Medieval Europe*, edited by Katherine Allen Smith and Scott Wells, pp. 137–49. Leiden: Brill, 2009.

———. "A Thirteenth-Century Coin Hoard Found in the Collection of the American Numismatic Society and a Penny from the Cluniac Priory of Souvigny." *Trésors monétaires* 8 (1986): 115–27 and plate 41.

———. "Two Medieval Women's Control of Property and Religious Benefactions in France: Eleanor of Vermandois and Blanche of Castile." *Viator* 41 (2010): 151–82.

———. "Were There Twelfth-Century Cistercian Nuns?" *Church History* 68 (1999): 824–64.

———. *Women and Monasticism in Medieval Europe: Sisters and Patrons of the Cistercian Order*. Kalamazoo: TEAMS, 2002.

———. "Women's Work in Family, Village and Town After AD 1000: Contributions to Economic Growth?" *Journal of Women's History* 19 (2007): 10–32.

Berman, Constance H., and Caroline A. Bruzelius. "Introduction." In "Monastic Architecture for Women," special issue, *Gesta* 31, no. 2 (1992): 73–75.

Bezant, Jemma. "Revising the Monastic 'Grange': Problems at the Edge of the Cistercian World." *Journal of Medieval Monastic Studies* 3 (2014): 51–70.

Bitel, Lisa M. *Isle of the Saints: Monastic Settlement and Christian Community in Early Ireland*. Ithaca, NY: Cornell University Press, 1990.

———. *Land of Women: Tales of Men and Gender from Early Ireland*. Ithaca, NY: Cornell University Press, 1998.

———. *Landscape with Two Saints: How Genovefa of Paris and Brigit of Kildare Built Christianity in Barbarian Europe*. New York: Oxford University Press, 2009.

Blanton, Virginia, Veronica O'Mara, and Patricia Stoop, eds. *Nuns' Literacies in Medieval Europe: The Hull Dialogue*. Turnhout: Brepols, 2013.

———. *Nuns' Literacies in Medieval Europe: The Kansas City Dialogue*. Turnhout: Brepols, 2015, and forthcoming Antwerp vol., 2017.

Blary, François. *Le domaine de Châalis, XIIe–XIVe siècles: Approches archéologiques des établissements agricoles et industriels d'une abbaye cistercienne*. Mémoires de la Section d'archéologie et d'histoire de l'art 3. Paris: Éditions du CTHS, 1989.

Blumenthal, Uta-Renate. *The Investiture Controversy: Church and Monarchy from the Ninth to the Twelfth Century*. Philadelphia: University of Pennsylvania Press, 1991.

Böhringer, Letha, Jennifer Kolpacoff Deane, and Hildo van Engen, eds. *Labels and Libels: Naming Beguines in Northern Medieval Europe*. Turnhout: Brepols, 2014.

Bois, Guy. *Crise du féodalisme: Économie rurale et démographie en Normandie orientale du début du 14e siècle au milieu du 16e siècle*. Paris: Presses de la Fondation nationale des sciences politiques; Éditions de l'école des hautes études en sciences sociales, 1976.

Bondéelle-Souchier, Anne. "Les moniales cisterciennes et leurs livres manuscrits dans la France d'Ancien Régime." *Cîteaux* 45 (1994): 193–337.

Bonis, Armelle. *Abbaye cistercienne de Maubuisson (Saint-Ouen-l'Aumône, Val-d'Oise): La formation du temporel, 1236 à 1356.* Saint-Ouen-l' Aumône: Conseil général du Val-d'Oise, Service départemental d'archéologie du Val-d'Oise, 1990.

Bonis, Armelle, and Monique Wabont. "Île-de-France monastique au Moyen âge: Conformité ou singularité des fondations cisterciennes?" In *Cîteaux et les femmes*, ed. Bernadette Barrière et al., pp. 19–34. Paris: Créaphis, 2001.

Bonnardot, Hippolyte. *L'abbaye royale de Saint-Antoine-des-Champs de l'ordre de Cîteaux: Étude topographique et historique.* Paris: Féchoz et Letouzey, 1882.

[Bonnin, Theodore?]. "Lettres de Saint Louis, constatant les adieux que le roi fit aux religieuses de Maubuisson en partant pour la Croisade, mars 1270." *Bibliothèque de l'École des Chartes* 17 (1857): 365, no. 13.

Borlée, Denise. "L'architecture des abbayes cisterciennes de l'Yonne: État des lieux et hypothèses." In *Les Cisterciens dans l'Yonne*, edited by Terryl N. Kinder, pp. 29–39. Pontigny: Amis de Pontigny, 1999.

———. "La Cour Notre-Dame." In *Les Cisterciens dans l'Yonne*, edited by Terryl N. Kinder, pp. 173–78. Pontigny: Amis de Pontigny, 1999.

Bouchard, Constance Brittain. *Holy Entrepreneurs: Cistercians, Knights, and Economic Exchange in Twelfth-Century Burgundy.* Ithaca, NY: Cornell University Press, 1991.

Bourgeois, Giselle. "Les granges et l'économie de l'abbaye de Nonenque au Moyen Âge." *Cîteaux* 24 (1973): 139–60.

Bourin-Derreau, Monique. *Village Médiévaux en Bas-Languedoc: Genèse d'une sociabilité (Xe–XIVe siècle).* 2 vols. Paris: L'Harmattan, 1987.

Bouton, Jean de la Croix. "L'Abbaye de Bonlieu." In *Mélanges à la mémoire du père Anselme Dimier*, edited by Benoît Chauvin, part 2, vol. 4, pp. 449–61. Arbois: B. Chauvin, 1982–87.

———. "L'établissement des moniales cisterciennes." *Mémoires de la Société pour l'histoire du droit et des institutions des anciens pays bourguignons, comtois, et romands* 15 (1953): 83–116.

———. "Saint Bernard et les moniales." In *Mélanges Saint Bernard: XXIVe Congrès de l'Association bourguignonne des sociétés savantes (8e Centenaire de la mort de Saint Bernard), Dijon, 1953*, pp. 225–47. Dijon: Marlier, 1954.

Bouton, Jean de la Croix, Benoît Chauvin, and Elisabeth Grosjean. "L'abbaye de Tart et ses filiales au moyen âge." In *Mélanges à la mémoire du père Anselme Dimier*, edited by Benoît Chauvin, part 2, vol. 3, pp. 19–61. Arbois: B. Chauvin, 1982–87.

Bove, Boris. *Dominer la ville: Prévôts des marchands et échevins parisiens de 1260 à 1350.* Paris: CTHS, 2004.

Boyd, Catherine E. *A Cistercian Nunnery in Mediaeval Italy: The Story of Rifreddo in Saluzzo, 1220–1300.* Cambridge, MA: Harvard University Press, 1943.

Branner, Robert. *St. Louis and the Court Style in Gothic Architecture.* London: A. Zwemmer, 1965.

Bredero, Adriaan H. *Bernard of Clairvaux: Between Cult and History.* Grand Rapids, MI: William B. Eerdmans, 1997.

Brenner, Elma. "Recent Perspectives on Leprosy in Medieval Western Europe." *History Compass* 8, no. 5 (2010): 388–406.

Brown, Peter. *Through the Eye of a Needle: Wealth, the Fall of Rome, and the Making of Christianity in the West, 350–550 AD.* Princeton, NJ: Princeton University Press, 2012.

Brundage, James. *Law, Sex, and Christian Society in Medieval Europe.* Chicago: University of Chicago Press, 1987.

Bruzelius, Caroline A. "Cistercian High Gothic: The Abbey Church of Longpont and the Architecture of the Cistercians in the Early Thirteenth Century." *Analecta Cisterciensia* 35 (1979): 1–154.

———. "Hearing Is Believing: Clarissan Architecture, ca. 1213–1340." In "Monastic Architecture for Women," special issue, *Gesta* 31, no. 2 (1992): 83–91.

———. *The Stones of Naples: Church Building in Angevin Italy.* New Haven, CT: Yale University Press, 2004.

———. *The Thirteenth-Century Church at St-Denis.* New Haven, CT: Yale University Press, 1985.

———. "The Twelfth-Century Church at Ourscamp." *Speculum* 56 (1981): 28–40.

Burton, Janet. *The Foundation History of the Abbeys of Byland and Jervaulx.* Borthwick Texts and Studies 35. York: University of York, 2006.

———. "Medieval Nunneries and Male Authority: Female Monasteries in England and Wales." *Women in the Medieval Monastic World,* edited. by Janet Burton and Karen Stöber, pp. 123–43. Turnhout: Brepols, 2015.

———. *The Yorkshire Nunneries in the Twelfth and Thirteenth Centuries.* Borthwick Papers, no. 56. York: University of York, Borthwick Institute of Historical Research, 1979.

Buczek, Daniel S. "Medieval Taxation: The French Crown, the Papacy and the Cistercian Order." *Analecta Cisterciensia* 25 (1969): 42–106.

Bynum, Caroline Walker. *Jesus as Mother: Studies in the Spirituality of the High Middle Ages.* Berkeley: University of California Press, 1982.

———. *Wonderful Blood: Theology and Practice in Late Medieval Northern Germany and Beyond.* Philadelphia: University of Pennsylvania Press, 2007.

Caby, Cécile. "Cisterciens en Italie septentrionale: Un nouvel éclairage historiographique." *Revue Mabillon* 13 (2002): 303–7.

Canivez, J.-M. "Cadouin." In *Dictionnaire d'histoire et de géographie ecclésiastiques,* edited by Alfred Baudrillart et al., 11:118–22. Paris: Letouzey et Ané, 1949.

Carbonell-Lamothe, Yvonne. "L'abbaye du Vignogoul." In *Les Cisterciens de Languedoc (XIIIe–XIVe s.),* pp. 269–81. Cahiers de Fanjeaux 21. Toulouse: Privat, 1986.

Carolus-Barré, Louis. "L'abbaye de la Joie-Notre-Dame à Berneuil-sur-Aisne (1234–1430)." In *Mélanges à la mémoire du père Anselme Dimier,* edited by Benoît Chauvin, part 2, vol. 4, pp. 487–504. Arbois: B. Chauvin, 1984.

Carpenter, Jennifer. "Juette of Huy, Recluse and Mother (1158–1228): Children and Mothering in the Saintly Life." In *Power of the Weak: Studies on Medieval Women,* edited by Jennifer Carpenter and Sally-Beth MacLean, pp. 57–93. Urbana: University of Illinois Press, 1995.

Les cartulaires: Actes de la table ronde organisée par l'École nationale des chartes et le G.D.R. 121 du C.N.R.S. Edited by Olivier Guyotjeannin, Laurent Morelle, and Michel Parisse. Paris: École des Chartes, 1993.

Cassidy-Welch, Megan. *Monastic Spaces and Their Meanings: Thirteenth-Century English Cistercian Monasteries.* Turnhout: Brepols, 2008.

Cawley, Martinus. "Four Abbots of the Golden Age of Villers." *Cistercian Studies Quarterly* 27 (1992): 299–328.

Cevins, Marie-Madeleine de. "Les implantations cisterciennes en Hongrie Médiévale: Un réseau?" In *Unanimité et diversité cisterciennes,* edited by Nicole Bouter, pp. 453–84. Saint-Étienne: CERCOR, 2000.

Chapin, Elizabeth. Les villes de foires de Champagne, des origines au *début du XIVe siècle.* Geneva: Slatkine Reprints, 1976.

Chauvin, Benoît. "L'intégration des femmes à l'ordre de Cîteaux au XIIe s. entre hauts de Meuse et rives du Léman." In *Cîteaux et les femmes*, edited by Bernadette Barrière et al., pp. 192–212. Paris: Créaphis, 2001.

———, ed. *Mélanges à la mémoire du père Anselme Dimier*. 6 vols in 3. Arbois: B. Chauvin, 1982–87.

———. "Papauté et abbayes cisterciennes du duché de Bourgogne." In *L'église de France et la Papauté (Xe–XIIIe siècle) = Die französische Kirche und das Papsttum (10.–13. Jahrhundert): Actes du XXVIe Colloque historique franco-allemand organisé en coopération avec l'École nationale des chartes par l'Institut historique allemand de Paris (Paris, 17–19 octobre 1990)*, edited by Rolf Grosse, pp. 326–62. Études et documents pour servir à une *Gallia Pontificia*. Bonn: Bouvier, 1993.

Chédeville, André. *Chartres et ses campagnes (XIe–XIIIe s.)*. Paris: Klincksieck, 1973.

Cheney, C. R. *Episcopal Visitation of Monasteries in the Thirteenth Century*. Manchester: Manchester University Press, 1931.

Chibnall, Marjorie. "'Clio's Legal Cosmetics': Law and Custom in the Work of Medieval Historians." In *Anglo-Norman Studies XX: Proceedings of the Battle Conference, 1997*, edited by Christopher Harper-Bill, pp. 31–43. Woodbridge: Boydell, 1998.

———. *The Empress Matilda: Queen Consort, Queen Mother and Lady of the English*. Oxford: Blackwell, 1991.

Christianson, Karen Ann. "Female Leadership and Male Submission: The Order of Fontevraud in Twelfth-Century France." PhD diss., University of Iowa, May 2009.

Cochelin, Isabelle. "Sainteté laïque: L'exemple de Juette de Huy." *Le Moyen Age* 95 (1989): 397–417.

Cohen, Meredith. "Metropolitan Architecture, Demographics, and the Urban Identity of Paris in the Thirteenth Century." In *Cities, Texts, and Social Networks, 400–1500: Experiences and Perceptions of Medieval Urban Space*, edited by Caroline Goodson, Anne E. Lester, and Carol Symes, pp. 65–100. Burlington, VT: Ashgate, 2010.

Collège des Bernardins, Paris. Website, accessed March 31, 2017. https://www.collegedesbernardins.fr/a-propos/huit-siecles-dhistoire.

Colvin, Howard. *The History of the King's Works*. 4 vols. London, HMSO, 1963.

Companion to Bernard of Clairvaux. Edited by Brian P. McGuire. Leiden: Brill, 2011.

Conner, Elizabeth. "The Abbeys of Las Huelgas and Tart and Their Filiations." In *Hidden Springs: Cistercian Monastic Women*, vol. 3, bk. 1, of *Medieval Religious Women*, edited by John A. Nichols and Lillian Thomas Shank, pp. 29–48. Kalamazoo, MI: Cistercian Publications, 1995.

Constable, Giles. "Forgery and Plagiarism in the Middle Ages." *Archiv für Diplomatik, Schriftgeschichte, Siegel- und Wappenkunde* 29 (1983): 1–41.

———. *Monastic Tithes: From Their Origins to the Twelfth Century*. Cambridge: Cambridge University Press, 1964.

———. *The Reformation of the Twelfth Century*. Cambridge: Cambridge University Press, 1996.

Cottineau, L. H., ed. *Répertoire topo-bibliographique des abbayes et prieurés*. 2 vols and supplément. Mâcon: Protat frères, 1935–39.

Courtet, René. "Histoire de l'abbaye des Iles, anciennement de Celles." *Bulletin de la société des sciences historiques et naturelles de l'Yonne* 120 (1988): 47–69.

Couvret, Anne-Marie. "Charte de Jean de Dampierre pour l'abbaye Notre-Dame de Saint-Dizier." *Cahiers Haut-Marnais* 131 (1977): 157–59.

Cowdrey, H. E. J. "Archbishop Aribert II of Milan." *History* 51, no. 171 (1966): 1–15.

Cray, Susan. "Matilda the Great, Countess of Auxerre, Nevers, and Tonnerre." Undergraduate honors thesis, University of Iowa, 1990.

Davis, Michael T. "Cistercians in the City: The Church of the *Collège Saint-Bernard* in Paris." In *Perspectives for an Architecture of Solitude: Essays on Cistercians, Art and Architecture in Honour of Peter Fergusson*, edited by Terryl N. Kinder, pp. 223–34. Turnhout: Brepols/ Cîteaux, 2004.

Degler-Spengler, Brigitte. "Die Zisterzienserinnen in der Schweiz." *Cistercienser-Chronik* 94 (1987): 124–32.

———. "Einleitung: Die Zisterzienserinnen in der Schweiz." *Helvetia Sacra* (Bern) 3 (1982): 507–74.

———. "The Incorporation of Cistercian Nuns into the Order in the Twelfth and Thirteenth Century." In *Hidden Springs: Cistercian Monastic Women*, vol. 3, bk. 1 of *Medieval Religious Women*, edited by John A. Nichols and Lillian Thomas Shank, pp. 85–134. Kalamazoo, MI: Cistercian Publications, 1995.

Delaforge-Marchand, Sandrine. "Édition du chartrier de l'abbaye de Saint-Antoine-des-Champs (1191–1256)." *École nationale des chartes: Positions de thèses de la promotion, 1994*. Paris, 1994.

Denifle, Henri [Heinrich]. *La désolation des églises, monastères, et hôpitaux en France pendant la guerre de cent ans*. 2 vols. in 3. Paris: Picard, 1897–99.

Desmarchelier, Michel. "L'architecture des églises de moniales cisterciennes: Essai de classement des différents types de plan (en guise de suite)." In *Mélanges à la mémoire du père Anselme Dimier*, edited by Benoît Chauvin, part 3, vol. 5, pp. 79–121. Arbois: B. Chauvin, 1982–87.

Dimier, Anselme. "L'architecture des églises de moniales cisterciennes." *Cîteaux* 25 (1974): 8–23.

———. "Chapitres généraux d'abbesses cisterciennes." *Cîteaux* 11 (1960): 268–73.

———. *Saint Louis et Cîteaux*. Paris: Letouzey et Ané, 1954.

Dimier, Anselme, and R. H. Delabrouille. *Notre-Dame-du-Lys*. Paris: Nouvelles éditions latines, 1987.

Diwo, Jean. *Les Dames du Faubourg*. Paris: Noël, 1984.

Donkin, R. A. *The Cistercians: Studies in the Geography of Medieval England and Wales*. Toronto: Pontifical Institute of Mediaeval Studies, 1978.

Donnelly, James S. *The Decline of the Medieval Cistercian Laybrotherhood*. New York: Fordham University Press, 1949.

Duba, William, and Chris Schabel. "A Documentary History of St Theodore Abbey." In *A Cistercian Nunnery in the Latin East: The History and Archaeology of St Theodore Abbey, Nicosia, Cyprus*, edited by M. Olympios and C. Schabel. Leiden: Brill, forthcoming.

Duby, Georges. *The Early Growth of the European Economy: Warriors and Peasants from the Seventh to the Twelfth Century*. Translated by Howard B. Clarke. Ithaca, NY: Cornell University Press, 1974.

———. *The Knight, the Lady and the Priest: The Making of Modern Marriage in Medieval France*. Translated by Barbara Bray. New York: Pantheon Books, 1983.

———. *Rural Economy and Country Life in the Medieval West*. Translated by Cynthia Postan. Columbia: University of South Carolina Press, 1968.

———. *The Three Orders: Feudal Society Imagined*. Translated by Arthur Goldhammer. Introduction by Thomas N. Bisson. Chicago: University of Chicago Press, 1982.

Duclos, H. *Histoire de Royaumon: Sa fondation par Saint Louis et son influence sur la France*. 2 vols. Paris: Ch. Douniol, 1867.

Du faubourg Saint-Antoine au bois de Vincennes: Promenade historique dans le 12e arrondissement; Exposition organisée par le Musée Carnavalet et la délégation à l'action artistique de la ville de Paris; Mairie annexe du 12e arrondissement 26 janvier–20 février et 19 mars–20 avril 1983; Musée Carnavalet, 26 avril–5 juin 1983. Exhibition catalog. Paris: Musées de la Ville de Paris, 1983.

Dupré, A. "Les Comtesses de Chartres et de Blois: Étude historique." *Mémoires de la Société archéologique d'Eure et Loir* 5 (1872): 224–27.

Dutilleux, A. *Notice sur l'abbaye de Joyenval.* Versailles: Cerf, 1891.

Duval-Arnould, Louis. "Les aumônes d'Aliénor, dernière comtesse de Vermandois et dame de Valois." *Revue Mabillon* 60 (1984): 395–463.

Egbert, Virginia Wylie. *On the Bridges of Mediaeval Paris: A Record of Early Fourteenth-Century Life.* Princeton, NJ: Princeton University Press, 1974.

Elkins, Sharon K. *Holy Women of Twelfth-Century England.* Chapel Hill: University of North Carolina Press, 1988.

Elliott, Dyan. "Alternative Intimacies: Men, Women, and Spiritual Direction in the Twelfth Century." In *Christina of Markyate*, edited by Samuel Fanous and Henrietta Leyser, pp. 160–83. New York: Routledge, 2004.

———. *Fallen Bodies: Pollution, Sexuality, and Demonology in the Middle Ages.* Philadelphia: University of Pennsylvania Press, 1999.

Erlande-Brandenburg, Alain. "Le tombeau de coeur de Blanche de Castille à l'abbaye du Lys." In *Art et architecture à Melun au Moyen Age*, edited by Yves Gallet, pp. 255–57. Paris: Picard, 2000.

Espace et Territoire au Moyen Âge: Hommages à Bernadette Barrière. Edited by Luc Ferran. Bordeaux, 2012.

Evergates, Theodore. *The Aristocracy in the County of Champagne, 1100–1300.* Philadelphia: University of Pennsylvania Press, 2007.

———, ed. *Aristocratic Women in Medieval France.* Philadelphia: University of Pennsylvania Press, 1999.

———. "Aristocratic Women in the County of Champagne." In *Aristocratic Women in Medieval France*, edited by Theodore Evergates, pp. 74–110. Philadelphia: University of Pennsylvania Press, 1999.

———. *Feudal Society in the Bailliage of Troyes Under the Counts of Champagne, 1132–1284.* Baltimore, MD: Johns Hopkins University Press, 1975.

Fanous, Samuel, and Henrietta Leyser, eds. *Christina of Markyate: A Twelfth-Century Holy Woman.* New York: Routledge, 2004.

Farmer, Sharon. "The Leper in the Master Bedroom: Thinking Through a Thirteenth-Century Exemplum." *Framing the Family: Narrative and Representation in the Medieval and Early Modern Periods*, edited by R. Voaden and D. Wolfthal, pp. 79–100. Tempe: Arizona Center for Medieval and Renaissance Studies, 2005.

———. *The Silk Industries of Medieval Paris: Artisanal Migration, Technological Innovation, and Gendered Experience.* Philadelphia: University of Pennsylvania Press, 2017.

———. *Surviving Poverty in Medieval Paris: Gender, Ideology and the Daily Lives of the Poor.* Ithaca, NY: Cornell University Press, 2002.

Field, Sean L. *The Beguine, the Angel, and the Inquisitor: The Trials of Marguerite Porete and Guiard of Cressonessart.* Notre Dame, IN: Notre Dame University Press, 2012.

———. *Isabelle of France: Capetian Sanctity and Franciscan Identity in the Thirteenth Century.* Notre Dame, IN: University of Notre Dame Press, 2006.

Field, Sean L., and M. Cecilia Gaposchkin. "Questioning the Capetians, 1180–1328." *History Compass* 12 (2014): 567–85.

Fiero, Gloria, Wendy Pfeffer, and Mathé Allain, eds. *Three Medieval Views of Women: "La Contenance des Fame," "Le Bien de Fames," "Le Blasme de Fames."* New Haven, CT: Yale University Press, 1989.

Flamare, H de. "La charte de départ pour la Terre-Sainte de Gaucher de Châtillon, baron de Donzy." *Bulletin de la Société nivernaise des lettres, sciences et arts* 13 (1886–89): 174–82.

Fontette, Micheline de. *Les religieuses à l'âge classique du droit canon: Recherches sur les structures juridiques des branches féminines des ordres.* Paris: J. Vrin, 1967.

Foot, Sarah. *Veiled Women.* 2 vols. Aldershot: Ashgate, 2000.

Fossier, Robert. "L'économie cistercienne dans les plaines du nord-ouest d'Europe." In *L'économie cistercienne: Géographie—Mutations du Moyen Age aux temps modernes,* pp. 53–74. Flaran 3. Auch: Comité départemental du tourisme du Gers, 1983.

———. *La terre et les hommes en Picardie jusqu'à la fin du XIIIe siècle.* Paris: Nauwelaerts, 1968.

Fourquin, Guy. *Les Campagnes de la région parisienne à la fin du Moyen Âge.* Paris: Presses Universitaires de France, 1964.

Freed, John. "Urban Development and the 'Cura Monialium' in Thirteenth-Century Germany." *Viator* 3 (1972): 311–27.

Freeman, Elizabeth F. "Cistercian Nuns in Medieval England: The Gendering of Geographic Marginalization." *Medieval Feminist Forum* 43 (2008): 26–39.

Gajewsky-Kennedy, Alexandra. "Recherches sur l'architecture cistercienne et le pouvoir royal: Blanche de Castille et la construction de l'abbaye du Lys." In *Art et architecture à Melun au Moyen Age,* edited by Yves Gallet, pp. 223–54. Paris: Picard, 2000.

Galbraith, Vivian H. "Monastic Foundation Charters of the Eleventh and Twelfth Centuries." *Cambridge Historical Journal* 4 (1934): 205–25.

Ganck, Roger, de. "The Cistercian Nuns of Belgium in the Thirteenth Century Seen Against the Background of the Second Wave of Cistercian Spirituality." *Cistercian Studies* 5 (1970): 169–87.

———. "The Integration of Nuns in the Cistercian Order Particularly in Belgium." *Cîteaux* 35 (1984): 235–37.

———. "The Three Foundations of Bartholomew of Tienen." *Cîteaux* 37 (1986): 49–75.

Gaposchkin, M. Cecilia. *The Making of Saint Louis: Kingship, Sanctity, and Crusade in the Later Middle Ages.* Ithaca, NY: Cornell University Press, 2008.

Garsonnin, Maurice. *Histoire de l'Hôpital Saint-Antoine et de ses origines: Étude topographique, historique et statistique.* Paris: Henri Jouve, 1891.

Gayoso, Andrea. "The Lady of Las Huelgas: A Royal Abbey and Its Patronage." *Cîteaux* 51 (2000): 91–115.

Gilchrist, Roberta. *Gender and Material Culture: The Archaeology of Religious Women.* London: Routledge, 1994.

Gill, Katherine. "*Scandala*: Controversies Concerning *Clausura* and Women's Religious Communities in Late Medieval Italy." In *Christendom and Its Discontents: Exclusion, Persecution, and Rebellion, 1000–1500,* edited by Scott L. Waugh and Peter D. Diehl, pp. 177–203. Cambridge: Cambridge University Press, 1996.

Gimpel, Jean. *The Medieval Machine: The Industrial Revolution of the Middle Ages.* New York: Holt, Rinehart and Winston, 1976.

Gold, Penny Schine. "Male/Female Cooperation: The Example of Fontevrault." In *Distant Echoes,* vol. 1 of *Medieval Religious Women,* edited by John A. Nichols and Lillian Thomas Shank, pp. 151–68. Kalamazoo: Cistercian Publications, 1984.

Golding, Brian. "Bishops and Nuns: Forms of the *cura monialium* in Twelfth- and Thirteenth-Century England." In *Women in the Medieval Monastic World*, edited by Janet Burton and Karen Stöber, pp. 97–121. Turnhout: Brepols, 2015.

————. *Gilbert of Sempringham and the Gilbertine Order c. 1130–c. 1300*. Oxford: Clarendon Press, 1995.

Gosso, Francesco. *Vita economica della abbazie piemontesi (sec. X–XIV)*. Analecta Gregoriana 22. Rome: Gregorian University, 1940.

Grant, Lindy. *Architecture and Society in Normandy, 1120–1270*. New Haven, CT: Yale University Press, 2005.

————. "Blanche of Castile and Normandy." In *Normandy and Its Neighbours, 900–1250; Essays for David Bates*, edited by David Crouch and Kathleen Thompson, pp. 117–31. Turnhout: Brepols, 2011.

————. *Blanche of Castile, Queen of France*. New Haven, CT: Yale University Press, 2016.

Graves, Coburn V. "The Economic Activities of the Cistercians in Medieval England (1128–1307)." *Analecta Sacri Ordinis Cisterciensis* 13 (1957): 3–62.

————. "English Cistercian Nuns in Lincolnshire." *Speculum* 54 (1979): 492–99.

————. "Stixwould in the Market-Place." In *Distant Echoes*, vol. 1 of *Medieval Religious Women*, edited by John A. Nichols and Lillian Thomas Shank, pp. 213–36. Kalamazoo, MI: Cistercian Publications, 1984.

Grélois, Alexis. "L'expansion cistercienne en France: La part des affiliations et des moniales." In *Norm und Realität: Kontinuität und Wandel der Zisterzienser im Mittelalter*, Vita Regularis: Ordungen und Deutungen religiosen Lebens im Mittelalter, edited by Franz J. Felten and Werner Rösener, 287–325. Berlin: Lit Verlag, 2009.

————. "Humbeline-Héloise: Variations autour de deux figures du monachisme féminin au XIIe siècle." In *Universitas scolarium: Mélanges offerts à Jacques Verger par ses anciens étudiants*, edited by Cédric Giraud and Martin Morard, pp. 329–46. Geneva: Librairie Droz, 2011.

Griffiths, Fiona. "The Cross and the *Cura Monialium*: Robert of Arbrissel, John the Evangelist, and the Pastoral Care of Women in the Age of Reform." *Speculum* 83 (2008), 303–30.

————. *The Garden of Delights: Reform and Renaissance for Women in the Twelfth Century*. Philadelphia: University of Pennsylvania Press, 2007.

————. "'Men's Duty to Provide for Women's Needs': Abelard, Heloise, and Their Negotiation of the *Cura Monialium*." *Journal of Medieval History* 30 (2004): 1–24.

Griffiths, Fiona J. and Julie Hotchin. "Women and Men in the Medieval Religious Landscape." In *Partners in Spirit: Women, Men, and Religious Life in Germany, 1100–1500*, edited by Fiona J. Griffiths and Julie Hotchin (Turnhout: Brepols, 2014), pp. 1–45.

Grundmann, Herbert. *Religious Movements in the Middle Ages: The Historical Links Between Heresy, the Mendicant Orders, and the Women's Religious Movement in the Twelfth and Thirteenth Century, with the Historical Foundations of German Mysticism*. Translated by Steven Rowan. South Bend, IN: Notre Dame University Press, 1995. Originally published as *Religiöse Bewegungen im Mittelalter: Untersuchungen über die geschichtlichen Zusammenhänge zwischen der Ketzerei, den Bettelorden, und der religiösen Frauenbewegung im 12. und 13. Jahrhundert* (Berlin: Ebering, 1935; followed by an edition with revisions made in additional chapters in 1961, identical to the edition of Darmstadt: Wissenschaftliche Buchgesellschaft, 1970).

Guyotjeannin, Olivier, Jacques Pycke, and Benoît-Michel Tock. *Diplomatique médiévale*. L'atelier du médiéviste 2. Turnhout: Brepols 1993.

Hall, Dianne. *Women and the Church in Medieval Ireland, 1140–1540.* Dublin: Four Courts Press, 2003.

Harvey, B. F. "Monastic Pittances in the Middle Ages." In *Food in Medieval England: Diet and Nutrition,* edited by C. M. Woolgar, D. Serjeantson, and T. Waldron, pp. 215–27. Oxford: Oxford University Press, 2006.

Henneau, Marie-Élisabeth, "Les Isles." In *Les Cisterciens dans l'Yonne,* edited by Terryl N. Kinder, pp. 163–71. Pontigny: Amis de Pontigny, 1999.

Herlihy, David. *Pisa in the Early Renaissance: A Study of Urban Growth.* Port Washington, NY: Kennikat Press, 1973.

———. "Treasure Hoards in the Italian Economy, 960–1139." *Economic History Review,* 2nd ser., 10 (1957): 1–14.

Hermite-Leclercq, Paulette l'. *Le monachisme féminin dans la société de son temps: Le monastérè de La Celle (XIe–début du XVIe siècle).* Paris: Cujas, 1989.

Hicks, Leonie V. *Religious Life in Normandy, 1050–1300.* Woodbridge: Boydell, 2007.

Higounet, Charles. *Défrichements et villeneuves du Bassin parisien, XIe–XIVe siècle.* Paris: CNRS, 1990.

———. *La grange de Vaulerent: Structure et exploitation d'un terroir cistercien de la plaine de France, XIIe–XVe siècle.* Paris: SEVPEN, 1965.

Hill, Bennett D. *English Cistercian Monasteries and Their Patrons in the Twelfth Century.* Urbana: University of Illinois Press, 1968.

Hoffmann, Richard C. *An Environmental History of Medieval Europe.* Cambridge: Medieval Textbooks, 2014.

Hydraulique monastique: Milieux, réseaux, usages. Edited by Léon Pressouyre, Paul Benoît, Armelle Bonis, and Monique Wabont. Paris: Créaphis, 1996.

Hyde, Elizabeth. "The Cistercian Priory of Nun Cotton." Paper presented at the Eleventh Conference on Medieval Studies, sponsored by the Medieval Institute, Western Michigan University, Kalamazoo, May 2–5, 1976.

Il monastero di Riffreddo e il monachesimo cistercense femminile nell'Italia occidentale (secoli XII–XIV): Atti del convegno Staffarda–Rifreddo, 18–19 maggio 1999. Edited by Rinaldo Comba. Cuneo: Società per gli studi storici, archeologici ed artistici della provincia di Cuneo, 1999.

Iogna-Prat, Dominique. *Order and Exclusion: Cluny and Christendom Face Heresy, Judaism, and Islam (1000–1150).* Translated by Graham Robert Edwards. Ithaca, NY: Cornell University Press, 2002.

Jamroziak, Emilia. *Survival and Success on Medieval Borders: Cistercian Houses in Medieval Scotland and Pomerania from the Twelfth to the Late Fourteenth Century.* Turnhout: Brepols, 2011.

Janauschek, Leopold. *Originum Cisterciensium.* Vienna, 1877. Reprint, Ridgewood, NJ: Gregg Press, 1964.

Johnson, Penelope D. *Equal in Monastic Profession: Religious Women in Medieval France.* Chicago: University of Chicago Press, 1991.

Jones, Sarah Rees. "Women's Influence in the Design of Urban Homes." In *Gendering the Master Narrative: Women and Power in the Middle Ages,* edited by Mary C. Erler and Maryanne Kowaleski, pp. 190–211. Ithaca, NY: Cornell University Press, 2003.

Jordan, Erin L. "Female Founders: Exercising Authority in Thirteenth-Century Flanders and Hainaut." "Secular Women in the Documents for Late Medieval Religious Women,"

Edited by Constance H. Berman and Michelle Herder. Special issue, *Church History and Religious Culture* 88, no. 4 (2008): 535–61.

———. "Gender Concerns: Monks, Nuns, and Patronage of the Cistercian Order in Thirteenth-Century Flanders and Hainaut." *Speculum* 87 (2012): 62–94.

———. "Patronage, Prayers and Polders: Assessing Cistercian Foundations in Thirteenth-Century Flanders and Hainaut." *Cîteaux* 53 (2002): 99–125.

———. "*Pro remedio anime sue*": Cistercian Nuns and Space in the Low Countries." *Women in the Medieval Monastic World*, edited by Janet Burton and Karen Stöber, pp. 279–98. Turnhout: Brepols, 2015.

———. "Roving Nuns and Cistercian Realities: The Cloistering of Religious Women in the Thirteenth Century." *Journal of Medieval and Early Modern Studies* 42 (2012): 597–614.

———. *Women, Power, and Religious Patronage in the Middle Ages.* New York: Palgrave Macmillan, 2006.

Jordan, William C. "The Cistercian Nunnery of La-Cour-Notre-Dame-de-Michery: A Community That Failed." *Revue bénédictine* 95 (1985): 311–20.

———. *Louis IX and the Challenge of the Crusade: A Study in Rulership.* Princeton, NJ: Princeton University Press, 1979.

Kantorowicz, Ernst. *The King's Two Bodies: A Study in Mediaeval Political Theology.* Princeton, NJ: Princeton University Press, 1957.

Kemel-Hilmi, Ahmet. "Women and the Pursuit of Power in the Thirteenth Century: The Case of Alice, Queen-Regent of Cyprus (1218–1232)." *Journal of Cyprus Studies* 13 (2007): 1–26.

Kerr, Berenice M. *Religious Life for Women, c. 1100–c. 1350: Fontevraud in England.* Oxford: Oxford University Press, 1999.

Keyser, Richard. "The Transformation of Traditional Woodland Management: Commercial Sylviculture in Medieval Champagne." *French Historical Studies* 32 (2009): 353–84.

Kienzle, Beverly Mayne. *Cistercians, Heresy and Crusade in Occitania, 1145–1229: Preaching in the Lord's Vineyard.* York: York Medieval Press, 2001.

Kinder, Terryl N. "Blanche of Castile and the Cistercians: An Architectural Re-evaluation of Maubuisson Abbey." *Cîteaux* 22 (1969): 161–88.

———, ed. *Les Cisterciens dans l'Yonne.* Pontigny: Amis de Pontigny, 1999.

Kinney, Dale. "Roman Architectural Spolia." *Proceedings of the American Philosophical Society* 145 (2001): 138–61.

Klein, Kerwin Lee. *Frontiers of Historical Imagination: Narrating the European Conquest of Native America, 1890–1990.* Berkeley: University of California Press, 1997.

Knowles, David. *The Monastic Order in England.* Cambridge: Cambridge University Press, 1940.

Knox, Lezlie S. *Creating Clare of Assisi: Female Franciscan Identities in Later Medieval Italy.* Leiden: Brill, 2008.

Krenig, Ernst Günther. "Mittelalterliche Frauenklöster nach den Konstitutionen von Cîteaux." *Analecta Sacri Ordinis Cisterciensis* 10 (1954): 1–105.

Kuhn-Rehfus, Maren. "Cistercian Nuns in Germany in the Thirteenth Century: Upper Swabian Cistercian Abbeys under the Paternity of Salem." In *Hidden Springs: Cistercian Monastic Women*, vol. 3, bk. 1 of *Medieval Religious Women*, edited by John A. Nichols and Lillian Thomas Shank, pp. 135–58. Kalamazoo, MI: Cistercian Publications, 1995.

Kwanten, A. "L'abbaye Saint-Jacques de Vitry-en-Perthois." *Mémoires de la Société d'agriculture, commerce, sciences, et arts du département de la Marne* 81 (1966): 93–109.

Lackner, Bede K. *The Eleventh-Century Background of Cîteaux.* Washington, DC: Cistercian Publications, 1972.

LaCorte, Daniel M. "Pope Innocent IV's Role in the Establishment and Early Success of the College of Saint Bernard in Paris." *Cîteaux* 46 (1995): 289–303.

Lawrence, C. H. *Medieval Monasticism: Forms of Religious Life in Western Europe in the Middle Ages.* 3rd ed. London: Longman, 2001.

Leclercq, Jean. "Cisterciennes et filles de S. Bernard à propos des structures variées des monastères de moniales au moyen âge." *Studia Monastica* 32 (1990): 139–56.

———. "Monachesimo femminile nei secoli XII e XIII." *Movimento religioso femminile e francescanesimo nel secolo XIII: Atti del VII convegno internazionale, Assisi, 11–13 ottobre 1979,* pp. 63–99. Assisi: Società internazionale di Studi Francescani, 1980.

Lehmijoki-Gardner, Maiju. "Writing Religious Rules as an Interactive Process: Dominican Penitent Women and the Making of Their *Regula.*" *Speculum* 70 (2004): 660–87.

Lekai, Louis J. *The Cistercians: Ideals and Reality.* Kent, OH: Kent State University Press, 1977.

———. "Le collège Saint-Bernard de Toulouse au moyen âge (1280–1533)." *Annales du Midi* 85 (1973): 251–66.

Lepointe, Gabriel. "Réflexions sur des textes concernant la propriété individuelle des religieuses cisterciennnes dans la région Lilloise." *Revue d'histoire ecclésiastique* 49 (1954): 743–69.

Lespinasse, René de. *Chronique ou histoire abrégée des évêques et des comtes de Nevers écrite en latin au seizième siècle et publiée pour la première fois.* Nevers: Fay, 1870.

———. *Le Nivernais et les comtes de Nevers.* 3 vols. Paris: H. Champion, 1909–14.

Lester, Anne E. *Creating Cistercian Nuns: The Women's Religious Movement and Its Reform in Thirteenth-Century Champagne.* Ithaca, NY: Cornell University Press, 2011.

———. "Gender and Social Networks in Medieval France: The Convents of the Country of Champagne." PhD diss., Princeton University, 2003.

Lester, Anne E., and William Chester Jordan. "La Cour Notre-Dame de Michery: A Response to Constance Berman." *Journal of Medieval History* 27 (2001): 43–54.

Leuzinger, Jürg. *Das Zisterzienserinnenkloster Fraubrunnen: Von der Gründing bis zur Reformation, 1246–1528.* Bern: Peter Lang, 2008.

Lewis, Andrew W. *Royal Succession in Capetian France: Studies on Familial Order and the State.* Cambridge, MA: Harvard University Press, 1981.

Leyser, Henrietta. *Hermits and the New Monasticism: A Study of Religious Communities in Western Europe, 1000–1150.* London: Macmillan, 1984.

Liber Largitorius: Études d'histoire médiévale offertes à Pierre Toubert par ses élèves. Edited by Dominique Barthélémy and Jean-Marie Martin. Geneva: Droz, 2003.

Limerick, Patricia Nelson. *The Legacy of Conquest: The Unbroken Past of the American West.* New York: W. W. Norton, 1997.

Linehan, Peter. *The Ladies of Zamora.* University Park: Pennsylvania State University Press. 1997.

Livingstone, Amy. *Out of Love for My Kin: Aristocratic Family Life in the Lands of the Loire, 1000–1200.* Ithaca, NY: Cornell University Press, 2010.

Lopez, Robert S. *The Commercial Revolution of the Middle Ages, 950–1350.* Engelwood Cliffs, NJ: Prentice-Hall, 1971.

Lower, Michael. *The Barons' Crusade: A Call to Arms and Its Consequences.* Philadelphia: University of Pennsylvania Press, 2005.

Lynch, Joseph H. *Simoniacal Entry into Religious Life from 1000 to 1260: A Social, Economic and Legal Study.* Columbus: Ohio State University, 1976.

Macy, Gary. *The Hidden History of Women's Ordination: Female Clergy in the Medieval West.* Oxford: Oxford University Press, 2008.

Mahn, Jean-Berthold. *L'ordre cistercien et son gouvernement des origines au milieu du XIIIe siècle (1098–1265).* 2nd ed. Paris: Boccard, 1951.

Makowski, Elizabeth. *Canon Law and Cloistered Women: Periculoso and Its Commentators, 1298–1545.* Washington, DC: Catholic University of America Press, 1997.

McGuire, Brian Patrick. "Cistercian Nuns in Twelfth- and Thirteenth-Century Denmark and Sweden: Far from the Madding Crowd." In *Women in the Medieval Monastic World,* edited by Janet Burton and Karen Stöber, pp. 167–84. Turnhout: Brepols, 2015.

———, ed. *A Companion to Bernard of Clairvaux.* Leiden: Brill, 2011.

McKitterick, Rosamund. *Perceptions of the Past in the Middle Ages.* Notre Dame, IN: University of Notre Dame Press, 2006.

McLaughlin, Mary Martin. "Heloise the Abbess: The Expansion of the Paraclete." In *Listening to Heloise: The Voice of a Twelfth-Century Woman,* edited by Bonnie Wheeler, pp. 1–17. New York: St. Martin's Press, 2000.

McNamara, Jo Ann. "Canossa and the Ungendering of the Public Man." In *Render unto Caesar: The Religious Sphere in World Politics,* edited by Sabrina Petra Ramet and Donald W. Treadgold, pp. 131–50. Washington, DC: American University Press, 1995.

Mecham, June L. *Sacred Communities, Shared Devotions: Gender, Material Culture, and Monasticism in Late Medieval Germany.* Edited by Alison Beach, Constance H. Berman, and Lisa Bitel. Turnhout: Brepols, 2014.

Menant, François, Hervé Martin, Bernard Merdrignac, and Monique Chauvin. *Les Capétiens: Histoire et dictionnaire, 987–1328.* Edited by François Menant. Paris: Laffont, 1999.

Mercier, Jean, "L'abbaye du Val des Vignes à Ailleville." *Mémoires de la Société academique, d'agriculture, des sciences, arts, belles-lettres du departement de l'Aube (Troyes)* 115 (1990): 135–52.

Mews, Constant J. "The Council of Sens (1141): Abelard, Bernard, and the Fear of Social Upheaval." *Speculum* 77 (2002): 342–82.

Mignardot, Andrée. *Michery: Histoire d'un village du Nord-Sénonais.* Michery: Mignardot, 1996.

Milis, Ludo. "Ermites et chanoines reguliers au XIIe siècle." *Cahiers de civilisation médiévale* 22 (1979): 39–80.

Miller, Tanya Stabler. *The Beguines of Medieval Paris: Gender, Patronage, and Spiritual Authority.* Philadelphia: University of Pennsylvania Press, 2014.

Minnis, Alistair, and Rosalyn Voaden, eds. *Medieval Holy Women in the Christian Tradition, c. 1100–c. 1500.* Turnhout: Brepols, 2010.

Miramon, Charles de. *Les "donnés" au Moyen Âge: Une forme de vie religieuse laïque, v. 1180–v. 1500.* Paris: Cerf, 1999.

Mollat, Michel. *The Poor in the Middle Ages: An Essay in Social History.* Translated by Arthur Goldhammer. New Haven, CT: Yale University Press, 1986.

Monasteria nova; Storia e architettura dei cistercensi in Liguria (sec. XII–XIV). Edited by Colette Bozzo Dufour and Anna Dagnino, directed by Valeria Polonio and Luisa Valle. Genoa: Donati, 1998.

Mooney, Catherine M. *Clare of Assisi and the Thirteenth-Century Church: Religious Women, Rules, and Resistance.* Philadelphia; University of Pennsylvania Press, 2016.

Moore, Robert I. *The War on Heresy.* Cambridge, MA: Harvard University Press, 2012.

Moreau, Édouard de. *L'abbaye de Villers-en-Brabant aux XIIe et XIIIe siècles: Étude d'histoire religieuse et économique.* Brussels: A. Dewit, 1909.

Moreau, Marthe. "Les moniales du diocèse de Maguelone au XIIIe siècle." In *La femme dans la vie religieuse du Languedoc (XIIIe–XVIe s.)*, pp. 241–60. Cahiers de Fanjeaux 23. Toulouse: Privat, 1988.

Mouret, Dominique. "Les moniales cisterciennes en France aux XIIe et XIIIe siècles: La diversité des origines, l'intégration à l'espace; Les cisterciennes et leur temps." Mémoire de Maitrise, Université de Limoges, 1984.

Mouret, Dominique, and Jean de la Croix Bouton. "Convers et converses de moniales cisterciennes aux XIIIe et XIVe siècles." In *Les Cisterciens de Languedoc (XIIIe–XIVe s.)*, pp. 283–312. Cahiers de Fanjeaux 21. Toulouse: Privat, 1986.

Mulder-Bakker, Anneke B. *Lives of the Anchoresses: The Rise of the Urban Recluse in Medieval Europe.* Translated by Myra Heerspink Scholz. Philadelphia: University of Pennsylvania Press, 2013.

———, ed. *Living Saints of the Thirteenth Century: The Lives of Yvette, Anchoress of Huy; Juliana of Cornillon, Author of the Corpus Christi Feast; and Margaret the Lame, Anchoress of Magdeburg.* Translations by Jo Ann McNamara, Barbara Newman, and Gertrud Jaron Lewis, and Tilman Lewis. Turnhout: Brepols, 2011.

Müller, G. "Generalkapitel der Cistercienserinnen." *Cistercienser-Chronik 24 (1912): 65–72, 114–19.*

Mundy, John H. "Charity and Social Work in Toulouse, 1100–1250." *Traditio* 22 (1966): 203–87.

Nichols, John. "History and Cartulary of the Cistercian Nuns of Marham Abbey, 1249–1536." PhD diss., Kent State University, 1974.

Nichols, John A., and Lillian Thomas Shank, eds. *Medieval Religious Women.* 3 vols. in 4. Kalamazoo, MI: Cistercian Publications, 1984–85.

Nolan, Kathleen. *Queens in Stone and Silver: The Creation of a Visual Imagery of Queens in Capetian France.* New York: Palgrave Macmillan, 2009.

Oliva, Marilyn. *The Convent and the Community in Late Medieval England: Female Monasteries in the Diocese of Norwich, 1350–1450.* Woodbridge: Boydell, 1998.

Oram, Richard D. "Breaking New Ground: The Monastic Orders and Economic Development Along the Northern European Periphery, c. 1070 to c. 1300." In *Religion and Religious Institutions in the European Economy, 1000–1800*, Acts of the 43rd Conference of the Datini Institute, Prato, May 8–12, 2011, edited by Francesco Ammannati, pp. 331–45. Florence: Firenze University Press, 2012.

———. *Domination and Lordship: Scotland, 1070–1230.* Edinburgh: Edinburgh University Press, 2006.

Oram, Richard D., and Matthew Hammond. "Life on the Edge: The Cistercian Abbey of Balmerino, Fife (Scotland)." *Cîteaux* 59 (2009): 5–167.

Parisse, Michel. "Des veuves au monastère." In *Veuves et veuvage dans le Haut Moyen Age*, edited by Michel Parisse, pp. 255–74. Paris: Picard, 1993.

———. *La Lorraine monastique au Moyen Âge.* Nancy: Université de Nancy, 1981.

———, ed. *Religieuses en France au XIIIe siècle.* Nancy: Presses Universitaires de Nancy, 1985.

Petit-Dutaillis, Charles. *Étude sur la vie et le règne de Louis VIII.* Paris: É. Bouillon, 1894.

Pfeffer, Wendy. "The *Dit des monstiers.*" *Speculum* 73 (1998): 80–114.

Pibrac, A. du Faur, comte de. "Histoire de l'abbaye de Voisins." *Mémoires de la Société d'agriculture, sciences, belles-lettres et arts d'Orléans* 22 (1881): 177–348.

Poly, Jean-Pierre. *La Provence et la société féodale, 879–1166: Contribution à l'étude des structures dites féodales dans le Midi.* Paris: Bordas, 1976.

Power, Daniel. *The Norman Frontier in the Twelfth and Early Thirteenth Centuries.* Cambridge: Cambridge University Press, 2004.

———. "Who Went on the Albigensian Crusade?" *English Historical Review* 128, no. 534 (2013): 1047–85.

Power, Eileen. *Medieval English Nunneries, c. 1275 to 1535.* 1922. Reprint, Cambridge: Cambridge University Press, 2010.

Prieur, Armande. "Histoire de l'abbaye Notre-Dame du Lys-la-Royale au diocèse de Sens." Thesis in Melun, AD Seine-et-Marne, 100J149. Also summarized in *École nationale des chartes: Positions des thèses de 1945* (Paris, 1945).

Raban, Sandra. *Mortmain Legislation and the English Church, 1279–1500.* Cambridge: Cambridge University Press, 1982.

Rackham, Oliver. *Ancient Woodland: Its History, Vegetation and Use in England.* New ed. Dalbeattie: Castlepoint Press, 2003.

Rawcliffe, Carole. *Leprosy in Medieval England.* Woodbridge: Boydell, 2006.

Renzi, Francesco. "The Bone of the Contention: Cistercians Bishops and Papal Exemption; The Case of the Archdiocese of Santiago de Compostela (1150–1250)." *Journal of Medieval Iberian Studies* 5 (2013): 47–68.

Richard, Jean. *Saint-Louis. Le justicier sans faiblesse.* Paris: Fayard, 1983.

Riddy, Felicity. " 'Burgeis' Domesticity in Late Medieval England." In *Medieval Domesticity: Home, Housing and Household in Medieval England,* edited by Maryanne Kowaleski and P. J. P. Goldberg, pp. 14–36. Cambridge: Cambridge University Press, 2011.

Riley-Smith, Jonathan. *The First Crusaders, 1095–1131.* Cambridge: Cambridge University Press, 1998.

Rissel, Hiltrud. "Entdeckung einer Inkorporationsurkunde für ein frühes Frauenkloster im 12. Jahrhundert." *Cîteaux* 39 (1988): 43–64.

Roisin, Simone. "L'efflorescence cistercienne et le courant féminin de piété au 13ème siècle." *Revue d'histoire ecclésiastique* 39 (1943): 342–78.

Rosenthal, Joel T., ed. *Medieval Women and the Sources of Medieval History.* Athens: University of Georgia Press, 1990.

Rosenwein, Barbara H. *Negotiating Space: Power, Restraint, and Privileges of Immunity in Early Medieval Europe.* Ithaca, NY: Cornell University Press, 1999.

———. *To Be the Neighbor of Saint Peter: The Social Meaning of Cluny's Property, 909–1049.* Ithaca, NY: Cornell University Press, 1989.

Roux, Simone. *Paris in the Middle Ages.* Translated by Jo Ann McNamara. Philadelphia: University of Pennsylvania Press, 2009.

Rudolph, Conrad. *The "Things of Greater Importance": Bernard of Clairvaux's "Apologia" and the Medieval Attitude Toward Art.* Philadelphia: University of Pennsylvania Press, 1990.

———. *Violence and Daily Life: Reading, Art, and Polemics in the Cîteaux "Moralia in Job."* Princeton, NJ: Princeton University Press, 1997.

Sainte-Marie de Boulaur: Histoire de l'Ordre de Fontevrault (1100–1908). Auch: Cocharaux, 1911–15.

Schneider, Ambrosius, et al. *Die Cistercienser: Geschichte, Geist, Kunst.* Köln: Wienand, 1974.

Schulenburg. Jane T. "Strict Active Enclosure and Its Effects on the Female Monastic Experience (500–1100)." In *Distant Echoes,* vol. 1 of *Medieval Religious Women,* edited by John A. Nichols and Lillian Thomas Shank, pp. 51–86. Kalamazoo: Cistercian Publications, 1984.

Seale, Yvonne. "*De Monasterio Desolato*: Politics and Patronage in an Irish Frontier Convent." *Journal of Medieval Monastic Studies* 4 (2015): 21–45.

————. "Reading the Premonstratensian Landscape: Women, Space, and Patronage in Northern France, c. 1120–1400." PhD diss., University of Iowa, 2016.

Septième centenaire de la mort de Saint Louis: Actes des colloques de Royaumont et Paris, 21–27 mai 1970. Paris: Belles Lettres, 1976.

Shadis, Miriam. *Berenguela of Castile (1180–1246) and Political Women in the High Middle Ages.* New York: Palgrave, 2009.

————. "Blanche of Castile and Facinger's 'Medieval Queenship': Reassessing the Argument." In *Capetian Women*, edited by Kathleen Nolan, pp. 137–61. New York: Palgrave, 2003.

Shadis, Miriam, and Constance Hoffman Berman. "A Taste of the Feast: Reconsidering Eleanor of Aquitaine's Female Descendants." In *Eleanor of Aquitaine, Lord and Lady*, edited by Bonnie Wheeler and John Carmi Parsons, pp. 177–211. New York: Palgrave, 2002.

Shortell, Ellen. "Erasures and Recoveries of Women's Contributions to Gothic Architecture: The Case of Saint-Quentin, Local Nobility, and Eleanor of Vermandois." In *Reassessing the Role of Women as "Makers" of Medieval Art and Architecture*, edited by Therese Martin, pp. 129–74. Leiden: Brill, 2012

Simons, Walter. *Cities of Ladies: Beguine Communities in the Medieval Low Countries, 1200–1565.* Philadelphia: University of Pennsylvania Press, 2001.

Sivéry, Gérard. *Blanche de Castille.* Paris: Fayard, 1990.

————. *Louis VIII: Le Lion.* Paris: Fayard, 1995.

Sorrentino, Janet. "In Houses of Nuns, in Houses of Canons: A Liturgical Dimension to Double Monasteries." *Journal of Medieval History* 28 (2002): 361–72.

Southern, R. W. *Western Society and the Church in the Middle Ages.* London: Penguin, 1990.

Spiegel, Gabrielle M. *Romancing the Past: The Rise of Vernacular Prose Historiography in Thirteenth-Century France.* Berkeley: University of California Press, 1993.

Stock, Brian. *The Implications of Literacy: Written Language and Models of Interpretation in the Eleventh and Twelfth Centuries.* Princeton, NJ: Princeton University Press, 1983.

Strocchia, Sharon T. *Nuns and Nunneries in Renaissance Florence.* Baltimore: Johns Hopkins University Press, 2009.

TeBrake, William H. *Medieval Frontier Culture and Ecology in Rijnland.* College Station: Texas A&M University Press, 1985.

Thompson, Kathleen. "Matilda, Countess of the Perche (1171–1210): The Expression of Authority in Name, Style and Seal." *Tabularia* (2003), http://tabularia.revues.org/1546.

————. *The Monks of Tiron: A Monastic Community and Religious Reform in the Twelfth Century.* Cambridge: Cambridge University Press, 2014.

————. *Power and Border Lordship in Medieval France: The County of the Perche, 1000–1226.* Woodbridge: Boydell for Royal Historical Society, 2002.

Thompson, Sally. "The Problem of Cistercian Nuns in the Twelfth and Early Thirteenth Centuries." In *Medieval Women: Dedicated and Presented to Professor Rosalind M. T. Hill on the Occasion of Her Seventieth Birthday*, edited by Derek Baker, pp. 227–52. Oxford: Ecclesiastical History Society, 1978.

————. "Why English Nunneries Had No History: A Study of the Problems of the English Nunneries After the Conquest." In *Distant Echoes*, vol. 1 of *Medieval Religious Women*, edited by John A. Nichols and Lillian Thomas Shank, pp. 131–49. Kalamazoo, MI: Cistercian Publications, 1984.

———. *Women Religious: The Founding of English Nunneries After the Norman Conquest.* Oxford: Clarendon Press, 1991.

Thouzellier, Christine. *Hérésie et hérétiques: Vaudois, Cathares, Patarins, Albigeois.* Rome: Edizioni di storia e letteratura, 1969.

Timbert, Arnaud, and Yves Gallet. "Une foundation royale du début du XIIIe siècle: L'abbaye Saint-Jean-Baptiste du Jard." In *Art et architecture à Melun au Moyen Age,* edited by Yves Gallet, pp. 201–21. Paris: Picard, 2000.

Toubert, Pierre. *Les structures du Latium médiéval: Le Latium méridional et la Sabine du IXe siècle à la fin du XIIe siècle.* 2 vols. Rome: École française de Rome, 1973.

Toupet, Christophe, and Monique Wabont. "L'abbaye cistercienne de Maubuisson (Val-d-Oise, France): Les réseaux hydrauliques du xiiie au xviiie siècle." In *L'hydraulique monastique: Milieux, réseaux, usages,* edited by Léon Pressouyre, Paul Benoît, Armelle Bonis, and Monique Wabont, pp. 135–55. Paris: Créaphis, 1996.

Turner, Frederick Jackson. "The Significance of the Frontier in American History." In *Frontier and Section: Selected Essays of Frederick Jackson Turner,* edited by Ray Allen Billington, pp. 37–62. Englewood Cliffs, NJ: Prentice-Hall, 1961.

Turner, Ralph V. *King John.* London: Longman, 1994.

Underhill, Frances A. *For Her Good Estate: The Life of Elizabeth de Burgh.* New York: Palgrave, 2000.

Van der Meer, Frédéric, ed. *Atlas de l'ordre cistercien.* Paris: Sequoia, 1965.

Van Engen, John. "The 'Crisis of Cenobitism' Reconsidered: Benedictine Monasticism in the Years 1050–1150." *Speculum* 61, no. 2 (April 1986): 269–304.

Van Houts, Elisabeth. *Memory and Gender in Medieval Europe, 900–1200.* Toronto: University of Toronto Press, 1999.

Venarde, Bruce L. "Making History at Fontevraud: Abbess Petronilla of Chemillé and Practical Literacy." In *Nuns' Literacies in Medieval Europe: The Hull Dialogue,* edited by Virginia Blanton, Veronica O'Mara, and Patricia Stoop, pp. 19–31. Turnhout: Brepols, 2013.

———. "*Praesidentes Negotiis*: Abbesses as Managers in Twelfth-Century France." In *Portraits in Medieval and Renaissance Living: Essays in Memory of David Herlihy,* edited by Samuel K. Cohn Jr. and Steven A. Epstein, pp. 189–205. Ann Arbor: University of Michigan Press, 1996.

———. *Women's Monasticism and Medieval Society: Nunneries in France and England, 890–1215.* Ithaca, NY: Cornell University Press, 1997.

Verdon, Laure. *La terre et les hommes en Roussillon aux XIIe et XIIIe siècles.* Aix-en-Provence: Publications de l'Université de Provence, 2001.

Verneret, Hubert. *Mahaut de Courtenay, 1188–1257: Comtesse de Nevers, Auxerre et Tonnerre.* Précy-sous-Thil: Éditions de l'Armançon, 2002.

Veyssière, Laurent. "Cîteaux et Tart, foundations parallèles." In *Cîteaux et les femmes,* edited by Bernadette Barrière et al., pp. 179–91. Paris: Créaphis, 2001.

Vongrey, F. and F. Hervay. "Kritische Bemerkungen zum 'Atlas de l'ordre Cistercien' von Frédéric van der Meer." *Analecta Cisterciensia* 23 (1967): 115–52.

Wabont, Monique. *Maubuisson au fil de l'eau: Les réseaux hydrauliques de l'abbaye du XIIIe au XVIIIe siècle.* Pontoise: Conseil général du Val-d'Oise, 1992.

Wacha, Heather. "La Puissance du Choix: Women's Economic Activity in Twelfth- and Thirteenth-Century Picardy." PhD diss., University of Iowa, 2016.

Waldman, Thomas A. "Abbot Suger and the Nuns of Argenteuil." *Traditio* 41 (1985): 239–72.

Warren, W. L. *King John.* Berkeley: University of California Press, 1978.

Weaver, Ellen F. *The Evolution of the Reform of Port Royal: From the Rule of Cîteaux to Jansenism.* Paris: Beauchesne, 1978.

Wheeler, Bonnie, and John Carmi Parsons, eds. *Eleanor of Aquitaine, Lord and Lady.* New York: Palgrave, 2002.

White, Stephen D. *Custom, Kinship, and Gifts to Saints: The Laudatio Parentum in Western France, 1050–1150.* Chapel Hill: University of North Carolina Press, 1988.

Wickham, Chris. *Early Medieval Italy: Central and Local Society, 400–1000.* London: Macmillan, 1981.

Williams, David H. "The Early Cistercian Nuns: 1125–1350." *Analecta Cisterciensia* 66 (2016): 177–475.

Wissenberg, Christophe. *Entre Champagne et Bourgogne: Beaumont, ancienne grange de l'abbaye cistercienne de Clairvaux.* Paris: Picard, 2007.

———. "Granges cisterciennes de l'Yonne: Constitution des domaines et aménagement de l'espace." In *Les Cisterciens dans l'Yonne*, edited by Terryl N. Kinder, pp. 50–71. Pontigny: Amis de Pontigny, 1999.

Wolbrink, Shelley Amiste, "Necessary Priests and Brothers: Male-Female Co-operation in the Premonstratensian Women's Monasteries of Füssenich and Meer, 1140–1260." In *Partners in Spirit: Women, Men, and Religious Life in Germany, 1100–1500*, edited by Fiona J. Griffiths and Julie Hotchin, pp. 172–212. Turnhout: Brepols, 2014.

Zerner-Chardavoine, Monique. "L'abbé Gui des Vaux-de-Cernay, prédicateur de croisade." In *Les Cisterciens de Languedoc (XIIIe–XIVe s.)*, pp. 185–204. Cahiers de Fanjeaux 21. Toulouse: Privat, 1986.

———. "L'épouse de Simon de Montfort et la croisade albigeoise." In *Femmes, Mariages, Lignages, XIIe–XIVe siècles: Mélanges offerts à Georges Duby*, pp. 449–70. Brussels: De Boeck Université, 1992.

ACKNOWLEDGMENTS

The research for this study was undertaken over a number of years in what were for a long time neglected archives and libraries of unpublished documents, particularly in Paris and in the French provinces. As I complete it, as I pore through long lists of manuscripts consulted and photographs taken, I have visions of archival reading rooms, of the light and rain in late October in Paris, of stays with nuns in Troyes, of driving around the countryside in search of archives and places sometimes long gone. The bump of the plane as it landed in Roissy, probably right on top of what had once been my nuns' granges of Aulnay, stimulated my sense of anticipation. I recognized placenames when I took the bus into Paris in the light of early morning.

Not only has this book occupied a long period in my life, but I have incurred numerous debts of gratitude to institutions, archivists, and interlibrary loan departments and librarians in the United States who have provided funds and research aid, as did the many graduate and undergraduate students who acted as research assistants. Financial and other institutional support came from the University of Iowa, Clare Hall, Cambridge, the Camargo Foundation, the Guggenheim Foundation, and the National Endowment for the Humanities. The University of Iowa Library has been a major asset to my work, as have the staff in the History Department and my colleagues there. The University of Pennsylvania Press and editors Jerry Singerman, Ruth Karras, Edward Peters, and Erica Ginsburg have been ever patient and deserve my most sincere thanks. So does Brenda Bolton, who decided to reveal herself as reader—she provided some great language for tricky situations. My very special thanks go to Gordon Thompson for making the maps. Thank you all.

In Paris and in the provinces of France, the archivists, librarians, fellow researchers, and students deserve special thanks. I'd like to recognize the role of genealogists in making archival depositories a funding priority, but also for their friendliness over lunches on terraces outside. There was also the hotelkeeper who explained to me some strategic tricks for using the Paris subway without encountering long walks underground. Again my thanks to them and all the archival employees who brought out entire collections of documents for my work. I have attempted to recognize specific courtesies in the notes and important studies in the bibliography, but the debts of gratitude over so many years are too numerous to list.

I would like to thank especially Professor Bernard Barbiche of the École des Chartes in Paris, who provided encouragement from an early date (and indeed transcriptions from papal bulls) and his wife Ségolène Dainville Barbiche, always welcoming friends in Paris, often meeting me for lunch or inviting me for dinner and introducing me to the archivists who were their students. Thanks also to fellow travelers: Chris Africa, Judy Aikin, Michelle Armstrong-Partida, Alison Beach, Lisa Bitel, Karen Christianson, Becky Church, Susan Cray, Kristi Diclemente, William Duba, Russ Friedman, Pat Goodwin, Lisa Harkey, Lisa Heineman, Mary Hoffman, Richard and Ellen Hoffmann, Erin Jordan, Jim and Blandina, Marie Kelleher, Linda Kerber, Erica Lindgren, Ray and Beth Mentzer, Michael Moore, Melissa Moreton, Salvatory Nyante, Wendy Pfeffer, Kelly Putnam, Becky Rogers, Miri Rubin, Martin Brett, and all my Cambridge friends, Chris Schabel, Yvonne Seale, Miriam Shadis, Sheri Sojka, Katherine Tachau, Richard Unger, and Heather Wacha. I also thank the nuns of Our Lady of the Mississippi for constant encouragement, and I hope to visit again soon. Finally, I wish to thank my students, colleagues, and friends who organized not one but two celebrations of my retirement. I am still basking in that glory.

My sad recognition and thanks to too many who did not live to see this volume in print but were instrumental in some way: Bernadette Barrière, Marjorie Chibnall, Victoria Chandler, Carin Green, Judith Goldfein, David Herlihy, Doris Hoffman, Bob H., Richard Kerber, Barbara Kreutz, June Mecham, Jo Ann McNamara, and Claire Sponsler.

Finally, to Ben and Natasha, David and Ginger, all my love and thanks, but particularly to David, who has cooked so many meals, and Ginger, who has kept me company at my desk for so many hours.

My thanks to Cambridge University Library for permission to use the illustration of MS Mm.5.31, fol. 113r. All other photos are my own. Thanks to David Williams for Figure 2.

I have sought assiduously and acknowledge permissions to reuse materials from my earlier publications from: Brepols for "Cistercian Agriculture in

Female Houses of Northern France" (2014); Brill for "Noble Women's Power as Reflected in the Foundations of Cistercian Houses for Nuns" (2009); Cistercian Publications for "Cistercian Nuns and the Development of the Order: The Abbey of Saint-Antoine-des-Champs Outside Paris" (1995); *Cîteaux* for "Cistercian Women and Tithes" (1998); *Magistra* for "Beyond the Rule of Saint Benedict (2007); to the Society for Medieval Feminist Scholarship for "Archives from Houses of Cistercian Nuns and Their Evidence for Powerful Thirteenth-Century Secular Women," *Medieval Feminist Forum: A Journal of Gender and Sexuality* 51, no. 2 (2015): 132–44; and "New Light on the Economic Practices of Cistercian Women's Communities," *Medieval Feminist Forum* 41 (2006): 75–88; the Society for Church History for "Were There Twelfth-Century Cistercian Nuns?"(1999); TEAMS for information on Las Huelgas, Port-Royal, Saint-Antoine, and Montreuil, from *Women and Monasticism in Medieval Europe: Sisters and Patrons of the Cistercian Order* (2002); the Western Society for French History for "Fashions in Monastic Patronage" (1990) and "Dowries, Private Income, and Anniversary Masses: The Nuns of Saint-Antoine-des-Champs (Paris)" (1993).